Praise for
THE ASCENT OF MEDIA

"*The Ascent of Media* is really about the ascent of man: from a species that started recording his life experience on clay tablets and now records it on computer tablets. In Mr. Parry's view, the future isn't a rejection of the past. It's just a natural evolution.
There are two reasons to read any book: To learn or to be entertained. With *The Ascent of Media*, Roger Parry manages to do both. We can't wait to see the movie."
David Bernstein and Beau Fraser, co-authors of Death to all Sacred Cows

"Whatever the technology, mankind has always enjoyed a good story.
The Ascent of Media tells a cracking story with a cornucopia of insights.
Read Roger Parry and you're equipped to imagine where digital media might take us next."
Peter Bazalgette, TV producer and President, Royal Television Society

"Media are going through huge changes. This book provides a thought provoking read and a terrific insight into where we are now and where media might go next."
James Palumbo, founder of Ministry of Sound

"The aptly titled *Ascent of Media* is a must for anyone with even a passing interest in today's vast and exploding world of media. From students of the industry to the leaders of businesses who may struggle to know how to spend their shareholders' advertising money wisely, Roger Parry provides insights into what is really happening in the digital chaos of the twenty-first century..."
Richard Wheatly, Chief Executive of Jazz FM

"*The Ascent of Media* is a wonderful overview of the history of all forms of media and the key people responsible for their development. It leaves the reader in no doubt as to its power to influence our opinions and emotions, leverage commercial and political messages, stimulate the senses and at the same time enhance our productivity."
Neil Blackley, director of Ingenious Media, former Head of UK and European Media Research, Merrill Lynch

THE ASCENT OF MEDIA

FROM GILGAMESH TO GOOGLE VIA GUTENBERG

ROGER PARRY

NICHOLAS BREALEY
PUBLISHING

London • Boston

To Benjamin

First published by
Nicholas Brealey Publishing in 2011

3–5 Spafield Street
Clerkenwell, London
EC1R 4QB, UK
Tel: +44 (0)20 7239 0360
Fax: +44 (0)20 7239 0370

20 Park Plaza, Suite 1115a
Boston
MA 02116, USA
Tel: (888) BREALEY
Fax: (617) 523 3708

www.nicholasbrealey.com

© Roger Parry 2011
The right of Roger Parry to be identified as the author of this work has been
asserted in accordance with the Copyright, Designs and Patents Act 1988.

ISBN 978-1-85788-570-5

Library of Congress Cataloging-in-Publication Data
Parry, Roger, 1953-
  The ascent of media : from Gilgamesh to Google via Gutenberg / Roger
Parry.
      p. cm.
  Includes bibliographical references and index.
  ISBN 978-1-85788-570-5
  1. Mass media--History. I. Title.
  P90.P3393 2011
  302.23--dc23

2011022264

British Library Cataloguing in Publication Data
A catalogue record for this book is available from the
British Library.

Contents

The number of books will grow continually, and one can predict that a time will come when it will be almost as difficult to learn anything from books as from the direct study of the whole universe.
Denis Diderot, 1763

The multitude of books is making us ignorant.
Voltaire, 1764

I deplore the putrid state into which our newspapers have passed and the malignity, the vulgarity, and mendacious spirit of those who write for them.
Thomas Jefferson, 1787

Telegraphs of any kind are now wholly unnecessary.
John Barrow, British Admiralty, 1816

The telephone has too many shortcomings to be considered as a means of communication.
Western Union, internal memo, 1876

The cinema is an invention without a future.
Louis Lumière, pioneer of photography, 1895

The radio craze will die out in time.
Thomas Edison, inventor of the phonogram, 1922

While theoretically and technically television may be feasible, commercially and financially I consider it an impossibility.
Lee De Forest, pioneer of radio, 1926

The VCR is to the American film producer... as the Boston Strangler is to women alone at home.
Jack Valenti, President, Motion Picture Association of America, 1982

Billboards will be abolished.
David Ogilvy, founder of Ogilvy & Mather, 1983

It doesn't matter how good or bad the product [the Kindle] is; the fact is that people don't read anymore.
Steve Jobs, co-founder of Apple, 2008

Greek philosopher Plato lived more than 2,000 years ago, but he has left us one of the most fascinating discussions of the role of media in society. In his book *The Republic*, he described the Allegory of the Cave, which served to stimulate debate about what was reality and what was perception. Imagine, suggested Plato, a group of prisoners who have been born and raised in a cave and chained in such a way that all they can see is a flat, white wall in front of them. Behind their backs burns a fire that gives off light and between the fire and their backs are a group of puppeteers, who use their hands to throw shadows onto the visible wall of the cave. The shadows are all that the prisoners know and see. Denied any other realities, they give different shadows names and endow them with human characteristics. They discuss among themselves the shadows' activities. They ascribe to the shadows motivations and give them a past and a future.

Now let one of our imaginary prisoners escape, said Plato. This person gets outside of the cave and discovers the existence of the actual world. He experiences the reality of day and night, sun and moon. He now understands that he has been a victim of the false reality created by the puppet masters. He returns to his fellow prisoners and tries to explain the truth to them, but they are unable to comprehend what he has seen and unable to relate to anything but the shadows. They reject his crazy ideas. For them their reality is the true one. He, the escapee, is now a dangerous and disruptive malcontent.

The Matrix is a film that explores the idea of humans trapped inside a wholly manufactured world created by computers. In it people make real life-and-death decisions based on false information. Another film, *The Truman Show*, has Jim Carrey's character live his entire life on the set of a television program. Every aspect of his environment is an illusion, but he is the only one deceived. Recent commentators have found Plato's cave a powerful analogy for the way in which mass media work on the public mind and the perception of reality.

Preface

This book began a few years ago, in a coffee shop in Palo Alto, California. Faced with several hours' wait before going to the nearby airport of San Francisco I started to write an article, trying to make sense of the economic hurricane blowing through the media industry, uprooting established structures and destroying traditional organizations. At that time Palo Alto felt like the eye of the media storm.

Drinking a cappuccino on University Avenue, I was a few hundred yards from where Google had its first real office, over a bicycle shop, and just as close to the first HQ of Facebook. The mouse and the internet were pioneered a short bus ride away, at Menlo Park. Apple created its magic devices down the road at Cupertino. Behind me was the tunnel under the rail tracks to Stanford University. For a media professional in the early twenty-first century it was like being a priest on a trip to the Vatican or a wine drinker visiting Bordeaux. Unremarkable though it looked (Palo Alto is a small college town), this was ground zero for the new digital media. I wondered what Plato would have made of it.

In the late 1600s the nascent newspaper industry had congregated on London's Fleet Street because of its proximity to the original book market of St Paul's churchyard; around 1910 Hollywood had the weather, space, and willing workforce to make movies; by the 1920s New York was the origin of much early radio broadcasting, as it was home to the most important paymasters, the advertising agencies. And now Palo Alto had become the place for digital media, because it brought together the computer scientists of Stanford, the technologists of Silicon Valley, and the venture capitalists of Sand Hill Road. It was an environment that encouraged the collision of ideas between software, engineering, and finance.

Over more than 3,000 years of development, mediated content has become increasingly important in making society function. It has been a story of constant growth in the amount and range of material available as media has taken up more of our time and become an ever larger part of the economy. The recent creative destruction initiated by the internet has been just one more, typically disruptive, era in the media story.

The advance of media has not been smooth, however, and the equivalent of the recent dot-com boom and bust has happened many times before. The development of electricity and railways led to the telegraph network in the 1850s, which, in turn, laid the ground for the telephone and, ultimately, the internet. Mass-market newspapers were born in the 1880s because of a combination of steam presses, automated typesetting, cheap newsprint, and advertising. Photosensitive film, clockwork motors, and the new working-class audience created cinema around 1910. And the vacuum tube, electromagnetic waves, and recorded sound enabled radio in the 1920s.

Each of these media revolutions produced a frenzy of financial speculation. Fortunes were made and lost, and preexisting media companies turned upside down. The first few years of each new technology created confusion and false starts and gave little indication of the media landscape that would finally emerge. This time it has been no different.

Nevertheless, now there is a better understanding of how digital media will fit into the broader picture. Old media formats have suffered disruption but are adapting to the changed conditions. New media are emerging to exploit screen-based, internet-enabled devices. By 2011, stimulated by a huge increase in sales of electronic readers, the value of ebooks sold monthly in America was greater than the amount spent on buying trade paperbacks[1]; film studios were beginning to make money out of streaming; record companies were finding legal solutions for downloading music; newspapers were experimenting with charging for online content; Google made record profits; and Facebook recruited its 600 millionth member. After the initial chaos a more ordered and reengineered media industry is taking shape. The technology is in place, so the challenge now is to develop the political and economic frameworks to allow creativity to flourish, reward innovation, and preserve quality.

In trying to understand all this, it became clear to me that looking back at the history of media can provide real insights into its future. Part One considers the building blocks of mediated content; namely, speech, music, images, and writing. Part Two analyzes the three forces that have shaped the media—politics, economics, and technology—and describes the people, organizations, and events that have defined the 16 main media types. Part Three speculates on the future of media in the context of past experience.

Media are going through a time of great change and are entering one of great opportunity. This book tells the story of their unstoppable ascent.

A NOTE ON SPELLING

This book has been written for a global audience with an Anglo/American perspective and uses American spelling throughout. In effect, *The Ascent of Media* has adopted Noah Webster rather than Samuel Johnson as its guide. The book argues that English is well on its way to becoming the global common language, but a major factor in its preeminence is its ability to adapt and adopt conventions driven by its users rather than originated by its home nation. Accordingly, it is likely, over time, that American spelling conventions will become the global norm and thus they are adopted here. Apologies to those who reside in the parts of the map still colored pink who might be upset.

A NOTE ON TYPEFACES

The text typeface used in this book is Minion Pro, designed by Robert Slimbach for Adobe. Highly readable, it was inspired by the classical, elegant typefaces used in the late Renaissance.

The typeface used for the headings is ITC Legacy Sans, the sans serif companion to a typeface designed by Ronald Arnholm based on Nicolas Jenson's fifteenth-century Eusebius.

PART ONE
Introduction | Media's Building Blocks

Media channels developed to move content from originator to recipient, from creator to consumer. That content is constructed from the building blocks of speech, music, images, and writing.

For early humans communication was one to one: the drawing, music, or speech was seen or heard directly.

Once writing and documents developed, the content became mediated. The communications capabilities of the originator were extended and remote audiences were able to be reached.

Printing, broadcasting, and the internet then expanded the audience and thus the size of manageable human society by a huge degree.

Ascent of Media

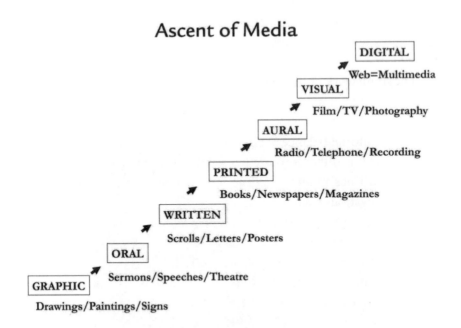

The ascent of media has not been neat and tidy. Successive eras do not have defined start and end dates. When a new medium comes along it does not simply replace the previous ones, it absorbs aspects of its predecessors and causes them to become modified. Old forms of media do not die out, they evolve. New forms adopt and adapt past conventions. Each era provides richer and more extensive communications than the ones before.

The media industry is now undergoing fundamental changes—revolution is not too strong a word—as the internet connects and empowers people and we move to an increasingly screen-based and interactive global communications culture. Digital technology allows information and entertainment to reach us instantly, at any place and any time. Most of us now have the tools to create content as well as to receive it. Media is moving away from the publication or broadcast by the privileged few to the exchange of ideas involving the enabled many.

Although it is less than 20 years since the web emerged, it has been hugely disruptive of conventional media, with the likes of Mozilla, Napster, Google, and YouTube turning traditional economics inside out. It has been wonderful for media consumers but challenging for media managers. However, the initial period of chaos and confusion is coming to an end.

The ascent of media is continuing its historical and relentless pattern of growth. We are seeing the start of a dynamic new era in which the convergence of text, audio, and video is creating a rich and compelling media mixture.

The framework of the internet has enabled the medium of the web. Digital technology, combined with new hardware like smartphones and new concepts such as Facebook, is changing the way we live. Notions of privacy and editorial balance are being challenged. The internet is barely adolescent, so it is difficult to predict what sort of media landscape will emerge when it has matured. While it took many decades for the full impact of innovations such as printing, the telegraph, and broadcasting to become apparent, we can now study the lessons from these past media eras to construct a guide to the likely future.

Media have come to play a central role in our lives. In the 1960s Canadian writer Marshall McLuhan described media as the extensions of man and talked of the creation of a global village. With the arrival of the internet and the web, his predictions have come true. "We have been hit hard by seismic shifts wrought by the web... Media is profoundly being transformed," said Steve Forbes, publisher of *Forbes* magazine, in a memo to his staff in 2009. This emphasizes the magnitude of the economic challenge posed by converting content into digital code.

The alphabet is itself a code that allows the sounds of spoken language to be expressed in simple symbols. Samuel Morse devised another code using dots and dashes to turn the alphabet into electric blips that could be sent

Key Media Formats	
Graphic	
c30,000 BC	Cave drawings
1415	Perspective
Oral	
c10,000 BC	Speech
534 BC	Athenian drama
Written	
c3,500 BC	Clay tablets
c100 AD	Codex books
Printed	
1450	Gutenberg bible
1843	Rotary press
Aural	
1876	Telephone
1877	Phonogram
1885	Radio
Visual	
1839	Photography
1895	Cinema
1926	TV
Digital	
1971	Internet
1993	WorldWideWeb
2010	iPad

down telegraph wires. These wires inspired the telephone and ultimately the internet. Morse created a communications revolution in the 1850s, but that was as nothing compared to what is happening today. Now all forms of content—sounds, pictures, text, and video—are being created, edited, stored, distributed, and consumed in coded digital form. Just 30 years ago this prospect was science fiction; now it is commonplace in every home.

Over many hundreds of years the media has become a huge, wealthy, and powerful industry, but it now faces fundamental issues. Long-established practices such as selling advertising, protecting intellectual property, and expecting consumers to pay for content are all being challenged. The tools and skills of content creation that were, until recently, only available to a small elite are now anybody's for the using. Expensive and exclusive distribution methods like printing presses and broadcast towers no longer present a barrier to entry. Any teenager has the technology in their bedroom to be William Randolph Hearst or Louis B Mayer.

According to the *Financial Times*, in the first decade of the twenty-first century the media industry had an annual negative return on assets of more than 4 percent, which compares very unfavorably with plus 7 percent a year 40 years ago.[1] Readers, viewers, and listeners are experiencing unprecedented choice and flexibility, but media companies and media professionals have been shocked by the pace of change and overwhelmed by the economic and technical challenges facing them. In the past the development of new media types has enabled or in same cases precipitated major changes in society. It is happening again.

MEDIA EVOLUTION

There is no escaping the all-pervasive influence of media. Whether we want news, information, or entertainment, half of our waking hours are taken up by the consumption of mediated content.[2] The mass media have been a feature of life since the 1920s when the term "media" was first coined, reflecting the addition of radio, talking pictures, and the gramophone to what had been the dominant technology of print.

Less than 100 years later the arrival of another new technology is driving change, so extreme that just because a medium is popular does not mean it is profitable. Digital production and distribution are as profound an event for media as were the inventions of Gutenberg, Morse, and

Marconi. Nevertheless, the arrival of new forms does not imply the extinction of the old. Traditional media have a remarkable ability to adapt and survive. A thousand years into the future, assuming the asteroids keep missing us and the super-volcanoes stay dormant, human beings will be reading books. That moment is too far removed for us to be sure of the book's exact format, its subject matter, or indeed its language. But it's a reasonably safe bet that books of some sort will still be around.

While media are continually evolving, their individual formats have a robust longevity and find new roles even after their period of being the dominant form has passed. Each medium has its golden age: it booms and declines but never disappears entirely. Media types mutate, they influence their successors, and what was once a channel of mass communication often metamorphoses into a niche form of art.

All media channels were once analogue and separate; now they are digital and converging. The typical office in the 1970s reverberated to the sounds of the typewriter, telex, and mimeograph machine. These communication tools are now gone, replaced first by the fax and then by word processing and email. To suggest that total replacement awaits newspapers, magazines, or books is too extreme, but in the face of high-speed broadband and advanced screen technology the status quo cannot possibly be sustained.

Radio was hit by the rise of the iPod and other MP3 players. Sales of music CDs slumped in the face of digital downloading. Newspapers saw classified advertising collapse as people shifted their notices for second-hand cars and houses to the web. And broadcast television has lost audience to cable, satellite, personal video recorders, and internet TV.

Although the traditional media formats are being challenged, most will adapt to operate alongside the new digital media. And the new media themselves are confronting the issues that have cropped up through history such as censorship, privacy, copyright, piracy, and ways of getting paid for content.

THE NEW ERA

The web has been taking over the role of many of its predecessors in terms of both consumers' time and advertising revenues. That is not to say that a website can reproduce the excitement and impact of a blockbuster movie on a big screen or the relaxation and pleasure of flicking through a top-quality glossy magazine on a beach. But it will radically change the economics of traditional media—indeed, it already has—which now have to find ways to reinvent their value proposition. While some media will continue to operate with a model financed solely by advertising, that pool of time-honored revenue is shrinking as online does a better job of targeting consumers. Some legacy media are experimenting with charging for their existing content online, although the most successful are those who design material specifically for the web audience rather than simply trying to sell their old product via a new media channel.

Traditional media resent and resist new arrivals. The BBC's first Director-General, Lord Reith, had trenchant views on the introduction of commercial television in the 1950s, describing it as "akin to the bubonic plague." Thirty years earlier newspaper owners had gone to great lengths to undermine Reith's own plans to develop BBC Radio. Jack Valenti, the long-standing president of the Motion Picture Association of America, was vehemently critical of any new development that might threaten the movie studios. In 1974 he told Congress that "Cable TV was a huge parasite in the marketplace" and in 1982 that "the VCR is to the American film producer and American public as the Boston Strangler is to women alone at home."[3] The web and digital media are viewed with equal concern. Rupert Murdoch, for example, accused Google and others of "theft" by aggregating news without payment.[4]

To predict what happens next we need to understand the impact of digital and screen technology. Speech was the medium that allowed human society to function, but it was limited to a small crowd in a single place at a specific time; it did little to extend man's reach. Writing and documents created a permanent record and thus extended communication over time and distance. Printing made books numerous and portable, which extended their impact further. The telegraph made long-distance messages instant. Radio and television extended our ability to hear and see at a distance, although initially these were ephemeral media that only happened in real time: unless you were tuned into a particular station and at a particular moment, the program was gone. But with digitization everything is now available to everyone, everywhere, and for ever. Media is now timeless and borderless and its distribution costs are near zero.

WHAT ARE MEDIA?

Put "media" into Google and you get more than one billion results. It's a very broad term. The search reveals that Media was an ancient region of Asia near the Caspian Sea that flourished about 1,000 years before the fall of Rome. It is roughly where the Kurds live today. That is the first recorded use of the word, but is only relevant to this story in that the region happens to be the source of what is now the English language.

The word "medium" is both an adjective and a noun. As an adjective it means average, with alternatives being "intermediate" and "middle." As a noun it is defined as "means," with the alternatives of "vehicle," "channel," and "mode." It is the use of medium as a noun that is the subject of this book. It is the vehicle by which words, images, information, and ideas are distributed. Content is *mediated* if it reaches us through the agency of a *medium*.

The Oxford English Dictionary defines media as "the main means of mass communication (esp. newspapers and broadcasting)." The American *Webster's* goes for "any means, agency or instrumentality of communication." The more contemporary *Encarta* has "the various means of mass communication thought of as a whole, including television, radio, magazines and newspapers."

Information can be conveyed to one person from another using a device such as a letter, the telephone, or email. This is point-to-point communication: a simple transmission. A one-to-one message is a narrowcast medium, as the recipient is usually targeted by the sender. Information or ideas can also be conveyed from the one to the many by a broadcast medium such as a newspaper or a radio or television program. This is the more normal sense of the term "mass media."

When you talk to a friend over a table, the medium you are using is, technically, air. The carriage mechanism for your words is the mixture of gases between you. But in the sense used in this book, the medium being employed is speech. The spoken word is the medium used to communicate your thoughts. The air is the physical medium that transmits the sound waves. The thought is the content.

When we "listen to the radio," it is the radio receiver itself that we hear emitting speech and music. The radio waves are also a medium, which allow the broadcast to happen although you cannot hear the radio waves themselves. You need the receiver to translate the electromagnetic pulses into sound waves your ears can recognize.

Most media act as a carriage mechanism for other, more basic media forms. At the simplest we have spoken words and hand-drawn images. Both of these can be argued to be, at their most fundamental, expressions of raw thought: manifestations of activity in the brain. They are building blocks of the more complex communications by which humans give instructions and express ideas. The written word is a tangible and permanent manifestation of transitory spoken language. It uses symbols—the alphabet—to communicate the thoughts expressed by speech.

Is music a medium? The answer must be yes, as it conveys a message. Music evokes emotion and thus creates communication. That little tone on your PC tells you Windows is starting up. Reveille says "wake up" to soldiers. The "Wedding March" signals the arrival of the bride as surely as a text message or an electronic sign.

THE BUILDING BLOCKS OF MEDIA

There are 16 main media channels, which are the vehicles used to convey the four basic elements of speech, music, images, and writing. These are the tools humans have developed to express our thoughts and emotions. The various media formats—books, newspapers, television, and so on—are the channels used to distribute this content more widely.

In effect, both images and music communicate from mind to mind without the need for language. They are visceral and direct. Anyone in the world, of any age or nationality, can respond to a picture or a tune. Spoken and written words only communicate after we have learned the code of a particular language. They transmit more complex ideas, but require education, preparation, and analysis.

SPEECH

Boxgrove in West Sussex, southern England, has given its name to a very early ancestor of ours: Boxgrove Man, whose remains were found there in 1994. These were big, muscular hunters, direct forerunners of modern human beings, who lived some 350,000 years ago. The evidence suggests they had the physiology to communicate using sounds and had, potentially, a high level of control over their vocal cords.[5] In 2004 more specimens of Boxgrove Man were found in Spain, which provided clear fossil evidence of advanced hearing and voice box development.[6] It is not unreasonable to assume that the human ability to communicate with sound, if not actually a spoken language, can be dated back to this time.

It is impossible to say with any certainty when intelligible speech developed. We know that written records of language started to appear about 6,000 years ago and we can be sure that spoken language must predate this by some considerable degree. But how did it start and what did it sound like? The problem with spoken as opposed to written language is that it leaves no trace in the historical record. Numerous theories have been developed to try to solve the puzzle of its origins.

Humans are unlike other mammals in that we do not (normally) use our teeth for hunting or fighting. Our mouths have become a specialized part of us with a big emphasis on communication. We are also unusual as we have developed two different hemispheres in our brain. In most people the left hemisphere is dominant and it is in there that the speech functions reside. Differential brain development seems linked to people having dominant left or right handedness and is also connected to manual skills such as tool

EXTENDING THE FIVE SENSES

Humans' perception of the world is based on the data obtained from our five senses: touch, taste, smell, hearing, and vision. These vary in the degree to which they access remote information and can be mediated.

Touch and taste are the most intimate and the least extensive of the senses. You have to be close to the observed subject for them to function. Touch needs direct contact. Taste is triggered by receptors in the mouth. Smell provides more extension and informs us about our near environment. Nothing communicates breakfast more emotively than the aroma of cooking bacon.

Both hearing and vision allow us to undertake a far more remote investigation of our environment. In our primitive past they were the vital senses for both hunter and prey. They let us experience what is happening at a distance, and they can be applied to specific objects, not only the general background. They can be focused. We talk about hearing (general) and listening (specific). We say that we see (broad) and we watch (narrow). Vision and hearing are the two senses most extended by the media. But it is hearing that leads to the most fundamental building block that sets humans apart from all other species: the ability to talk.

making. Somewhere in our ancient history the use of tools and the development of speech are linked.

Speech seems to happen in humans in a rather miraculous fashion. Babies learn it by imitation. Individuals who may be regarded as wholly illiterate, in that they are unable to read and write, can be highly articulate speakers. Many animals have a voice and can communicate with sound, but only humans use language, which is a set of rules to allow people to understand each other correctly.

The origins of language

The source of modern English can be traced back to an ancient language called Proto-Indo-European, spoken about 10,000 years ago by people living in the area of what is now Turkey—near the region of Media. This is the original linguistic root from which developed Hindi, German, Russian, and Latin, and hence French, Italian, Spanish, and so on. The links between these languages and the existence of a common ancestral tribe are well proven and accepted.

English is an odd creation, in that it represents the recombination of two of the main language groups, taking its origins from both Germanic and Latin sources. It thus has a very large vocabulary and often enjoys both a German and a Latin version of the same idea. One intriguing example of this is with respect to food. Cow (the animal) comes from old German *cu*. Beef (the meat) comes from Latin *bos*. Sheep (the animal) come from German *scep*, mutton and lamb (the meat) both come from Latin.

But what happened between the sophisticated early Indo-European languages of 10,000 years ago and what we assume were the largely inarticulate grunts and snuffles of Boxgrove Man some 300,000 years earlier? How did we get from what linguistics expert Guy Deutscher calls the "me Tarzan" stage to the oratory of Cicero and the poetry of Shakespeare?[7]

A great leap forward

About 50,000 years ago there seems to have been a sudden and very rapid development of humans as a species. At that point Cro-Magnon man appears in the fossil record. They would have looked almost identical to modern humans and had well-developed vocal cords, tongue, and mouth. They certainly had the physical equipment to speak but, tantalizingly, we can have no way of knowing whether they did. However, archeological evidence shows a greatly increased incidence of communal activity and shar-ing of tasks: art, jewelry, and tool making. These early humans were able to work collectively and they did to a much greater extent than their imme-diate ancestors. Anthropologists term this "the great leap forward" and many suggest it was the development of language that enabled this social cooperation to occur.[8]

A mathematical analysis of the 504 currently recognized major lan-guages by Dr. Quentin Atkinson suggests they can all be traced back to people living in sub-Saharan Africa around 50,000 years ago who devel-oped the basic sounds that are the building blocks of all languages.[9]

Some academics argue that hand gestures, rather than sounds, were the beginning of human communication and that speech later came to accompany them.[10] These initial words would have been complements to the manual signs. In Guy Deutscher's fascinating book *The Unfolding of Language*, he argues that speech started with basic "thing" words (rock, water); "doing" words (run, eat); and "pointing" words (this, that), and that all subsequent grammar—the welter of adjectives, adverbs, pronouns, and the rest—can be seen as a natural development of these initial basic direc-tions.[11] Noam Chomsky, the celebrated American linguistics expert, has argued that human children have an inbuilt ability to recognize the struc-ture of language and that all languages share the same basic logic. It is this innate ability that enables children to learn a language so rapidly.

Language has both an interaction function to help humans organize joint tasks ("Let's all push this boulder from the same side at the same time") and a transaction function to pass knowledge on to others in the group and to subsequent generations ("The big yellow things are called lions. They bite"). The earliest words were probably onomatopoeic. Bang, wind, scream, and cry each sound like the phenomenon they describe. Over time they have become modified, so words like dog and cat may have started with their roots in the sound made by the animal but changed with use.

The next level of language development simply requires the tacit agreement of a group of people that a particular sound denotes a com-monly observed thing: sun, moon, or hill. And then, a bit more sophisti-cated, another sound describes an action: walk, run, jump.

Once it moved beyond the primitive, spoken language allowed us to describe and communicate ideas and abstract notions as well as merely descriptions. A central question is which comes first: thought or speech.

Is speech the articulation of thought or do we need the existence of words to help us think in abstract terms? If you do not know the word for freedom, can you understand the concept? The color red is still the color red and a rock is still a rock even if we call it something different. It exists as a tangible thing. But good, bad, and evil are concepts defined by language. Outside of the human consciousness they do not exist.

The power of the spoken word

Speech has obvious limitations as a medium. The listener needs to be within earshot to get a true, first-hand version. Communications could be passed over distance by way of a messenger, but he or she had to remember the message and might get it wrong. Nevertheless, stories could be maintained over time by the oral tradition of poetry and songs handed down from one generation to the next.

The two great epic poems by Homer, the *Iliad* and the *Odyssey*, were probably created about 3,000 years ago. Created is a better term than written, as it is likely, according to historian Robin Lane Fox, that originals were not recorded as text and that what we have today is the effort of much later scribes, who heard them from itinerant storytellers touring the ancient world reciting, extending, and modifying the epic tales that had started life as poetry readings in Athens.[12]

Long after the invention of printing, the spoken word remained the main means of communication, as most people could not read. The minister in church, the orator in the public square, and the master in school used speech rather than text to communicate. The pulpits of the medieval Catholic Church have been described as the mass medium of their day.[13] Shakespeare's grammar school at Stratford-upon-Avon emphasized the practice of rhetoric and made extensive use of plays and poetry to teach.

MUSIC

Music is a fundamental communications tool, an arrangement of sounds and silences, which probably predates speech and certainly predates writing as a means of getting a message across. Even those of us who cannot read a note of music nor have any idea of the structure of composition can whistle a tune. The ranks of successful rock stars with no formal musical training are legion. You do not have to understand the technology of music to be moved by it. Music stimulates emotions and communicates ideas. It can make us happy or sad, brave or nostalgic. It can help us get to sleep. It can be romantic; it can be military.

The archeological record demonstrates that primitive human societies had the ability to make music long before they used writing. Musical collaboration probably played an important part in the development of speech. The evocation of emotions through music must have developed out of imitating natural sounds such as birdsong and animal calls.

The first attempts to control sound would have been using the human voice to reproduce familiar noises. The development of percussion instruments would have been a natural extension of the sounds made when using early tools like hammers. The earliest manmade musical instruments are flutes made from vulture bones in Germany about 35,000 years ago.[14] Purpose-built drums have been around for at least 5,000 years and had an important signaling function, as well as encouraging soldiers in battle and slaves at work. The notion of variable pitch would have come from experiments with humming and whistling and by using primitive wind instruments such as flutes.

Pitch is the frequency of vibration of a sound. High frequencies are high pitched and low frequencies are low pitched. A long string when plucked will emit a lower-pitch note than a short string. Likewise, a long bamboo pipe when blown across will produce a lower pitch than a short one. A range of carefully selected bamboo pipes will provide the full range of musical notes. Variation of pitch is a naturally occurring event, like wind blowing through trees. The description of musical scales and the organization of notes into octaves is a human attempt to make sense of this natural phenomenon.

A musical note is simply a sound at a particular frequency

THE MATHEMATICS OF MUSIC

In Chinese mythology music was invented by Ling Lun about 5,000 years ago. He was said to have been given a mission by the Emperor to find a set of bamboo pipes that would exactly reproduce a perfect set of tones from which all other instruments could be tuned. Having found the ideal set of pipes, he cast a set of 60 bells for the imperial palace to reproduce each perfect note. The underlying mathematics of Chinese musical theory—as described by Ling Lun's bells—is more or less the same as that recorded by the Greeks 2,000 years later.

played for a certain length of time. A chord is a combination of notes. Harmony is a combination of notes and chords that work well together and that people find pleasing. Most people will say that music written in a major key (one type of combination) sounds happy and positive, whereas that in a minor key sounds sad and concerning.

Combinations of notes that have certain ratios between their frequencies are either pleasing or annoying. In an octave, the ratio of the note C and G is about 2:3. It is called a "perfect fifth" and sounds attractive. The notes C and B have a ratio of about 10:19 and the combination jars on the ear.[15] It is this ability to create an emotional reaction that makes music such a powerful media building block. Most societies link music to their gods and it has always had a strong association with magic. That music played a major part in ancient ritual is clear from written records and stories. Pictures 5,000 years ago depict musical instruments being played. The word "music" itself comes from ancient Greece, where education was broadly divided into *gymnastica*, which was physical, and *musica*, which was cultural and intellectual, the latter activities being those arts inspired by the Muses. What we now call music had a much broader definition then, including poetry and drama.

In religious ritual music heightened the experience and gave structure to the service. In war it was used to inspire the armies and communicate orders in battle. In physical labor it was employed to control and inspire effort. It also has a central role in folklore and religion. Joshua is said to have used trumpets to bring down the walls of Jericho. Krishna played a flute to stop the rivers flowing. Orpheus could use his lyre to charm animals. The Pied Piper of Hamelin employed music to great effect on the city's rats.

Prosody is the study of the rhythm and melody of spoken lan-

STRINGS OR WIND?

Music has always had some deep and complex link with human thinking, social organization, and even politics. In ancient Greece the followers of Apollo were conservative and classical, favoring simplicity and objectivity. They were associated with stringed instruments, particularly the lyre. By contrast, the members of the cult of Dionysus were the romantics. They were emotional and sensual and subjective. They favored wind instruments. This separation was an early version of Roundheads and Cavaliers: a great human political divide manifest in music.

guage and recent studies have suggested a close link between music and speech. Research from Germany demonstrated that babies recognize the musical qualities of their mother's speech and interpret emotional meaning (such as praise or disapproval) as much from the rhythm of the sounds as from the words themselves. Research also shows that our native language has a significant impact on the way we hear and interpret music. People bought up with tonal languages like Mandarin, where meaning is derived from the way a word is expressed, seem to have a much higher incidence of perfect pitch than those bought up with a language like English, where each word tends to have a unique meaning.[16]

IMAGES

Words are not always required to convey complex and abstract meanings. An image can be a universal communication. The ubiquitous smiley face ☺ transcends differences between language, culture, and education. We all know what it means. It is an emoticon. Symbols like this communicate to us intuitively. The smiley symbol, now available in any word-processing package, started out as three simple punctuation marks on early computer screens : -) which pulled together give a sideways smiling face :-). This usage was invented by (presumably bored) computer technicians at Carnegie Mellon University in 1982 to indicate emails that were intended as a joke. It was an early attempt to convert a text-based medium into something more graphic and user friendly.

The ☺ symbol is used by some people as shorthand at the end of messages for the notion of "I agree." At this point it becomes a rebus, a symbol that stands for a word or group of words and is usually recognized in any language—for example, the ♥ of I ♥ New York. Other images used to communicate on a universal basis are the little icons employed almost the world over to indicate male ♂ and female ♀ or the stylized airplane showing the road to the airport.

Images are powerful communicators. They include everything from sketches to still photographs; from comic graphics to maps and fine art. Images can be both media in themselves and part of other media forms. Early paintings and sculpture often had a clear set of religious, political, and social messages.

We like visual communications. The pie chart is now a familiar part of many newspapers. We use icons to control our smartphones. Commercial brands, long-running musicals, television series, and even cities now feel the need for a distinctive logo. A worldwide audience understands exactly what is implied by the five Olympic rings, the Nike Swoosh, New York's Big Apple, or the white mask of *Phantom of the Opera*. No words are needed. As communication becomes more global and as attention spans become shorter, the role of the image will only grow.

Development of the image

Creating a basic image requires some physical skill, but less training and certainly less social development than using language. An image may be two-dimensional like a drawing or three-dimensional like a sculpture, but in all forms it can convey rich elements of emotion as well as basic information.

Drawings of animals on the walls of caves became abundant from about 30,000 years ago. It seems that our ancestors devoted a lot of effort to creating likenesses of the beasts with which they hunted and worked. There are more than 200 caves with art in France and Spain dating from this period, so we can safely assume that the use of images was widespread and fundamental to early human communication.

The Chauvet in Southern France, for example, has accurate likenesses of rhinoceroses, bears, bison, lions, and horses. By the time we get to 17,000 years ago the artists who drew in the Lascaux caves in South West France show an amazing sophistication of form and perspective.

From these early experiments humanity went on to develop drawing far more rapidly than writing. An alphabet is, after all, simply speech communicated through drawn images, so it needed the development of a structured, spoken language combined with a high level of graphical skill before writing could happen.

Once papyrus and parchment became common, artists applied their skills to the pictures in books and the illustrated manuscript became the main visual art form. Pigments, oil paints, and inks allowed greater sophistication and the development of engraving meant that multiple copies could be made.

An early practical use of engraving was the map, which used drawing to show the representation of spatial relationships, important for recording and conveying military and trading information. It was a powerful image-based medium and the first attempt to represent a concept rather than just depict an object.

From the 1840s onward, photography allowed the capture of an image by a chemical process. Once it had become established, painters became more interested in investigating the artistic opportunities of their craft rather than merely seeking to depict reality. Digital photography allows almost unlimited manipulation of images, which has made them a ubiquitous element of most media.

WRITING

While speech allows instant communication, writing allows information to be preserved over time. About 5,500 years ago an unknown member of a long-gone civilization called the Harappan etched some symbols onto a clay pot in what is now modern Pakistan. We think, but do not know as we cannot read them, that the symbols indicated the contents of the pot. These fragments are the earliest-known surviving example of writing.[17] Some 4,000 years later we know that a scribe called Sin-liqe-unninni made a copy of the oral legend of King Gilgamesh on clay tablets in a language called Sumarian using a writing technique called cuneiform.[18] He is cited as the world's first-named author of a story and subsequent scholarship means that we are able to read what he wrote.[19]

Versions of the Gilgamesh story were recorded in hieroglyphs on scrolls of papyrus at the Great Library at Alexandria. This intellectual marvel of the ancient world was founded somewhere around 300 BC and contained some 500,000 scrolls.[20] The great collection suffered many indignities and in about 43 BC much of it was destroyed by fire, possibly by accident, or possibly by Julius Caesar in an act of vandalism. Later, in about 600 AD, legend suggests that the rest was used as fuel for the city furnaces to heat public baths when the new rulers decided that these written records had little cultural value compared to access to hot water.

Alphabets

The earliest writing techniques such as cuneiform and hieroglyphics made use of pictures to convey meaning. They were limited, as the number of ideas that could be communicated was constrained by the lack of available images. Cuneiform symbols were a series of cuts made with a wedge-shaped reed. Egyptian hieroglyphics had about 700 images.

The phonetic alphabet—the direct ancestor of the letters on this page—emerged about 3,000 years ago. It was invented by the Phoenicians to solve the problem of representing many words with only a small number of symbols. Letters represent the smallest sounds that can be combined, the subatomic particles of language. Each bit of sound is called a phoneme. Syllables are like the atoms; words themselves are the molecules; and sentences are the complex compounds.

The Roman alphabet, as used in the English language, consists of 26 letters that create some 45 recognizable phonemes. Combinations of letters in English can give phonemes that in other languages might have a letter of their own. CH and TH, for example, are phonemes for which no single English letter can stand. The letter C in English can be a hard pronunciation as in "card" or soft as in "ceramic"—two phonemes from one letter depending on the context.

An alphabet is simply a written way to build and record the sounds of a spoken language. In Malaysia, for example, the Malay spoken language appears in both Arabic and English alphabets. The single spoken language sounds the same, but the two written representations use different symbols.

The future of writing

The English of Shakespeare and even more so Chaucer is hard to

NO WORDS

The Chinese written language is not an alphabet but is based on logograms. A logogram is a symbol that represents an entire word or idea. An example close to home would be the logogram for the number 7. In English we say *seven*, in French *sept*, in German *Sieben*, and in Italian *sette*. But in written documents in any of these European languages the symbol 7—the logogram—can be used. A native of each country could read the written number in the others' documents but they may well not understand the spoken or written word.

Similarly, different Chinese dialects have developed different sounds for the same idea, but the logogram is the same in all cases. So different are the dialects that it can be hard for the speaker of one to understand another, although they can all read the same script. The problem of writing in Chinese is that a typical author needs more than 2,000 separate symbols (out of a possible 60,000) to communicate effectively.

read today, although that of Bunyan and Defoe is easier. In Elizabethan times (the late 1500s) a major language transition was underway. Latin was used in most documents and was fixed in form and meaning by virtue of having been written down for generations. However, the spelling, grammar, and meanings of spoken English were evolving rapidly as immigrants arrived and people made the language up as they went along. It is said that Shakespeare created, or at least was the first to write down, some 1,700 new words. It was only with the spread of printing that the English language became fixed and standardized.

At the risk of upsetting the Academie Française, it seems hard to imagine that English will not become the world's common written language even if local oral traditions survive. There is just too much momentum. English is most people's second choice of language and it is more computer friendly than Chinese logograms. Most people have to learn English if they wish to communicate with those in other countries.

In his book *Globish*, Robert McCrum notes that about 80 percent of home pages on the web are "in some form of English." He adds:

> Constantly in flux, at the mercy of fashion, whim and caprice, the indefinable genius—the word is hardly too strong—of the English language has always been to adapt itself, like mercury, to every new contour.[21]

The trend toward English is illustrated by the actions of leading Japanese internet giant Rakuten, that country's version of Amazon and eBay combined. It has adopted an English-only policy for internal meetings, documents, emails, and even building signage in Tokyo. The founder, Hiroshi Mikitani, says the company has done this in pursuit of its plans to be truly global and that "it is a huge issue for Japan [to be] the only country with all these well educated people who cannot speak English."[22]

Nevertheless, the English of the year 2100 is likely to be quite a bit different from the language of this book, because it will reflect the fluid development of the spoken word. Writing will also become more visual. We can already see the huge influence of text messaging and web pages. The following sentence may look ugly but most readers will understand it:

C U L8r @ the ♫. Lets hope for ☼. Band is rly wkd. Txt me ☺

Writing started as a way of using made-up images to communicate speech. Images are internationally comprehensible so this use of more graphics is an inevitable development for a world language.

RICH MEDIA COMBINATIONS

The media experience becomes richer when two or more of the building blocks are combined. And some people experience an unusual crossover of media stimuli that gives clues as to why combinations work so powerfully. If you look at a letter of the alphabet and you always see it as a certain color, or if a particular number evokes a specific taste or music a particular smell, then you suffer from, or perhaps are blessed with, synaesthesia. As many as 1 person in 100 experiences this. Composer Richard Wagner, artists Wassily Kandinsky and David Hockney, and writer Vladimir Nabokov are all recorded as having this ability.

Active synaesthesia organizations have now been set up around the world. In simple terms, the condition may be described as an abnormal set of connections in the brain. Researchers say that it is prevalent in creative people, has a strong genetic link, and that the ability to develop language derives from making associations between sounds, colors, and smells.

As with other neurological phenomena like color blindness or perfect pitch, synaesthesia may be present in all of us. It can be triggered by the use of drugs like LSD. People often use references to synaesthesia by combining senses, like "a bitter wind" or "a loud pattern." The ability to trigger multisensory responses in media is of huge interest, as it could be what makes certain works of art or music so popular and so evocative.

The 16 media types described in this book are, for the most part, combinations of the building blocks. Books use writing and drawing, radio uses speech, and music and magazines use text and images. The greatest overall emotional impact comes from live performance such as theatre, a movie, or a rock concert, where speech, music, images, and text are all combined with touch, taste, smell, and, at times, mass hysteria.

Society needs media to help it function. Media allow us to share ideas and experience and to collaborate. In a speech about creativity,

Maurice Saatchi, one of the world's most famous advertising professionals, observed:

> Creative people can take the three humble tools at their disposal—words, pictures and music—and carve from them weapons that will change the world.[23]

Society has been shaped by the media that have developed to serve it and our lives would be utterly different if the media did not exist. We are now at one of the great turning points of the media industry. The rest of this book explains how we arrived here.

PART TWO
Evolution | The Media Journey

From the earliest drawings on the walls of caves to writing on clay tablets through to the technical revolutions of printing, broadcasting, and the internet the experience of consuming media has become more complex and intense.

Each new technology creates new media formats that both add to and modify what went before. Each new media type has brought its own creative opportunities. Part Two describes the forces that have fashioned the media industry.

Shaping the media

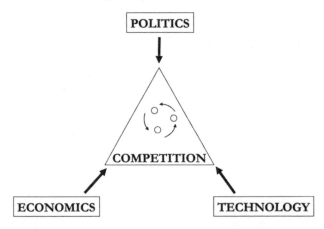

Media have been shaped by the interplay of politics, economics, and technology—the "PET" theory of media. When a new technology emerges it can often be adapted to transmit mediated content. In its early days this new medium will be shaped by political controls, and modified by the economics of subscription and advertising revenues.

As we began to see in Part One, the vast range of media we enjoy today has resulted from thousands of years of development. Primitive words allowed us to talk with the fellow occupant of our cave, but we needed to communicate further than the person standing next to us. That is how we started developing media. Smoke signals, drums, reflecting mirrors, and semaphore flags were all ways to extend our reach over distance. Carvings on clay tablets, hieroglyphs on city walls, and the oral tradition of epic poetry were ways of communicating over time.

Long before they were able to write them down, poets and dramatists created chronicles to be memorized. A popular poem had the potential to reach tens of thousands of people through itinerant storytellers. The theatre is an extension of the spoken word, which took speech from one to one to some to many. The play in performance was the broadcast medium of Shakespeare's time. The social comment of *The Merchant of Venice* or the political messages of *Richard II* would have reached a huge audience via the Globe Theatre.

For several thousand years media was limited to speech and hand-written documents. The Roman senator who recorded his thoughts on scrolls in his library was using writing to communicate over time. The Roman general who sent written instructions to his troops on the front line was extending his geographic reach. But both addressed a small audience, wax tablets had limited capacity, parchment and scribes were expensive.

In his treatise on Politics, written around 350 BC, Aristotle argued that the ideal size of a city was limited by the degree to which its people could share information.[1] One way of interpreting this is that the size of a well-functioning society was limited by the size of the crowd who could hear an orator's speech at the same time. Those spoken words were, in effect, unmediated. The crowd heard them directly. Media has developed to extend the effective size of the crowd.

In the 1440s Johannes Gutenberg made a breakthrough and his printing press made information widely available. Its impact was on distribution more than creation. The free thinking of the Renaissance took limited and expensive manuscript books out of the churches and put printed copies into the universities and schools. This drove the rapid development of science, art, and culture.

Nevertheless, it was not until after England's Glorious Revolution in 1688 that print became widespread, cheap, and legal. News sheets were produced by an emboldened merchant class wanting to express their views and by the 1700s print technology was everywhere. The transmission of radical ideas was at the heart of the Revolutions in both France and America.

Once newspapers arrived, the role of the theatre as a communication medium changed and its focus was more entertainment than propaganda. Print would reign supreme as the information channel for 200 years until radio came along in the 1920s to, once again, take the spoken word to a mass audience.

In their first 30 years, radio stations offered a full range of news, documentaries, variety shows, and music. However, when television became popular they retreated into specialized formats. Cable TV accelerated the process and in 1981 The Buggles' song "Video Killed the Radio Star" launched MTV. In spite of television's reach, 25 years later radio star Howard Stern signed a new $500 million contract to do his (outrageous) thing on Satellite Radio. The radio star was alive and well and very highly paid, and radio had reinvented itself as pure entertainment.

At the turn of the twentieth century websites blossomed and dot-com companies boomed and then bombed. But the fastest-growing advertising medium, in terms of dollars spent, was posters. This millennia-old medium had reinvented itself with improved illumination and low-cost printing.

So the story of media unfolds against the backdrop of the development of humanity. Social history and media history influence one another. Media are both a mirror and a window. They reflect the events around us and can also be a major force for social change. And the media themselves are continually evolving, driven by politics, economics, and technology.

POLITICS

Politicians have a love–hate relationship with the news media. They want to use it to increase their popularity and to get elected, but they fear it as a platform for their opponents. And they worry, in extreme cases, that it might promote civil unrest. Many politicians would like to be able to control the media and in totalitarian dictatorships that is exactly what they do.

This is nothing new. Early manuscripts that did not please were banned by the Catholic Church and books that offended were burnt in public. The British monarchy controlled printing by granting a monopoly to the Stationers' Company. Oliver Cromwell closed the playhouses when his Puritan regime took over London. Some 300 years later, Hitler closed the theatres after he invaded Poland.

Governments can exercise control either directly by ownership or indirectly by taxation and regulation. Various techniques from the official censor; laws of treason, slander, and libel; licenses; and specific media taxes have all been used.

The electromagnetic spectrum is a limited resource and without some form of state allocation of frequencies to radio and television, chaos would result. However, regulators have often gone well beyond the technical allocation of bandwidth and tried to control content in addition.

As international satellites and the web have rendered domestic broadcast control meaningless, governments are seeking ways to manage web activity as well, although given its global nature this is proving to be difficult. In the 1500s attempts by France to impose strong regulation on local printing resulted in a thriving unregulated French-language publishing community in the nearby Netherlands; 600 years on, similar things are happening online.

State control

In practice, whenever we use the term "censorship" today we nearly always take it to mean an attempt to review, in advance of publication or broadcast, a document or program and prevent it being made public. The notion of political censorship (ideas) as opposed to state security (secrets) and moral protection (offensive material) is often characterized as being at odds with freedom of speech, as in nontotalitarian societies one of the roles of the media is to monitor and control government.

Moral censorship—to prevent undesirable material falling into the hands of children, for example—is accepted and to a degree desirable, although in Western society only the most extreme ideas and images are regarded as illegal. From a moral point of view pretty much anything can be shown, said, or portrayed in controlled media such as theatre and cinema to which access can be restricted. Newspapers and television are expected to exercise more self-restraint, as they are more widely accessible. The rise of the web is producing particular challenges, as the mechanisms to control it are not available and, in reality, it is available to anyone of any age.

CENSORSHIP

Censorship, be it military, political, or moral, is as old as media themselves. The most powerful medium in ancient Athens was the voice of the marketplace orator, the most potent of whom was Socrates. Afraid of his influence and unhappy with his message, the rulers of the day made him drink poison—an early example of draconian government control. The word and the practice of censorship date from ancient Rome, where the *censores* were a type of Roman magistrate who were given the duty of looking after the *regimen moram*, the general conduct and moral behavior of the citizens. The idea was also found in ancient China, where royal officers were appointed to monitor the behavior of government officials.

ECONOMICS

Media organizations exist to move content from the originator to the consumer. Often consumers are willing to pay for what they receive, but advertisers are also prepared to pay for the privilege of sending a message to those consumers. These means that media companies are not typical businesses, as the ability to "sell" their audience gives them an unusual source of income.

In addition, unlike most of human enterprise, some media owners do not have to make a profit. Media is seen by many governments as a social benefit and thus they are prepared to subsidize or even pay for it. Books and newspapers in many countries are free of sales tax. Theatres and the film industry receive grants. Many nations pay for a state broadcasting company.

Assessing what it is that motivates people who work in media organizations is also not straightforward. There is a lot more to it than money. It is a complex mixture of artistic fulfillment, altruism, and the need to make a living. Media workers are often driven by the desire to achieve a channel for their output and recognition by their peers. There is no other industry that gives itself quite so many awards. If there is an overriding philosophy for most media people, it is probably some variant of the old MGM slogan *ars gratia artis*—"art for art's sake"—implying that creative people work for the joy of creation rather than some broader social, political, or economic purpose.

A quest for "monopoly"

There are two basic parts to the business of media: production and distribution. Each requires different skills and technologies, but over time most media owners have tried to own both so that they could control the whole process. The structure of any one media industry has often been driven by a desire to obtain a vertical monopoly. The early printers were also publishers who created books to keep their presses busy. Publishers were frequently booksellers as well. They opened shops to provide a market for their output where they could control prices. In the days before copyright it was the printer rather than the author who effectively owned the value of the book.

The most obvious example of vertical integration is the movie business. At the height of the Hollywood studio system in the 1940s, the five so-called majors owned the studios, the cameras, the film laboratories, the stars' contracts, the distribution companies, and the cinemas.

For much of the history of media it was ownership of the distribution channel (theatres, presses, broadcast towers, and so on) that gave media owners their monopoly power. Digital technology and the web have changed all that, fundamentally upsetting conventional media economics.

The buzzword for managers of media companies for some years has been "convergence." Everything becomes everything else. Telephones become televisions. Televisions become retail outlets. Music players become web browsers. Websites become radio and television stations. "Content is King" said Bill Gates in 1996, implying that ownership of the transmission medium is not as important as owning what goes out on it. And it is increasingly true that it is content that marks out success or failure rather than ownership of the distribution channel. Being a traditional press baron confers far less power when every home computer and, indeed, mobile phone allows unrestricted web access.

Low or no marginal costs

When you buy a coffee in Starbucks or a loaf of bread in a grocery store, you are engaged in a very straightforward consumer transaction. Someone has grown the coffee or the wheat, processed it, transported it, and, in the case of Starbucks, paid someone to make it in an expensive city-center location. The money you pay covers all these costs and leaves profit. If a lot more people buy coffee or bread, the cost per cup or loaf goes down a bit through economies of scale, but only a bit because each product has substantial physical or labor content.

When you buy a newspaper or magazine you are involved in a very different transaction. The cost of creating the newspaper is the same whether there is 1 reader or 1 million. The writers, photographers, and editors will have to work just as hard no matter how many people read their product. Printing and distribution costs will, of course, vary by the size of circulation, as they are physical elements of each copy sold. If you can sell more newspapers then each marginal reader is almost pure profit; but if you charge too much you will lose readers to cheaper alternatives. If your circulation goes down normally your advertising income will follow. Getting the right balance is a fine art and managers of newspapers study price elasticity with great care.

With broadcast media the economics are even starker. The cost of making a radio or television program is fixed by the type of show. The infrastructure of broadcast towers is fixed. The cost of serving the extra, marginal viewer or listener is essentially zero. This means that as the audience grows the cost per viewer or listener goes down, while the advertising value goes up. Extra audience is a double win, which is why ratings are monitored with such enthusiasm.

However in media, unlike other businesses, you can choose to have a zero price as you can just "sell" your audience. Some newspaper owners, typically those with daily titles in big cities, choose to offer their papers for free, as the cost of collecting the small cover price is so high that it is not worth doing and the larger circulation makes the advertising income alone profitable.

Hit driven

Because the marginal viewer or reader is disproportionably profitable, media managers spend a lot of time looking for "hits" to capture more people. In practice, in many media businesses, some 80 percent of the profit will come from just 20 percent of the titles or stars. The "hits" are crucial but hard to find. Public taste is unpredictable and picking winners is a tricky business, which often makes media owners very conservative and encourages them to stick to confirmed performers.

The two original media businesses, theatre and book publishing, were both capital intensive and risky. A play had to be written and produced before it was unveiled to the audience. Likewise, a book had to be physically printed and distributed to booksellers. If the play or book was not popular, the initial investment was wasted.

This is why media entrepreneurs adopted the "proven hit" formula from early on. A house playwright like William Shakespeare reduced the risk to The Globe. His name on the playbill ensured an audience. Early book publishers sought to reduce the risk by offering bibles and religious texts, which served a proven market, or by seeking subscriptions in advance so they knew they had orders before they printed the book.

The early newspapers hedged their bets. Many of the readers were known to the publisher and became loyal subscribers. Once a title had a following it was not subject to the same hit-and-miss risk as a single book or play. In addition, with bigger audiences and regular editions, newspapers could obtain advertising income.

The film business has the most challenging experience of managing hits. Its product is a one-off that is expensive to make. This encourages the star system and sequels. A big name or recognized formula reassures an audience, as people are reluctant to commit two or more hours of their time and their money to an unknown quantity.

The web and digital distribution are offering solutions to the "hits-only" problem. The concept of the "long tail" of accessible, niche titles has been well explained in the book of the same name by Chris Anderson.[2] A typical large bookstore might carry 40,000 titles. An online operation such as Amazon can offer more like 400,000. Books and magazines can now be stored digitally and printed on demand. This means that distribution costs are reduced and books that are out of print will become available again.

Network effects

The beneficial economic impact of a network can be seen throughout media history. In simple terms, a network effect is the increase in value of a media product as the result of linking it to numerous users. A commonly quoted example is the fax machine. A single fax machine (no matter how good it is) is useless. A second fax machine owned by a supplier, customer, or friend makes the first one more useful. If everyone has one then it becomes a vital tool and the cost of buying one is likely to go down substantially because of manufacturing economies of scale. The telephone and the telegraph also exhibit classic network effects.

Early newspapers experienced a strong network effect as they reproduced each other's news stories (often without attribution), which made their own publication more valuable. Each title benefited from the sharing of content and the practice led to the establishment of news agencies like Reuters, Havas, and the Associated Press, which meant that newspapers could share the services of a network of foreign correspondents.

Furthermore, network effects defined the structure of radio in the US, as local stations (operating under a local license) quickly found that sharing programming and selling joint advertising produced huge benefits. Radio signals are localized because of the physics of broadcasting, but individual local stations can rarely afford large program budgets. Once linked together they can simultaneously broadcast to the whole country, allowing costs to be shared and advertising to be sold on a national basis.

Broadcast networks require transmission mechanisms to join stations together. Communications networks—linking numerous one-to-one users—need some form of exchange mechanism. The structure of the internet is a direct descendant of the mail-sorting rooms and telegraph exchanges of the 1700s and 1800s. And the web is the ultimate example of the benefits of a network effect. As each incremental person logs on the network becomes more valuable.

SORTING AND SWITCHING

The initial postal services were couriers who rode from one royal palace to another. The first telegraph lines were point to point, mostly along newly constructed railway tracks. In these early phases the main users were the palace officials for the post and station masters for the telegraph. However, once postal routes and telegraph networks linked numerous places, the demand to communicate was huge. This required messages to be continually directed and redirected. This led to the invention of sorting offices in the case of the mail and switching centers for the telegraph, with lines temporarily connecting locations by pulling plugs in and out.

Advertising

The earliest advertisements used the earliest medium: speech. Ancient orators who gathered people together to tell stories must surely have used the opportunity to slip in the odd commercial. Certainly by the time we were writing on walls the medium was being used for commerce. From the excavations at Pompeii we find enough examples of commercial messaging to suggest it had been around a long time before then. Printed advertising handbills, promoting taverns and entertainment, appeared very soon after Gutenberg produced his first Bible. God may have got in first, but Mammon was close behind.

Display advertising is where whole pages or half pages of a newspaper or magazine are purchased to promote a brand generically, often without a specific sales proposition. Display did not really feature in the economics of media until the 1800s, when a combination of mass readership and branded packaged goods came together to create the conditions for it to be of value.

Income from classified advertising has been important to media since the late 1700s. Particularly in the US, newspapers developed right from the start as advertising-supported vehicles. After the War of Independence, the fledgling US government encouraged the spread of newspapers as an aid to building a democracy and unifying a federal nation. It did this by subsidizing the postal delivery of papers, thus creating a mass readership. Subscriptions had to be relatively inexpensive, so advertising played a major role in financing publication. In particular, the fast-growing city-based mail-order firms like Sears Roebuck needed to advertise to reach the largely rural consumers who rarely made a visit to the store. In

1800, according to media historian Paul Starr, 20 of the 24 daily papers published in America had the word *Advertiser* in their title.[3]

Initially all papers designed and sold their advertising themselves. However, as retailers and manufacturers grew more numerous and wanted design experts to make their messages stand out, the profession of advertising agent was created. The first was in 1841 when the American Newspaper Agency was founded in Philadelphia by one Volney Palmer. Its role was to sell space on behalf of local papers and to create eye-catching advertising for its clients. Perhaps the most venerable name in advertising, J Walter Thompson, started in 1864 when J Walter hung out his shingle in New York to sell space on behalf of magazines. He invented the idea of separating the creative department from account executives.

Agencies traditionally took a 15 percent commission from their media customers—newspapers and magazines—and worked for their manufacturing clients for nothing. The publishers were happy as this added to their sales efforts. The advertisers saw the commission as part of their overall cost of media. Nevertheless, it was an anomalous relationship where the client was not charged for creative work done and the agency had an inbuilt incentive to make the client's media budget as large as possible. In recent years this structure has broken down. Creative agencies are now paid by clients to develop ideas and

CLASSIFIED ADS

Early advertising in newspapers was what we now call "classified," as it attempted to sell specific goods and services rather than to promote a brand. The first advertisement for coffee appeared in *The Publick Adviser* in 1657 promoting a London coffee house:

In Bartholomew Lane *on the back side of the Old Exchange, the drink called* Coffee, *which is a very wholesom and Physical drink, having many excellent vertues.*[4]

The term classified comes from the practice in early newspapers of grouping together types of product or service in columns, hence putting them into classes. It was regarded as an important service to readers as well as a useful source of income. *The Times of London*, founded in 1788, carried classified advertising on its whole front page right up until 1966.

Classified advertising is a huge business and is of particular importance to media with a local focus, as their audience tend to be interested in selling things to each other.

media-buying agencies are paid an agreed fee to negotiate the best possible terms and capture discounts from media owners.

Advertising is not a medium in itself but is an integral part of most media and indeed the economic driving force. Without it the media industry would be fundamentally changed and most media would look, sound, and feel very different.

The creative skills of media professionals have influenced the look of advertising and, in return, the work of advertising copywriters and art directors has influenced the media. Many of the early posters mimicked works of art. Many familiar ideas for television commercials are borrowed from classic film sequences. Going the other way, the tight editing and careful scripting style of the classic 30-second commercial have done much to influence the look and feel of music videos and television shows.

Websites in their millions have been launched on the assumption that advertising will be their source of revenue. The argument runs that more eyeballs will lead to more income. It was the chase to establish a high-profile web presence, first-mover advantage, which drove the dot-com boom of the early 2000s. In reality, of course, the total pool of advertising is limited. While there has been a substantial shift of commercial spending away from old media toward online, the total volume of advertising has hardly risen. The net result is that many old-media formats have become unprofitable, but many new-media services also run at a loss as the advertising income is now spread too thinly.

TECHNOLOGY

The main advances that have driven the technical evolution of media are the same as those that have enabled industry generally: mechanization (printing), steam power (mass production), and electricity (telephony and broadcasting). And, more recently, the adoption of digital techniques looks like being the most profound event in media history. Nevertheless, new media are not solely a function of technology; they frequently follow from discoveries that were intended for other purposes. The way a new medium actually evolves is heavily influenced by what is happening in society at the time.

While it was the combination of movable type, a converted wine press, and oil-based inks that allowed printing, it was the use of books by the church reformers and the newly founded universities that created demand. By the 1700s movable type was being widely used for political pamphlets, but it was the development of joint-stock companies, international trade, and the rise of a merchant class that led to a demand for regular news publications.

In the mid-1800s, the process of making cheap paper from wood pulp was perfected about the same time as the invention of the steam-powered rotary printing press. However, it was the newly created consumer goods industry with branded products that led to the development of advertising, which, when combined with increased literacy, funded mass-market publications.

In the 1850s the telegraph utilized the newly discovered properties of electricity. But it was the development of railways that allowed the laying of telegraph wires along the new tracks and also created the need to schedule trains.

Radio required the discovery of electromagnetic waves. But it was intended as a form of wireless telegraph for ships at sea, and only much later did it become a medium of entertainment and information, because radio-set manufacturers wanted to create a market. Similarly, television combined radio with cathode-ray tubes to send pictures, but it was the rise of a consumer society and a huge increase in a wealthy middle class in the 1950s and 1960s that paid for it. Media professionals did not drive the demand for television; that was consumers and advertisers.

The internet started as a way for defense establishments to link their remote computers together in the 1960s. Academics discovered the joys of email in the 1970s. However, it was in the 1980s with the drive of Microsoft to put a computer on every desk, the development by Apple of user-friendly graphical interfaces, and fiberoptic cables that the web as we now experience it emerged.

ADVERTISING

The late 1920s saw an explosion of commercial broadcasting in America, much of the advertising on which was tasteless and misleading. Major broadcasters such as NBC imposed conservative policies that limited advertisers to more muted forms of sponsorship. But by 1932 the US Congress ordered the Federal Radio Commission to investigate the benefits and problems of radio. The resulting report come to the firm conclusion that without advertising the medium could not develop. The shape of what is now commercial broadcasting was thus established.

Technology diffusion

The pace at which new media are taken up varies. Two American academics, Everett Rogers and Frank Bass, have led the field in understanding the factors that influence the rate at which a new technology reaches the market. The differing speeds of uptake are partly a function of price, but mostly of how desirable, or indeed necessary, the service provided is seen to be. The theory identifies groups in the population such as innovators and early adopters who have a much greater propensity to try new technologies.

Radio was relatively slow to be adopted, as the early sets were expensive and primitive and there was limited content. Black-and-white television was the same, slowed also by the fact that radio was already in place and by the Second World War. Color television was much faster, as it was a superior substitute for what was already in the home and much of the original black-and-white equipment needed replacing at a time of economic boom. The video-cassette recorder offered a unique consumer benefit with no substitute. The CD player was a greatly superior alternative to records and offered extensive new content. The take-up of cellphones was relatively slow as the fixed line alternatives were good enough for many of the occasions when people wanted to make a call.

The internet itself has been relatively slow to reach 50 percent of the population, as in its early days it was not seen as a "must-have" and lacked compelling content, but the takeup of services such as Facebook has broken all records in terms of speed of diffusion as the network of the web was already in place. The extraordinary uptake of MP3 players could not have happened until after the internet had achieved critical mass to distribute digital files.

Number of years to achieve 50% penetration of US households[5]

Radio	28 years
Black-and-white TV	24 years
Color TV	18 years
VCR	12 years
CD player	11 years
Cellphone	14 years
Internet access	10 years
MP3 players	6 years

COPYRIGHT

The concept of copyright is where politics, economics, and technology come together. It is at the heart of making the creation of content a successful business and career.

The idea of patents over inventions has been around since the 1400s when the Republic of

Venice recognized various glass-making methods as patent. However, before mechanical printing—that is, before Gutenberg—the notion of being able to own the right to a story or idea was not really an issue. The cost of producing copies of books was very high and the number of copies very small. Most of the texts were religious or scientific, so it seemed reasonable that any value created should go to the book's manufacturer rather than the original author, who was often not an identifiable single individual in any event. Early writers like Chaucer had no protection in copyright. They worked for patrons, Chaucer himself being famously granted "a gallon of wine a day for life" by King Edward III.

The original idea of copyright was a mechanism to enforce the monopoly of printing enjoyed by the members of the Stationer's Company. At the time William Shakespeare was writing his plays, around 1600, there was no legal way for an author to own the rights on his work. Anyone could make copies, which is one reason he never published the texts in his lifetime; he made his money from the tickets at live performances.

However, in response to lobbying from writers in 1710, the British Parliament enacted the so-called Statute of Anne, subtitled "An Act for the Encouragement of Learning, by vesting the Copies of Printed Books in the Authors or purchasers of such Copies." The idea was that to encourage writers to share knowledge and produce entertainment, they must be allowed to obtain an income no matter who chose to publish the work. The author, not the printer, would own the copyright and it would stay with them for 28 years. At the time this was a radical idea, but it proved successful and paved the way for the professions of author and journalist and led to the development of the novel as an art form.

In the US, copyright legislation was written into the Constitution in 1787. Perhaps tellingly, the American Copyright Clause made much more explicit the industrial importance of intellectual property. Its stated objective was: "To promote the Progress of Science and useful Arts, by securing for limited Times to Authors and Inventors the exclusive Right to their respective Writings and Discoveries."

The notion that a creative artist owns the right to reproduce their work has been extended to the visual arts and to sheet music, then to records, radio, television, and film. The duration of an author's or composer's rights has been extended time and again over the past three centuries, driven by vocal lobbying by the creative community.

CROSSING THE LINE

When being entertained, we often need to cooperate with the medium concerned to achieve a suspension of disbelief. It is our own imagination that allows us to believe that the actors on a bare stage presenting *Henry v*, in what Shakespeare called the "Wooden O," are engaged in the battle of Agincourt. Or that Superman can leap tall buildings or that Dorothy went to Oz. We want to believe, so we do.

Nevertheless, this can have a less attractive dimension. Video games have become so compelling that many people spend more time playing them then on any other media. Fantasy games involving the control of characters in artificial worlds have proved to be the most addictive. Online role-playing games are building a fanatical worldwide following. People often spend all weekend online and a player in South Korea died after an unbroken 50-hour session. Players can earn in-game money by doing tasks like slaying dragons and then spend it on virtual products such as advanced weapons. In China a real-life murder was committed by a player who suspected another one of stealing his in-game possessions.[6] Plato would have been fascinated by this collision of fantasy and reality.

This has an artistic aspect, too. There are times when an author, actor, or director wishes to remind us that we, the audience, are part of a mutually created illusion. In effect they want to get us to agree, for a moment, to cross the line and recognize the artifice at work. Theatre directors call this "breaking the fourth wall," but it occurs in all media.

Letting the audience in on the act is not a new idea. In the seventeenth-century play *The Knight of the Burning Pestle* by Francis Beaumont, actors are located in the audience and open the production by complaining about the subject matter of plays. Shakespeare has Puck address the audience directly at the end of *A Midsummer Night's Dream* to say he hopes they have enjoyed the action. Characters in television or film dramas occasionally look straight to camera to address the audience. The blurring lines of truth and fiction and reality versus fabrication are also behind both the popularity of, and the controversy over, programs such as *Big Brother*.

Copyright law in the UK and the US is continually changing to keep up with new technologies. For example, the 1911 UK Copyright Act gave films protection as "works of dramatic art" or as a "series of photographs." It was not until the 1956 Act that they were protected as films in their own right. The same Act introduced copyright law to television, which previously had had no protection.

The advent of digital media has made it simple not just to copy but to make a perfect clone of the original of any digital product. This can be done anywhere in the world and distributed at almost no cost. Such developments have called the whole issue of copyright into question.

THE MEDIUM IS THE MESSAGE

Hidden away in a car park at the University of Toronto is a small mock Tudor building, which houses the McLuhan Program in Culture and Technology. It is a modest legacy for the man who did more than any other to influence thinking about how the modern media really work.

In 1964 Canadian academic Marshall McLuhan wrote the now iconic *Understanding Media*. Unfortunately, this is one of those books that was much discussed but not all that much read. This is a pity, as it was a fascinating, if rather bleak, analysis. It provided a prescient forecast of how media would develop and, in places, is almost religious and mystic in tone. Reading it today, it is a shock to realize it was written more than 40 years ago. It is a book about communications theory and the cultural

THE MEDIUM IS THE MASSAGE

By 1967 McLuhan's *Understanding Media* had become a bestselling cultural sensation, but there was much confusion about the exact interpretation of his ideas. To explain them he teamed up with a leading graphic designer to create a book combining images and text. They planned to use his famous "medium is the message" phrase as the title, but when it came back from the typesetter a mistake had been made and it read "The Medium Is the Massage." McLuhan, who loved playing with language and enjoyed the juxtaposition of ideas, adopted the error as neatly emphasizing his thesis that it is not just the content but the medium itself that is a sensory experience that works directly on us and changes society. He also liked the idea that it echoed, in a punning way, his notion that media were entering an era of the "mass age."[7]

impact of media rather than an economics or business book, but it gave us one of the famous media phrases—"the medium is the message"—which is resonant but surprisingly difficult to explain.

Broadly, the idea is that a new medium has an effect on the way society works because of the existence of the medium itself. The impact of the medium is more than its content. In McLuhan's own words, and demonstrating an obvious love of puns, he says:

> the instance of electric light may prove illuminating. Whether the light is being used for brain surgery or a night-time game of baseball is a matter of indifference. It could be argued that these activities are in some ways the "content" of electric light. This fact merely underlines the point that the medium is the message because it is the medium [electric light] that shapes and controls the scale and form of human association and action.[8]

In another explanation, journalist James Harkin uses a McLuhan quote to show the importance of the medium itself by saying that content is simply "the juicy piece of meat carried by the burglar to distract the watchdog of the mind."[9]

McLuhan also argued, and indeed it is the subtitle of his book, that media are the "extensions of man," saying that media have, in effect, extended the central nervous system of the individual and or society. He said that it was the creation of a medium itself rather than its content that had the impact. The development of newspapers supported democracy and thus changed for ever the role of monarchy. The arrival of radio provided a forum for leaders like Hitler, Stalin, Churchill, and Roosevelt to reach an entire population directly, which changed the nature of political leadership. Television in the home changed the way in which families live and interact and the web changed the nature of retailing.

Understanding Media was preceded by two years by McLuhan's other major book, *The Gutenberg Galaxy*. In this he argued that the new broadcast media marked the end of the original mechanical book and print-based era. Modern media, he said, were creating "the global village." Given that he was working some 30 years before the internet, he would have found quite extraordinary the way in which websites have made his comments come true.

GOLDEN AGES OF MEDIA

Pictures – 500 to 1600
Before printing, pictures were the main way to record ideas. When books became dominant, art reverted to being mainly decorative.

Theatre – 500 BC to 100 AD and 1580 to 1750
A central part of Greek society, theatre declined in the dark ages. With the Elizabethans it again became the main way to communicate.

Books – 1550 to 1820
Books did not reach a wide audience until well after printing. They became the main communications medium until overtaken by newspapers.

Postal systems – 1750 to 1860
Mail coaches were a vital part of Georgian life. Then the telegraph took over and the letter became more of a social grace.

Posters – 1890 to 1920
The urban poster in Paris started the boom and it continued until the 1920s' color magazines reduced its advertising value.

Newspapers – 1820 to 1930
The earliest publications had a limited readership. Steam-powered presses gave newspapers mass circulations and huge power until radio.

Magazines – 1880 to 1960
Color printing made magazines attractive to advertisers. They survived radio, but declined in the face of TV.

Cinema – 1910 to 1955
The golden age started with the opening of movie theatres in most towns and ended with the arrival of TV.

Comics – 1935 to 1955
Comics flourished with low-cost printing and a desire for escapism after the Second World War.

Radio – 1925 to 1955
The power of radio started with the creation of institutions like NBC and the BBC and continued until the audience switched to television.

Television – 1955 to 2010
Broadcast TV became dominant once it was in more than 50 percent of homes but its prominence declined after cable, satellite and the web.

2.1 | Theatre

Live theatre was both the original mass medium and the first multimedia experience. In Athens 2,500 years ago, a new production was the central cultural event of the city. Everybody went. Everybody talked about it. It knitted society together. In Victorian times, before cinema and television, theatre going was a grand spectacle with huge venues. Audiences in the thousands watched elaborate productions with live animals and explosive effects. Now theatre is more of a niche experience, but it remains the source of much of the creative experimentation that inspires other media.

The theatre **extends** the spoken word, often combining it with music and images. **It** is planned, directed, and manipulated to tell a story in a compelling way. A play communicates ideas and elicits an emotional reaction. Theatre is an organized, public extension of fireside narratives and religious ritual. It was also the first communications medium to persuade an audience to part with money to watch it. Theatre is a robust medium and against a backdrop of social and technical change it has continually reinvented itself.

Theatre is not always thought of as a medium, as it does not provide an obvious transmission mechanism like ink on paper or a broadcast signal. But in the days before printing presses and radio towers, it was the main way to communicate ideas from the one to the many. The act of getting people together for a shared event made it the only mass medium before printing other than the church pulpit. It was the channel through which ideas, ideologies, stories, characters, and history reached a wide audience. It is also the origin of much current popular culture. The slobby Homer Simpson and his cunning son Bart, who dominate many of the world's television channels, can trace their characters back to the medieval players of the *commedia dell'arte* and through them to their origins with Roman playwright Plautus. *The Simpsons* has 2,000 years of theatrical heritage.

THE PHYSICAL EXPERIENCE

Theatre requires very little technology. It is the human voice projected to an audience who are seated or standing within earshot. The medium simply needs a stage for the actors to work on and an area for the audience to watch.

The first theatres in ancient Greece were small, natural valleys where the audience sat on the banks and the actors appeared on a flat area below them. By Roman times it was normal to purpose-build a theatre, but the format of two basic areas, the stage and the seating, remained the same. The Elizabethan outdoor theatres, like the famous, and now reconstructed, Globe, allowed the audience almost to surround the stage. They were modeled on the courtyards of inns where the experiments in early English drama took place. Indoor theatres started appearing in the late 1500s. By the 1700s many presented the newly invented medium of Italian opera, which needed to accommodate the orchestra in a pit. This led to the audience being more cut off from the players.

Electric lighting arrived in the nineteenth century and amplified sound came in the twentieth. In recent times sophisticated equipment such as revolving stages and hydraulic lifts has allowed for far more spectacular productions. But the core experience of the theatre remains the thrill of seeing human beings in real-time performance, knowing that what you are watching is happening live and that no two shows will ever be quite the same.

THE ORIGINS OF DRAMA

Theatre as entertainment and education started in an organized way about 2,500 years ago in ancient Greece. Before that, rituals in dance and chant were a feature of religious ceremonies. A sense of "theatre" is what made these events impressive. It added shock and awe to a religious gathering. Whatever else Stonehenge was used for, it was certainly an early form of theatrical venue.

Dionysus, the Greek god of fertility, was the patron of vineyards and wine. Not unsurprisingly, he was one of the most popular deities and a major annual festival was held in his honor. At this event a chorus of about 50 people sang and chanted to amuse the audience. These performances became organized competitions—the *American Idol* of ancient Athens. At some point they started to feature a single performer who would stand in front of the chorus and recite solo verse. In 534 BC one of these competitive events was won by a priest or "actor" called Thespis. The concept of the theatre and the profession of thespian were, allegedly, born in that year.

The Greeks had clear ideas about the drama representing conflict. The earliest organized form was the tragedy, which was a contest of humanity against some unchangeable force of nature. Usually it pitched man against the immortal gods and thus had a predetermined and often bad outcome for the human participants. Frequently the protagonists would fail in their endeavors because of some fatal character flaw—often that of hubris, meaning excessive pride. The comedy (which comes from the Greek meaning "revel") was a form that developed later and depicted conflict between people themselves. The plot and humor resulted from simple human misunderstanding in a domestic setting, which was more easily resolved than battles with the Olympians. The comedy had an earthy and lighthearted feel to it and relied on highly recognizable social stereotypes.

Early Greek public drama competitions were major events. The normal structure was three tragic plays followed by a comedy. Entry to the event was free and the competition was paid for by the city government and wealthy patrons. Some historians claim that the winner's prize was a goat; the word "tragedy" may come from the Greek word for "goat," which is *tragos*.[1] Equally, it may simply refer to the religious festivals that predated the dramas, as they featured a goat sacrifice.

The three best-known Greek playwrights, who participated in the competitions around 400 BC, were Aeschylus, Sophocles, and Euripides. They wrote of gods, heroes, and fools and created many of the characters, plot lines, and theatrical conventions we still recognize.

The Greek approach to drama, with its twin elements of tragedy and comedy, has dominated the thinking of generations of playwrights. The dramatic masks worn by the chorus in ancient Greece to depict comic and tragic characters remain the symbols of theatres to this day.

The original layout of theatres has also been sustained down the centuries. The ancient *theatron*—in Greek "a place for seeing"—was set in a dip between hills, which provided seating to watch the action below. The orchestra was a large flat area for the chorus to dance and chant. In the early venues there was no stage and the auditorium was where the audience sat to listen.

When the Romans conquered the Greeks they adopted many of their theatrical traditions, but in a grander way. They built theatres with raised stages to allow a

DEUS EX MACHINA

In the time of the Greek playwrights Euripides and Sophocles, some 2,400 years ago, the audiences liked neat and tidy endings. Some writers achieved this by highly contrived story lines, but Euripides was fond of having an actor, portraying a god, being lowered onto the stage to sort out any remaining complications with divine insight and the powers of a deity. The crane-like device that did this was called a *machina* and the event was called "a god from a crane," hence *deus ex machina*. Even in Euripides' time some critics found it an annoyingly trite way to bring things to a close. The use of an unexpected character or event to tidy up a plot is now referred to using the same phrase.

better view and made far less use of the orchestra area as the original links with religious ceremony and chorus became lost. In about 200 BC one of the most celebrated Roman playwrights, Plautus, borrowed most of his plots and characters from the Greeks but updated them to Roman tastes. He was as prolific and famous in his day as Shakespeare was in his, and the texts of 21 of his plays still survive. Indeed, Plautus is the source of many of the plots and ideas that Shakespeare and others later adapted. In particular, he created stock characters such as the miser, the self-important soldier, the sly servant, and the identical twins. These comic personalities became so familiar to the Romans that they developed special masks for each to aid recognition and encourage a cheer of approval and anticipation when the character took the stage.

As the Roman Republic turned into the Empire, the original Greek style of drama lost its popularity. Urban Roman theatre audiences turned to short farces and crude comedies based on highly exaggerated caricatures of drunken clowns, sly servants, and lusty old men. In these entertainments it is easy to see the origins of the *commedia dell'arte*, which would become the main theatrical form of medieval Italy. One of the central characters was the cunning slave who outsmarted his owners. The style continued into modern times into farce and provided the inspiration for Frankie Howerd's *Up Pompeii!*, a television comedy series set in Roman times.

The theatre of the later Roman Empire lost all contact with the civic purpose of the Greeks. In the spirit of "bread and circuses," performances became an event in the Coliseum rather than the exploration of social structure and characters on a stage. Hence increasingly the paying public were treated more as spectators who watched outrageous performances rather than as an audience who listened to ideas. The theatre as an art form fell into disrepute to such a degree that public performances were periodically banned and educated society turned its back on theatrical events.

MYSTERY PLAYS: RELIGIOUS EDUCATION

With the decline of the Roman Empire the theatre, like many aspects of classical life, vanished for many hundred of years. During the so-called dark ages theatrical performances were almost unknown until the Christian Church revived the medium as part of its communications efforts. At some point during the twelfth century "miracle plays" started to appear as an adjunct to church services and as a way of telling the main Bible stories, not in Latin but in the vernacular language. One of the first, which was performed in French, was called "Adam" and illustrated the messages in Genesis. In England these evolved into the much more ambitious mystery plays or mystery cycles, which may have got their name because they were enactments of religious mysteries but also because they were performed by members of trade guilds, who were supposed to have mastered their craft, hence mastery or mystery plays.

Such plays became very popular from about 1400 AD and were a central element of Easter and Christmas festivals. A team drawn from each trade took responsibility for an appropriate story. In the famous York Cycle, for example, the shipwrights did the building of the Ark, the goldsmiths the arrival of the three kings bearing gifts, and the bakers enacted the Last Supper. The Chester Cycle of 1540 records 26 plays. The Nativity was done by the thatchers and the Crucifixion by the ironmongers and ropers.[2] At the very least, it appears that the Church authorities may have had a sense of humor and the Guilds a keen nose for the benefits of commercial sponsorship. The performance of these plays was free, but the players would seek to make a living from selling the audience food and drink and other goods. The players set up mobile stages called pageants, which allowed the audience to move from stage to stage to see all the different stories in the overall cycle.

The mystery plays had clear Catholic and popish origins. Inevitably, they quickly lost popularity at the time of Henry VIII who, in the mid-1500s, had issues with the Roman Church so decided to found his own, the Church of England. He wanted an altogether more secular drama. This set the stage—excuse the pun—for the blossoming of the English theatre and the arrival of playwrights like Christopher Marlowe, Ben Jonson, and William Shakespeare, all against the background of the Italian Renaissance.

RENAISSANCE THEATRE: CLASSICAL BUT DULL

In the fifteenth and sixteenth centuries scholars and intellectuals throughout Europe were fascinated with all things Greek and Roman. A newly wealthy merchant society attempted to recreate the classical age, and the theatre was no exception. The Latin texts of plays by authors such as Plautus, Seneca, and Sophocles were available in libraries, as were detailed

descriptions of the design of Roman theatres and of the staging and cos-
tumes used in classical productions. The Roman architect Vitruvius had
left extremely full notes on how to build and run a theatre, and he has continued to be the main single influence on theatre design today. Many
attempts were made to recreate his classical constructions. The greatest
surviving example is the Teatro Olimpico in the Italian city of Vicenza,
designed by Palladio, which was completed in 1585. It opened with a production of *Oedipus* by Sophocles.

The artists and architects of the Renaissance developed the notion
of the formal stage and the use of painted scenery. The theatrical productions of this period in Italy tended to be very serious and academic, in an
attempt to recreate what people imagined, probably wrongly, to have been
classical Roman entertainment. They were dull, worthy, boring, and long.
To make these heavy-going evenings less taxing, producers invented the
idea of the *intermezzi*, quick, fun, and often spectacular presentations using
elaborate sets and featuring singing and dancing. From these evolved the
idea of opera as a dramatic form.

SHAKESPEARE & CO.: MASS ENTERTAINMENT

The English were less interested in theatre design and classical purity and
were more focused on the plays themselves. The subjects were much more
down to earth and many of the characters were drawn from British history
or everyday life. In his play *Henry IV*, Shakespeare defined and celebrated
the strong characteristics of the Welsh, Irish, Scots, and English that dominate much of British humor to this day. In *The Merry Wives of Windsor*
he handed out similar treatment to the values and character of the middle
classes.

Plays were often based on classical stories but staged using the folk
traditions of the mystery cycle and the earthy, but anglicized, characters of
the *commedia dell'arte*. They were a popular entertainment in the newly
constructed baronial halls of the Elizabethan nobility. This led to the idea
of using the courtyards of inns as temporary venues to reach the mass population. However, these spaces, designed for unsaddling horses, were not
large enough for the growing audience. By the 1570s the idea of money
lending had arrived from Italy and in 1576 an entrepreneur called James
Burbage, probably benefiting from the newly invented loans, established

the first purpose-built auditorium. It was known simply as The Theatre in Finsbury Fields, outside the walls of the City of London. The name was taken from the Greek, but the design owed more to the coaching inns of England than the hillsides of Athens. The location was chosen to avoid the bureaucratic controls of the City government.

After 21 years of successful performances, the lease on The Theatre expired and the landlord, a strict Puritan, refused to renew it. Richard Burbage (James's son) was the leading actor of his time and he arranged a clandestine demolition of The Theatre. Its oak beams were transported across the River Thames to Southwark where, in 1599, it was rebuilt again outside of the strict controls of the City of London and renamed The Globe. It grew in fame with William Shakespeare as its writer in residence.

The Globe and its rivals, like The Rose and The Curtain, made conscious efforts to cloak themselves in the glamor and respectability of the ancient traditions while presenting contemporary and often controversial modern themes. Classical stories were updated with modern characters. The buildings they were performed in, while quintessentially English, were decorated in what was imagined to be a Greek or Roman style. For the Elizabethan audience the rapid development of theatres was probably as exciting and marvelous as the arrival of cinema seemed in the early twentieth century.

While the open-air theatres appealed to a mass audience, they suffered from the effects of the weather. Smaller indoor venues like the

COMMEDIA DELL'ARTE

In the mid-1500s Italy and France were criss-crossed by bands of traveling players who staged impromptu performances based on stock characters and basic human themes, such as young lovers frustrated by a scheming older relative. The *commedia dell'arte* (loosely translated as the plays of professional artists) became the main entertainment of the town as shows were put on in marketplaces and street corners. The focus was on the skills of the actors as opposed to the writers. Traveling bands often included jugglers, acrobats, and musicians, who would perform comic interludes between the main parts of the story. The stock characters have left their impression on modern theatre, film, and particularly pantomime. The antics of the servants—the *zanni* in Italian—have given us the word "zany" in English and set the style of many of the early silent films, while the amoral Punchinello evolved into Mr Punch.

MASTER OF THE REVELS

Tudor monarchs enjoyed the newly emerging art of theatre and appointed a member of the royal household to organize such events, the Master of the Revels. From the time of Henry VII onward this official paid for and previewed potential royal entertainment. By the time of Elizabeth I theatre had become a major public spectacle and the role was extended to controlling what was allowed on the commercial stage; in effect, the official censor.

The most famous Master of the Revels was Edmund Tilney, who officiated from 1578 to 1610 so was in charge throughout Shakespeare's career. When the Puritans closed the theatres the office was abolished and when stage entertainment returned its control was undertaken by the Lord Chamberlain. This continued for 300 years until stage censorship was abolished by The Theatre Act of 1968, reflecting the liberal spirit of the times.

Blackfriars Theatre were set up in empty buildings to appeal to a more select, educated, and richer audience. Plays written for them tended to be more subtle and less rowdy. The open-air theatres normally featured bare stages, a minimum of props, and limited scenery. The enclosed theatres used extravagant settings and effects.

It was in this period that many of the conventions of the modern theatre were created. Burbage and a few others were major stars, whose names on a playbill drew the crowds. The structure of plays was a prologue (to ensure the audience knew what was going on), a few big dramatic monologues to give the star something to showcase their talents, and scenes for clowns to give the leading actors and the audience a break. Most productions also ended with the cast dancing a jig to mark the transition from the artificial world of the stage and the play back to the harsher reality of Elizabethan society.

Theatre in England thrived under Elizabeth I and subsequently James I and Charles I. But when the Royalists lost the English Civil War and Charles I lost his head, the actors lost their royal patrons. The humorless Puritans, under Oliver Cromwell, seized power and the theatres were closed by law. A new dark age had arrived, albeit a brief one.

RESTORATION COMEDIES: ARISTOCRATIC AMUSEMENTS

When the British bored of Cromwell after 20 years of seriousness, they bought back the monarchy in the form of Charles II in 1660. The Restora-

WHY IS SHAKESPEARE FAMOUS?

William Shakespeare was one of a group of successful and popular playwrights working around 1600. Contemporaries included Ben Jonson, Christopher Marlowe, Francis Beaumont, and John Webster. Beaumont has a tomb in Westminster Abbey and Jonson had his collected works published in his own lifetime. By contrast, Shakespeare's plays were not printed until seven years after his death and he was buried, in relative provincial obscurity, in Stratford-upon-Avon. Whether the Bard really is the greatest ever playwright is up for debate, but he is certainly the most famous because it suited people to make him so.

Shakespeare's friends and fellow actors John Heminges and Henry Condell collected his works in the now famous First Folio in 1623. Whether their motives were to create a memorial or something more commercial (1,000 folios were sold at £1 a time), we do not know for sure. But the act of publication created the Shakespeare "brand" and laid the cornerstone for what has become a global industry.

With the Restoration of the monarchy after the Puritan-versus-Cavalier Civil War, people needed entertainment in the newly reopened theatres and Shakespeare fitted the bill as an authentic English voice. In particular, his plays had great roles and thus actors liked to be in them. Thomas Betterton, for example, enjoyed huge success in the late 1600s as Hamlet, Macbeth, Lear, and Falstaff. He idolized the author and made a pilgrimage to Stratford to learn more. He passed on his findings to one Nicholas Rowe, who in 1709 wrote a major biography of Shakespeare.

The leading player in making Shakespeare what he is today was another great actor, David Garrick. Shakespearean scholar Jonathan Bate has characterized the 1730s as the decade as when "the cult of Shakespeare took root," pointing out that about a quarter of all the plays performed in London were by him.[3] Garrick arrived in London just after this and started making his name as a Shakespearean star. A genius at public relations, he had himself painted by one of the great portrait artists, William Hogarth, playing the role of Richard III. This painting was the first of many showing scenes from the Bard that contributed to Garrick's fame and the iconic Shakespearean image. Garrick also invented the idea of an annual Shakespeare Jubilee to be held in Stratford, which greatly helped raise Garrick's own image and created the Stratford-based Shakespeare trade that thrives to this day.

tion was a huge national party and newly reopened theatres were at the center of it. In the two decades of forced closure, many of the old theatre buildings had been demolished or ruined. A new generation of theatrical entrepreneurs took their inspiration from what had been happening in Italy and France. The old open-air venues of Shakespeare and Marlowe now seemed unfashionable and uncomfortable. The Restoration brought three features of British theatre that are still highly visible: the proscenium arch stage, mobile painted scenery, and actresses.

Restoration plays were current, controversial, funny, and daring. They reflected the relaxed sexual and moral climate of the age. The use of young women rather than the boys who had previously played the female parts created the profession of actress and made great stars of the likes of Nell Gwynne. Ironically, many of the actresses specialized in playing while dressed as men. These so-called breeches roles were popular as comic devices and also as an excuse for seeing women dressed in tight, figure-hugging men's clothes. The diarist Samuel Pepys makes numerous references to visiting and revisiting theatres to see a particular actress perform.

Restoration comedies were aimed at the small, elite, fashionable, aristocratic London audience and lacked the broad-based appeal of their Elizabethan forebears. They were stories of contemporary aristocrats featuring modern issues and manners. However, they were ephemeral. Plays had very short runs as the small but demanding audience was quickly bored.

Running theatres was a precarious profession. Charles ii licensed only two theatre companies, the King's and the Duke's, which became fierce competitors for writers, actors, and audiences. Both constructed splendid new theatre buildings that were designed by Sir Christopher Wren. Both in the end had significant financial problems created by overambitious productions and poor cost control; a familiar experience for anyone running a theatre business to this day.

After the Glorious Revolution in 1688, the last flamboyant king of the Stuart dynasty was ousted and the more serious-minded and austere William and Mary took the throne. The period of the bawdy plays, aimed at the idle, urban elite, came to an end and theatre had to reinvent itself once again.

ACTOR-MANAGERS: SERVING THE NEW MERCHANTS

From 1700 onward European and British society saw a reduction in the power and influence of the old aristocracy and the rise of educated and wealthy merchants. Cultural taste and social etiquette were driven by the ideas and activities of this increasingly confident group of middle-class business people. Theatre changed to reflect the demands of this fast-growing audience.

The British stage became dominated by actor-managers who responded to their new customers with updated classics and also a string of new plays by contemporary writers reflecting the burning issues of the time. In the mid-1700s David Garrick was the pioneer, changing the way both plays were performed (more naturalistic) and theatres were operated (more comfortable). Garrick and the actors who followed him, such as John Philip Kemble and Sarah Siddons, made their reputation with Shakespeare, but reflected the new audience by staging more fashionable subjects. The Georgian theatre of the 1700s produced great writing on social and comic themes, which resulted in plays that are still performed today and characters and plots that continually reappear in film and television. Some of the best known are Oliver Goldsmith's *She Stoops to Conquer* and Richard Sheridan's *The Rivals* and *School for Scandal*. The latter introduced the unfortunate Mrs Malaprop, whose constant misuse of language was a none too subtle dig at the affectations of the rising lower-middle classes.

DAVID GARRICK

David Garrick was by far the most influential actor-manager of the mid-1700s. He emerged as an overnight success in 1741 playing the role of Richard III in a very naturalistic way, in stark contrast to the bombastic and declamatory style then in fashion. The writer Alexander Pope commented: "that young man never had his equal as an actor, and he will never have a rival."

Garrick became the manager and owner of the Drury Lane Theatre, taking the lead role in many of his own productions. He introduced footlights, ended the age-old practice of letting the audience sit on the stage, and moved his musicians from the gallery above the actors down into what we now call the orchestra pit. He turned his theatre into a great financial success by understanding the tastes of the new Georgian merchant classes. When he died in 1779 he was buried in Poets' Corner in Westminster Abbey—an honor not given to another actor until Sir Laurence Olivier in 1989.

PANTOMIME

The word *pantomimus* was used by the Romans for a solo performer who acted all the parts of a short story to music, but as a dramatic form this vanished in the dark ages. By the 1700s the characters of the *commedia dell'arte* had come to England in shows called Harlequinades. The Harlequin character was shown as having magical powers and carried a large magic wand called a "slapstick," which when hit against other actors or scenery would appear to transform them. It is from this that we get the term "slapstick comedy." Storylines developed for the Harlequinade include *Jack the Giant Killer* in 1773 and *Aladdin and his Wonderful Lamp* in 1788. The name "pantomime" was resurrected and the format as we now know it started when the famous clown Grimaldi appeared in the first production of *Cinderella* at Covent Garden in 1820.

The 1843 Theatre Act abolished the monopoly of performance enjoyed by Drury Lane and Covent Garden. This allowed other theatres to stage their own pantomimes and led to many traditional stories being converted to this format. The idea of the "principal boy" (played by a girl) and his mother the "dame" (played by a man) are Victorian inventions.

Pantomime has become a popular and traditional Christmas event in the UK, with well-known comedians taking the part of the dames and well-known actresses appearing as the principal boys. The idea has never really caught on in the US, where the big musical rather than the pantomime is the popular holiday show.

VICTORIANS: EMPIRE AND MELODRAMA

By the time Victoria came to the throne, Britain was building a global empire and enjoying a huge increase in wealth. Theatre became a true mass medium again and a worldly wise and much larger audience wanted spectacle and amusement. Huge theatres were constructed and huge productions were needed to fill them. The so-called father of melodrama was the French writer/director Guilbert de Pixérécourt, who combined music with dramatic effects such as simulated volcanoes, floods, and earthquakes to produce a popular and accessible spectacle. His approach enthralled London, where the big theatres became regular presenters of melodramatic events. Shows featured ships in tanks, herds of live animals, and lavish scenery.

The traditional theatre of drama was championed in the 1820s by Edmund Kean, one of the first to be described as a classical actor. He performed a string of Shakespearean hits, once again at the Drury Lane. Both Edmund and his son Charles were successful in America; the theatre was becoming an increasingly transatlantic medium, with the best productions appearing in both London and New York. A big show made more money with a US/UK tour and the interplay between "Broadway" and the "West End" dates back to then. One of the first successful American actors in London in the early 1860s was Edwin Booth, whose younger brother John Wilkes Booth gained unfortunate notoriety when he assassinated President Abraham Lincoln during a production of *Our American Cousin* at Ford's Theatre in Washington, DC in 1865.

By the late 1800s the leading classical actor was Henry Irving, who operated the Lyceum Theatre. He was a typical larger-than-life thespian and the first actor to be given a knighthood. His personal manager was the author Bram Stoker, who is thought to have based his Count Dracula character on Irvine's appearance and manner.

In addition to serious theatre and mass spectaculars, the Victorian audience wanted funny, light, contemporary drama, which was offered by playwrights like Oscar Wilde with *The Importance of Being Earnest*.

MUSIC HALLS AND MUSICALS

In Georgian and Victorian times the "legitimate" theatre of Garrick, Kean, and Irvine appealed to the educated middle classes, while the less intellectually inclined enjoyed the melodrama and pantomime. But following the industrial revolution, a huge working class in both the UK and the US had also emerged who had money to spend and wanted to be entertained in a manner suiting their tastes.

By the mid-1880s music halls were being built all over Britain, offering variety shows with jugglers, singers, ventriloquists, and magicians. They had started as small venues—essentially extensions of public houses—but the new ones were huge auditoria. Vaudeville was a similar phenomenon in the US. Before cinema and television the music halls were the popular mass entertainment and an increasing gap opened up between the audience they served and the more "high-brow" theatre. Major music halls like the Coliseum in London or The Palace in New York were purpose-built.

This was also the age of the hippodrome: huge venues with facilities for circus acts and live animals. The London Hippodrome, built in 1900, featured a 100,000-gallon water tank. The artist immortalized in the song

CIRCUS

Although the term "circus" dates back to the chariot racing and trick horse riding at the Circus Maximus in Rome, the form of entertainment we are used to today is a much more recent idea starting in the late eighteenth century with specialist equestrian acts. It reached its zenith with "Barnum and Bailey's Greatest Show on Earth," which toured the world around 1900.

Like music hall, traveling animal circuses declined in popularity through the twentieth century, because of the rise of cinema and television. But in 1984, two Canadians came up with the idea of a circus based only on human acts and formed the Cirque du Soleil. The show initially needed Canadian government support, but after a few years it developed a successful worldwide franchise. Several Cirque du Soleil shows are running all the time in Las Vegas. It is the spirit of Barnum and Bailey without a horse or a lion in sight.

"The Daring Young Man on the Flying Trapeze" was Jules Leotard, a French acrobat, who invented his own figure-hugging costume that was adopted by dancers worldwide and now carries his name.

Many of the songs that are a familiar background to British and American culture, such as "It's a Long Way to Tipperary," "Burlington Bertie," and "Alexander's Rag-Time Band" are music hall or vaudeville compositions. Famous names included the Marx Brothers, Jack Benny, WC Fields, Harry Lauder, and Marie Lloyd. Serving the same audience as the music halls were the traveling showmen such as William Cody, who mounted worldwide tours of his cowboy spectacular "Buffalo Bill's Rough Riders." This featured among other attractions the female sharpshooter Annie Oakley and the real Indian Chief Sitting Bull.

In addition to spectacle, the mass audience also wanted something more accessible than Italian opera. The idea of the comic or light opera was taken to its greatest success by Gilbert and Sullivan, who combined catchy tunes with satirical lyrics and glamorous staging.

RESPONDING TO THE MOVIES: REALISM

In the twentieth century music hall and vaudeville lost out in a big way to cinema and radio, with many of their established stars and much of their audience moving across to these new mass media. The serious or "straight" theatre did better in holding its patrons, however. Around 1900 in London and New York there was interest in the works of new, foreign authors such as Anton Chekhov (Russian)—*The Seagull, Uncle Vanya,* and *The Cherry Orchard*—Henrik Ibsen (Norwegian)—*The Wild Duck, Hedda Gabler,* and *The Master Builder*—and George Bernard Shaw (Irish)—*Captain Brassbound's Conversion, Man and Superman,* and *Major Barbara.* These writers depicted real life and showed the political and social issues facing real people. They wanted acting to be naturalistic and the settings contemporary. Shaw in particular was seen as a champion of social reform and was fascinated by social mobility. His story about a poor flower girl being schooled to appear like a member of the aristocracy was told in the play *Pygmalion,* which later became the musical and film *My Fair Lady.*

REPERTORY THEATRE

The first Repertory Theatre in the UK was The Gaiety in Manchester. It was opened in 1907 by Annie Horniman, who had previously founded The Abbey in Dublin. The idea was to have a resident acting company that would present several different plays in rotation to give a local community access to a wide range of productions and authors.[4] There might be three different plays a week, a matinee of one and an evening performance of another. The system mixed traditional Shakespeare and Sheridan with the prolific output of new writers. This was a very different approach from the long-standing actor-managers who would go on tour with the same production for many months.

"Rep" theatres opened in many provincial towns in the UK and in the US, where they are called "stock." They were considered a valuable training ground for actors because of the huge pressure of learning and performing so many different roles in a short period.

The approach to acting in this realistic and natural theatre was very different from the dramatic and declaratory style of the leading Victorians. The greatest influence in this new movement was the Russian director Constantin Stanislavski, who put actors through the most rigorous rehearsal process and insisted that they understood the underlying motivations of the character they were playing. These ideas were particularly taken up in America and resulted in what is now called "method acting." This style of performance lent itself to the cool, close-up media of cinema and television. Many of the leading screen actors learned their craft on the stage in this way.

SHOCK, SURPRISE, SENSATION, AND SOPHISTICATION

As talking pictures became established in the 1920s and television was on the horizon, theatre underwent another revolution. A new generation of writers and directors wanted to experiment with audience interaction and to test the boundaries of artistic acceptability. Also emerging was a new group of stage and lighting designers, who wanted theatre to become an unsettling and challenging experience. If television and film were to be domestic and popular, theatre would be wild and demanding.

Edward Gordon Craig and Josef Svoboda experimented with minimalist sets and stark lighting, which most modern theatre goers have come to accept as normal but which in the 1920s and 1930s were a shock. This approach complemented the work of writers such as Luigi Pirandello—*Six Characters in Search of an Author*—and Bertolt Brecht—*The Threepenny Opera* and *Mother Courage*. Brecht developed the idea of theatrical alienation, wanting to shock the audience out of cosy complacency.

There was also renewed interest in the craft skills of theatre, which moved intellectually up-market with well-written, carefully structured plays. In the UK contemporary themes and manners were explored by writers like JB Priestley—*An Inspector Calls*—Noël Coward—*Private Lives*—and Terence Rattigan—*The Winslow Boy*. A few years later in the US dramatists explored even more controversial and challenging issues and hitherto taboo subjects. Eugene O'Neill—*The Iceman Cometh*—and Arthur Miller—

THE MOUSETRAP

This mystery story by detective writer Agatha Christie can claim the crown of the world's longest-running play. Written as a radio play in 1947, it is a typical whodunit that pioneered the format of the group of potential suspects gathered in a country house awaiting the denouement of the mystery. Perhaps the real mystery is why it has survived for more than 60 years in the highly competitive commercial theatre of London's West End. The title *The Mousetrap* has an impeccable theatrical pedigree, being a reference to the play within a play in Hamlet that the Prince uses as a device to trap his uncle into an admission of murder.

Death of a Salesman—wrote about the challenges people faced in their everyday lives. Commercial travelers, alcoholics, and corrupt politicians became the stuff of drama. These American pioneers were echoed in the UK in the 1950s by the so-called kitchen sink dramas of writers like John Osborne—*Look Back in Anger* and *The Entertainer*, a play that documented the decline of the music hall. On the art-house end of the theatre spectrum writers such as Samuel Beckett—*Waiting for Godot*—and Eugène Ionesco—*Rhinoceros*—baffled audiences with challenging and revolutionary themes, which are sometimes called the "Theatre of the Absurd."

New York's Broadway and London's West End thrived on a huge range of new writing and modern ideas. However, theatre audiences were in decline in the years after the Second World War. The stage format best suited to compete with Hollywood and television for mass appeal was the musical. Starting with *Show Boat* in 1927, Broadway producers began to experiment with big budgets and the genre thrived with *Oklahoma!*, *South Pacific*, and *West Side Story*. This model of long-running musical spectaculars was taken to new levels by Andrew Lloyd Webber with shows such as *Cats* and *The Phantom of the Opera*.

THEATRE IN A DIGITAL AGE

The medium of theatre is thriving in the twenty-first century. It is no longer the center of society as it was in Athens nor does it reach the mass audience of Elizabethan and Victorian times, but it has evolved to serve a series of niches with great success. Authors such as Tom Stoppard—*Rock 'n' Roll* and *The Coast of Utopia*—and Alan Bennett—*The History Boys* and *The Habit of Art*—have delivered plays rich in concepts and language. They introduce ideas that feed into other media. Acting companies such as The Globe, the National Theatre, and the Royal Shakespeare Company continue to find new and exciting ways to bring classic authors to a younger generation. New playwrights explore contemporary themes. Multimillion-dollar musicals like *Miss Saigon* and *The Lion King* have helicopters landing on stage and a stampede of wildebeest. Hugely innovative productions like *War Horse* and *His Dark Materials* reintroduced puppetry alongside live action.

Major theatre in the English-speaking world is now concentrated in, but not exclusive to, the West End of London and Broadway in New York. It is here that the most popular and expensive shows can be seen. "Off-

Broadway" is the US equivalent of the smaller London playhouses that offer less mass-market shows.

Theatre in ancient Greece was government funded and free to whoever wanted to watch. Today most cities have some form of state- or charity-funded theatre, as it is considered an important cultural contribution to the community. Theatre is a classic example of the idea that as a mass medium becomes marginalized, it becomes a form of art to be nurtured and supported.

Unlike film, which can make money in many ways after the initial theatrical showing, and television, which delivers a big enough audience to sell advertising, theatre needs to cover its costs from one audience. Fortunately the relatively small number of people who patronize the theatre are willing to spend a lot on tickets and are keen to see new productions. The somewhat larger numbers who seek out the big musicals tend to follow proven hits, which is why some shows have become virtual tourist fixtures in the larger London and New York theatres. Inevitably, this leads to a conservative commercial approach in terms of artistic policy and casting.

Over the years the economic reward has moved around between authors, producers, directors, and actors, although for most of the time actors have been the main draw. Producers have always taken the financial risks and now spend a lot more time on tax planning and fundraising than casting. Funding often comes from individuals, "angels," who take the risk of limited profits in return for the pleasure of being part of the production team. Authors will do well if their text becomes a long-running, much-performed classic or is made into a film, but most playwrights do not get rich. Actors get the recognition and experience, and the willingness of the stars of cinema and television to appear live on stage confirms theatre's continued importance in showcasing talent.

In relative terms theatre is elitist and a minority taste, but it still retains huge cultural influence. As a medium that requires people to pay at the door, it offers a robust business model in an age when so much entertainment is free. Live performance thrives because its audience wants the sense of being present at something original. In a world of virtual media there is something very human about being entertained by real people.

2.2 | Books

Daniel Maclise, Caxton Showing the First Specimen of His Printing to King Edward IV at the Almonry

The book has enjoyed an extraordinary journey. It started, in a form hardly recognizable today, as the way to store the epic poems of Greek mythology and to record the household accounts of the wealthy. It evolved into an elite object of Christian veneration, then became the first, and for a long time the dominant, mass medium. As the main device of human communication for two millennia, it spawned a huge range of genres that have shown remarkable resilience in the face of newspaper publishing, broadcasting, and the web. The book did for text what the theatre did for the spoken word. It extended the reach of authors, taking ideas to a wider public and preserving them over time. The book is now successfully adapting to digital production and distribution.

Over its 2,000-year history the book industry developed the commercial template from which other media have taken their lead. The familiar split of tasks between creating content (the author and illustrator), production (the publisher and printer), and distribution (the bookbinder and bookseller) all evolved out of the book trade. The issues of copyright, intellectual piracy, censorship, advertising, and commercial sponsorship were all first encountered by books.

Books, as we experience them today, include a vast array of formats and purposes. They can be a quick entertainment on a plane journey; a luxurious object of decoration on a coffee table; a source of ideas in a kitchen; a store of facts; an instruction manual; or simply something we like to look at on our shelves even if we never read them. Increasingly books are sold as digital files for use on specially designed readers like the Kindle and the Nook, which offer a title as an alternative to, or for some people in addition to, the traditional printed form.

The book remains the medium of choice for the origination of ideas by the individual creative writer. While alternatives such as newspapers, radio, television, and film need the collaboration of teams, the book allows the lone author to work in their own way. And the book is frequently the base from which other media properties are built.

Despite the dot-com boom in the 2000s the book (in all its forms) has probably been the fastest-growing heritage medium in terms of number of units produced. In 2011, in America alone, more than 300,000 new titles were scheduled to be published as traditional printed books—more than had ever been printed in a 12-month period before. To this must be added in the year more than 2 million nontraditional books such as those made available only as ebooks and as PDF files that are printed on demand.[1] The book, as a media format, is in extraordinarily good health and is writing itself a new chapter in the digital media age.

STORES OF KNOWLEDGE

The Great Library of Alexandria in Egypt was created to hold, catalogue, and provide easy access to all the literature of Greek civilization; it was the Google of its time. As ancient society grew the oral tradition was no longer adequate to communicate and preserve the explosion of ideas. The handwritten scroll was created to be the means by which information was stored.

The first librarian, Zenodotus, lived around 230 BC. Among other things he is credited with turning Homer's epic oral poems, the *Iliad* and the *Odyssey*, into manageable documents. At its height the library was said to have contained some 400,000 scrolls with all the knowledge, wit, and wisdom of the ancient world. They were called tomes, rolls of papyrus reading, in most examples, from top to bottom. In many cases they would have been the sole copy of a political text, scientific theory, play, or story. These fragile documents were normally wound around a smooth piece of wood and were designed as storage devices rather than a distribution medium.

However, as more people wanted and could afford them, multiple versions were made of the more popular works. A room full of literate slaves made copies as the text was dictated. Wealthy individuals created their own libraries that carried great prestige. These rich bibliophiles then traded the scrolls among themselves. The profession of secondhand bookseller is as old as the idea of the book itself.

THE FORMAT OF THE BOOK

When the very early Romans wanted to write things down, perhaps a lesson in school or even something as mundane as a shopping list, they used a wooden tray filled with wax, which they called a tablet. They prided themselves that this was a huge technical advance on the conquered barbarians, who simply scratched messages on bits of wood and bark. But the tablet was cumbersome, so later on, once they had conquered Egypt, they used papyrus made from reeds found in the delta of the river Nile. Once processed into a fabric it has similar properties to modern paper.

The main rival to the library at Alexandria was in the city of Pergamum in modern-day Turkey. When papyrus became expensive through overharvesting, the scribes of Pergamum developed an alternative made from treated sheepskin called parchment. Several leaves would be collected together and kept between hard wooden covers. This was the first book in the format we now recognize, a collection of pages. They called it a *codex* (plural *codices*), Latin for a "lump of wood," which is roughly what it resembled. The word "book" itself is derived from the Old English word *boc*, originally beech bark, a material used for primitive writing long before the Greeks and Romans.

The early Christian Church seized on the codex as the best format for protecting and displaying copies of their Gospels, as it helped distinguish them from the scrolls that they felt characterized the pagan religions of the Romans and Greeks and from those used by Jewish clerics. The Christians felt the format gave their Gospels an extra sense of value, importance, and permanence. It made the sacred texts, the books themselves, objects of veneration. This was the beginning of the end for the scroll—perhaps the eight-track stereo of its day.

The size of an original piece of parchment was, in simple terms, the size of a flattened-out sheep. This was too big for easy use and by convention it was normally folded in half to create what was called a folio (from the Latin *folium*, leaf). This created two large pages that could be written on on both sides, thus creating four usable faces of a size that could be bound and carried with ease. Quarto was a skin folded twice to create four pages and octavo three folds to create eight pages. These terms described the size of the resulting book. Even after the widespread use of paper made from rags, which could be any size, this terminology of book construction remained in use.

OBJECTS OF ART

Before the invention of printing, books were handmade, labor-intensive, and highly valued objects. To own and use a book you had to be rich enough to pay for it and educated enough to read it. For the first 1,000 years of book history the early Christian codices were objects of art as much as of learning. With very few exceptions it was only the Church that had the resources to create such valuable items and secular, nonreligious works were rare.

The factory floor of the medieval book business was the *scriptorium*, a room where monks would laboriously make copies of texts deemed to be of value. There was competition among various religious orders for the best and most magnificent collections. Surviving examples from the eighth and ninth centuries such as the Lindisfarne Gospels and the Book of Kells show the effort and skill that were applied to creating religious texts and getting one up on the neighboring abbot.

As education became more widespread and people traveled more, the demand grew for books on more general themes to impart knowledge and expertise. Roman and Greek scientific and philosophical manuscripts started to make their way to northern Europe, often as scrolls in the kitbags of soldiers returning from the Crusades. By the time of the twelfth century secular scribes and bookbinders set to work on the production of commercial books, mostly in Latin and Greek, on a wide range of nonreligious topics.

These early books combined three separate craft skills: those of the calligrapher, the illuminator, and the bookbinder. We now tend to think of books as contiguous products with a clear beginning and end, but early books were far more a collection of individual, carefully crafted pages. A book was simply a way of storing a group of leaves that may have been originated by different people in different places over a number of years or even decades. The early secular book was a protective container of varied content rather than a coherent intellectual product. By 1300 the profession of bookbinder was well established and records show these artisans grouped around the area of London that is now Fleet Street, as this put them close to the booksellers who ran their markets around the old St Paul's Cathedral.

As the books moved out of the monasteries and into the universities and royal courts, they found a new audience. Original literary works in the vernacular (the language of the streets as opposed to Latin) started to be written and read. Dante wrote the *Divine Comedy* in Italian in the early 1300s; Chaucer wrote *The Canterbury Tales* about 50 years later in English. Both became famous

GUTENBERG

Johannes Gutenberg was born in the German city of Mainz around 1400. He trained as a goldsmith and started several businesses, including making mirrors for pilgrims to allow them to capture the healing properties of religious relics in the reflection. In 1439 he invited local investors to join him in a secret project he called "art and enterprise." Gutenberg used his metalworking skills to develop movable lead type and combined this with a converted wine press and a new form of oil-based ink. By 1450 he was producing small printed documents and over the next few years he printed at least 180 copies of his masterpiece bible. He designed the typeface to look like script handwritten by the monks to maximize his sales.

However, like many media pioneers Gutenberg hit financial problems and was declared bankrupt. He remained involved in various printing projects and in 1465 was given official recognition and a state pension, which included a grant of 2,000 liters of wine. He died three years later. It is not known whether he drank the wine in time.

CAXTON

William Caxton brought the business of printing to England. Born in Kent in about 1420, he became a successful merchant in Bruges and then went onto Cologne, where he learned the new skill of letterpress and movable type. He made a translation of a popular French romance called *Stories of Troy*, which was the first book printed in English. On the back of this success he set up a printing press at Westminster in 1476. He went on to print more than 100 different books, of which one of the best known was the English-language version of *The Golden Legend*, a highly fanciful collection of the lives of the saints. Caxton's translations brought European culture to the previously rather insular English aristocracy and his texts became sources for Shakespeare.

When he died in 1492, Caxton's machines transferred to his partner Wynkyn de Worde, who had a particular interest in typography and introduced the italic script to England. De Worde published more than 400 titles specializing in popular, less expensive books. In 1500 he moved his print operations to London's Fleet Street to be close to the bookbinders, thus initiating a printing tradition that lasted until the twenty-first century.

throughout Europe. In the days before the creation of copyright laws anyone could make facsimiles of the text, so authors relied on patronage rather than royalties. The commercial *scriptoria* made their money because of the beauty and rarity of their product rather than its content. The demand for books of all types was well established by the mid-1400s.

PRINTING

Printing, the process of reproducing an image from an original, started in China around 800 AD and by 1300 there were many thousands of pages in existence, mostly created using carved wooden blocks that reproduced both text and drawings. In Europe the breakthrough came in Germany, when Johannes Gutenberg converted a wine press to allow him to print high-quality pages—the letterpress technique. Other printers quickly copied his methods. With the flourishing of the universities from the mid-1400s the demand for printed books on subjects other than religion grew. Experts on the arts, sciences, politics, and theatre all produced works. Private collectors began to emerge and building private libraries became a fashion again.

England was a slow starter in printing but an important market for books. As with wine, the English became connoisseurs rather than producers. Latin and Greek texts were imported in large numbers, so much so that the early book business in London was called the "Latin trade."

The production of books in the vernacular had a profound effect on the standardization of spelling and grammar. Before printing the spoken language had a very loose structure, but once numerous copies of a book originated from the same set of metal type, it acted to fix spelling and meaning once and for all. By 1500 the dark ages were over, the Renaissance had begun, and the bibliophile and library traditions of Rome and Greece were being recreated, but with printed books rather than handwritten scrolls. By 1600, it is estimated 200 million books had been published.

PAPER MAKING

Clay tablets in southern Europe, wood bark in the north, and bamboo slabs in China were clumsy media: fragile, hard to inscribe, hard to carry. To improve on this many ancient societies created specialist light-weight writing materials—broadly called *tapa*—by cooking the pulp of plants and trees and drying it on frames to create sheets that could be marked with charcoal and primitive inks. Papyrus was the most successful of these.

The combination of papyrus and hieroglyphics made a major contribution to the development and management of the Egyptian and later Roman empires. Written records allowed the development of a bureaucracy and social control, as well as the transmission of military orders and information. It is sometimes argued that when the papyrus stocks ran out the Roman Empire started to fail, as communications between remote outposts became more difficult.[2]

Although the Egyptians gave paper its name, the techniques of making it came from China. It started around 100 AD with a discovery credited to Chinese court official Ts'ai Lun, who developed a process of combining wood bark and rags allegedly inspired by watching bees and wasps build nests.[3] The manufacturing technique made its way to Italy via Korea along the medieval trade routes. A huge number of variations developed, all involving cooking and drying fibers. A water-powered paper mill is recorded in the German city of Nuremberg in 1390—the start of mass production.[4]

Paper making came relatively late to England, with the first record of a paper mill not until 1495. It was located near Hertford and owned by

PROHIBITED BOOKS

In the early days of hand-produced books, the vast majority were made by or for the Church or the monarch, so the need to censor unapproved material was very limited. Unofficial documents that met with disapproval were almost always anonymous and were simply destroyed. There was no need to have any additional control mechanisms. However, as soon as Gutenberg's press allowed mass distribution of texts, the Church and various governments started to control the free flow of printed material that now could come from many sources and regularly crossed national borders.

In 1559 Pope Paul IV came up with the idea of a list of banned books, the so-called *Index Librorum Prohibitorium*. The plan was to prohibit texts that might undermine morals or contained "theological errors." As it turned out, the list included a number of works of science that challenged the then conventional views of how the universe worked and God's role in it. The Index remained in place until 1966 (that is not a misprint) when it was abolished by Pope Paul VI. In the UK it was the Crown rather than the Church that was most active in controlling publishing and it did this through licensing.

John Tate. Tate paper became famous and was used to print *The Canterbury Tales*. For several hundred years English paper making remained a cottage industry. By 1800 there were 430 paper mills in England and Wales turning out some 10,000 tonnes of paper a year and consuming such huge quantities of rags that many boatloads of old cloth had to be imported to meet the demand.[5] By the mid-1800s a combination of new industrial processes allowed cheap paper to be made from wood pulp, which opened the way for the development of large-circulation newspapers, "penny dreadful" magazines, and cheap mass-market books.

FONTS AND TYPEFACES

Before the invention of printing all documents were written by hand. Manuscript writing was a skill and each scribe tended to develop their own hand or writing style. Thus, as with a composer or artist, each might be recognized by their technique, which might reflect their location and their training. For example, the Book of Kells (the gospels written in Latin) is a collection of more than 300 pages created during the eighth century and is regarded as the highpoint of medieval illustrated manuscripts. It is in a style called "insular majuscule," which refers to the way of writing adopted in the islands of Britain—insular for islands and majuscule for capital letters.

The Holy Roman Emperor Charlemagne wanted to create a more standardized form of writing throughout his extensive empire. In 781 AD he commissioned a special edition of the Gospels in what became known as the Carolingian (after Charlemagne) script. He worked with the Abbot of the monastery at Tours in France producing many hundreds of documents in this script over the next 20 years. The script features lowercase letters as well as capitals and became the inspiration for many of the typefaces we use today.

Over the next few hundred years the skill of the elegant Carolingian script was lost and most religious documents started to be done in black-letter style, which was cruder and clumsier. This was partly done for fashion, but mostly because it allowed the scribes to fit a lot of writing into a small space, reflecting the high cost of parchment. It was this style that was most popular at the time Gutenberg was starting to work, so he turned it into his first font, which is now called Gothic.

The word "font" comes from the Middle French *fonte* meaning to pour. Type was originally made

BOOK BURNING

One step beyond prohibition of a book was its public destruction. The burning of books had a ceremonial role, a statement of where true power lay and a demonstration of official disapproval. Official book burning happened long before printing. It was done in ancient China and numerous examples are on the record in Egypt and Rome.

In modern consciousness the German Nazi Party burning books in an open square in Berlin is one of the most shocking and enduring images, partly because it has been captured on film. It also has the most awful symbolic impact. It is painfully ironic that the German playwright Heinrich Heine wrote in 1821: "Where they burn books, they will end in burning human beings." In Spain Franco's fascists were also keen on burning books, notoriously doing so in Corunna in 1936.

The most famous literary treatment of book burning is Ray Bradbury's 1953 novel *Fahrenheit 451*, the title being the temperature at which paper catches fire. The story is of a dystopian future society where all books are banned as subversive and a fireman is a public official whose job it is to destroy any books that are discovered. And it is still happening—Russian Nationalists burned Ukrainian history books in 2010.

LICENSING OF PRINTING

From the start of printing in Britain, the state sought to control it. British monarchs in the early 1500s took a very simple approach to censorship: if anything was to be printed it had to have prior royal approval. To print anything without such approval was a crime. However, as the volume of books grew this became unwieldy, so Henry VIII devised a private-sector solution that was implemented by his daughter, Mary I.

The Stationers' Guild had been around since 1403 as a trade association for the craft skills of bookbinding and bookselling. In 1557 it was granted a Royal Charter to become the Stationers' Company. This gave its members the monopoly over all book production. It was a private-sector extension of the royal veto, which was an elegant solution to control increasingly large numbers of publications. It became illegal to print a book without a license from the Company, whose members entered an approved text into the Stationers' Register establishing their right to make copies of it. This is the origin of copyright, although ownership of the copyright vested only in members of the Company—excluding authors and playwrights.

Initially printing (under the close eye of the Crown) was only allowed in London. In 1586 the Star Chamber court extended this to one press in each of Oxford and Cambridge, the origin of the famous University Presses. This prepublication control continued in England until 1695, when the Licensing Act expired. This made publication of journals critical of the government far easier and led to magazines like *The Tatler* and *The Spectator*. The new freedoms also led to a rash of newspapers in the then British colony of America and laid the ground for the development of ideas that led to the American Revolution.

when molten lead was poured into a mold to create a single letter of a particular design. When an alphabet of letters in the same style is created it is called a font or typeface.

The artists and merchants of the Italian Renaissance found black-letter style heavy and oppressive and when printing spread to Venice in the late 1400s, they developed new typefaces to suit the mood of the times. As with architecture and art, they looked back to classical times and rediscovered the clean simplicity of the Carolingian script and out of this developed two new letter styles, Roman (in 1470) and Italic (in 1501). Both are in use to this day.

As literacy spread, efforts were made to standardize handwriting as well as printing. Approved formats were developed and teaching materials produced by engraving sample words onto plates of copper. This form of standardized handwriting became known as copperplate. The most successful of the copperplate training manuals was *The Universal Penman* by George Bickham, which is still in print 250 years later.

CHAPBOOKS

Within 50 years of the invention of printing, one of the most popular applications for it were "broadside ballads." These were the lyrics of popular songs and stories printed onto one side of a low-quality paper, hence "broadside," sold in the streets by pedlars and priced at half a penny. They were used by families and groups of laborers to entertain themselves, being read or sung out loud. Broadsides had started to circulate in handwritten form before printing, but movable type made them far more common. One of the earliest big sellers was the *Ballad of Robin Hood* in 1506.

However, after licensing was introduced it meant paying a stamp tax of 4 pence per sheet. Some printers followed this rule; others risked prison and printed anonymously; others responded by cramming in far more text to make the levy seem less onerous. They did this by folding the big broadside sheet into four or eight pages and printing on both sides. This densely worded publication became the so-called chapbook, sold by the chapmen, itinerant dealers. Their name came from the Old English verb *cheap*, meaning to trade or barter; places like Cheapside and Eastcheap were the sites of markets.

The price of chapbooks was much higher than broadsides in order to pay the stamp tax, but they contained a lot of words and were still well within the reach of the ordinary working man. They were crude, rude, and lewd—the supermarket tabloids of the sixteenth century.

Chapbooks were hugely popular for 200 years. They were a medium that allowed folk tales and myths to be written down. The story of St George and the Dragon was popular and Shakespeare used chapbook stories as sources for his plays. A couple of centuries later, Robert Burns is said to have been inspired into Scottish nationalism by the chapbook story of William Wallace. In the American colonies (which still paid English taxes) equivalent cheap books told sensational tales of white women settlers abducted by Indians. Surviving American examples include an eight-page illustrated version of Robinson Crusoe and, demonstrating an eye for popular taste and tight editing, one entitled *Only the Good Bits of Moll Flanders*, in effect an early version of *Reader's Digest*.[6]

Unlike the upscale and more professional codex publications, chapbooks were not bound and not intended as collectables. They were ephemeral and they were fun. Thousands of examples survive nevertheless and it can be seen that many were printed in a slapdash fashion. Pieces of old, worn, and broken type were used. Many had woodcut illustrations that employed the same lurid pictures in numerous different stories and often bore no relation at all to the text they illustrated.

A close cousin of the chapbook, also designed for popular consumption, was the almanac. These were extended calendars containing information such as the phases of the moon, tide tables, and horoscopes.

A LIBRARY IN EVERY HOME

While the chapbook and almanac were entertainment for the masses, the better-off started to collect books as objects of interior decoration and symbols of sophistication. Merchants and gentleman farmers aspired to the sort of library that had once been the preserve of kings and archbishops. By the 1700s the Georgians, on both sides of the Atlantic, were buying, reading, and storing books on an almost unimaginable range of subjects. Early books had been created at the whim of a patron or paid for by the author. They now started to be published by printers and booksellers keen to employ their machines and shop space and make a profit. Encouraged by the new copyright laws, authors started to see writing as a profession. Books, like all luxuries, moved down the social scale. By the early 1800s they were adornments to any middle-class household. For the Victorians a modest home library was a crucial social statement. It was a store of knowledge, a source of information, a means of self-education, and a form of entertainment; rather like the internet today.

For the early Victorians books were still expensive and handmade on letterpress machines. However, by the mid-1800s the same mechanical printing and paper-making technologies that would transform the newspaper and magazine industries were making books available to everyone who wanted them.

PAPERBACKS

In the 1700s and 1800s the upper middle-class reading public and booksellers were happy with the expensive hardcover format. It was attractive and durable and had second-hand value. Poor people could not read, so there was no mass market. However, from about 1820 onward things began to change. New inventions in manufacturing made paper printing and binding much cheaper. Literacy was more widespread. Much improved transport allowed large numbers of books to be moved around quickly. If cheap books could be produced in greater numbers, they would find a new audience.

WH SMITH

WH Smith is a familiar sight in British high streets, train stations, and airports. It has played a central role in the distribution of both books and newspapers for more than 200 years. It was started as a simple newsstand in London in 1792 by a Mr HW Smith, changing its name to WH Smith in 1846 when the founder's grandson William Henry took over. He opened a bookstall at London's new Euston station and the following year signed a major and, in retrospect, brilliant contract to have a monopoly of book selling on the London and North Western Railway. As the Victorian traveling public clamored for entertainment on the trains, WH Smith was the sole outlet for publishers of the new low-cost "yellow backs." Not only did its deal give it a book monopoly, it allowed free rail transport for all WH Smith stock, which made it the most powerful distributor of newspapers as well.

The dime novel

Carey's Library of Choice Literature was launched in America in 1838 with reprints of English novels that were sold a chapter at a time. No copyright was paid to the British authors, the paper was cheap, and subscribers received chapters through the mail at the special low rates designed for newspapers. The US Post Office, lobbied by traditional booksellers, then decided that the publication was a "book" not a newspaper and it would be charged at a higher rate. This decision destroyed the economics of the subscription library overnight.

Another American entrepreneur called Park Benjamin came up with what he claimed was a weekly paper called *Brother Jonathan* and this time obtained lasting Post Office approval. *Brother Jonathan* carried works by the likes of Charles Dickens (who did not get paid) and quickly had more than 30,000 subscribers. Dickens, like other British writers, was able to capitalize on his US popularity by doing lucrative American speaking tours. This was a Victorian response to illegal copying that would be repeated by the music business 150 years later.

The success of *Brother Jonathan* led others to follow, again without payment to authors, and similar publications started to be sold at railway stations and in general stores as well as by post. Publishers would wait for boats to arrive from England, pirate new editions of recent books in the harbor, and have them reprinted in the cheap American format within hours. A book that might have cost a pound in London cost pennies in New York. The publications were called "pamphlet novels" and met with much disapproval. English geologist Sir Charles Lyell commented:

> Many are of the opinion that the small print of the cheap editions in the United States will injure the eyesight of a rising generation, especially as they are often read in railway cars, devouring whole novels, printed in newspapers in very inferior type.[7]

However, other low-cost US publications like *New World* started to commission original work that they did pay for, by American writers including Nathaniel Hawthorne, Washington Irving, and Edgar Allan Poe. The format started to get so popular that booksellers and publishers once again lobbied the US Congress, which in 1843 changed the rules to increase postal rates. The pamphlet novel trade had run its course.

Further advances in printing technology made soft-cover publications even cheaper. In the US the Beadle Brothers exploited this by selling their books for ten cents, coining the term "dime novel." They commissioned home-grown American stories, mostly about the Wild West. The first, published in June 1860, was *Malaeska, the Indian Wife of the White Hunter*, which had previously appeared in installments in magazines. The dime novel format became a huge success and once again they started to reprint European authors without payment or permission; in a way their success was the source of their ultimate downfall.

Magazine baron Frank Munsey recognized the public taste for good stories at low prices. He commissioned new American writers, focused on crime and romance, and developed his so-called pulp fiction magazine *Argosy*, which was cheaply printed on paper made from wood pulp. Then in 1891 the US Congress finally approved an international copyright law. The combination of legally enforced royalties and competition from the likes of *Argosy* ended the dime novel era, but the taste for mass-market books had been established.

Yellow backs

UK publishers watched events in America with some disapproval, although in the end they developed low-cost books themselves. The spread of the railway network in the mid-1800s led to a huge increase in travel by all classes of people. Victorian train passengers wanted to be entertained and publishers came up with the idea of "yellow backs," which sold at much lower prices than conventional books.

As in the US, new technologies of mechanized printing and cheap paper made it economic to create long print runs of cheap small books. They had bright yellow covers

PUBLIC LIBRARIES

From their earliest days books (indeed scrolls) were collected together in libraries. Monasteries, universities, schools, towns, and larger private homes all had collections, but they were very restricted in access. In the 1700s like-minded individuals clubbed together to form subscription libraries to create shared collections. One of the first was the Library Company of Philadelphia, founded by Benjamin Franklin in 1731. The London Library was founded much later, as most wealthy people in London had their own collections and did not need the subscription model.

By the 1800s, social reformers were starting to argue that making books available to all citizens was an important political act. As a relatively new country with a strong commitment to public education, the United States led the trend and the first free public library opened in Salisbury, Connecticut in 1803. While in the UK the public library movement was given official support by the 1850 Public Libraries Act, in the US private philanthropy was the driving force. The biggest donor was Andrew Carnegie and in the 20 years after 1900 more than 1,700 public libraries were opened in the US and more than 200 in the UK using his endowment.

illustrated with vivid artwork, and cost about 2 shillings when a typical bound novel might be 15 shillings. Publishers realized they had found new customers and a new market without reducing the sales in the original one.

Yellow backs were mostly reprints of popular British novels, whose authors welcomed this additional new income. In another innovation they often carried advertisements to help cover costs and keep their sale price down. Because these books were produced with factory-made paper and cheap bindings, they have tended to age very badly. Not many have survived, but there is a collection of some 400 yellow back titles in the Fisher rare book library of the University of Toronto.

Penguins

While dime novels and yellow backs had shown that there was a market for cheaper books, the First World War and then the Great Depression made paper scarce. In 1935 British publisher Allen Lane took the spirit of the yellow back to a new generation of readers with an innovative paperback brand, which he called Penguin. According to the company (now owned by publishing giant Pearson), the idea originated when he was at Exeter railway station having visited the author Agatha Christie and found there was nothing to read. He hit on the notion of an inexpensive, quality novel that would sell for sixpence: "the same price as a packet of cigarettes."

His idea was not unique. Albatross Books in Germany was already publishing a low-cost, high-quality format. This had an Albatross as its symbol and color coded its books by genre; just as Penguin would do. Inspired by this, Lane's secretary came up with the name "Penguin" as being "dignified but flippant," and his office junior was sent to London Zoo to sketch penguins to provide a logo for the covers.[8]

At that point the soft-cover format was associated with lurid novellas. Allen Lane wanted his books to have a quality feel, but also to stand out on the shelves. Garish cover art implied trashy fiction, so he went for a radical solution of no pictures, just the title and the author's name in black print on white with two colored bars above and below: orange for fiction, green for crime, and blue for biography.

Other publishers thought the quality paperback format would fail, so Lane was able to buy rights to books cheaply. One of his first was Ernest Hemingway's A *Farewell to Arms*. In the event the public loved his idea and an order from mass-market retailer Woolworths for 63,000 copies guaranteed success. Within 10 months of launch there were one million Penguin paperbacks in print.

THE NOVEL

It would be possible to devote a whole book to trying to define exactly what constitutes a "novel" and where the term originated. At its simplest, a novel is a work of fiction, a book that tells a story with characters and a plot as opposed to being a work of reference, record, propaganda, or education.

Adults and children love stories and the medium of the book told them from the very beginning. By the time the illustrated manuscript was the main form of record, we have stories like *Sir Gawain and the Green Knight*, which dates from the thirteenth century, and the various legends of King Arthur. These sagas of mystical beings and heroes were usually called "romances," but they were fantasies with strong religious overtones rather than works of fiction about real people. Like the Greek myths before them, they were the written record of what had been essentially fireside performances.

The Spanish writer Miguel de Cervantes wrote *Don Quixote* in 1605 and this is regarded by many as the first true novel. It is a complete story and its theme is a real man driven mad by his unrealistic belief in the very sort of fantasy world described in the medieval romances. The book is seen as an indictment of the prevailing form of fantastical literature. Cervantes certainly used the term "novel" himself for a collection of his short stories written in 1613.

In England, works of allegorical fiction became popular, although these were still religious or political publications rather than human-interest stories. Famous examples include John Milton's *Paradise Lost* (1667) and John Bunyan's *Pilgrim's Progress* (1678). Playwright William Congreve published a short book he called "a novel" in 1691, but it was more a modern morality tale like his much more famous plays.

There is a good case to be made that talented writers had little motivation for writing works of fiction until the concept of intellectual property was established, since patrons were unlikely to commission such a book. It may just be a coincidence, but the first book to be regarded as a real novel in English is *Robinson Crusoe*, published by journalist Daniel Defoe in

1719, less than 10 years after copyright became protected by English law. This has all the classic elements of a novel. Its lead character is a real person with whom the contemporary audience could relate. It has a strong plot and story arc, dealing with contemporary issues and illuminating the human condition, and is set in an intriguing and exotic location. The eighteenth century was the "Age of Enlightenment" when philosophers like John Locke were arguing that the real human "self" could only be understood by direct experience and empirical experiment—exactly the sort of enlightenment that is experienced by the hero of a novel as they make their way through the book.

After Defoe had demonstrated the commercial viability of writing a novel, the floodgates opened for writers who expanded on the genre: Jonathan Swift's *Gulliver's Travels* (1726), Samuel Richardson's *Clarissa* (1747), and Henry Fielding's *Tom Jones* (1749). All of these established the format of a story told through the eyes of real people and describing their response to life's experiences.

Perhaps as a reaction against the rational thinking of the Enlightenment, a popular and escapist form of literature called the "gothic novel" emerged. This combined elements of fantasy and the supernatural seen from the perspective of the main character and with a strong story line. One of the best known, *The Castle of Otranto*, was written in 1764 by Horace Walpole, the son of the then prime minister. The gothic genre reached its high point with Mary Shelley's *Frankenstein*, published in 1818. In the same year Jane Austen produced a popular parody of the style in *Northanger Abbey*. Here the main character (a bit like Don Quixote before her) suffers from having read too many gothic stories.

BOWDLERIZATION

The Victorians were enthusiastic moral crusaders and developed a strong prudish streak. Some classics of literature were felt to be too racy, and all foreign publications were suspect. In 1818 one Thomas Bowdler produced *The Family Shakespeare*. He took out what he felt to be objectionable words or ideas to make the text "acceptable to women and children" and to remove passages "which cannot with propriety be read aloud in a family." For example, in his version Lady Macbeth's scream of "Out damned spot" is altered to "Out crimson spot." In Henry IV the prostitute Doll Tearsheet was simply removed. Bowdler gave his name to "bowdlerization," meaning to amend text with a moral purpose.

The structure of the novel started out as the story of man's progress through life. It has developed into an unlimited range of subgenres such as romantic, detective, westerns, science fiction, and fantasy and it provides the basis for much of the material in cinema and on television. Strong characters and a compelling story are the fundamentals of all drama. If anyone was in any doubt about the contemporary power of the novel, the 1 billion plus sales of the Harry Potter books should be evidence enough.

THE DICTIONARY

The *Oxford English Dictionary* (OED) defines itself as "a book that lists (usually in alphabetical order) and explains the words of a language or gives equivalent words in another language." There have been hundreds of dictionaries over the years, but the most famous and enduring were those of Dr Johnson, Noah Webster, and the OED itself.

Lists of words have been found dating back 4,000 years to the early cuneiform tablets. The Romans and Greeks had scrolls of definitions. The Rosetta stone is, in effect, a translation dictionary, as it repeats the same message in three languages. The first English-language attempt was a list of 8,000 words in 1592 and the first alphabetically indexed English dictionary came in 1604. The English language was being written down and read like never before, but there was no standard work of reference, no ultimate authority, to explain exactly what words meant or, perhaps more importantly, how they should be spelled.

Dr Johnson

The London publishing community was acutely aware of the need for a set of standard definitions, so its members clubbed together to commission Samuel Johnson to write one. Dr Johnson was already a well-known journalist and he agreed to accept a substantial fee of 1,500 guineas to compile the definitive dictionary. He started in 1746 with an initial (and unrealistic) promise to finish in three years. It was known at the time that the Academie Française had contracted with 40 scholars to write the definitive dictionary of French and expected it would take 40 years to do so. It took Johnson only nine years to write his masterwork. And, in an extraordinary feat of endurance, he did it all by himself. The resulting text was vast. It contained more than 40,000 definitions and these were supported by more than

100,000 literary references. Physically the book was also huge. In fact it was two books, each approximately 18 inches by 20 inches and printed on heavyweight, luxury paper. Right from the start, it was intended to be an impressive and desirable physical object, as well as a defining work of scholarship. Johnson's biographer James Boswell commented:

> the world contemplated with wonder so stupendous a work achieved by one man, while other countries had thought such undertakings fit only for whole academies.

Johnson's approach was highly original, as he did not just list words but tried to give them meaning and context. And as a committed mischief maker, he had a dry sense of humor. Witness two of his entries:

> Oats: a grain which in England is generally given to horses, but in Scotland supports the people.
> Lexicographer: a writer of dictionaries; a harmless drudge that busies himself in tracing the original and detailing the signification of words.

Johnson's dictionary was very expensive (£4 10 shillings in 1755, which would be many hundreds of pounds today) and it was only printed in relatively small numbers. However, it quickly achieved great fame and prestige and remained the definitive British source of reference for some 150 years. For Johnson himself the dictionary was not a great financial success. He did not receive royalties, so got nothing beyond his original fee. Despite his fame he was always short of money, but in 1762 a grateful nation did grant him an annual pension of £300 to recognize his contribution to the language.

OED

The *Oxford English Dictionary* was a substantially bigger project than Johnson's and in stark contrast to the one-man-band approach it was an early example of collaborative user-generated content—a Victorian Wikipedia. It was begun as a project by London's Philological Society in 1857. They felt that Dr Johnsons's *magnum opus* was out of date and recruited an army of volunteers to fill in slips providing quotations to illustrate the meaning of words, including the many thousands that had emerged since Dr Johnson went to press in 1755.

Within four years the Philological Society team had accumulated more than 100,000 slips and many hundreds of contributors had signed up. One of the most prolific was an American surgeon called William Minor, who had been confined to the British lunatic asylum Broadmoor after committing a murder. As it turned out, he was one of the most effective dictionary compilers.

The sheer scale of the undertaking overwhelmed its originators. In 1879 the Oxford University Press agreed to take over the whole affair from the amateurs. By 1882 there were 3.5 million quotations and by 1885 OUP had decided to move operations out of London to Oxford to manage the enterprise more effectively.

The first part of the dictionary, words beginning with A, was published in 1888, but it took a further 40 years to complete the project with the last book, volume 12, coming out in 1928. The project was never a financial success, but it became, and remains, the ultimate guide to the English language – at least the variants spoken and written in England. The United States had commissioned its own great book.

Webster's

After 1776, the leaders of the newly independent colonies felt that American English needed its own dictionary champion. Rather than adopting Dr Johnson, they looked to a school teacher called Noah Webster, an influential member of the Connecticut elite who had studied at Yale. He was a friend of Alexander Hamilton and a strong supporter of the Federalist Party, which wanted a strong federal government and a distinctive American culture. Winning political independence from Britain was one victory. Webster and his friends wanted clear cultural independence as well.

Webster had written several guides to American grammar. His 1786 publication *The American Spelling Book* became a bestseller and his fascination with words helped create the peculiarly American phenomenon of the spelling bee. In 1806 he published *A Compendious Dictionary of the English Language*, which aimed to provide a definitive and prescriptive guide. It was in this that he institutionalized what are now accepted American spellings for words such as color (British version colour), honor (honour), and center (centre). He felt that these made more sense in the simpler form. It is Webster's lead that is followed in the spelling of this book.

FRANKFURT BOOK FAIR

Every year in October some 250,000 people visit Frankfurt to celebrate the book business. The Book Fair has been running for more than 500 years, since the time that Frankfurt was the center of German printing and publishing—just a few miles from where Gutenberg set up his first press. In 1650 the Frankfurt fair lost the number one position to Leipzig, where the local politicians were more commercially minded. However, after the Second World War Leipzig found itself in the Soviet block and in 1950 Frankfurt once again become the principal global showcase for books. Right from its origin it was an opportunity for printers and publishers to buy and sell manuscripts that had originated in one region but might have value in another. It has evolved into the main international marketplace where all the elements of the book trade meet and do deals.

Exactly like Johnson before him and the OED afterwards, Webster's dictionary was not a financial success. He had to mortgage his home to bring out a second edition and after he died the copyright was lost, so now any reference book in America can put Webster in its title even if it has no link to the original.

THE BOOK TRADE

The means of getting books into the hands of their readers has changed greatly over time and is now changing faster than ever. The distribution and retailing issues, first confronted by the book trade, have set the model for other media to follow. Before mechanical printing there was a limited trade in secondhand books and it was only after printing that the professions of bookbinder and bookseller really got going.

Binding

When we buy a book today, be it from a high-street bookstore or online, we think of it as a single product purchase. Before about 1850 we would have been expecting to make two separate transactions: buying the printed leaves of a book from a printer and then organizing the binding—designed to our taste and library decoration—from a professional bookbinder. It was not unknown for a rich collector to have an entire library of purchased books rebound to fit in with his own domestic style and décor. One of the first great private library builders was the French aristocrat Jean Grolier, who by 1525 had more than 3,000 books, most of which had Italian bindings.

Bookbinding was, and is, the process of physically assembling the pages and placing them between suitable covers, a convenient way to protect and present the leaves of text and illustrations. It was registered as a trade in London from around 1300, but the profession's real craft skills started to be seen in Italy in the 1500s. It was there that most of the styles and techniques that persist in quality books were developed.

As the whole process of book production, printing, and binding was mechanized, the craft skills of the binder became redundant and the art in books became more about cover design than physical construction. The technique of perfect binding—gluing pages directly into a spine without heavy stitching—was invented in 1895, although it was not applied to paperback books until 1931 in Germany. It was adopted by Penguin as the mark of a quality paperback.

Selling

By the 1800s bookshops were a feature of every town. They were a source of new information, a vital marketplace for secondhand volumes, and, to an extent, part of the home furnishing trade. Nevertheless, by the middle of the twentieth century small, independent operations would probably not have been economic propositions but for the love and attention of their owners, who enjoyed the work and accepted low rates of pay. In the UK they were protected by the Net Book Agreement and in America by the complex structure of regional wholesalers.

As with other forms of retailing in the 1980s and 1990s, the big book chains like Barnes & Noble, Borders, and Waterstones introduced centralized buying and

NET BOOK AGREEMENT

In 1900 booksellers in Britain entered into an unusual pact. They agreed that the publishers could set the retail prices and that all booksellers would stick to them. Those who broke the rules would be denied supplies. This goes against the retailing of almost all other goods, where the shopkeeper buys at a wholesale price of x and then sells to his customers at x plus as much as he can get away with. The logic was that good margins would be made on bestsellers and the surplus used to finance less popular but more worthy works. Despite constant protests, the agreement remained in place for nearly 100 years. After it was abolished in 1997 there were dire warnings of the collapse of literature, but in fact books became cheaper and sales actually went up, although many small bookshops did close.

BARNES & NOBLE

In 1873 Charles Barnes set up a book printing company in Illinois. In 1917 his son established a bookstore in New York as a partnership with Clifford Noble. The company has been a consistent innovator in book retailing. It was the first to advertise on television, the first to offer discounts, and the first bookstore to sell CDs, DVDs, and computer games. It was also the first to open cafés in a joint venture with Starbucks. In 2011 the chain was bid for by media conglomerate Liberty, attracted by its ownership of the popular ereader the Nook and by its success at selling customers profitable ebook titles in its shops.

distribution, which made them more cost effective than the small independent shops. For some years they flourished, selling books as if they were any other mass consumer product. But the arrival of the internet changed all that. Many book buyers wanted to browse a wide range of printed titles. A big shop might have 40,000 on display, but the online operator Amazon offered 400,000. The online merchants could make searching for individual titles and authors much simpler, and by passing on their huge economies of scale offered even lower prices.

Unable to compete on price and range, the chain stores have stumbled. Borders went bankrupt, and Barnes & Noble and Waterstones were both sold in 2011 at well below their peak stock market values. The dramatic growth of the ebook, the book as a digital file, has put high-street and main-street booksellers under even more pressure. Consumers have flocked to acquire electronic readers and having bought the technology they want things to read. The demand for downloadable, digital content exploded. By 2011 Amazon was selling more titles in electronic formats than traditional hardbacks and paperbacks combined.

In terms of bookstores we are likely to see a return to the origins of specialist book retailing, where well-presented, small shops offering a quality retail environment are staffed by expert bibliophiles who make recommendations for reading based on personal knowledge. Titles not immediately on the shelves can be instantly downloaded to the customer's ereader or printed to order. The Espresso Book Machine produces a 300-page paperback, perfect bound in a four-color cover, in less than 5 minutes at a cost of about £3 or $5. It means that backlist titles will never go out of print and a niche request can be fulfilled instantly.

The days of the bookshop as a warehouse with expensive storage shelves on the high street and a supermarket-style approach to promoting heavily discounted titles are over. But the huge waste from unsold books being returned to publishers or pulped is also probably gone. The book trade will once again focus on providing a cultural service, not just on selling cheap bestsellers.

THE PUBLISHING PROFESSION

The early book printers had made an investment in equipment and staff and they needed to keep their machines busy, so they began to experiment with commissioning new types of books. They wanted to make those books and their authors famous, so the profession of publisher—or book entrepreneur—was born. These first publishers had to take risks. They gambled that a book would find a market and that they would make a profit. It was very different from the printer, who sold his labor by the hour, and the bookseller, who took a small margin on each transaction.

Longmans was founded in 1742 with a focus on history and education. Debrett's was established in 1769 to provide books for the landed gentry. Macmillan was founded in 1843 to promote literature, with authors like Thomas Hardy and Rudyard Kipling. In the US in 1924, Simon and Schuster began by publishing books of crossword puzzles. The pioneer book publishers had to confront all the issues now so familiar to most media owners: the management of talent, copyright piracy, libel, spiraling marketing costs, and predicting public taste.

Publishing, more than anything, is about separating the wheat from the chaff: making the best material available to a wide audience. The

> **WATERSTONES**
>
> In 1982 a senior employee of WH Smith, Tim Waterstone, left to set up his own eponymous chain of bookshops based on the idea of expert service, an attractive retail environment, and a wide range. The business thrived, but in the 1990s was taken over by music retail group HMV, after which it adopted a centralized, chain-store approach. The competition from Amazon and supermarkets offering deep discounts on bestsellers put the chain under pressure and after a collapse in profits it was sold, in 2011, to a Russian billionaire with the stated intention of returning it to a focus on local markets and expert service.

challenge of technology allowing unlimited output was observed even in the fifteenth century. The Director of the Harvard University Library, Robert Darnton, has published a fascinating collection of essays called *The Case for Books*. In the introduction he quotes from the translation of a letter written in 1471 by an Italian scholar, Niccolò Perotti, just 20 years after Gutenberg started printing:

> I have lately kept praising the age in which we live because of the great, indeed divine, gift of the new kind of writing which was recently brought in from Germany. In fact, I saw a single man printing in a single month as much as could be written by several persons in a year... It was for this reason I was led to hope we should have such a large quantity of books that there wouldn't be a single work which could not be procured because of scarcity. Yet I see things turned out quite differently from what I had hoped. Because now that anyone is free to print whatever they wish they often disregard that which is best and instead write merely for the sake of entertainment, what would be best forgotten or, better still be erased from all books.[9]

More than 400 years on and the challenge of the unlimited blogosphere reflects Perotti's lament. The role of the publisher, even with the advent of the ebook and digital printing, is to select from a huge number of offers a product that pleases and will find a market. The publisher's brand acts as a promise of performance to reassure both retailers and buyers.

A GLORIOUS FUTURE FOR BOOKS?

The book looks set to embrace the digital age and thrive. The increasing challenge to other, heritage printed media like newspapers (daily) and magazines (weekly) is that their online audiences expect a publication schedule that is continuous. Readers want their news and comment laced with video and they want it now. But the book is a media formula that takes a bundle of content, a story or an argument, and freezes it in time. It is a collection of ideas and information presented as a complete whole. And we the readers seem to like this, whether it is offered between the hard covers of the time-honored codex format—familiar for 2,000 years—or on the screen of a specially designed reader like a Kindle or a Nook.

And unlike other media such as film and music, the book is under less threat from the streaming of digital files. Renting a three-minute song from a cloud-based catalogue or watching a movie on a whim fits with the technology's capabilities and our lifestyles. Streaming a digital book makes less sense. The readership will normally be too small to generate advertising. Books are often read over a long period, kept as points of reference, and loaned out to friends. Downloaded files with copyright protection fit these needs in the same way physical books do. Book files will probably continue to be purchased to download, owned, and retained, because they fulfill a similar role to their printed forebears. As Jeff Bezos, founder of Amazon has said, "Kindle is never going to have the same smell as a book, never going to have the same tactile feel. But you do lose yourself in the story, the same way you do in a physical book."[10]

In addition, the traditional book is an artifact, as Bezos suggests. As well as being a medium of data transfer it has, since its earliest days, been an object of pleasure to be handled, stored, admired, and often offered as a gift. With film or music it is the content itself we value more than the vehicle of delivery. With books many of us collect for the pleasure of the collection. High-quality photography, graphics, and printing produce an overall product that cannot be replicated in digital form. Home libraries are as popular as ever and are one of the most prized possessions in the fast-growing Chinese market.

In later chapters we will see the oft-repeated lesson that most old media forms do not die out but evolve to respond to new technologies. As the oldest mass medium, the book has been a pioneer in this process. While the roles of authors, publishers, and booksellers are changing, they will be modified, they will not disappear.

As an original medium to create characters, showcase concepts, or develop an argument, the book is hard to beat. In fiction it allows pure imagination to be shared between author and reader. In nonfiction it remains a powerful way to organize and communicate new ideas. The book was the first mass communications tool and its final chapter as a mass medium is a long time from being written.

2.3 | Pictures

The phrase "a picture's worth a thousand words" has the ring of timeless wisdom about it. In fact it was coined in the 1920s to promote the purchase of outdoor advertising on streetcars in America. However, the power of the image as a communications medium was well understood long before a copywriter captured it with a pithy slogan. A picture of a crying child, a cute baby animal, or a spectacular sunrise evokes a whole set of complex responses that would take a very long time to communicate in print.

Pictures now play a key role in most other media, particularly newspapers, magazines, and websites. Moving pictures are, of course, the essence of television and film, but this chapter is about the use of images as a standalone medium in their own right. It covers drawings, paintings, photographs, maps, and graphics. These are the two-dimensional images employed as media to convey a message. A picture is created for a reason. It can be the most basic line drawing made with a stick of charcoal or a complex montage of photography, paint, and printed graphics. It is acting as a medium of communication with the objective of transmitting information or ideas—it is trying to tell us something.

LOOKING AT PICTURES

We read a book or a newspaper in the way the author or editor intended us to. With a particular chapter or article, we tend to begin at the beginning and work our way through to the end. It is hard to follow the story if we jump around. But a picture (or a photograph or even a map) presents itself in a very different way. When confronted with the image we can start where we want to. When you first encounter the *Mona Lisa*, what do you notice: the eyes, the smile, or the hair? In Picasso's *Guernica*, is it the overall effect, the face of the bull, the stance of the horse, or the images of the people? In the iconic photograph "Raising the Flag on Iwo Jima," are you drawn to the flag itself, the soldiers, or the debris on the hilltop? Different people react in different ways.

As viewers, we have far more control of the way we interact with an image than we do with a text or a film. We start with the bits that interest us and that gives us the context against which to judge the rest. Infrared technology can track where a person's eyes look when they see an image. For instance and perhaps not surprisingly, men and women look at pictures of fashion models in a different way and move their eyes over the image in a different order. Women look first at hair and teeth; men look, initially, at different anatomical features.

All pictures are a form of illusion, as they use techniques to persuade our minds to see an image. A painting or drawing uses the language of visual art to communicate in two dimensions. A sculpture does the same in three dimensions. A photograph can be seen as simply capturing a moment of reality by recording reflected light, but in most cases there is some degree of artifice that gives the photographer the same control as the artist. In practice, photographs are produced rather than simply "taken." Similarly, a map is not only showing us the relative location of things, it conveys social and political ideas. A graphic is rarely intended as a neutral device—it presents data in such a way as to support an argument.

ELEMENTS OF THE IMAGE

Our mind interprets what we see in an image based on our education, experience, and culture. With language there is relatively little ambiguity; the words smile or frown, for instance, mean pretty much the same to any listener. What is implied by an image of the same things is far more subjective. Images are an insight into the mind that interprets them, hence the use of the Rorschach ink blot to test an individual's psychological state.

The phenomenon of pareidolia describes the way in which we see images in what are actually random patterns, such as the "man in the moon." We talk about the idea that some makes of automobile look sad and others happy. We see animals in clouds and in the night sky we see the characters implied by the constellations. Our minds interpret what we see to find a pattern that relates to our world.

In simple terms, images are made up of lines, shape, and color, which in various combinations produce a powerful effect.

Line

A line can be thick or thin, straight or curved, angular or wavy. We have learned to interpret lines, so even the most subtle differences convey meaning. To a great extent our brain chooses to see patterns and messages because of the way in which we interpret things. Draw a circle with a dot in the lower half and we see a face. Add a couple more dots and we see eyes. Make the lower dot a line and we see a smile. A basic drawing like this contains very little hard information. Our brain fills in the gaps.

In the conventions of manga comics, simple symbols are used for an entire emotional state. A sweat drop on the face shows embarrassment. Three dots (an ellipsis, ...) over the head show silence. An experienced manga reader knows and appreciates this visual language.

Shape

Basic shape implies meaning, largely for cultural reasons. Certain shapes elicit particular emotions. A circle is calming, artistic, complete, and serene. A square is aggressive, military, scientific, and rational. A triangle shown with its point facing up and its long side down looks secure, grounded, and safe, like a pyramid. But turn it though 180 degrees and stand it on its point and it looks precarious, risky, and impermanent, like an arrow in flight. The dimensions of the Golden Mean make us happy and evoke harmony and balance.

Color

Humans see color in the context of an overall image rather than as an absolute and unchanging fact of the environment. We see colors because the retinas in our eyes contain three types of cell, each of which responds to different wavelengths of light. The images we receive stimulate these cells to different degrees. The information from each cell type is then processed in the brain so that we see the colors. Humans are called tri-chromats, because we have three different types of color-sensitive cells. Some fish and birds are tetra-chromats, as they have four. So-called color blindness happens when one of these cell sets is not working.

The most important aspect of color in media is its physiological or emotional effect. The impact of color on our mood is highly subjective and strongly linked to other cultural factors. In the

THE GOLDEN MEAN

Take a blank sheet of white paper and draw on it a simple rectangle. Make the short side 10 cm and the long side 16.2 cm. It produces a very pleasing effect. It should: you have just drawn an image based on the idea of the divine ratio.

In the late 1400s an Italian monk called Luca Pacioli published a book called *On Divine Proportion*. In it he explained that the ratio of 1.62:1 appeared in nature and created a perfect relationship. He was fortunate to have his book illustrated by Leonardo da Vinci, which made it a big hit with artists and architects, who started to use the theory in all branches of the visual arts. It was the governing idea in the size and layout of many books.

The concept of the golden mean in mathematics dates back to Pythagoras and Fibonacci, but it was Father Pacioli who assured its place in the creation of images. A golden triangle, by the way, looks like a dunce's hat with an angle of 36° at the top and two equal angles of 72° at the bottom.

Anglo-Saxon world we think of blues as calming and cool. Reds are seen as hot and active. Yellow is happy; brown is sad. In the UK or US red is associated with danger or anger, in China with luck and gifts.

The way color is used in language is rich with associated emotions. We see red and feel blue. We are green with envy and cowards have a yellow streak. The decision to use a particular color in an image is therefore loaded with meaning.

LITHOGRAPHY

Lithography is literally writing on stone. It is a chemical process that works because of the mutual repulsion of oil and water and was discovered in 1796 by an Austrian called Alois Senefelder. An image is painted onto a stone surface, originally smooth limestone. An acid solution is then used to etch the image into the stone, which is now a printing plate. If oil-based ink is rolled onto the stone it can be pressed against a sheet of paper to produce a very high-quality printed copy. This technique was vastly superior to the old ways of engraving and it opened up a huge new market for commercial art and maps.

In the 1830s the process was refined to make color prints by using multiple stones, one for each color. By the 1870s it had been combined with photographic techniques using metal plates. This was the key technology that allowed mass-produced maps and enabled the poster industry in France in the 1880s. Further improvements led to offset lithography, which is at the heart of most modern printing processes and is used for newspapers and magazines.

THE TECHNOLOGY OF IMAGES

Drawing is creating images with lines and shading. Painting is doing the same with pigment dissolved in a liquid. Printing is the reproduction of an original using ink to create lines and shades. Photography was a chemical—and is now also a digital—process of capturing reflected light. As technology has advanced the use of images has become more varied, widespread, and sophisticated.

Drawing and painting

Early cave drawings were done with readily available chalk and charcoal. Painting needs a pigment, a material that changes the color of light when it is reflected. Thus a blue pigment absorbs red and green light so the surface it is on looks blue. Original pigments came from naturally occurring minerals, sometimes straight out of the ground. Carbon produced black, zinc white, cobalt blue, and iron red. The pigment needs to be applied using a carriage medium that evaporates, leaving the color in place. This was originally water, but most early painting was done using tempera, which meant mixing a pigment with the yolk or white of an egg. Frescoes are done by mixing pigment with water and putting it onto wet plaster; when the plaster dries the image is captured. The Romans used oil paint to decorate their shields, but it was not until the 1400s that oil-based paint was widely used by fine artists and enabled a much more dramatic use of color in pictures.

Engraving and printing

Being able to paint or draw on a wall or a canvas creates a permanent record and allows an audience to view the result, but it is a one-off. The viewer has to interact with the original in situ. To reach a much bigger audience the image needs to be able to be reproduced. The creation of mechanical copies predates by far the development of movable type printing.

- Woodcuts are the most ancient and simplest form of image reproduction. The technique is believed to have been used first in China around 600 AD and was widespread in Europe a few hundred years later. The parts of the wood intended to carry the ink are left raised and those intended to appear white are cut away. Before movable type was invented woodblocks were used to print text as well as images.
- Wood engraving is the same idea, but rather than use softwood with parts cut out, here the end of hardwood is cut across the grain to produce a much sharper image that can be used to print many more times. Engraved hardwood blocks were often used along with movable metal type to create the illustrations in early books.
- Copperplate and, later, steel plate techniques of engraving are the opposite of woodcuts. A sharp instrument is used to gouge out part of the plate; the ink collects in this groove and is then transferred to the paper. The printing of a copperplate image was done independently from the text. Hence in early books the illustrated plates were bound into the volume later or sometimes sold alone. Publishers still call pages of pictures in a book "plates" to this day.
- Lithography requires an image to be etched onto a stone or metal surface, which is then used to transfer ink to paper. It started as a

way to make maps and posters and is now the basis for most high-volume printing.

⊓ Photogravure provides a permanent way to print a photograph with a rich range of tones that produces a very high-quality image. The photographic negative is chemically etched into a flat copper plate, which is then covered in ink and pressed against paper. Rotogravure is a similar but lower-quality process using a drum, which used to be used to print the black-and-white pictures in newspapers.

⊓ Digital printing allows images to be created using software and then sent to a laser printer, which reproduces it to a much higher degree of accuracy than most of the analogue techniques. In high-speed, high-volume industrial applications such as newspapers, the physical printing is still done using an offset litho process, but the print plates are made directly from the computer with no intervening stages.

Photography

Photography is the process of capturing an image onto a medium using a chemical reaction. For the first 150 years this medium was light sensitive paper or transparent film. Since the 1990s the image has been more usually recorded in a digital format.

The pioneers of photography could only make images in black and white, as they relied on the chemical properties of silver salts, which went a varying shade of black depending on how much light they had been exposed to. The first really viable color film did not arrive until 1935 with the launch of Kodachrome.

Digital photography was developed in the 1970s with solid state computer chips that turned light directly into digital information. The first commercial digital camera was marketed by Fuji in 1988 and the first Kodak came along in 1991. Digital allows much more flexible handling of the photographic image in terms of storage and transmission. It also enables almost unlimited manipulation of the image, which is fun for photographers but has led to real concerns about the veracity of photographs, as it is almost impossible to tell whether a picture has been doctored.

Computer graphics

Artists have been able to create graphic images by hand for thousands of years, but with the arrival of computers a whole new range of opportunities became available. The computer graphics interface (CGI) started to be investigated in the 1960s. Before then input to a computer was via a keyboard and punch cards and output was words and numbers on a screen or a printout. In 1963 a conference paper described the use of a graphical display monitor using a light pen input device. The same year the computer mouse was invented. Apple used a GUI (graphical user interface) in its Lisa computer in 1983. In the same decade hardware company Silicon Graphics launched its graphical workstation and software firm Adobe started selling its Photoshop image-manipulation program.

The power of graphics as a communication tool was demonstrated by Mosaic, the image-based browser that really launched the web in 1993. Computer graphics now dominate the world of design and even fine art. The technology also allows for a huge range of computer games and animated films.

HALFTONE PRINTING

Early printing was done by placing black ink on white paper to create an image. As letters were a simple line, they reproduced very clearly. Pictures, on the other hand, were printed in a crude way. An artist had available a huge range of shades, but an early printer could only mimic these by using lines on a wood block engraving.

The concept of halftone was first proposed by photography pioneer William Fox Talbot in the 1850s. Through an optical illusion the human eye sees a high density of small black dots as very dark, whereas a lower density of black dots looks light. Based on this, any shade of gray can be created by printing varying amounts of dots.

In 1873 the *New York Daily Graphic* published what it claimed to be the first ever reproduction of a photograph using the process. By the 1890s it had been perfected. This allowed the widespread use of photographs and boosted the sale of popular graphic newspapers.

The technique is extended into color printing by using three colored inks and black. Printers call the three inks cyan, magenta, and yellow. Black is called key, as the other colors are aligned to fit to it. This is why it is common to find the letter CMYK and three colored bars along the edges of many newsprint pages. This is the printers' device to align the color plates.

EVOLUTION OF THE PAINTING

Our ancient ancestors drew what mattered to them: the animals in their world. Cave paintings taught children how to survive and allowed the organization of hunting expeditions. For Egyptians and Romans the day-to-day life of the military and the imperial families provided the practical subject matter for paintings and the imagined lives of the numerous gods formed the spiritual element. Hieroglyphics were pictures that provided a record of historical events and were a way of communicating instructions.

The early Christian Church wanted icons for worship, wall paintings for storytelling, and illustrated manuscripts for study. Medieval bishops knew exactly what they wanted when they commissioned frescoes. Imagery was a central part of the Church's overall communications program. In the centuries before printing, paintings—along with sermons from the pulpit—were the mass media of their day. The scenes of heaven and hell on the walls of churches in northern Italy now look to us to be almost comic or cartoon-like in nature, but at the time they sent a powerful message about social order, acceptable behavior, and the importance of the Church.

The secular authorities also commissioned images to enhance their social position and celebrate their victories. The Bayeux Tapestry, which dates from just before 1100 AD, commemorated the successful Norman invasion of England and was almost certainly commissioned by the brother of the

PERSPECTIVE

In 1415 Italian architect Filippo Brunelleschi demonstrated the mathematics of perspective based on original Roman ideas. Prior to his time the size of subjects in paintings had depicted the relative importance of the people rather than actual spatial relationships. Artists knew that this did not look real, but they did not know how to solve the problem. Brunelleschi showed that lines coming toward the viewer would all converge on the same vanishing point and that simple geometric principles dictated the relative size of people or buildings, depending on where they were in relation to each other. He demonstrated his ideas by exhibiting his painting of the newly built Baptistery of the cathedral in Florence next to the real building. Image and structure looked nearly identical. The artistic community of Florence was enthralled and quickly adopted the technique, which was a major factor in creating the look of Renaissance paintings.

victor William the Conqueror. It is a clear use of art as both propaganda and historical record.

By the time of the Renaissance, a wealthy merchant class had emerged in Italy who wanted enlightenment as well as religious inspiration. Artists had new technologies to play with like oil-based paints and perspective. Religious subjects remained popular, as the Church still had most of the commissioning money, but pictures were becoming part of most people's daily lives. The tools of painting and drawing were used to educate in the new sciences as well as to produce decoration. Early forms of reproduction also meant that images were not just one-offs on a wall but could be copied. As Marshall McLuhan points out in *The Gutenberg Galaxy*, the technique of printing images predated the introduction of movable type. The use of woodblocks enabled "exact repeatability." He observes:

> The printing of pictures (and diagrams) however unlike the printing of words from movable type brought a completely new thing into existence—it made possible pictorial statements that could be exactly repeated... This repetition has had incalculable effects upon knowledge, thought, science and technology.[1]

Leonardo da Vinci was very aware of the importance of drawings in science, which is why for him words alone were not enough. He wrote:

> The more minutely you describe the more you will confine the mind of the reader, and the more you will keep him from the thing described. And so it is necessary to draw and to describe.[2]

Images also started to become important in the homes of the rich. When the merchants acquired wealth they wanted what had been the preserve of royalty: immortality on canvas. The Dutch School of artists such as Rembrandt and Vermeer was commissioned to produce flattering images of their patrons surrounded by their possessions and families.

By the Baroque and Romantic periods, patrons did not only want representations of themselves, they also demanded huge-scale visual entertainment. Grand homes and palaces needed grand pictures, so in the seventeenth and eighteenth centuries art was big business. Painters of that time can be compared to today's rock stars.

The development of lithography in the 1780s allowed images of paintings to be reproduced in good quality. This led to popular works becoming familiar images in many homes. Some painters were thus encouraged to become even more theatrical in both size and subject. The monumental art of French painter David in the 1800s was as vital in building the image of Napoleon and his Empire as television coverage would be today for a president.

By the late 1800s photographs were common and representational paintings lost their magic. One school of Victorian painters responded by trying to tell stories within their picture frame and, in some ways, their popular art occupied what is now the role of television: bringing the world and its events into people's homes.

Other artists explored the fundamental nature of images and light, resulting in the Modern art movement. The Impressionists were interested in optics and the depiction of emotion. Georges Seurat and the pointillists painted in the same way color printing would later work, using a huge number of individual colored dots. Cubists explored the depiction of three dimensions in two.

Some art developed as political commentary. Picasso's *Guernica* was far more than simply decorative; it was one of the most articulate and effective antifascist statements of its time. Picasso himself was in no doubt about his motives:

> In the panel on which I am working, which I shall call *Guernica*, and in all my recent works of art, I clearly express my abhorrence of the military caste which has sunk Spain in an ocean of pain and death.[3]

During the twentieth century films, television, and comic books came to dominate the visual landscape. Artists such as Andy Warhol and Roy Lichtenstein responded with highly commercial but clearly painted images, which became "pop" art. The media of painting and drawing were not replaced by printing, photography, and film; they simply changed to respond to the new competitors.

PHOTOGRAPHY AS ART

In 1935 German philosopher Walter Benjamin wrote what was to become a very influential essay, "The work of art in the age of mechanical reproduction." In this he explains the idea that traditional works of art enjoyed an "aura" derived from their being a unique manmade object with a recorded provenance and timeline. The implication was that with the widespread availability of photography, this aura would not apply to mechanically reproduced images. In practice this has not been the case, as many famous photographs have taken on a strong sense of artifact: "Raising the Flag on Iwo Jima," the Yousuf Karsh portraits of Albert Einstein or Marilyn Monroe, the dramatic image of St Paul's Cathedral as bombs exploded around it. These are iconic photographs and people seek out a signed "original" even though the image itself is available to an almost unlimited degree.

Were a photograph to exist of Lisa del Giocondo, the subject of da Vinci's *Mona Lisa*, it would be a very

CAMERA OBSCURA

Camera obscura is Latin for dark chamber. If light reflected from an object passes through a small hole in a wall, then an image of that object will appear (upside down) on a surface placed at a distance from the hole. This can be seen best if the object is in bright sunlight and the hole is in something like a window shutter. This combination happens naturally in rooms and the phenomenon of the *camera obscura* must have been observed frequently in antiquity, with the earliest reference being from China in 500 AD. The first detailed record of the use and explanation of the technique comes from an Islamic physicist and mathematician called Ibn al-Haytham, working in Egypt in 1020 AD when he described the operation of such a room, used to study the eclipse of the sun. His book, *Kitab al-Manazir* (the Book of Optics), was of great influence in Europe.

The principle of the *camera obscura* was described by Leonardo da Vinci in 1490. In the 1700s artists used portable *camera obscuras* to replicate highly detailed scenes for them to copy and paint over. Canaletto was perhaps the most famous exponent of the technique. These devices evolved into so-called pinhole cameras that captured the image on light-sensitive paper. By the 1800s the use of lenses and mirrors allowed very good images to be created in specially built rooms and it became fashionable to construct them as tourist attractions throughout Europe and America.

different artifact from the painting. We would know that the photograph was an exact moment in time, we would assume that the background was really there, and we would infer the sitter's mood at the moment the shutter clicked. But we would also know that the image we were looking at was probably one of many thousands of copies of the original negative. The painting of the same woman in the Louvre is a "creation." We know that it happened over a period of time; four years in this case. We know that Leonardo's hand held the brushes and we assume that the interaction between subject and artist led him to build an impression of her character that he captured in the enigmatic smile.

Photographic pioneers saw their technology as simply a way of faithfully recording a "real" image. In 1846 Fox Talbot published a book of photographs called *The Pencil of Nature*, commenting that the pictures were "...natural images... impressed by the agency of Light alone, without any aid whatever from the artist's pencil."[4]

However, later commentators recognized the role of the photographer as similar to that of the artist. American author Susan Sontag wrote a set of essays in 1977 called *On Photography*. She observed that the sheer ubiquity of photography was becoming an intrusion into human privacy and pointed out that only if a photographer does not participate in a scene can they be truly said to have recorded an event rather than to have authored one. If the photographer intervenes in any way, then

CHEMICAL PHOTOGRAPHY

During the 1820s and 1830s various techniques were developed to capture an image. All relied on light-sensitive chemicals based on silver. In 1826 French inventor Nicéphore Niépce used silver and chalk on paper. In 1839 Louis Daguerre used silver and iodine on metal. Both recorded a single positive image. By 1841 British scientist William Fox Talbot had a method that captured the image as a negative on a glass plate and from this any number of positive prints could be made. The daguerreotype produced a much sharper picture but was a one-off original. Fox Talbot's calotype was a less good reproduction but it allowed unlimited copies. The daguerreotype dropped out of use by the 1860s and refinements of the Fox Talbot method were made by American George Eastman, who in 1884 replaced photographic plates with a roll of light-sensitive film and in 1888 patented the portable camera under the name Kodak.

the nature of the event is staged and the photograph is a record of the interaction rather than a dispassionate observation. The recent controversies over Robert Capa's war photographs have reignited this debate. *On Photography* raises questions about the degree to which the existence of photography as a process caused society to change and to become more concerned with transitory images than with mundane and permanent reality.

Because photography captures a "real" image we tend to think that a photo has less artifice than a painting or drawing, but in fact the photographer can exercise huge control. The resulting printed picture, whether exhibited in a gallery, a magazine, or a book is just as much "created" as is a painting. Sontag also observed that the still picture could be more powerful than film and television:

> Photographs may be more memorable than moving images, because they are a neat slice of time, not a flow. Television is a stream of unselected images... Each still photograph is a privileged moment, turned into a slim object that one can keep and look at again.[5]

The emotional power of photographs often comes from the knowledge that, even if staged, they represent real things happening to real people. In Phnom Penh, the capital of Cambodia, there is a huge exhibition of black-and-white photographs of victims of the Killing Fields, displayed in the old school where the pictures were taken. They have an extraordinary effect as the faces look out at the camera recording their arrival in the processing prison; we now know that every one of the thousands of subjects was killed.

We now expect most photographs to have experienced some degree of digital enhancement, which means that we trust them far less as a medium of record. According to the *Financial Times* the beginning of the digital age of manipulated images can be dated to 1982, when the highly respected *National Geographic* magazine used a digitally altered photograph of the pyramids on its cover:

> The digital age has transformed and enlivened the medium of photography. But it has also provoked a crisis, bringing into question the medium's relationship to reality and its role as a documentary and artistic tool.[6]

However, in the days of chemical photography many of the most iconic pictures turned out to have been staged in some way. As former newspaper editor Harold Evans points out in *Pictures on a Page* (written in the pre-digital age), a number of people are involved in making decisions about a photograph in a newspaper:

> The camera cannot lie; but it can be an accessory to untruth. The photographer may begin it, selecting the moment and the composition which suits his belief... Next there is the unseen influence of the picture editor. He can select, suppress, distort. He can juxtapose images to provoke derision. He can blow up a single frame in a hundred and crop it to give a tiny detail the greatest significance; the yawn in a crowded political meeting rather than the candidate in the centre of a warming crowd.[7]

The photographer is adding their comment in the same way that a good travel writer provides insight into familiar locations.

MAPS

Maps do not have the obvious editorial or entertainment qualities of newspapers or television and they are not usually included in a list of media. Nevertheless, they certainly are a medium in that they are a device through which information and ideas are communicated from the one to the many and preserved over time. Maps seem, at first sight, to be a simple description of reality, but in practice they often contain elements of invention and concealment.

Maps use two-dimensional symbols to represent features that occur in three dimensions. But exactly what is represented is as much a matter of culture, politics, and the cartographer's objectives as it is of pure geography. The symbol representing a river or a hill normally depicts a physical fact. The geographic feature exists and can be visited. Anybody from any culture—or indeed from another planet—could link these basic symbols to a topographic reality. However, the symbol for a church has a less clear-cut role. Barring accidents the building will exist where the map shows it to be, but the fact that the construction is a church can only emerge from understanding and accepting a social and more specifically religious meaning. To the uninformed observer it is just a big building and many other big buildings will not be marked or described.

Maps also commonly show buildings like post offices and (in the UK) public houses; presumably because these are felt to be useful locations that the map reader may wish to visit, and they are useful in way finding. But these selections reflect a social role more than a physical presence. The map creator is making value judgments about their audience's needs. Very few American maps show bars, for instance.

Crude maps showing relative locations of places go back more than 4,000 years but were little more than basic diagrams. The early Greeks took pleasure in applying the newly developed skills of mathematics to trying to depict their world accurately. Herodotus traveled the Mediterranean and his map of the inhabited world from 450 BC is surprisingly accurate. The height of Greek cartography was reached by Ptolomy around 150 AD, when he produced a map of the known world based on the principle that the globe was spherical and incorporated knowledge of China, India, and Africa. He mapped the course of the Nile in some detail, but was unaware of the existence of America or Australasia.

By contrast, the Romans were much more focused on the location of their roads and forts. They used maps for military control rather than the pursuit of knowledge, being concerned with military efficiency and property rights rather than a holistic explanation of how the world was put together.

The most ambitious attempt at a topographically accurate map is the "Map of Roger," created by an Arabic cartographer called Edrisi for King Roger of Sicily in 1154. This would be the basis of most world maps for many hundreds of years.

The medieval church used the form of a map to try to explain the development of religion and its role in the world. There are some 1,000 *mappa mundi* still in existence, two of the most famous being that in Hereford Cathedral and the similar Ebstorf Map in Germany. Both show a world with Jerusalem at its center and the location of many biblical events. These huge works of art from the thirteenth century described a crude version of Europe, Asia, and Africa, but were explanations of the Christian belief system in diagrammatic form as much as they were geographic maps.

Of all the skills that languished during the dark ages, cartography may have been the most neglected. Map making as a science did not reemerge until the Renaissance, with the most famous exponent being Gerardus Mercator in Holland, who responded to the huge increase in ship-born exploration by coming up with a mapping technique using the so-called Mercator Projection in 1569. This allowed ships' captains to plot straight-line courses between ports, but actually resulted in a distortion in the real size and shape of landmasses when drawn. It is this projection that still dominates the presentation of world maps to this day and gives a false impression of the real, relative size of the continents.

From the seventeenth century the technology of copperplate engraving allowed very accurate maps to be printed in large numbers. They became part of everyday commercial life and also a tool of government. Maps started to show things that did not exist at all on the ground, such as national, state, or country boundaries. Author George Orwell, of *1984* fame, wrote in an essay:

> Maps are tricky things, to be regarded with the same suspicion as photographs and statistics. It is an interesting minor manifestation of nationalism that every nation colours itself red on the map. There is also a tendency to make yourself look bigger than you are which is possible without actual forgery since every projection of the earth as a flat surface distorts some part or other. During the Spanish Civil War, maps were pinned up in the Spanish villages which divided the world into Socialist, Democratic and Fascist states. From these you could learn that India was a democracy, while Madagascar and Indo-China were labelled "Socialist".[8]

THE ATLAS

Atlas was the Titan of Greek mythology who held the world on his shoulders. The map maker Mercator borrowed his name in 1570 and was the first to apply it to a collection of maps in a book. Mercator went on to produce his own world atlas in 1578 by updating the work of Ptolomy and Edrisi, using his own mathematical projections of relative locations. However, it was not a popular success, as the buyers and collectors of maps wanted the fanciful adornment of the medieval *mappa mundi* rather than Mercator's pure science and reason.

The most comprehensive analysis of the role of maps as media is by JB Harley, who says:

Every map is linked to the social order of a particular period and place. Maps do not simply reproduce a topographical reality; they also interpret it... As much as guns and warships, maps have been the weapons of imperialism... Maps were used to legitimise the reality of conquest and empire... They helped create myths which would assist in the maintenance of the territorial status quo.

Harley also has some fascinating observations about what he calls the "silences" in maps, where features like the slums of Victorian London or the American Indian-owned territories of the pre-Civil War US were simply left blank, as the politics of overtly depicting them was not acceptable to the map makers or their patrons.

A vivid example of the points made by Orwell and Harley was the so-called Morgan's Map of London in 1682, which depicted the city after the Great Fire as a well-ordered and beautiful urban paradise. It took six years to make and was hugely detailed and geographically accurate, but simply left out things like prisons and workhouses. It also showed a magnificent rebuilt St Paul's cathedral that in fact was not there.[9]

Because of their political importance, most countries undertake mapping via a government agency. In the UK it is the Ordnance Survey and in America the US Geological Survey that are regarded as the most authoritative sources. With aerial photography and global positioning satellites the physical accuracy of maps is no longer in doubt, but the presentation can still be highly subjective. Perhaps more than any other medium, the information on maps should not be taken at face value.

SATIRE MAPS

By the 1870s the technology of color lithography allowed color maps to be mass produced in huge numbers. This opened up a new, popular market and it was met by combining the skills of the map maker and the political cartoonist. The leading exponent was Fred Rose, who in 1877 created the now famous Octopus map, which showed the nations of Europe as national caricatures. England was John Bull, Germany a Prussian soldier, and France an attractive woman. Russia was a huge, threatening octopus with tentacles strangling other countries. While the map was geographically accurate, its main message was political.

GRAPHICS

The painting is a created image, the photograph captures a moment in time, and the map is a representation of spatial relationships and political information. The graphic is a nonverbal communication of what may be a complex idea. Graphics work because they show the relationship between variables in a simple and immediate way. However, unlike pictures or photographs they may need training and education to understand them, as to some extent reading graphics is like learning a language.

Florence Nightingale—"the lady with the lamp"—is famous as the campaigning nurse who fought for better medical treatment for soldiers during the Crimean War. One of the main devices she used in her campaign was graphics. In 1858 she was elected the first ever female member of the Royal Statistical Society of London. Her main objective was to draw attention to the poor living conditions of the military and she collected data to prove that soldiers suffered higher mortality rates than civilians whether they were in battle or not. She needed to convey this idea in a compelling way and developed a type of graph called a "Nightingale Rose" to explain it. According to *The Economist*:

> Nightingale hoped charts would liven up her publications; the queen [Victoria], she thought, might look at the pictures even if she did not read the words.[10]

A couple of years after Florence Nightingale in 1861, a French engineer called Charles Joseph Minard used what is often cited as one of the best graphics ever. It shows the rate of loss of manpower in Napoleon's army as he advanced toward, then retreated from, Moscow. It displays several variables in a single two-dimensional image: the army's location and direction, showing where units split off and rejoined; the declining size of the army that emphasizes catastrophic moments like the crossing of the Berezina River; and the low temperatures during the retreat. The fame of this graphic is slightly ironic, as it was Napoleon who said, in praise of graphics, "a good sketch is better than a long speech."

In 1953 two researchers, Watson and Crick, cracked the mystery of the structure of the DNA molecule: the building block of life. It was a masterful feat of biology, but in communicating this complex idea to the world they were hugely assisted by a drawing. Crick explained the biochemistry and made a rough sketch of what he thought it might look like; his wife, Odile, who was a professional artist, created a simple but elegant graphic of the concept of the DNA double helix. It was this image, as much as the science, that captured the world's attention and has been described as "possibly the most important scientific drawing of the twentieth century."[11]

The London Underground map is not really a map at all but a schematic representation of the relative positions of the various stations and the intersections of the various lines. It was done to help passengers work out how to use the system rather than accurately to show the locations of stations. Before 1932 the London Underground maps attempted geographic reality, but a railway draftsman called Harry Beck realized that as most of the lines ran underground and could not be seen or accessed from the surface, much of the information was not relevant. The diagram he created, which we still use today, owes more to the conventions of circuit diagrams than to cartography.

The popularity of graphics is clearly demonstrated by the extraordinary rise of software programs such as PowerPoint from Microsoft. Almost no business, government, or academic presentation is now made without the bars and lines of a computer-generated chart.

A SYMBOLIC SOCIETY

We live in an increasingly visual age. Nearly all media contain images; even radio stations regularly direct listeners to look at their website. We find it easy to understand messages that only appear as symbols. Particularly in Western culture, we perceive all media according to the mantra of "show not tell." Television and film depend more and more on visual sequences; modern novels describe images and events by visual analogy. They let the reader draw their own conclusions in contrast to the more wordy descriptions found in Charles Dickens and Anthony Trollope. We think far more visually than the Victorians. The huge rise in popularity of manga comics and Japanese *anime* can partly be linked to the extremely visual nature of the graphic novel.

Digital technology allows everyone to capture and manipulate images. No great craft skill is required to illustrate a message or a document. Artists have pushed the boundaries of depicting form and color purely for their aesthetic responses rather than as attempts at representation. A painting is more true art now than ever before. It really is an attempt to communicate emotions and ideas directly from image to brain.

Devices like the Apple iPhone and iPad make more use of symbols than text to control the device and to communicate. The new developments of surface computing and voice recognition will probably see the end of the keyboard and the mouse as the main ways of interfacing with computers. It would be naive to say that the written word is under threat, but future generations are likely to make far more use of the spoken word and the image.

Iconic images are just as important now as they were in the Renaissance, but in the twenty-first century they are more likely to be commercial logos than religious scenes. And one form of picture is regarded as the purest type of advertising: the poster, which is the subject of the next chapter.

2.4 | Posters

Putting information onto walls has been a communications device since before books were invented. Cave paintings conveyed a message to anyone passing by. Egyptian priests inscribed their temples. There was graffiti in Roman times. Medieval shop signs and early theatre bills shaped the commercial medium of posters, which is now a major advertising business with some $30 billion a year being spent around the world. Like other media, the poster or "out-of-home advertising" is undergoing a technological revolution, but unlike most of the others might be a beneficiary, rather than a victim, of digital technology.

The poster is often described as the purest communications medium. It exists solely to display an advertising message. It has a single, specific purpose. The perfect poster is said to have no more than eight words, use only three main colors, and have only one striking image. It must be possible to read and understand the whole poster in 6 seconds—the time it takes to drive or walk past.

Posters are now familiar as home decoration and particularly as a cheap adornment to students' walls. Often the images displayed started life as commercial or propaganda messages, but increasingly the poster is created as an item of art in its own right. As a commercial tool, out-of-home advertising competes with, and influences, other media types and is both an alternative for and a complement to advertising in broadcast and print.

The medium of posters is where art, design, and commerce most directly collide. Newspapers, cinema, and television would still exist without advertising, as some of us would pay to get them. But without promotional budgets the outdoor medium would disappear entirely as, by definition, its only role is to deliver its message.

Public signage goes back thousands of years and its commercial use has a long, if undistinguished, history. However, as an industry and a medium, the poster only really started in the late 1800s when new technologies in printing, the development of branded goods, and the desire by politicians to clean up the look of cluttered cities combined to create mass communication in public places.

The outdoor advertising industries in Europe and America have developed in very different ways and the root of the variation can be traced back more than 100 years to the decisions of urban planner Baron Haussmann to make Paris beautiful and, later, of car manufacturer Henry Ford to make automobiles for the mass market.

The companies that erect and service outdoor sites often describe themselves not as media owners but as "contractors." Many started out as offshoots of building firms and property developers. The work of physically putting up the posters was often handed to tradespeople like window cleaners and painters, who had the ladders and the head for heights. Their task was akin to hanging wallpaper, albeit on a giant scale. The creative work of producing striking images and compelling text was mostly done in advertising agencies. As digital technology has undermined the economics of most traditional media, outdoor has been the fastest-growing advertising channel after the web itself. The oldest medium has been enjoying a comeback.

MESSAGES ON WALLS

Gnaeus Helvius Sabinus was a candidate for political office in Pompeii in 79 AD. We know, because some of his election notices, written on the walls of the town before it was buried in volcanic ash, have survived.[1] Another rather poignant message of the same period reads: "A copper pot was taken from this shop. Whoever brings it back will receive 65 sesterces."[2] Both were early illustrations of public communication. But even some 1,000 years before a Pompeian shopkeeper was appealing for help retrieving stolen goods, Egyptian officials were carving government messages into obelisks. These notices—official graffiti really—were not posters as we now understand them. They were simply written announcements that happened to be put up in a public place.

The idea of outdoor advertising, the combination of images and a few well-chosen words, started life as signage for medieval shopkeepers. In 1393 King Richard II made it law that innkeepers in London must display a painted sign to identify their establishment to its customers and his officials. As most people were illiterate, it needed to be a picture rather than a name. Inn signs have survived in the UK to this day. One of the most popular, the "White Hart," was Richard's own heraldic symbol.

Hand-drawn and roughly painted shop and inn signs became a feature of the growing cities across Europe. The arrival of movable-type printing in 1450s allowed the publication and distribution of handbills, which were usually passed from person to person but also could be stuck up on walls. As literacy was limited, they remained very basic and mostly told people where to find merchants rather than trying to sell anything in particular.

For businesses to invest in outdoor advertising they needed a commercial incentive, something to sell to a big market. The rise of retailing and branded goods in the 1800s went hand in hand with the development of the commercial poster. Until 1853 advertising in newspapers in the UK was heavily taxed. This made unregulated outdoor displays an attractive low-cost medium and public places became festooned with printed and hand-drawn notices. No end of gimmicks were tried. Engravings from the

1820s show the streets of London full of men and boys carrying signs. These "peripatetic placards," as Dickens called them, dressed in outlandish clothing and often wore very high hats with commercial messages written on them. An example of a street scene from 1820 is quoted by David Bernstein in his book *Advertising Outdoors*:

> Formerly people were content to paste handbills on walls but now they were ambulant. One man had a pasteboard hat, three times as high as other hats, on which is written in great letters "Boots at 12 shillings a pair".[3]

"Placard men" walked the streets and "chalkers" scribbled messages on walls and pavements. The vast majority were promoting events that charged admission, such as exhibitions, zoological gardens, and theatres rather than offering goods for sale. A small number of early brands were developing and one was Warren's Blacking, a patent product to clean shoes. The owner, Robert Warren, experimented with various types of advertising, including boys dressed up as tin cans marching down London's Strand promoting his polish. As a child the author Charles Dickens had worked at Warren's London factory and he remained a keen observer of the commercial scene. He described the placard carriers on London's streets as a piece of human flesh between two slices of pasteboard, leading to the modern term "sandwich board" men.

As advertisers became more aggressive they started to use horse-drawn vehicles to display advertising. A contemporary writer in 1834 described them:

> Chests like Noah's Ark, entirely pasted over with bills, of the dimensions of a small house, drawn by men and horses, slowly parade the streets.[4]

These created congestion and were seen as a hazard to pedestrians. *Punch* magazine commented in 1845:

> Go where you will, you are stopped by a monster cart running over with advertisements, or are nearly knocked down by an advertising house put on wheels.[5]

In the UK these specialist vehicles were finally outlawed by the Hackney Carriage Act of 1853, which also established the rules of the London taxi service and coincided with the repeal of advertising tax on newspapers. However, despite the huge proliferation of outdoor signage it was still not a real medium, nor was it a real business. There was no effective control of where messages were posted and, for the most part, there was no payment to the owner of the wall or field that supported the sign.

By the mid-1800s theatres and music halls normally displayed posters known as "playbills" outside their buildings. Theatre owners, in search of extra income, also sold the space on the stage curtains for advertising, establishing the idea of paying a venue owner to reach his audience and requiring the creation of large-scale artwork featuring commercial messages. Circuses and other traveling shows followed suit and made use of cheaply printed sheets showing their proposed offering. In the rural parts of America these bills were stuck onto large pieces of wood, which were described as "bill-boards" and displayed in towns ahead of the show's arrival.

In 1850 the great circus showman Phineas T Barnum made widespread use of professionally created billboards to advertise the arrival in America of his singing sensation the "Swedish Nightingale," Jenny Lind. Her tour was a smash hit. The advertising used the same images reproduced in various places and it worked. By the 1860s anyone who owned a potentially valuable space started to seek to be paid for the right to exhibit a poster.

FROM SIGNS TO SOPHISTICATION

The combination of a newly wealthy middle class and a fast-growing manufacturing industry with products to sell created a need for the dynamic, public promotion of brands. Black-and-white newspapers could not meet the demand. Advertisers wanted a broader, more creative and colorful canvas. The stage was set for the development of outdoor advertising as an industry and onto it walked a French artist called Jules Chéret. He took the established process of single-color lithography and improved it by using three large stones, one for each primary color. By the 1880s this enabled him to reproduce an extraordinarily rich variety of colors and tones, which were marveled at by the population of Paris. This revolutionary printing

JULES CHÉRET

Jules Chéret was apprenticed to a lithographer and was interested in painting. He studied printing in London and went to art school in Paris. It was the combination of the two skills that led him to adapt the lithographic process to allow color printing and to create posters for musical halls and theatres like the Folies Bergère and the Moulin Rouge. Chéret realized that a poster did not need to be as literal as a notice and could create desire for a product by simply showing an attractive scene. He specialized in flamboyant images of gaily dressed, laughing young women, which were used to sell everything from cigarettes to bicycles, hair tonic to wine. In the 1880s his style dominated the streets of Paris. In 1890 he was awarded the Légion d'honneur for his contribution to commercial art and is widely regarded as "the father of the poster."

process made it worthwhile for great art and investment to go into creating compelling messages in the shape of large urban posters.

This novel advertising medium found an eager audience on the newly constructed streets of Paris, where the City government had commissioned Baron Haussmann to lay out a spectacular network of boulevards and avenues with an emphasis on all things modern, such as street lighting and railway stations. They wanted to create an image of dynamic cosmopolitan creativity, to control unregulated commercial messages, and to seek new sources of revenue for the municipal coffers.

The City of Paris actively encouraged the building of public advertising structures such as the Morris Column to display the new lithographic posters. In addition, by 1881 it created official "posting places" on walls and imposed advertising regulations that led to the standardization of formats and sizes. Authorized, well-presented poster sites at railway stations were encouraged as both decoration and a source of official income. Artists like Henri de Toulouse-Lautrec and Pierre Bonnard were commissioned to provide work that would stand out on the streets, entertain the population, and enhance the image of the advertiser. By 1894 the Parisian poster was sufficiently admired that a major exhibition of French advertising art was staged in London.

In England in 1886 the renowned artist John Everett Millais had painted a portrait of his grandson Willie James blowing bubbles from a clay pipe. In a novel and highly controversial deal, the picture and its copyright were acquired by the Pears Soap Company for £2,200 (a major fortune at the time) and used in one of the earliest poster campaigns. Pears Soap was a bestseller; Willie became a famous face and went on to a glittering career in the Royal Navy. The first "poster boy" suffered no harm from his childhood exploitation, although the artistic community heaped criticism on his grandfather for "selling out" to the commercial world.

In the US there was less concern with art and more with impact and sales effectiveness. And brands were very important in the fast-growing American economy, where the profession of advertising agent was developing. J Walter Thompson opened his advertising agency in 1878. Ivory Soap and Quaker Oats both began advertising in 1879. The Coca-Cola brand appeared in 1886.

In America, the urban center was less important than the newly constructed intercity roads. Early pioneers included the Foster and Kleiser Company, which developed the idea of a standardized billboard size to offer a consistent format for statewide or even national campaigns.

The giant roadside billboards of the American road system were often too big for printed posters and the profession of sign painter flourished,

THE MORRIS COLUMN

In 1855 the City of Berlin decided that it needed to clean up the huge proliferation of illegal signs. A local inventor, Ernst Litfaß, came up with the idea of a purpose-built column to act as an advertising medium to stop the fly posting on walls. The City gave him a monopoly to put up 100 columns. In 1868 the City of Paris went one better and a local printer, Gabriel Morris, designed a poster column specifically for promoting cultural events. Initially used for theatres and books, later for films and magazines, the columns became an integral part of Parisian streets.

In *A la recherche du temps perdu*, Marcel Proust says he rushed out each morning to enjoy the "dreams offered to my imagination... by the colorful posters, still wet with glue." In the film *The Third Man*, the villain, Harry Lime, is seen using one of the Litfaß columns in Vienna to escape into the sewers. This started a myth that the Parisian columns were secret entrances for the Metro. In fact, both types simply contain street-cleaning equipment although in recent years some of the bigger ones have been used to house public toilets.

FOSTER AND KLEISER

Walter Foster and George Kleiser established their outdoor advertising company in Portland Oregon in 1901. They took the lead in creating a professional industry out of what was chaotic and uncontrolled bill posting. They pioneered standard-size structures, which reduced printing costs and provided advertisers with a promise of quality and consistency. They introduced the giant hand-painted billboard and during the First World War their specialized artists were employed to paint camouflage on military structures. In 1917 they established their own gardening department to ensure the ground in front of their boards was properly planted and maintained. In 1932 they were the first to use live models as part of a billboard display in Hollywood and in 1934 they employed full-time painters to continually update Dow Jones stock market news on a board in the financial district of San Francisco.

with many boards being painted in situ to a pre-agreed design. It was not until the 1970s that printing techniques on vinyl started to make the sign painter redundant.

WARS: POSTERS AS PROPAGANDA

The First World War gave a huge boost to the use of posters, as they were seen by all sides as an ideal propaganda tool. Before radio and television and without the need to argue politics with the owners of newspapers, governments were able to communicate directly with their people by placing messages up on the side of buildings, many of which were already government owned. The Great War (1914–18) needed large numbers of men in uniform and that meant mass recruitment. It produced the iconic "Your Country Needs You" image of Lord Kitchener staring directly out of the poster with an accusingly pointed finger. This was blunt, direct, and effective. In the early days of the war much was made of the symbolism of mythical heroes, saints, and religious scenes to get popular support for joining the conflict.

By the armistice in 1918 the poster campaign had become accepted as a highly effective communications tool. Tens of thousands of official poster sites had been established. Thousands of people had learned the skills of mixing images and words. The commercial world noticed and by the 1920s creatively designed, full-color posters on carefully maintained panels—as opposed to the by now illegal flysheets—became an important complement to growing radio and magazine advertising.

Because of the increasing value of the sites, private landlords, farmers, transport companies, and local authorities all wanted to be paid if their space was used for advertising. The modern structure of the industry developed in the 1920s and 1930s, with the poster contractors signing long-term leases for public spaces, commonly 5 to 10 years, and then seeking to rent those spaces out on a short-term basis to advertisers. Many of the sites that now display posters were legally established in this period.

By the Second World War improved education, radio, and cinema newsreels had created a generation that needed more sophisticated handling when it came to calls to fight for one's country. The posters were more subtle, focusing less on naked patriotism and more on encouraging industrial production and emphasizing national security. They also made far more use of cleverly crafted language, with slogans like "Loose lips sink ships," "Careless talk costs lives," and "Dig for Britain."

One unexpected by-product of the Second World War was the amount of air-raid damage and the resulting postwar building boom. In the UK cities were dotted by bomb sites and the authorities started to grant permission to surround them with advertising hoardings to hide the morale-sapping devastation. A beneficiary of this was ex-army officer Rory More O'Ferrall, who founded the poster firm that bore his name. In Paris there was less damage, but the government decided to create a city-wide franchise for putting up hoardings to hide the sites of public works. A grateful nation gave the contract to a hero of the Resistance, Eugène Dauphin, who again founded an eponymous poster firm.

The main by-product of the war in America was the creation of the Interstate Highway system in the 1950s, which drove new roads through farmers' fields and saw those farmers reap a significant income by putting up giant highway billboards.

POSTER BATTLEGROUNDS

By the 1950s magazines were able to offer low-cost, full-color printing. Creative people in advertising agencies started to look on posters as a poor cousin to other commercial media. In the 1950s, the original graphic art of the poster was frequently replaced by photography, so rather than creating anything new and original the poster medium was simply used to reproduce images and messages from other print campaigns. It had lost its creative edge.

In addition, the physical structure of the poster industry was under attack from environmentalists and civic planners, who saw it as visual pollution. Politicians in Europe and America sought to contain the spread of outdoor structures and to remove many of those already in place. As early as 1933 the writer Ogden Nash had been a critic, with his poem "Song for the Open Road":[6]

I think that I shall never see,
a billboard lovely as a tree.
Perhaps, unless the billboards fall,
I'll never see a tree at all.

The war years brought other priorities, but by the 1960s politicians were taking action. In France in 1964 the government started a program to reduce the number of roadside poster sites, which was the catalyst for French entrepreneur Jean-Claude Decaux to come up with his idea of placing advertising on bus shelters.

Taking its lead from France, the US Congress approved the Highway Beautification Act in 1965, which sought to reduce the number of billboards. And in the UK there was a tightening of planning laws to require that all advertising sites obtain official planning

JEAN-CLAUDE DECAUX

In 1964 French entrepreneur Jean-Claude Decaux had a simple but brilliant idea. He made an offer to the city of Lyon that he would supply and clean its bus shelters if it let him put advertising on them. Decaux had worked for a poster company and had seen many conventional billboards torn down as they were deemed to serve no useful public purpose. His vision was that outdoor advertising and civic pride needed to work hand in hand. Lyon agreed and over the next 30 years most cities around the world followed its example. Decaux branched out into other types of so-called street furniture, which provided public amenities. Automatic toilets, street lighting, recycling bins, bicycle racks, and municipal information panels were all funded by advertising. Decaux recruited leading designers and is regarded as having led the renaissance of the modern outdoor industry. His company expanded to become the largest in the world, making him one of the richest business leaders in France and in the 1990s, in a fitting nod to history, he took over the Morris Column business in Paris.

permission. It is somewhat ironic that one of the greatest critics of posters has been one of advertising's greatest practitioners: David Ogilvy. The founder of Ogilvy & Mather liked lists and in his 1983 book *Ogilvy on Advertising* he gave 13 predictions for the future of his industry. Number 4 was "Billboards will be abolished."[7] Despite his disdain for the medium, Ogilvy gave advice for creating great outdoor campaigns, saying that an effective poster needs to be a "visual scandal"—it needs a combination of images and words to capture attention and pique curiosity.

It was during the 1980s that the outdoor industry learned the art of social payback. More and more sites were on land owned by the state, so the income derived went back into government coffers. The costs of running airports, bus networks, tram systems, and railways were all reduced by income from the advertising they displayed.

HIGHWAY BEAUTIFICATION ACT

In 1965 Lady Bird Johnson, the wife of the then President, championed a new law in Congress called the Highway Beautification Act. It was one of the first examples of environmental legislation and was designed to protect American roads from what was seen as the "blight" of billboards. In reality the Act had unintended consequences, as the small print required state authorities to pay compensation to billboard owners if their boards were removed. The Act did reduce the rate at which billboards went up, but it meant that existing sites became more valuable through scarcity. In effect it created a licensed monopoly for existing billboard owners, which is one of the main reasons the American outdoor industry is so hugely profitable today.

Posters are regarded as public property and thus are likely to be criticized by special interest, religious, and other groups. A particular battleground has been the advertising of tobacco.

Increasing health consciousness led to the banning of cigarette advertising on television in the UK in 1965. The US followed suit in 1971, but advertising on posters was allowed to continue. This reflected the belief that television had more impact, but overlooked the fact that everyone, including children, was able to see posters. The main reason, of course, was that government regulated television so imposing a ban was easy. Also, many arms of local government and public transport benefited from the income from tobacco posters and they were reluctant to lose this.

The television ban was a boom period for the outdoor contractors and the tobacco companies became the best customers for posters, with the Marlboro Man becoming an industry icon. Tobacco was banned from billboards in America in 1997, but the poster sites remained and other advertisers were eager to take over such visible and valuable locations.

In the UK cigarette posters were allowed to continue until as recently as 2003, but with numerous rules about what messages could be used. This led to the somewhat surreal and baffling Silk Cut campaign showing massive images of cut purple silk, with nothing more on the poster than the statutory health warning that smoking was bad for you.

In France the outdoor industry enjoyed an artificial boost in the 1970s when the government prevented supermarkets from advertising on television. The motive was to help support local newspapers, but local outdoor advertising was an unexpected beneficiary. The ban ended in 2006 and it was expected that many poster sites would become uneconomic, but, as with tobacco in the US, the locations had been established in the minds of advertisers and were quickly adopted for other messages.

The poster industry did suffer greatly from the growth of television, however. In the US small local businesses, often family owned, started to combine in a wave of mergers, which often resulted in one organization developing a near monopoly of a city. In the UK small local companies tried to develop joint sales techniques. The ten largest grouped to form British Posters, which offered advertisers national campaigns and tried to keep prices high by what amounted to collusion. The UK competition authorities forced the breakup of British Posters in 1981.

AN UNEXPECTED BOOM

Rather to the surprise of advertising professionals, in the 1990s the outdoor industry found a new lease of life. A number of factors contributed. One was that other media, in particular television, had become so numerous and fragmented that outdoor was seen as the best way to reach the whole population at low cost. It earned a new title as "the last broadcast medium." Another was the rise of street furniture, which provided many new, high-quality urban panels. Yet another factor was the humble fluorescent tube.

The use of tubes mounted in special boxes meant that a poster could be backlit rather than illuminated from the front by spotlights. This gave a much sharper image and allowed illuminated panels to be put in places that had previously been impossible, where either planning permission for lamps was refused or it was physically difficult to site them. In particular, back illumination revolutionized bus shelters and made them a far more valuable advertising vehicle. The price of a shelter panel as an advertising site more than trebled once backlighting was installed. Posters that had been essentially wasted for much of the time could now be clearly seen in the dark winter months and during the night.

Print technology had also greatly advanced. The so-called "6 sheet" posters that were used in shelters and similar structures could be now printed in one go on large flat-bed machines. This made them cheaper and much easier to hang. With these advances municipal authorities quickly worked out the value of the franchises they controlled. They demanded, and obtained, huge guaranteed payments from the operators who wanted to run the advertising on their streets, stations, and airports.

Other innovations helped to make posters a more flexible and valuable medium. Audience measurement, which had been primitive compared to broadcast media, was greatly improved. Those sites that were shown to have a large audience and those where people had to linger, such as near traffic lights and railway stations, started to be fitted with scrolling devices so that one panel could show up to five different images, each for short periods.

Another printing innovation, which proved particularly valuable in America, was the use of vinyl. This meant that huge images could be printed

MEASURED IN SHEETS

The professional language of the poster industry in the UK describes the various formats in term of their size in "sheets." The terminology started in the 1920s. A single sheet was 30 inches by 20 inches, which was the largest size that could be printed by the machines of the time. This size was used on the back of buses and in shop windows. The "4 sheet" (simply a single image split into four sections) was used on early bus shelters. Typical city street posters are now called "6 sheets," even though modern machines allow printing in a single action. The "48 sheet" is the familiar size on the edge of towns and the "96 sheet" is the largest size and analogous to the smaller-format US billboards.

AUDIENCE MEASUREMENT

The value of a poster is a direct function of the number of people who see it. During the 1990s the outdoor industry greatly improved its audience research. Sites were graded not just in terms of the number of cars or people who passed by them but also how visible they were, the angle to the road, whether they were obscured by trees, and the demographics of the people passing by. Sites close to a shopping center tended to deliver a very different audience than those by a sports stadium or located in a city's financial district. Packages of poster sites were developed that could deliver a certain defined audience, which made the medium far more attractive to media buyers used to having the wealth of audience data provided by newspapers and television.

in one go and stretched across massive billboards that previously had to be painted by hand. Vinyl "skins" could also be moved from site to site, which developed the idea of "rotation," moving a particular message around a city over a period of months to extend its advertising reach. Vinyl also allowed the creation of giant banners, which started to be used in major building projects to conceal scaffolding and hide construction activities.

A new level of professionalism and accountability was introduced. Even on small conventional sites, both posters and frames were barcoded so that an advertiser could be told exactly where and when the message had been displayed. Prior to this there was always the suspicion that advertisers did not get exactly what they paid for and, short of visiting every site themselves, they could not easily check things out.

The big outdoor franchises became major business investments. The contracts for all the bus shelters in London, New York, or Paris were worth billions of dollars in sales over their 15-year life. Bidding for these franchises required huge technical resources and very significant investment. Only the major international players could afford to be in the game.

All these changes started to make the outdoor industry one that needed international expertise and lots of capital resources. The typical small, local operations that had characterized the poster business could not compete in this environment. An aggressive period of consolidation resulted in most countries ending up with only two or three big outdoor operators. Across the world the outdoor advertising industry became dominated by three companies: CBS, Clear Channel, and JC Decaux.

The 1990s were in some ways a second golden age for the outdoor industry. Spending on posters grew rapidly; in some markets it more than doubled over the decade. Far from being a victim of the dot-com boom, around the year 2000 the most basic medium of outdoor was a major beneficiary. The new internet companies, awash with cash from venture capitalists and IPOs, wanted to make their brands famous. Often they had only a very limited commercial story to tell, so the objective was to see their name up by the side of the road. Outdoor advertising was the obvious solution and billboards along Highway 101 to Silicon Valley became prime real estate. They were seen as the Super Bowl slots of the poster world and sold at huge prices.

A problem for the outdoor operators is they became victims of their own success. Encouraged by the boom, the big companies bid higher and higher amounts for the key franchises around the world and signed contracts with rich promises of revenue guarantees. As advertising prices in print and broadcast came down in the face of web alternatives, outdoor also experienced a slump, although its costs remained high from the contested auctions for prime sites.

DIGITAL DISPLAY

For some years no conference on the future of outdoor advertising has been complete without a clip of the shopping mall scene from the Stephen Spielberg film *Minority Report*. This showed Tom Cruise surrounded by digital billboards and holographic projections that recognized his presence and tried to advertise to him individually. It was science fiction, but it showed what the medium of posters could easily become: screen based and personalized.

Illuminated advertising signs are not new. Again, it was the French who led the way with electric displays using neon gas. Since their first commercial exploitation in 1923 they have spread across the world. Large-format illuminated boards using LEDs (light-emitting diodes) started to be widely installed in the 1980s. Now other screen technologies, such as back projection, plasma, and LCDs (liquid crystal displays), are also in use. Travelers on the London Underground experience coordinated video messages that follow them as they go up and down on the escalators. In New York full-motion video is available at many subway entrances.

Until recently only the most high-profile and high-value sites could justify the investment in digital displays, but costs have come down so digital screens are a viable option in a large number of locations. This has the potential to transform the medium. The days of the man with a ladder and a bucket of paste are numbered. The digital image can be created centrally and sent to the site by cable or satellite link. The same site can be used to display a series of images one after another and these can be changed to run different campaigns at different times of day. The same location on a busy commuter road might show advertising for coffee in the morning and beer at night, with a retailer using it in the middle of the day. Bluetooth technology is able to identify cellphones in the vicinity, measuring the audience and delivering personalized electronic coupons to the phone's owner.

The result will be that sites in the best locations will become especially valuable and the cost of operating them will actually drop once the initial investment in the digital display has been paid back. There is a certain irony in the fact that the oldest medium may be the one to benefit most from the digital revolution.

2.5 | Postal Systems

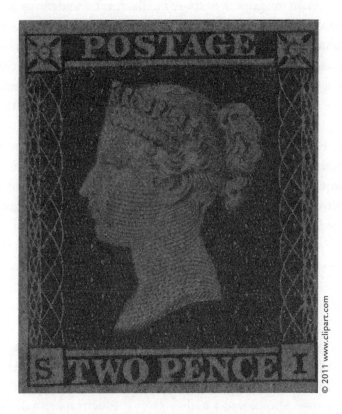

For thousands of years the letter—the written or printed word carried from one person to another—was the favored way to send a message. It is the postal system that makes the letter (and its reply) an important communications medium and has been the blueprint for the architecture and operation of many other media forms. The structure and economics of the telegraph, the telephone, radio, television, and the internet all have their origins in the way the post was organized. The debates in the twenty-first century about building the information superhighway and the desirability of making high-speed broadband available to all are simply reruns of nineteenth-century postal issues.

What makes the post, or the mail, such a key part of the development of media is the system it created for moving information around. It was the first example of powerful network effects in communication and first raised the issue of the social benefits of making access to information universal and how to charge for that. Decisions to use the postal system to subsidize the distribution of books, magazines, and newspapers had profound effects on the growth of those media. It is no understatement to say that postal systems nurtured the concept of nationhood. Indeed, in postrevolutionary America, creating the national postal system was a conscious policy to reinforce the newly minted idea of the United States.

The postal system is simply a way of getting a document into the hands of a named person at a distant location. However, more than that it creates a medium to allow the transmission—in a sense, the broadcast—of news and information. In each country as it developed, the post office became the way the nation was brought together in media terms. Early newspapers and magazines with small circulations depended on the post to reach far-flung readers and to get stories from their correspondents. Many carry an echo of this in their name, hence *The Newsletter*, *The Post*, and *The Mail*.

Electronic media distribution and the development of email are now radically changing the traditional role of the mail service. As the importance of the letter as a communications tool decreases, the system is being reinvented as a distribution mechanism for online shopping.

In the UK and US we are used to the idea that the postal

SHERLOCK HOLMES

One of the endearing features of Sir Arthur Conan Doyle's Sherlock Holmes stories is the frequency of arrival of mail to 221B Baker Street. There were multiple deliveries each day, up to 12 in certain parts of London in 1880. And the speed and ease with which Holmes and Watson could send letters were amazing—posted in the morning, the letter was with the recipient by the afternoon, the reply back by evening. The postal system also played a major role in Holmes' detective work. In 13 of his 60 reported cases, his knowledge of postal franking techniques plays a part in the solution.[1] The great detective was, by the standards of the day, never out of touch. Mail to the Victorians was a modern and exciting mass medium. Conan Doyle must have felt about the post much the way we do about the iPhone and the BlackBerry.

service charges us a fixed sum in advance (an adhesive stamp), that we can put our letter into any mailbox and the system will deliver it to any address in the country within a day or two. This straightforward idea is supported by extremely complex logistics systems and for much of its history the post did not work this way at all.

COURIER SERVICES

The earliest-known letters were found in Egyptian tombs from 4,500 years ago. They were addressed to recently deceased relatives and requested practical help with everyday problems such as property disputes. They were written on pottery bowls or papyrus. Obviously no postal system was required, as they were simply placed in the tomb. In Roman and medieval times there are huge numbers of documents written from one person to another. They are "letters" in that they conduct a one-sided conversation from the sender to the recipient, although they were not conveyed though a postal system, they were simply delivered person to person.

The Chinese and the Persians had well-organized message-delivery systems operating more than 2,000 years ago. The Romans built on these ideas to create the *cursus publicus*, which roughly translates as "public courier." It was developed by the Emperor Augustus and provided a military messenger service to help him communicate with distant governors and control the fast-growing empire. At intervals along the emerging Roman road system they located camps where fresh horses were kept, so that an imperial messenger could ride from place to place, pick up a new animal or hand his messages on to another rider. Historians estimate that the couriers could cover 150 miles in a day and a night. Their function was mostly to provide a flow of military information, but, for a price, wealthy citizens could also send documents to follow up on business and family issues. When the Roman Empire collapsed and the roads became disused, the courier service could no longer function.

POST HASTE

In the dark ages when Europe developed its small city states out of a landscape of warring tribes, there was little need for long-distance messenger services. Armies carried their information with them and people could

THURN UND TAXIS

The Taxis were an ancient, aristocratic European family who founded a courier service in Italy based on the Roman model. In 1490 they were granted a communications monopoly by the Habsburg Empire. By the 1500s they operated a European-wide courier network based in Brussels. By 1659 their services had been adopted by the Holy Roman Empire, which made the family "Princes of the Empire," and they changed their name to Thurn und Taxis. At their zenith they employed 20,000 couriers, had staging posts on all major roads, and operated specially designed Taxis post coaches, which have given their name to the modern taxi cabs.[2]

Over time the Taxis family business developed to become the main continental European postal network and in 1852 they issued their own stamps, using the symbol of a coiled post horn. Their operations were absorbed into the German state post office, Deutsche Post, in the late 1800s; the post horn is still part of the logo.

walk across a small town. But by the 1300s trade was beginning and required information to flow between cities. The word "post" derives from the staging posts set up along main roads to allow couriers to change horses, in the same way the Romans did. Moving mail quickly along these roads was called "post haste." The word "mail" comes from the Old French *male*, meaning bag, which over time became the term for a bag of letters carried by the courier and, more recently, for the letters themselves. The two terms "mail" and "post" have become intermixed. In the UK the Royal Mail delivers the post and in the US the Postal Service delivers the mail.

As trade grew, each of the great continental European Empires—the Spanish, the French, and particularly the Austro-Hungarians—set up their own elaborate courier systems of post roads and staging posts.

THE ROYAL MAIL

In England from early medieval times the kings had well-organized messenger routes to serve their needs, but there was no attempt to create any accessible public services. The last thing the ruling class wanted was the people communicating with each other; in any case most of the people could neither read nor write. In 1516 Henry VIII established the position of Master of the Posts to manage the process of messengers and staging posts. In 1635 Charles I made the, previously exclusive, Royal Mail courier service available to the public of Britain, at a cost, with the recipient of a package having to pay a substantial fee. In 1660 Charles II went further and created the General Post Office. This allowed a limited distribution of documents on a variety of established mail routes, but it was really nothing more than a messenger hand delivering a packet person to person. There was no concept of a central sorting office and the vast bulk of traffic remained for the government.

In 1680 a London merchant called William Dockwra started a private mail service offering local collection and delivery within the city for a penny a packet using a central sorting office. Letters were prepaid and deliveries were as frequent as one an hour. Dockwra was so successful that he was prosecuted for breaching a state monopoly and his service closed down in 1682.

For the next 200 years the British mail system continued to grow but remained a specialized service for the wealthy and the well connected. Mail coaches were introduced in the 1780s and started to make regular runs throughout Britain. The first mail-carrying train was introduced in 1830. However, while the development of paved roads, railways, and regular steamship routes was making transport of mail much quicker, the mail system remained stubbornly old-fashioned and inaccessible. The cost of sending a package was paid by the recipient and the price was hugely complex, based on weight, size, and distance. Many recipients refused to pay, which meant lost revenue and packages having to be returned. The Post Office employed a huge number of clerks just to work out the appropriate charges.

THE STAMP THAT CHANGED THE WORLD

When Victoria became Queen of England in 1837 there was a desire to modernize everything and make society more democratic. The Victorians were obsessed by improving the population and increasing literacy. They wanted to find a way to get Britain communicating. In political terms it was the Victorian version of "broadband for all," the equivalent of encouraging investment in a national fiberoptic cable network. The solution to the cost and inefficiency of the Royal Mail was a masterstroke of political and social engineering: the Uniform Penny Post. The idea was dreamt up by a teacher called Rowland Hill who inspired an Act of Parliament to reform postal charges and then oversaw the development of the adhesive

THE PILLAR BOX

In 1852 novelist Anthony Trollope was sent to the Channel Islands by Sir Rowland Hill. His task was to find a convenient way for the islands to organize their mail. Up to that point mail had to be taken to the local post office, but Trollope came up with the idea of a free-standing cylindrical box with a slot in it for posting letters into.

The first pillar box was installed on the island of Jersey in 1852; the first in London came in 1855. Until 1874 there was no standard color, but then "pillar-box red" was introduced to provide maximum visibility. The red pillar box became such a symbol of the British Post Office—there are now more than 100,000 of them—that when the Republic of Ireland was created in the 1920s, it repainted all of its boxes green to show independence from the UK.

stamp. The now famous "Penny Black" was introduced in May 1840. Pillar boxes to collect mail appeared in London in 1855.

The core and revolutionary idea was that the charge for a letter would be the same no matter how great the distance of its journey. This was based on Hill's detailed analysis that most of the cost of the Royal Mail was not in the transport but in the handling, charging, and accounting systems. He calculated, correctly, that a low price and a simple process would so greatly increase volume that the low price would be more than compensated for by increased usage. In the 1830s the Royal Mail carried about 70 million items a year. By 1840 in the first year of the Penny Black that figure had more than doubled to some 170 million. By 1870 it was 900 million and by 1901, when Victoria died, more than 2.5 billion items were carried annually.[3] As the UK was the first nation to create stamps, no one thought to put the country's name on them; it isn't there to this day. Hill's ideas were copied by postal services across the world and the economic concepts of creating a network based on a single price are the underpinnings of broadcasting, telephony, and the internet.

THE US EXPERIENCE

In America the equivalent of the Royal Mail started in 1692. Under British rule postal monopolies were set up in various independent colonies. Each was very much a law unto itself. In 1737, for example, Benjamin Franklin was appointed postmaster of Philadelphia – something he found very convenient as it helped him to distribute, on heavily subsidized terms, the newspapers he printed and published. Franklin went on to become joint postmaster for all the colonies collectively and started a system of setting up post roads to connect the major cities, from Maine in the north to Florida in the south. This network played a vital part in creating a sense of shared purpose and common identity between the individual colonies and went a long way toward promoting the idea of an independent "United States."

In the run-up to the American Revolution, the British dismissed Franklin from his post for his pro-independence stance. However, at the Second Continental Congress in 1775, he was appointed first Postmaster General of the newly constituted United States of America. It was Franklin who put in place most of the policies and structures that created the modern postal organization. By 1792 Article One of the new US Constitution gave the Post Office the power to establish local offices and post roads in all states and the role of Postmaster General was considered such an important position it was designated one of the officials in direct line of succession to the Presidency.

THE PONY EXPRESS

The Pony Express was a key link in moving mail across America from the east to the west coast. It looms large in the mythology of mail, but actually only operated for 18 months, from April 1860 to October 1861—less time than the run of the subsequent television series of the same name that made it famous.

The Pony Express route ran some 2,000 miles from Missouri to California and was supported by nearly 200 stations about 10 miles apart. The first mail pouch left Washington, DC on April 3, 1860 and arrived in San Francisco on April 14. The riders were selected for their weight—less than 125 lb—and each carried 40 lb of mail and equipment. The close proximity of the relay stations allowed each horse to cover most of the 10 miles at a gallop. In March 1861 a combination of Pony Express and the fast-growing telegraph network got the text of President Lincoln's inaugural address from Washington to San Francisco in 7 days and 17 hours.

However, by October 1861 telegraph lines had been built all the way from east to west with no gaps and the Pony Express closed down two days later. It was short lived but played a vital role in making California feel part of the Union. Its operations, its name, and its logo were sold to Wells Fargo.

Unfortunately, the US Post Office quickly became a source of political patronage. Party cronies were given senior jobs and the organization was prone to inefficiency and corruption. For much of the nineteenth century it was a big money loser, but it was supported by the Federal Government as it was felt to be a key part of nation building. A conscious decision was made to offer cheap carriage to newspapers in order to promote democracy. The newspaper subsidy led to distortions in the way other media were sold.

In his book *Democracy in America* (published in 1835), Alexis de Tocqueville marvels at the way even the rural farmer was able to receive his daily newspaper and thus be fully informed about political events. As the railways spread so did the Post Office. The first adhesive stamp was introduced in 1847 bearing the image, appropriately enough, of Benjamin Franklin. The US introduced a uniform rate in 1863, which, as in the UK, led to a huge increase in use of the mail.

THE NATURE OF THE LETTER

The act of writing something down preserves a message over time. The very earliest documents were created to record ownership and to educate an upcoming generation. The crucial importance of the postal system is that it allowed writing to communicate over distance. Initially this was to meet the needs of military commanders to issue orders, then of merchants to conduct trade, and then, much later, for ordinary people to build and maintain relationships. It was this ability to let people communicate directly with each other that worried governments and led many of them to be very slow to open up mail services to everyone.

The Universal Penny Post was far more important than merely instituting a change in pricing policy. It made letter writing accessible to the middle classes and the ordinary working man. It led to a huge increase in literacy and in curiosity about the wider world. Letter writers became aware that their correspondence might come to have historical value. Authors, particularly politicians, kept copies of their letters and it became highly fashionable to reprint, in book form, all the communications of a high-profile individual toward the end of their career. It is hard to imagine that a lifetime of emails would have the same interest or romance.

POSTCARDS

The postcard as a vacation souvenir or a thankyou note may now seem prosaic, familiar, and old-fashioned. But its story is a perfect demonstration of how a new communications craze was created by public demand and satisfied by entrepreneurial zeal.

Before the picture postcard was invented there was no mechanism for sending a short, informal message telling the recipient the location and activities of the sender. Twenty-first-century users of Twitter will instantly recognize the attraction the postcard held to its Edwardian fans. Having incurred the fixed cost of establishing postal services, the authorities were keen to find any way to put more volume through their organizations, and for post offices around the world the postcard was a valuable extra source of revenue. It is exactly the same economic argument as an airline or hotel wanting to sell all available seats or rooms, or cellphone operators offering text messaging, and has been used to promote Christmas cards, birthday cards, and more artificial card-sending occasions like Mother's Day.

In 1861 an American inventor in Philadelphia patented the concept of a prestamped, prepaid postal card, which he sold to a Mr. Lipman who marketed them as "Lipman's Postal Card: Patent Applied For." This continued for 10 years before the service was taken over by the US Post Office. The cards were a cheap way to send a short message but had no pictures on them. The first experiments with commercial picture cards—which had to have an official post office stamp attached to them separately—occurred in Austria in 1869. The French followed with photographs of the Eiffel Tower, then the Germans and Swiss with mountain scenery. The first in America came in 1893 with pictures advertising the Chicago World Fair.

To start with, one side of the card was both picture and blank space, the other kept clear for the address. The purchaser scribbled a short note next to the picture. An account of postcards comes from a contemporary journalist, George Robert Sims, who visited a Swiss mountain in 1900:

> directly we arrived at the summit, everybody made a rush for the hotel and fought for the postcards. Five minutes afterwards, everybody was writing for dear life. I believe that the entire party had come up, not for the sake of the experience or scenery, but to write postcards and to write them on the summit![4]

SEASIDE POSTCARDS

An eccentric offshoot of the picture postcard was the peculiarly British phenomenon of the saucy seaside postcard, many of which were drawn by graphic artist Donald McGill. By the 1930s the British working classes had discovered the joys of train and coach travel and of the beaches of the newly developed seaside resorts. This group's tastes in humor were catered for by cartoon cards with captions full of sexual innuendos and double entendres, and cartoons of stock funny characters like the young wife and the naive vicar (which, with their echoes of the *commedia dell'arte* approach, are close cousins of the Benny Hill school of comedy). In 1954, the then-80-year-old McGill was convicted and fined under the Obscene Publications Act following complaints from humorless local government officials. This, almost inevitably, resulted in his cards becoming collectors' items.

In 1902 the British Post office allowed both the address and a message to be written on one side of the card. This was the "divided-back" card, which left the whole of the front free for a picture and greatly accelerated the popularity of the format. The Americans allowed the same in 1907 and what deltiologists (postcard collectors) call the golden age of postcards began.

From then on many millions of cards were sent each year. The UK Post Office estimates that 6 billion were sent between 1901 and 1910, about 200 per person.[5] The public warmed to this new, low-cost communications opportunity. It was tangible and physical. It proved they had traveled and it was like sending a piece of the location back to friends and family. It was far cheaper and more fun than a telegram and the restricted amount of space meant that little literary effort was required; unlike a letter, which could be a challenge.

George Eastman's Kodak Company got in on the act by allowing people to create postcards from their own snapshots and in 1939 introduced the Kodachrome card, a full-color photograph with a gloss finish. This became the leading postcard technology after the Second World War.

PIGEON POST

Mail has been moved by car, train, boat, airplane, and rocket, but one of the most enduring mail carriers has been the homing pigeon. Rock pigeons have an innate ability to find their way back to their nests. They can fly at

30 miles per hour and navigate journeys of 100 miles or more. This ability made them a natural message carrier. Egyptian sea captains used pigeons to announce their arrival in port 3,000 years ago. The Greeks had a pigeon system to communicate the names of Olympic winners and Julius Caesar used them in his conquest of Gaul. In the 1700s and 1800s stockbrokers and merchants made extensive use of pigeons to share trading information, although they were not a postal service, simply a point-to-point courier.

Matters got much more organized in 1840 when Charles-Louis Havas (who founded the eponymous news agency) organized a regular Paris to London pigeon service. A few years later Paul Reuter used pigeons to cover a gap in the German telegraph network.

Perhaps the most famous and well-documented pigeon post was in 1870, during the siege of Paris in the Franco-Prussian war. The Prussian armies encircled the city and cut the telegraph lines. To get mail out the French postal service used balloons filled with coal gas; to get it back it used pigeons. According to the University of Houston:

> In all, 66 balloons left Paris carrying information to France beyond the German lines. Most flights were made at night. In all, the balloons delivered 102 passengers and 11 tons of mail. The mail amounted to 2½ million letters. The balloons also delivered 400 carrier pigeons for return mail.[6]

The pigeons were Paris-based racers. Some were carried out before the siege and taken as far as 150 miles away to Tours. Messages, both official documents and private letters, were copied by a photographic microfilm process onto lightweight paper and attached to the pigeon, which then flew the route back to Paris and its loft. Some 95,000 messages were sent this way. The service created huge interest in the UK, *The Times* of London reporting on November 19, 1870:

> The pigeon post is gone off, with sheets of photographed messages reduced to an invisible size, and which in Paris are magnified, written out, and transmitted to their addresses. They are limited to private affairs, politics and news of military operations being strictly excluded. But the Prussians, it is said, with their usual diabolical cunning and ingenuity, have set hawks and falcons flying round Paris to

ZIP and POST CODES

ZIP stands for "Zone Improvement Plan." It was adopted by the US Post Office in 1963 to encourage people to identify the recipients of letters with a simple numeric code rather than a complex address. The ZIP is five numbers that uniquely describe a location; for example, 10001 is New York City. As technology advanced the ZIP could be printed as a barcode, allowing it to be scanned by an optical reader.

In the UK the postcode dates back to Sir Rowland Hill, who broke London into 10 districts that were then subdivided into areas like SW19 (Wimbledon) and W8 (Kensington). In the 1960s a system of six letters and numbers was devised for the same reason as in the US, to allow the introduction of optical readers that could sort mail more rapidly.

Both ZIP and postcodes are extensively used by the marketing industry, not for sending letters but for segmenting the income and buying habits of consumers.

strike down the feathered messengers that bear under their wings healing words for anxious souls.[7]

THE FUTURE OF HOME DELIVERY

The mail network was of huge importance to social development. In 1860 American writer Edward Everett commented:

I am compelled to regard the Post Office, next to Christianity, as the right arm of modern civilization.[8]

The original role of the postal service, to move letters, was largely overtaken by the telegraph, the telephone, and, most recently, email. Almost any form of message or document is now sent more quickly and more cheaply in electronic form.

However, while the internet takes away it also gives. The huge growth in home shopping needs a means of getting goods to purchasers. Mail services are increasingly reverting to the role of the original couriers, but with goods rather than information—moving packages from one place to another, with the recipient paying the bill based on weight and size rather than a basic fixed price. The post may be losing its media role, but its contribution to media history has been immense.

2.6 | Newspapers

It is the newspaper, more than any other medium, that conjures up images of political power, journalistic scoops, and ruthless media barons. Newspapers have made and broken politicians, changed society, and amassed great wealth and influence for their owners. It is appropriate to start this chapter with quotes, as they are the stock in trade of reporting journalists—a profession invented in the 1700s to serve the emerging news-paper industry.

"Newspapers are the fourth estate."
Edmund Burke (1729–97)

"Four hostile newspapers are more to be
feared than a thousand bayonets."
Napoleon Bonaparte (1769–1821)

"Never pick fights with people who buy
their ink by the barrel."
Mark Twain (1835–1910)

Edmund Burke was a prominent British statesman at a time when the three great political "estates" that controlled the country were the Church, the nobility, and the House of Commons. During a Parliamentary debate Burke allegedly looked up at the newly created reporters' gallery and observed: "Yonder sits the Fourth estate—and the most important of them all." Napoleon recognized the need to keep public opinion on his side, despite having used military might to become the emperor of most of Europe. And Mark Twain was acknowledging the raw political and economic power exercised by the ruthless US newspaper barons at the height of the "yellow journalism" wars.

Newspapers have historically been the most partisan of the media and have frequently been owned by people who wanted to get their own political views across. As nations moved from being monarchies to aristocracies and then to open democracies, the newspapers played a crucial role in supporting or rejecting elected politicians. As the first mass medium with huge influence, they became the early battleground for issues of moral and political censorship and faced the challenge of balancing editorial independence with commercial considerations.

A WINDOW ON THE WORLD

In ancient Rome, *acta diurna* (daily events) were handwritten lists posted in prominent places. These contained information of public interest such as battles, scandals, executions, and political happenings. The Chinese had a similar system called *tipao*, which by about 600 AD were being copied onto primitive paper from ink-covered wooden blocks, making them the first printed news medium. All societies from then onward have produced some form of publication to tell citizens what is going on. In their early days these were nearly always government controlled, their circulation was limited, and their political and commercial impact modest. The bulk of the population did not have a use for news sheets as they could not read, so for them the main source of information was the village gossip, the traveling entertainer, or the town crier.

Things did not change that much after Gutenberg started using his printing press in the mid-1400s. While the technology existed, the demand was limited. Some would-be publishers did produce single-page pamphlets and eyewitness accounts of great battles. These were popular with the educated few and were also read out loud at public meetings. However, they were one-off reports, not regular newspapers. The pamphlets expanded into publications of several sheets, although these were normally created anonymously and distributed clandestinely to avoid retaliation against anyone distributing information the government did not like. Private newsletters were in use in the late 1500s by members of aristocratic families, but these were more an extended form of mail rather than a true publication. In the end it was the demands of commerce that led to the newspaper we now recognize.

ALMANACS

The format of the newspaper emerged long before the medium itself in the guise of the almanac. These documents, really pamphlets, started long before printing was invented as collections of calendars showing days of the week with astrological tables and star charts. They were used to help plan agricultural planting and more broadly to manage a household, by recording useful information such as the medicinal properties of plants. They also started to be used to make predictions about the future and are sometimes called prognostications. Handwritten almanacs are described by Bacon in the 1200s and Chaucer in the 1300s.

One of the earliest applications of printing was to make the almanac format available to a much wider public; Gutenberg himself produced one soon after publishing his famous bible. As early as 1500 the *Kalender of*

OLD MOORE'S ALMANACK

Dr. Francis Moore was a court physician to Charles II who some time around 1700 produced a pamphlet of herbal remedies, with advice on the best time of day and year to take them based on astrological tables. He called his publication *Vox Stellarum*, the voice of the stars. He also made weather forecasts and other predictions. After his death in 1715 the copyright of his work, by then known as *Old Moore's Almanack*, was taken over by the Stationers' Company. It became a regular and highly popular combination of household and gardening information spiced with predictions. At the height of its fame in the late 1700s it was selling more than 400,000 copies a year. It continues in publication to this day.

Shepherdes was being printed in Paris with woodcut illustrations. Printed almanacs proved to have huge popular appeal. Most publishers produced several different titles to make full use of their machines and staff. Benjamin Franklin published one in America called *Poor Richard's Almanack*.

In pursuit of their household management role, some publishers included pages printed with the days of the week but containing blank pages for handwritten notes and observations, the start of the personal diary. By the 1600s some almanacs contained advertising, mainly for patent medicines and medical devices such as spectacles.

As newspapers and magazines developed, the almanacs become less relevant and many of their features such as predictions were taken over by other publications in the form of horoscopes.

THE REGULAR PRINTED PAGE

The idea of regular news publications started in the independent city states of northern Italy. The *gazeta* was a small gold coin used in the Republic of Venice and in the late 1500s it was the price of a weekly news sheet produced by the Republic itself to inform its citizens of events in other cities and countries that might be relevant to their trading activities. A *gazeta* was also the admission price to a meeting where the contents of the sheet were read out for the benefit of the illiterate. The name later became used for newspapers around the world.

There is endless debate about what constitutes the first real newspaper in modern form. The argument is impossible to resolve, as it is a matter of definition. Regular publications started to appear in Europe just after 1600. A *Zeitung* (the German word for news sheet) was published in what is now the Netherlands in 1609. Copies survive of a 1610 news sheet from Basle, Switzerland. A number of Dutch printers produced fairly regular *corantos* (meaning currents or flows) with international news useful to shipping companies. The first continually published English-language periodical in London was the *Weekly Newes*; or, to give it its full and rather cumbersome title, *Corante, or weekely newes from Italy, Germany, Hungary, Poland, Bohemia, France and the Low Countreys*. This started in 1622 and was careful to report on mainly foreign events, carrying very limited English news or politics. To do otherwise would have incurred the displeasure of the government, which insisted that printers did not comment on affairs of state.

These early publications were simply collections of individual reports, with no attempt at creating a logical editorial style or approach. They were opportunistic money makers for printers when they were not publishing much more profitable books.

In the run-up to the English Civil War in 1642, there was a breakdown in the authority of Charles I. This led to a great relaxation of censorship and many pamphlets appeared serving up controversial domestic news and political gossip. They also promoted rising political activism and became the voice of organizations like the Diggers, the Levellers, and the Ranters. They started to look like newspapers, featuring headlines to make stories feel more important and woodcut illustrations. Nevertheless, this early flowering of proto-journalism was quickly stamped out by Oliver Cromwell after his Roundheads seized power and imposed their strict Puritan regime, which believed that having no published news made public control much easier.

The first real newspaper in England came after Cromwell had been deposed, when the restored Charles II and his court fled to Oxford in the autumn of 1665 to escape the plague in London. Wanting something to read and fearing that the somewhat unreliable news sheets coming up from London might be infected with germs, the court authorized the university, which had the technology and skills, to publish the *Oxford Gazette*. Borrowing the name from its Venetian forebears, it was a regular and reliable source of information. It proved a hit, so when the court moved back to London it changed the name to the *London Gazette* and it has been in publication ever since. The edition for the first week of September 1666 carries a particularly racy description of the Great Fire of London, starting with the words:

> The ordinary course of this paper having been interrupted by the sad and lamentable accident of Fire lately happened in London...

As the Industrial Revolution got underway, there was a dramatic increase in both literacy and commercial activities. This new mercantile class wanted information to help with their businesses. Local communities also wanted their own media to reflect their growing sense of self-government. The word "newspaper" begins to appear in English around 1670.

However, the Stuart monarchy still kept publications under tight government control out of fear of public unrest and the rise of another Cromwell. In the event it happened anyway and the so-called Glorious Revolution of 1688 saw the overthrow of James II and the installation of the more conservative Dutch couple William and Mary. It was the moment power really shifted away from the old order. And it had a profound effect on the media of the day, as it meant the population at large felt they now controlled their own destiny and wanted news and information to help them elect and supervise their leaders. The print licensing laws were relaxed and the newspaper industry was born.

The *Worcester Post Man* started in 1690, the *Edinburgh Gazette* in 1699, and the *Norwich Post* in 1701. Edward Lloyd ran a coffee house in London's Lombard Street that became a center for shipping merchants. In the 1690s he started *Lloyd's News*, which later became *Lloyd's List*, arguably the first business newspaper. It is still going in electronic form. Just down the road from him the first national title was the *Daily Courant*, which was published in 1702 from rooms above a pub called the White Hart in London's Fleet Street. This started a newspaper tradition that would last for nearly 300 years.

The *Courant* was a single printed page with two columns and it featured mainly foreign news as, at the time, it was still illegal to report speeches in Parliament. Papers like this were seen as an alternative to the sermons from the pulpit. They were devices to explain current events, in contrast to books, which were seen as repositories of knowledge.[1]

Over the next few years huge numbers of newspapers and magazines were launched. Daniel Defoe (author of *Robinson Crusoe*) founded the

Weekly Review in 1704. Jonathan Swift (*Gulliver's Travels*) was editor of the *Examiner*, which started in 1710. Many of today's great titles had their foundation in this period: the *Belfast Newsletter* was launched in 1737, *The Times* in 1785, and *The Observer* in 1791. The *Newsletter* can claim an extraordinary scoop as the first British paper to publish the American Declaration of Independence. A copy of the document stopped in Belfast on its way to London and was "borrowed" and printed by the paper before it officially reached George III. The court first read the constitution of the new created USA from an Irish newspaper.

EARLY NEWSPAPERS IN THE US

In America the development of newspapers followed a parallel track

THE SCOTSMAN

After the Napoleonic wars an Edinburgh-based solicitor, William Ritchie, and local customs official Charles Maclaran felt that existing newspapers were in league with the English political establishment and exhibited unblushing subservience. They launched *The Scotsman* on Scots poet Robbie Burns' birthday—January 25, 1817—as a Saturday journal at a cost of 10 pence, of which 4 pence was the notorious Stamp Duty. As the railway network developed in the 1860s and the stamp duty was repealed, *The Scotsman* became a 1 penny daily and got wide distribution to become the voice of Scotland. By 1905 the paper was so successful that it built one of the grandest office buildings in Britain on Edinburgh's North Bridge, which serves today as The Scotsman hotel.

to the UK. However, they became much more significant much more quickly, as politicians and businessmen alike saw them as one of the key elements in creating the spirit of the nation by offering support for a fledgling democracy and a growing economy.

The first American newspaper appeared in Boston in 1690, when the Colonies were still under rule from London. It was entitled *Public Occurrences*, but was banned by the British after just one edition. It took 14 years for the colonists to have another go and in 1704 the *Boston News Letter* was tolerated by officials, although the Massachusetts Governor reserved the right to censor its contents. In 1721 a certain James Franklin started the *New-England Courant*, but within a year he had clashed with the authorities and was thrown in jail. A colonial court decreed: "James

DECLARATION OF INDEPENDENCE

Despite the availability of many printers the actual document of the American Declaration of Independence was hand written by a professional scribe. This original text was then printed on July 4 1776 by one John Dunlap who produced 24 identical copies that were distributed to soldiers and politicians and reproduced in newspapers. They were known as "Dunlap's broadside". It was these mechanical reproductions that gave the Declaration its mass circulation, rapid impact and political power even though the Founding Fathers had relied on the more traditional medium of pen and parchment for the historical record.

Franklin be strictly forbidden... to print or publish the New-England Courant." To get around this his younger brother Benjamin took over and had much sport at the British government's expense, writing under the pen name Silence Dogood. Ben Franklin enjoyed being a newspaper magnate and a few years later took control of the *Philadelphia Gazette*.

Franklin and others used their newspapers to campaign vigorously against what they saw as the inequities of British rule. All the American colonies soon developed their own titles: the *New York Gazette* in Albany in 1725, the *Maryland Gazette* in Annapolis in 1727, and the *Virginia Gazette* in Williamsburg in 1736. By 1765 Boston had four papers, New York City three, and Philadelphia three, two printed in English and one in German. Most of these papers, while critical of authority, broadly accepted the colonial line. The notable exception was the *New York Weekly Journal*, started in 1733 by a German immigrant, John Peter Zenger. He was very critical of the Governor of New York and in 1775 was put on trial for seditious libel. The judge ordered a conviction, but Zenger's lawyer made his case about "the defense of liberty." The local jury refused to convict and this sent a clear message to the British that America was going its own way.

Another colonial flash point was the Stamp Tax. Enacted by the British Parliament, this was due to come into force in America in 1765, but would have made newspapers far too expensive for a mass audience. Editors campaigned against it and after the imposition date ignored it. The tax proved uncollectible in America and was later repealed. The campaign of defiance under the slogan "no taxation without representation" was, in some ways, a dry run for the Boston Tea Party, which was planned in the home of the editor of the *Boston Gazette*, Benjamin Edes, in 1773. American newspapers played a vital role in creating the community of merchants and politicians who became the Founding Fathers.

After American Independence Congress passed the Post Office Act of 1792 to support the newspaper industry, which provided special discounts to carry newspapers by mail. This, in effect, subsidized the medium on the grounds that it helped to build national identity and freedom of speech; in stark contrast to Britain, where newspapers were heavily taxed. This crucial subsidy did much to encourage privately owned regional and rural media in America.

In the early years of the American Republic newspapers thrived, but tended to be aggressively politically aligned. Two parties grew up, the Federalists and the Republicans (rather confusingly the forerunners of today's Democrats), who battled each other in the pages of rival papers owned by fervent supporters. So aggressive did it all become that in 1798 President John Adams passed the Sedition Act, leading to numerous prosecutions for antigovernment articles and arguably making American papers less free than their British counterparts. Freedom of the press itself became a major political issue and was championed by Thomas Jefferson, who beat John Adams in the 1800 election. Jefferson observed:

> Nothing in this paper is true, with the possible exception of the advertising, and I question even that... But if I had to choose between government without newspapers, and newspapers without government, I wouldn't hesitate to choose the latter.[2]

THE PENNY PRESS

The forces that came together to turn newspapers into a mass medium were the combination of improved education, steam-powered presses, the manufacture of newsprint, and the development of branded goods. All four elements needed to happen together, and this occurred first in America.

Cheap newspapers were promoted by ambitious entrepreneurs who saw the opportunity to make much more of the medium than using it as a mere political campaigning tool with the social elite. The first to take the plunge was the 22-year-old Benjamin Day, who launched in New York with

TYPESETTING

By the 1800s the art of the typographer was well established. Publications chose a typeface they liked (and in some cases owned) and letters, numbers, and punctuation marks were cast in metal, the resulting images being kept in large wooden racks. By convention the capital letters were kept in the upper drawers—the upper case—and the small letters in the lower racks—the lower case. A skilled profession of compositors developed. They were required to undertake a seven-year apprenticeship and could put together pages of books and newspapers with extraordinary speed.

Nevertheless, a printer working in the early 1880s was undertaking a very similar task to his medieval forebears and Gutenberg would certainly have recognized the process. This was all changed with the invention of the Linotype machine in 1886 by a German immigrant to America called Ottmar Mergenthaler. His machine kept brass stamps of all letters and numbers from a particular typeface in racks. A keyboard operator could then call up these letters as required, which were arranged, by the machine itself, into a mold into which hot metal was poured to produce a complete line of text (hence the "line-o-type"). Once it cooled and set this so-called slug of lead text, along with others, was fitted into a frame called a galley. When a complete frame was ready a few pages were printed and were called galley proofs. These were checked for accuracy and if necessary changes could be made to the tray of print. Once ready, the trays were placed into a printing machine and thousands of copies could be run off at high speed.

Phrases that were used again and again would be cast into a single slug called a cliché or stereotype—words that have found their way into the English language to characterize lazy journalism.

The process of making up printing plates from hot metal became the dominant newspaper technology for about 100 years. The arrival of computers and digital plate making in the 1980s made the old hot metal process uneconomic and large numbers of printers redundant. Digital technology has taken the last barriers to entry out of printed media. Anyone with a computer can now produce the same quality of book, magazine, or newspaper as the largest corporation in the world.

the *Sun* in September 1833. At a time when most papers were 6 cents, he offered the *Sun* for 1 penny a copy. He stated:

> The object of this paper is to lay before the public, at a price within the means of everyone, all the news of the day, and at the same time offer an advantageous medium for advertisements.[3]

Apart from cost, Day had other innovations. His *Sun* was much smaller than other papers and thus easier to read on the new public transport. He also broke with the tradition of home delivery by offering the *Sun* to news vendors at 67 cents per hundred copies, thus letting them keep a 33 cent profit, which greatly increased his circulation. In the year he launched, New York had 11 old-style papers with a combined daily sale of some 26,000. Within two years the *Sun* sold nearly 20,000 by itself making it the largest newspaper in America. The *Sun* was unashamedly aimed at popular taste and started some great, but not so laudable, journalistic traditions.

In 1835 it perpetrated the great moon hoax, which suggested that life had been found on the moon and included fabricated and fanciful lithographs of fantastic alien creatures. The fictional story was, quite wrongly, attributed to a famous (and real) astronomer, Sir John Herschel. In 1844 the *Sun* published another wholly untrue story, dreamed up by none other than Edgar Allan Poe, about a hot-air balloon crossing the Atlantic in three days. In 1897 it somewhat redeemed itself with the now famous editorial "Yes Virginia There is a Santa Claus," reassuring an 8 year old that St. Nicholas was worthy of being believed in. It was also the *Sun* that employed the city editor who came up with the seminal journalistic observation "When a dog bites a man that is not news, because it happens so often. But if a man bites a dog, that is news!." The *Sun*'s great rival was the *New York Herald*, which became for a period the world's most popular newspaper when it was owned by the gregarious James Gordon Bennett.

By contrast, in England the newspapers remained a more elite medium as circulation was held back by the Stamp Tax, which kept prices high. *The Times* introduced a steam-powered flatbed printing press in 1814. However, even when the mechanical production of low-cost paper from pulp started in the 1840s and the high-speed rotary press was invented by American Richard March Hoe in 1843, the circulation of *The Times* and its rivals remained tiny by American standards.

STAMP TAX

This notorious British tax had a major impact on all printed media. It was first introduced in England in 1694, during the reign of William and Mary, as "An Act for granting to Their Majesties duties on Vellum, Parchment and Paper towards carrying on the war against France." In 1712 it was specifically applied to newspapers and magazines and rapidly extended to cover advertising as well. The motivation was as much to limit publication as to raise revenue. The real intention was made clear when Lord North observed that the demand for newspapers arose from a "foolish curiosity" and newspapers were therefore a "luxury" that could withstand higher taxation.[4]

By the early 1800s British Stamp Duty had reached the significant sum of 4 pence a copy, which made newspapers and magazines too expensive for any but the well-off. London's Fleet Street was the home to many newspapers partly because of its proximity to Somerset House, which is where they had to go to get the pages stamped. Some editors risked (and received) prison sentences for publishing without paying the tax. Others campaigned vigorously against it. The brothers Leigh and John Hunt started *The Examiner* in 1808 and printed on their front page that the Stamp Duty was a "tax on knowledge." Leigh Hunt—a friend of Lord Byron and Mary Shelley—was imprisoned for his efforts but continued to edit *The Examiner* from jail.

By the mid-1800s the tax had been reduced to a penny a page for news but still a shilling a page for advertising. This led to the rapid growth of posters, handbills, and men carrying sandwich boards to meet commercial demand. In 1855, after years of campaigning, newspapers and advertising were exempted from Stamp Tax, producing huge rises in circulation.

By the 1830s there were some UK penny papers like those in the US. However, to evade the Stamp Tax they came "unstamped" and thus were illegal and often radical in their politics. These so-called paupers' papers preceded pirate radio by some 100 years. One of the most famous was the *Poor Man's Guardian*, which sold more than 20,000 copies a week in the 1830s. Its masthead was the first to carry the slogan "Knowledge is Power." The repeal of the Stamp Tax in 1855 enabled UK newspapers to become a mass medium.

THE AGE OF THE BARONS

Once papers achieved mass circulation, they because valuable businesses and provided their owners with great political influence as well as significant wealth. America, with its huge market, subsidized distribution, and plentiful advertising, led the way and the first so-called press barons emerged.

Joseph Pulitzer was an immigrant from Hungary. He settled in St. Louis and got a job on a local German language paper, which he later bought and used to found the *St. Louis Post-Dispatch*. In 1882 he purchased the then loss-making *New York World*, which he revitalized with sensational journalism and popular features like the Yellow Kid cartoon. Under his ownership the circulation rose from 15,000 to 600,000. Although Pulitzer was associated with sensational journalism, toward the end of his life he took a much more serious view of the profession and used his money to fund the Pulitzer Prizes, which remain, to this day, the most prestigious awards for journalism and literature.

The real-life subject of the iconic film *Citizen Kane* was William Randolph Hearst. He was the heir to a vast mining fortune and in 1887 he took over the *San Francisco Examiner*, which his father had won as payment for a gambling debt. He invested in modern printing equipment and star writers and made it the city's dominant paper. In 1895 he acquired the struggling *New York Morning Journal* and embarked on a huge circulation war with Pulitzer's *New York World*. Hearst created the first huge media empire, and in the run-up to the Second World War was a close confidant of presidents, prime ministers, and dictators. He was twice elected as a congressman and his personal life was every bit as outlandish as that of his film counterpart.

Frank Munsey, who was called the "great executioner of newspapers," believed that the newspaper industry needed substantial consolidation and as early as 1893 said:

> In my judgment it will not be many years—five or ten perhaps—before the publishing business of this country will be done by a few concerns—three or four at most.

He bought numerous New York papers—*Sun*, *Press*, *Herald*, *Tribune*, and *Globe and Mail*—and closed or merged them all together. He did not tell

YELLOW JOURNALISM

In the late 1890s Pulitzer and Hearst vied for success with rival popular papers. Both featured sensation, crime, and outrage and limited color printing, and both plumbed the depths of popular taste with huge headlines, salacious pictures, and dubious stories. Pulitzer introduced a hugely popular comic strip called Hogan's Alley, featuring a bald kid in a yellow shirt. Hearst fought back by hiring away the cartoonist to draw the same character in his paper; Pulitzer responded by finding another artist to do the strip. Both papers now featured rival yellow kids, and the idea of "yellow journalism" was born as a term for chasing a competitor down market.

the editor of the *Herald* the paper was being combined with the *Tribune* until he handed him the announcement for typesetting. He was an unpredictable owner and was famous for firing reporters for being too fat or left handed. Journalists called him "the most hated publisher who ever lived."[5]

Less known today but even more colorful was James Gordon Bennett, Jr., publisher of the third big-city daily the *New York Herald*. In 1869 he funded Henry Stanley to find Dr. David Livingstone, who was lost in Africa. He also paid for an expedition to the North Pole and, after he moved to Paris, founded the *International Herald Tribune*. His personal style was eccentric bordering on manic. He once arrived at a society party so drunk that he urinated in the fireplace in front of all the guests. Coverage of his exploits by other newspapers led to the common expression "Gordon Bennett!" as an exclamation of surprise or disbelief.

By comparison the British press owners were a far more serious lot. In the UK the first great baron was Alfred Harmsworth, later Lord Northcliffe, whose empire was taken over in the 1920s by his brother Harold Harmsworth, later Lord Rothermere. The two brothers had an extraordinary feel for popular taste. Harmsworth's first big success was the magazine *Comic Cuts* in 1890 and he used the profits to launch the *Daily Mail* in 1896. This was an unashamedly downmarket publication with short, simple pieces and themes aimed at amusing the newly literate lower middle class. It cost a half penny when most other papers were a penny. It gave away huge cash prizes to readers and pioneered promotional marketing. During the Boer War in 1900 the *Daily Mail* was selling more than a million copies a day. It was one of the first British papers to generate significant advertising income, which allowed it to keep its cover price well below that of its rivals.

The *Daily Mail* was such a success that Pulitzer invited Harmsworth to New York to edit a special edition of the *New York World* at the start of the twentieth century. Harmsworth, who loved innovation, experimented with a smaller printing format for the special edition and in so doing invented the concept of the half-sized newspaper. The term "tabloid" was being used at the time extensively in advertising by the pharmaceutical industry to describe compressing medicines into a smaller dose than a normal tablet. It captured the public imagination and was adopted as the description of the new small paper.

In 1903 the Harmsworth brothers purchased the loss-making *Sunday Dispatch*, which they turned into Britain's biggest-selling Sunday paper, and relaunched the ailing *Daily Mirror*, the UK's first tabloid with an emphasis on picture stories. They specialized in rescuing papers in trouble, buying *The Observer* in 1905 and *The Times* in 1908. Like his American counterparts, Harmsworth enjoyed total control of his numerous titles. He was a great advocate of new technology like the telephone and electric light. He was so keen on the new industry of motor vehicles that for a time he banned the *Daily Mail* from reporting automobile accidents lest this should stifle demand for cars.[6]

In the battle to serve the interests of middle-class Britain, the great rival to the *Daily Mail* was the *Daily Express*, which was built up to become the UK's leading daily paper by another press baron, Max Aitken, a Canadian who became Lord Beaverbrook. In his history of the British press Roy Greenslade comments:

> The idiosyncratic, iconoclastic Beaverbrook, inheritor of the Northcliffe mantle, ran his papers as organs of personal propaganda, poking his nose into the business of his rivals, making political mischief, courting publicity and revelling in his notoriety.[7]

Born in Ontario, Aitken made a fortune in Canada, then moved to England where he acquired the ailing *Daily Express* in 1916. In 1918 he started the *Sunday Express* and in 1923 bought the *Evening Standard*. These three papers provided him with a platform for his political and social views. He was a passionate supporter of the British Empire and free trade and was

COMSTOCK LAWS

The official logo of the New York Society for the Suppression of Vice shows a self-righteous-looking man in a stovepipe hat enthusiastically throwing books onto a fire. The picture may represent Anthony Comstock and it certainly celebrates his views and actions. Comstock was a postal worker who lobbied Congress to make it illegal to send obscene, lewd, or lascivious material by mail. This became law in 1873, the so-called Comstock Act. He created the Society for the Suppression of Vice as a vehicle to allow him to embark on a moral crusade against anything he deemed pornographic. This was a private-sector organization, funded by the YMCA, that took it upon itself to enforce laws that it felt the police were slow or loath to use. He also campaigned against lotteries and contraceptives and had some anatomy books banned on grounds of obscenity. In 1905 he fell out with the Irish playwright George Bernard Shaw by reporting a production of *Mrs Warren's Profession* to the police. Shaw wrote to the *New York Times*:

Comstockery is the world's standing joke at the expense of the United States. Europe likes to hear of such things. It confirms the deep-seated conviction of the Old World that America is a provincial place - a second-rate civilization after all.

In his 43-year career as self-appointed moral guardian, Comstock estimated that he destroyed 160 tons of obscene material and convicted more than 3,600 people.[8]

violently against the idea of a European Community. He was one of the most politically active newspaper owners. In the First World War he was Minister for Information and in the Second, Minister for Aircraft Production.

While the golden age of newspapers may be over, the barons still exist as heads of bigger and more diverse media groups. And they still engage in battles. In the first decade of the twenty-first century another colonial media entrepreneur, the Australian Rupert Murdoch, took on the 4th Lord Rothermere. Both invested many tens of millions of pounds competing with each other to see who could give away the largest number of free newspapers to commuters in London. In the end both admitted defeat and Rothermere sold his remaining London paper to a Russian billionaire for £1, who promptly made it available for free. And in New York Rupert Murdoch, having taken over the *Wall Street Journal*, chose to pick a long and expensive fight with the Sulzberger family, who founded and owned the *New York Times*, to see which would become the most influential title in America.

THE PROFESSION OF JOURNALISM

The owners of the early newspapers were a combination of printer, publisher, and polemicist. News gathering was a matter of listening to what business people, politicians, and travelers newly returned from an event had to say and printing it. Comment and opinion was simply the view of the owner. But as newspapers became an industry, they created a new profession of journalism and particularly of reporting. The word "journalist" first appears in 1665, when it was applied to someone who wrote a journal that was made public. The term "editor" in relation to a newspaper started to be used in 1712.

By the mid-1700s many writers tried to make a living from books, magazines, and newspapers. A number of them lived on London's Grub Street (now called Milton Street, just north of Moorgate). One of the more famous associates of the area was Samuel Johnson, later of dictionary fame. Grub Street became associated with the idea of hack writers who would do any sort of literary work for money. The *Grub Street Journal*, which started in 1730, was a popular weekly devoted to satirical attacks on the new profession of journalism.

Early high-profile newspapermen such as John Wilkes, who ran the radical *North Briton* in the 1760s, or John Walter, who founded *The Times* in 1785, would have been described as publishers or even politicians. The idea of journalism as a profession does not appear until 1833, coinciding with the launch of the *New York Sun* and steam-driven mass circulations. With multiple daily editions, newspapers could no longer be created by a jack-of-all-trades printer/publisher/editor and a new division of labor emerged between news-gathering staff, the editors who selected material, and those selling advertising. The use of the word "reporter" in a news context seems to date from this time as well. It had long been in use in the legal profession for one who recorded court proceedings. In the 1830s newspapers started to carry sensationalized reports of courtroom action and adopted the same term for their writers on the spot.

The early journalists and reporters were frequently anonymous or simply referred to as "our correspondent." This was partly to protect them from political reprisals and probably had the added benefit that an editor could simply make up stories or steal from another paper without any attribution. The idea of news reports being protected by copyright did not arrive until the late 1800s.

A major factor leading to the employment of reporters was the telegraph network, which allowed their eye-witness accounts to get back to the paper quickly and provided editors with a competitive advantage. Before the telegraph most news of battles came from the returning armies themselves. In the same way that the first Gulf War in 1991 could be said to have been the making of the 24-hour news channel CNN, there were two wars in the mid-1800s that really established the idea of the star reporter in newspapers: the Crimean War (1853–56) and the US Civil War (1861–65).

One of the first big reporting names was William Howard Russell, who covered the Crimean War for *The Times*. He was at the ill-fated Charge of the Light Brigade and his reports of dreadful battlefield conditions caused a public outcry that brought down the government and drew attention to Florence Nightingale and her nurses and the lack of medical facilities. The American Civil War was an even more important journalistic event. As the battle lines moved north and south the telegraph wires moved with them and reports from the front were regarded as of vital political and economic importance. As many as 150 war reporters marched alongside the troops. Up-to-date news of conflicts in Georgia sold newspapers in New York.

The role of the journalist has changed to reflect the available technology and the objectives of the newspaper. The concept of the scoop—an exclusive story that is published ahead of a rival's—dates from 1884 when the telegraph was in common use and the numbers of readers of papers were influenced by accessing news fast and first. With the development of the telephone the drive for speed became even greater and the mythology and glamor of the newshound developed. The acceptance of journalism as a real profession started in 1883 with the creation of the Chartered Institute of Journalists in the UK. By 1912 Columbia University in New York had a postgraduate journalism program.

As radio and then television and most recently the web have become primary sources for breaking news, the role of writers on newspapers has moved more to opinion and commentary, and the subjects they cover more to lifestyle and entertainment. There are many fewer full-time news

TYPEWRITERS

The typewriter—the archetypal journalist's tool—became one of the most important devices of the twentieth century, but there was no eureka moment in its invention. Writing machines were patented from about 1800 onward, many designed to help blind people. One that sits in London's Science Museum and dates from 1829 is called a typographer. In 1867 a team of Americans patented the Sholes and Glidden Typewriter, which had the first example of the QWERTY keyboard. It was manufactured by the gun makers Remington, but was not a great success as it only printed capitals. A few years later in 1878 the company produced the Remington 2, which also had lower-case letters, and the typing revolution began.

The QWERTY arrangement was designed to reduce the physical clashing of the metal bars that held each letter. Keys were located to ensure that common letter combinations did not use adjacent bars. With this set-up even the fastest typists rarely suffered jams. As a promotional gimmick the keyboard also had all the letters of "typewriter" along its top row, which allowed salesmen to demonstrate the brand name of their new machine by typing on just one line. French and German typewriters used the same principle, but to reflect the difference in spelling the keyboards are subtly altered—in France it is AZERTY and in Germany QWERTZ.

With the arrival of word processors the original logic of a QWERTY keyboard no longer held. A range of alternative layouts was suggested, of which the best known is the Dvorak Simplified Keyboard, patented by an American academic in 1936. Its supporters claim it has significant ergonomic advantages, but it has never caught on for the simple reason that the number of QWERTY machines in use—the installed base—is so large that most people do not want to be sidetracked by learning an alternative.

reporters and many more columnists. And those reporters who remain are often focusing more on long-term investigations rather than basic daily news gathering. The idea of journalists urgently whispering their copy down the telephone to beat rivals is long gone.

The activity of investigative reporting reached its zenith in America in the early 1970s when Bob Woodward and Carl Bernstein of the *Washington Post* painstakingly unearthed the Watergate scandal that led to the resignation of President Richard Nixon. And in the UK in the late 1970s, the *Sunday Times* under editor Harold Evans campaigned for compensation for victims of the drug thalidomide.

The growth of the web led to the phenomenon of citizen journalists and bloggers. No news organization can be in as many places as the public, so increasingly the most compelling photographs and eye-witness reports come from readers and viewers rather than professional journalists. With the arrival of Web 2.0 the role of the newspaper professional is changing to be more that of content coordinator rather than originator.

NEWS GATHERING AND NEWS AGENCIES

It is a pleasing symmetry that in today's digital world many newspapers make significant use of unpaid contributors. This is exactly the way they started in the 1700s, with letters sent in by diplomats and expatriates to give the latest news from their location. As they started to compete for readers, newspapers needed fresh news and most employed reporters to get it. However, it became very costly and wasteful for them all to gather the same news at the same time with different people, so some form of syndicated service was the obvious answer.

In America in the 1840s information from Europe arrived via transatlantic passengers, so editors sent reporters out in small boats to meet the ships on their way to dock to get the news first. For each paper to have its own boat became pointless and expensive, as they all ended up with the same stories. Thus they started to cooperate and in 1848 they formalized the arrangement as the Harbor News Association and purchased a boat they named *Newsboy* to obtain information on a collective basis. When a telegraph line was laid in 1849 between New York and Halifax (a port on the coast of Canada where most of the ships made initial landfall), it made sense for the pooled news to be collected by a shared agent using the new line. This led to the creation of the first "wire service" and what is now Associated Press or AP.

As the telegraph network spread across America, the Western Union company developed, in effect, a private monopoly of electronic transmission that offered preferential rates to AP members and refused to carry any other newswire service. A newspaper in a city that was a member of AP enjoyed significant advantages over those who were not. As a result, an AP franchise became a very valuable asset. When Pulitzer purchased the loss-making *New York World*, he was mainly motivated by being able to obtain its AP license for New York.

The UK equivalent of AP is the Press Association, which was set up by a group of provincial papers in 1886 to enable them to obtain international news. In Europe, the initiatives for news agencies came not from collectives of publishers but from individuals who saw an opportunity. Charles-Louis Havas started an agency in 1835 to offer the French press translations of stories from other European papers. He soon extended this to operating a carrier pigeon network between London and Paris. One of his employees, Paul Reuter, applied the news agency idea to the new technology of the international cross-border, telegraph.

Reuter was very inventive and realized that in 1850 the growing telegraph network had a significant weakness. Messages could not go directly from Berlin to London, as the lines did not run between Germany and Belgium. Reuter got permission to use a carrier pigeon service to bridge the gap and started a lucrative trade. In 1851 the Belgian

THE FIRST PRESS RELEASE

In October 1906 the Pennsylvania Railroad suffered a major accident in Atlantic City. Ivy Lee, the company's advertising consultant, convinced his client to distribute what he called a "press release." He invited reporters to the scene of the accident and provided a special train to get them there. The *New York Times* was so impressed with this innovative approach that it printed the press release in full as a "Statement from the Road." In the weeks that followed, public officials and other newspapers effusively praised the railroad company for its openness and honesty. The following year some anthracite coal operators in the US hired Lee to represent them during a strike. When he mailed out his second press release, some journalists called it an advertisement disguised as a story sent to manipulate news coverage. In response, Ivy Lee issued a Declaration of Principles that stated: "This is not a secret press bureau. All our work is done in the open. We aim to supply news." The press release has now become a staple of communications management.[9]

telegraph network was completed and Reuter moved to London to set up a news agency. He chose London as it was a financial center and the main link to America. It would also soon become the submarine telegraph capital of the world, and Reuter's motto was "follow the cable." He built his business by hiring reporters to follow armies across Europe and report back, via telegrams, on the progress of various wars. As the telegraph network expanded, so did his company and the Reuters telegram became a crucial part of most newspapers' foreign coverage. In 1865 he gained a world-shaking scoop by obtaining advanced information of the assassination of Abraham Lincoln. He sent a reporter to intercept the US mail boat in the Atlantic before it reached the coast of Ireland, then wired the news to his clients.

Reuters went on to thrive, not just in its news service but in providing financial information. In time it moved from private hands and, like AP and PA, became owned collectively by a group of publishers. In 1984, when Reuters obtained a stock market listing, it proved a huge payday for British newspapers, which used the windfall to pay for new printing technology.

Some news agencies specialized in just one area of information. In 1882 Charles Dow and Edwards Jones set up near the New York Stock Exchange to produce handwritten financial newsletters for subscribers in the Wall Street area. They happily described their news sheets as gossip. In 1889 they expanded the service by creating a printed afternoon newsletter, which they called the *Wall Street Journal*. This went on to become America's national business newspaper.

THE RESPONSE TO BROADCASTING

Until the 1930s the press barons on both sides of the Atlantic enjoyed their fame and power through the print-based monopoly they held over news, information, and advertising. Cinema provided entertainment, but until radio and television were established the newspapers owned the news and delivered the mass audience. If politicians wanted to reach people they needed the newspapers, hence the influence of the proprietors.

Radio, television, and more recently the web have all proven better media than newspapers for delivering news quickly. They are immediate and have more impact through sound and pictures. Most people now get most of their news from an electronic or digital source. Nevertheless, newspapers responded by evolving and finding new roles in the broadcasting environment.

Traditional broadsheets moved toward analysis and opinion. Some invested heavily in investigative reporting, so they themselves made news rather than reporting it. Mass-market tabloids started to devote much of their coverage to television and to sports and film personalities. They created popular features: horoscopes, competitions, and pictures of topless models. Saturday and Sunday papers began to distribute free color magazines, many with lifestyle themes such as home decoration, cooking, and gardening. And although overall newspaper circulations have declined significantly since the Second World War, advertisers have remained attracted by the targeted audiences delivered.

Local newspapers proved robust in the face of television, as they were able to offer specific classified advertisers a much more cost-effective way of reaching local communities to sell cars and houses and to offer jobs. The arrival of listings websites has, however, posed a major threat to this classified revenue and local papers urgently need to reinvent their model if they are to survive.

The digital technologies that have created problems have also provided opportunities to create and distribute papers in a new way. For instance, *USA Today* was started in 1982 with the intention of being a national paper in a country where all the others were regional. It exploited the new distribution opportunities of satellites to allow simultaneous printing in several cities. It also used computerized typesetting to create a fresh look at a much lower cost than a conventional operation. In layout and approach it consciously competed with television. Color on every page provided strong photographs and snazzy graphics; short articles and lots of data combined with a much improved newspaper navigation system using key colors on various sections and pages to help readers find their way around. *USA Today* focused on analysis, explanation, interpretation, and background rather than on breaking news. It was widely distributed in airports, stations, and hotels and aimed at the business traveler. Circulation quickly grew to more than 2 million.

THE OBSERVER

To demonstrate that media brands can have a long life but a baffling variety of objectives, take the example of the world's oldest surviving Sunday paper, *The Observer*, which started in 1791. It was founded with clear commercial motives by WS Bourne, who believed that the establishment of a Sunday newspaper would earn him a rapid fortune.[10] Within a few years he was deeply in debt and the paper became first a scurrilous gossip rag then a government propaganda sheet. During the 1800s, under a series of owners, it became increasingly serious and lost circulation when it sided with the north in the American Civil War (not a popular position in England at the time). It was taken over by a new owner, Frederick Beer, who installed his wife Rachel as editor. Under her control *The Observer* enjoyed a great scoop when it revealed that the evidence at the heart of the infamous Dreyfus Affair was forged. The paper then passed into the hands of Lord Northcliffe, who installed as editor the colorful JL Garvin, an unconventional but hard-line Tory who did much of his work over the telephone from his country home. The paper changed owners yet again when it was bought by the fabulously wealthy Astor family. David Astor took over as both editor and proprietor and made *The Observer* the voice of liberal Britain, employing among others author George Orwell. By 1977 it had been sold to an oil company and then to the mining tycoon Tiny Rowland. Rowland used it as a personal propaganda weapon in his battle with Mohamed Al-Fayed over ownership of the Harrods department store, going so far as to print a midweek edition of the Sunday title when it suited him. In 1993 it was taken over by the Scott Trust, which made it a stablemate of the left-wing daily *The Guardian*. The oldest Sunday paper in the world has gone from capitalist gamble to socialist charity via everything in between.

SAME ROLE, NEW TECHNOLOGY

In a digital age people still like newspapers and many millions are sold every day. However, increasingly the motivation to settle down with a paper has less to do with getting the news and more with the pleasure of reading a trenchant comment or a humorous column in a format that is easy to pick up and put down. The hard news on the front page is often very old by the time it has been printed.

When the main competition was television, newspapers held up well as the broadcasters were linear media with limited airtime. The structure of programs was set by schedulers, which could be frustrating to viewers. With the arrival of the web, particularly the mobile web, newspapers face a greater challenge. News now appears when, where, and how the users want it. Nevertheless, although the web represents a threat it is also an opportunity. Newspapers are trusted brands with huge experience of obtaining and processing information. Newspaper sites are amongst the most visited web locations. Some, such as the *Wall Street Journal*, successfully charge subscriptions. Others will follow.

WAPPING

In 1986 the four-centuries-long association of Fleet Street and newspapers came to an end when Rupert Murdoch moved production of all of his British titles—the *Sun*, *News of the World*, *The Times*, and the *Sunday Times*—from their traditional locations to the newly created plant in Wapping. The newspaper industry had become rife with archaic working practices and dominated by trade union rules. Reporters (National Union of Journalists) wrote the articles. Print workers (National Graphical Association) operated the linotype machines. Less-skilled staff (Society of Graphical and Allied Trades) worked on composition. And technicians (Electrical, Engineering and Plumbing Union) kept everything running. Unions negotiated incredibly generous overtime pay and members got paid without even turning up. Nonexistent workers signed in for pay packets under names like Mickey Mouse. Productivity was awful, so operating costs were astronomical. Under the smokescreen of launching a new London paper, Murdoch set up a state-of-the-art print plant and installed hundreds of computer terminals, which allowed journalists to do all aspects of writing and production themselves. A deal was done with the electricians to conduct all the machine operations. Although the printers went on strike for a year, accompanied by often violent demonstrations, Murdoch did not lose a single night's production. Following his lead all the other national papers took on the unions, which allowed the introduction of new technology and gave papers a new lease on life.

LIBEL

Licensing of printing sought to restrict publication in advance to protect the stability of the state. Copyright law protects the intellectual property of the author by demanding payment for its use. Libel is there to protect and compensate the subject of a media story from unfair defamation. The Romans had the idea that a defamatory public statement could be punished by civil penalties. Early English law recognized the idea of defamation and the Statute of Westminster in 1275 outlined the crime of *scandalum magnatum*, which essentially was the spreading of false rumors about senior state officers. Private individuals who felt they had been defamed could seek redress from an ecclesiastical court that recognized the sin of "bearing false witness" and would require a guilty party to do penance by wearing a white shroud and carrying a candle.

The libel laws we recognize today were not drafted until well after printing was established. They were enforced by the notorious Star Chamber Court of the 1500s, which treated libel as a criminal breach of the peace and could hand out draconian custodial penalties. As newspapers and magazines developed they wanted to avoid being bullied by the Star Chamber approach. They lobbied for a more balanced system. The ensuing Libel Act of 1792 allowed a jury of ordinary people to judge the truth or otherwise of an allegation. The law has stayed that way more or less until today.

Newspapers today are better technical products than at any time in their long history. They are better written, with more photographs and more graphics. Huge technical advances have brought production and distribution costs down to a fraction of what they were in the 1950s. The newspapers do their job well. Unfortunately, other media do parts of it even better.

The industry will shrink but not vanish. Individual titles will buck the trend and those with the most innovative approach will continue to find enthusiastic readers, even if much of their content is produced by the readers themselves and much of their income is derived from online advertising. As the web advances newspapers are likely to return to their roots as a relatively expensive luxury for the more affluent and more politically engaged.

2.7 | Magazines

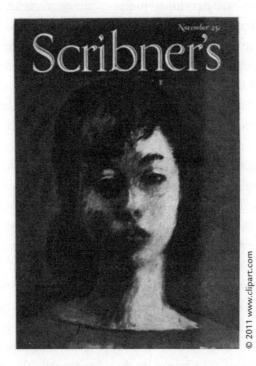

Magazines offer a treat to provide relaxation, entertainment, and special information. They are a personal indulgence—the media equivalent of a box of chocolates. The medium covers a huge range of products with a very broad set of purposes and has a significant overlap with newspapers and comics. The earliest magazines were, in effect, cheap books without hard covers. This category started in the 1700s as a format to disseminate political opinion and went on to become the main vehicle for advertising branded goods as they developed in the 1800s. It pioneered the use of photography and graphics and then reinvented itself with the arrival of television.

The term "magazine" covers a vast range, from mass-market glossy weeklies like *People*, available at supermarket checkouts, to *Beecraft*, a monthly by post serving beekeepers. *Vogue* reports on the world's fashion and lifestyle. *The Economist* (which confusingly calls itself a newspaper) is a global forum for business and political debate. The parochial village magazine, produced on a photocopier, is *the* guide to local life. Specialized scientific journals may only be published once a year.

Magazines have developed to foster communication between groups of people based on geography or common interests or shared professional skills. Because groups are continually changing, growing and shrinking, magazines reflect this, and many are launched and closed each year. More than other media type, the magazine business thrives on creative destruction. Although a few mass-circulation titles still survive, the once huge sellers like *Life*, *Saturday Evening Post*, and *Picture Post* have been overtaken by television.

Successful magazines tend to have an association with strong-minded individuals: Daniel Defoe with his *Review*, Henry Luce with *Time*, Tina Brown with *The Tatler* and the *New Yorker*, Jann Wenner with *Rolling Stone*, Tony Elliott with *Time Out*. The publication becomes, to some extent, an extension of the personality and interests of the editor/publisher/owner.

The English word "magazine" is derived from an Arabic term *makazin*, a storehouse, and by the 1600s had been adopted by the English to describe a warehouse for military shells and ammunition. Its first recorded use in a publishing context was in London in 1731, when it appeared in the title of the *Gentleman's Magazine*, promoted as a "store of useful information." The name made it to America 10 years later in the shape of the *General Magazine*, published in Philadelphia by Benjamin Franklin.

To distinguish magazines from books and newspapers we tend to think in terms of their technology and format. Typically, today's magazines are printed in full color on heavy, glossy paper, and are shorter than a book but more illustrated and luxurious than a newspaper. However, they started as one step up from the pamphlet or leaflet and were very much the poor relation to the book.

The early magazines were printed in the same way as book pages, but rather than being bound in hard covers they were distributed as a collection of a few folded sheets. Illustrations from engravings were widely used from the late 1700s, but photography did not appear until the late 1800s. It is really only since the 1930s that technology and economics have allowed magazines to develop the look and feel we are familiar with today. To our Victorian and Georgian ancestors magazines were much more practical and basic, more like today's *Private Eye*, *Spectator*, or *The Week* than *Hello!* or *Vanity Fair*.

COLLECTIONS OF CONTENT

Newly created institutions of learning like the Royal Society (which promoted science in England) developed the idea of regular journals to inform their members of discussions and presentations at their meetings. These proceedings were not felt substantive enough to warrant publishing a book, but were too specialized to be of interest in a newspaper. In 1665 the Royal Society published the first edition of its *Philosophical Transactions*. It is still produced today and is the oldest journal in the English-speaking world.

The first commercial publishing venture that aimed to make money from a regular print run was the *Athenian Mercury*, which started in 1691 and sold in London twice a week for a penny a copy. It encouraged readers to send in questions, which were answered by the expert members of the Athenian Society (actually the publisher and his friends). Crucial to its success was the newly developed penny post, established in London in 1680 to offer same-day delivery. This allowed numerous recently opened coffee shops to subscribe to the publication as a service to their customers.

A very early political magazine in the UK, in format if not in name, was *The Review* or, to give its full title, *The Review of the State of the British Nation*, which appealed to a particular set of political views but carried opinion and analysis rather than news reporting. It launched in 1704 and ran for a decade until it closed in 1713, made uneconomic by Stamp Duty. *The Review* was the brainchild of Daniel Defoe. In his youth Defoe was a very active and politically liberal pamphleteer, so his periodical was a logical extension of his campaigning activities. Interestingly, this first periodical was described as "not a newspaper dealing in facts but a journal of opinion and discussion"[1]—a distinction that remains valid to this day.

Defoe's *Review* was the immediate forerunner of a more famous and durable title, *The Tatler*, which exploited the London coffee house culture by having correspondents who frequented them to report on what was being said in them and by whom. The early editions shared the *Review* format, which looked much more like a collection of pamphlets than a book: just four pages, dense type, no illustrations, no pictures, no display advertising. They were vehicles of ideas and gossip and they made economic sense as they were being purchased by the same group of people who featured in them; remarkably similar to the approach of the much glossier *Tatler* of today.

The first real modern magazine both in name and in concept was the *Gentleman's Magazine*, which cost sixpence (expensive at the time). Copies of the original are on still on display on the website of Oxford University's Bodleian Library.[2] The first edition includes woodcut illustrations, an ode to Prime Minister Robert Walpole, and an essay on the problems of witchcraft. It was intended as a collection of items many of which had first been printed elsewhere. The title was the invention of Edward Cave, a post office official from outside London, who realized that the new postal network could reach a huge provincial audience who were not coffee house regulars. He also chose to report proceedings from Parliament—technically illegal at the time—which found an enthusiastic provincial audience. Dr. Johnson was one of Cave's rule-breaking parliamentary reporters.

Once the format and distribution method were established, many hundreds of others followed in both the UK and America. Nevertheless, they remained a minority taste among the educated wealthy few. Magazines were to continue this way for more than 100 years: written by the elite, read by the same elite. They were mostly serious, aimed at an educated and political, commercial, or scientifically active audience. Compared to newspapers, which were becoming more popular and fun, most magazines were worthy and quite hard work. This went on until four things combined to create the products we are more familiar with today: improved education, industrial printing, advertising of consumer brands, and photography.

REACHING THE MASS MARKET

As literacy spread people wanted to know more about the world around them and as class barriers began to come down the newly affluent sought ideas about how to dress and how to live. They also wanted to be entertained by short stories without the trouble of reading a book. Some felt the need to understand more about the issues behind the newspaper headlines. Rotary presses allowed mass publishing and the development of brands and advertising offered a way to pay for it all. Magazines were creations of commerce.

However, it was not all erudition. Cheap paper allowed the cost per copy to come down dramatically. This led to the creation of the so-called penny dreadful in the 1830s, a collection of lurid short stories aimed at a mass audience. These were typically printed on just eight sheets of paper and had sensational criminal themes. The response of the educated classes was remarkably similar to the reaction toward types of reality television and video games today. These sensational weeklies aimed at teenagers and young adults developed into slightly more respectable, but still cheap and popular, magazines, of which the best known was *Boys of England*, which ran for more than 3,000 issues.

THE SEVEN CURSES OF LONDON

This is an extract from as essay in 1869 by James Greenwood about the penny dreadful magazines:[3]

I allude to those low-minded, nasty fellows, the proprietors and promoters of what may be truthfully described as "gallows literature." As a curse of London, this one is worthy of a special niche in the temple of infamy, and to rank first and foremost...

...The main difficulty is that the tens and hundreds of thousands of boys who stint a penny from its more legitimate use to purchase a dole of the pernicious trash. At the present writing I have before me half-a-dozen of these penny weekly numbers they include, The Skeleton Band, Tyburn Dick, The Black Knight of the Road, Dick Turpin, The Boy Burglar, and Starlight Sall.

...Which of us can say that his children are safe from the contamination? Boys well-bred, as well as ill-bred, are mightily inquisitive about such matters... Let us for a moment picture to ourselves our fright and bewilderment, if we discovered that our little boys were feasting off this deadly fruit in the secrecy of their chambers!

At the more established end of the market, Charles Dickens arranged for some of his novels to appear in serial form in magazines he controlled. *Hard Times* and *Great Expectations* were both first published this way. *Strand Magazine* in the UK started in 1891 and developed a huge audience by following Dickens' example and publishing popular fiction in

PULP MAGAZINES

The origin of so-called pulp publishing—sometimes called pulp fiction—was a New York magazine called *Argosy*, launched by Frank Munsey in 1896, which combined the technology of steam-driven presses with cheap paper made from wood pulp. These magazines were the natural successors of the original dime novel and the penny dreadful and the precursors of the mass-market paperback and action hero comic. *Argosy* was created in the most inexpensive way possible by hiring cheap authors and using bulk printing on low-cost paper with no illustrations, not even on the cover. It sold for 10 cents and quickly built a circulation of half a million.

By the 1920s the pulp format had become more sophisticated. Covers were created on better paper with a smooth finish—called slicks—and a lurid illustration to reflect the content, which was sensational crime and science fiction. Often the covers were designed first and the author told to write a story to match the alluring picture. Inside the body of the magazine the cheap paper and fast printing made high-quality illustration impossible, so the techniques of cross-hatching and pointillism were used to produce basic images. This would greatly influence comic book design and was reflected much later in the Pop Art of Roy Lichtenstein. Buck Rogers and Zorro were among the pulp heroes, although most of the magazines were anthologies of separate stories rather than about specific characters. Paper rationing in the Second World War and the arrival of television led to the demise of the classic pulp magazine.

installments. It was famously the vehicle by which Sir Arthur Conan Doyle introduced Sherlock Holmes to the public, and at its height sold 500,000 copies a week.

As these magazines had to promote themselves to new readers rather than relying on a small, loyal elite, they developed striking and well-illustrated front covers to entice a purchase from the rapidly expanding network of newsstands. Perhaps the most famous example of this was the *Saturday Evening Post*, which started in America in 1821 but did not find a mass readership until late into the 1800s with a mixture of popular fiction and cartoons. In particular, it made use of cover art, which by the 1900s featured many works by Norman Rockwell. He drew *Post* covers for some 50 years, creating a defining archive and portrayal of American domestic life.

In the US, titles such as *McClure's* and *Munsey's* also adopted the new technology, slashed their prices, increased their print runs, and popularized their content. They changed their economic model away from high cover prices to chasing big audiences subsidized by advertising. *McClure's* commissioned fiction from the likes of Rudyard Kipling, Robert Louis Stevenson, and Mark Twain. It is also credited with creating the genre of "muckraking" journalism with its exposure and criticism of Standard Oil's monopoly. *Munsey's* was widely criticized for having "pictures of half-dressed women," but by the 1880s was selling 700,000 copies a month.

ADVERTISING TRANSFORMS ECONOMICS

Most early magazines carried no display advertising, but by the 1700s they began to have a very limited amount of classified notices, promoting goods and services relevant to the magazine's specialized readership. As graphic design, photography, and color printing changed the editorial look and feel of a publication, they opened up opportunities for mass-market display advertising to promote newly developed consumer brands. In 1853 the British government abolished the advertising tax. The change in commercial behavior was immediate. For newspapers advertising was a welcome bonus, but for many magazines it became the rationale for being in existence at all. Hundreds of titles were launched purely to be advertising vehicles.

By the late 1800s full-page advertisements were a common magazine feature and with them a subtle but crucial economic shift occurred. The commercial income meant that a reader was of value to the publisher not just because they paid a subscription, but because their attention could be "sold" to an advertiser. Rich readers were worth more than poor ones and women, who made many of the purchasing decisions about the newly invented brands, were suddenly a key audience. Indeed, for popular magazines with a big readership, the income from advertising became so large that the cost of the publication to the reader—the cover price—was frequently less than the cost of production. Thus developed a virtuous circle where the bigger the circulation, the greater the advertising income; and the greater the income, the lower the cover price, which stimulated further sales.

In the huge domestic American market this led to a business model of very low-cost subscriptions and large advertising volumes. This has lasted for more than 100 years, although the sale of magazines at newsstands and shops is far less important in the US than in Britain, where the smaller scale of the market makes cover prices a more significant part of the equation. Abundant advertising also meant that magazines were designed with groups of consumers in mind. Almost any hobby or special interest group could sustain a title if specialist advertisers wanted to reach them.

WOMEN'S MAGAZINES AND MORE

Magazines aimed at women were a particular feature of the new consumerism of the nineteenth century. Specialist female titles had been around since the early 1700s, *The Ladies' Diary* and *The Ladies' Magazine*, which offered fashion news and embroidery patterns. By the 1850s, when it became clear that it was women who ran households and made commercial decisions, a new genre of publications appeared to serve them. These were aimed at domestic management and were keen to sell newly branded soaps, foods, and household equipment.

In 1852 Samuel Beeton (and his soon to be far more famous spouse, Isabella Beeton) founded the *Englishwoman's Domestic Magazine*, which was all about running a household and being a well-dressed, middle-class wife. In 1860 they made a trip to Paris to see the fashions their readers would not normally be able to afford. They came back with the idea of publishing color fashion plates (which were individually tinted by hand) of what to wear and how to wear it, setting a style that has dominated women's publishing ever since. Mrs. Beeton wrote a series of articles for the magazine on cooking and running a house, which in 1861, in an early form of brand extension, were published as *Beeton's Book of Household Management*. This has never been out of print and is regarded as the definitive insight into the Victorian household.

In the US, *Good Housekeeping* was started in 1885 with the intention of helping the housewives of Massachusetts live fuller lives. Since then there have been thousands of women's titles aimed at every age group, class, and interest. The publishing empire of Martha Stewart has its roots in these Victorian magazines.

Playboy, launched in 1953, was probably the first magazine to be aimed specifically at men's sexual interests. Prior to this mainstream publishers had targeted men via business, hobbies, or sport. *Playboy* became an industry of men's clubs and later television channels. However, in commercial terms the women's market was much bigger and it stayed that way until the 1980s, when the concept of the "lads' mag" was created, one of the first being *For Him Magazine*, later shortened to *FHM*. Many others quickly followed, such as *Loaded* and *Maxim*, which trod the fine line between being soft porn like *Playboy* and serving a general audience. What they did achieve was to open up a whole new market of men's health and lifestyle that advertisers were keen to reach. Once again, the needs of advertising defined the magazine market more than any other factor.

HENRY LUCE

One of the most influential people in the world of magazines was Henry Luce, who founded *Time*, *Fortune*, *House & Home*, *Life*, and *Sports Illustrated*. He was born in China in 1889 and educated in England. He arrived in America aged 15 and later graduated from Yale. He launched *Time* in 1923 with the objective of providing a weekly digest of the world's news. It was an immediate success. He was editor-in-chief of all of his magazines and demanded constant innovation and high standards of journalism and photography. Under his leadership Time Inc. grew to be the world's largest magazine publisher and ultimately, after a series of mergers, became Time Warner the world's largest media company.

PICTURES ON A PAGE

Magazines are the most visual of the print media and they have the printing technology to make pictures look really good. What many of us think of as the defining characteristic of the glossies is great images. Photographers like Annie Leibovitz defined the style of *Vanity Fair*, as did war photographer Robert Capa for *Life*. The fashion, perfume, and luxury goods brands, the commercial mainstay of many magazines, use magazines as they are the only medium that can reproduce the ultra high-quality images that define these products.

Public demand for pictures is not new. The *Illustrated London News* started in 1842 and was an immediate success, launching with engravings of the war in Afghanistan and a train crash in France. The novelty of pictures made *ILN* the must-have medium of its day. It outsold most newspapers and had a huge readership for big events such as the Great Exhibition (1851) and the Crimean War (1853), for which it created

VOGUE

In 1892 the new aristocracy of the US got their own magazine when *Vogue* was launched in New York, with the support of the Astors and the Vanderbilts. It was stylish but not a success. In true American tradition, it was an upwardly mobile entrepreneur from St. Louis with the exotic name of Condé Montrose Nast who purchased it in 1909 and made it a success. He raised the price, introduced high-quality paper, and commissioned leading artists to create his covers. The first editor was the highly eccentric Edna Woolman Chase, who insisted that her staff wear black silk stockings, white gloves, and never open-toed shoes. She wrote to one employee who tried to kill herself:

We at Vogue *do not throw ourselves under subway trains. If we must, we take sleeping pills.*[4]

Vogue introduced photographic covers in 1932 and, in effect, invented the profession of fashion model. It also pioneered the concept of targeted advertising, with Nast saying in the 1930s:

I can bait the editorial pages to lift out of the millions of Americans the 100,000 cultivated people who can buy luxury goods.[5]

pictures from the front using the first generation of war artists as reporters. In the US *Leslie's* had a similar role. This was started by Frank Leslie, an ex-employee of *ILN*. It regularly sold 100,000 copies, often more when there was a good story on the Civil War (1861), which it covered with some 12 reporters at the front.

The capturing of photographic images started in 1837, but it was not until nearly 100 years later that full-color printing technology allowed high-quality reproduction. Photographs of the world and global events created a new and very popular magazine format. In the US, *Life* ran from 1936 to 1972; in the UK, *Picture Post* was the main title from 1938 to 1957. These publications made the photographer the star and the pictures the main reason for buying them. The arrival of television proved a mortal blow for these photo-journalism titles, as the immediacy of moving images in the home was so much more compelling.

However, when used in a different way, the photograph continues to be a great success. *National Geographic* was founded in 1888 by the National Geographic Society as a learned journal, but quickly became a vehicle for high-quality photography of the exotic and unusual. As each new media technology came along, *National Geographic* responded with its own brand extensions. Its eponymous television channel is one of the most consistently popular and it has become a feature of many people's home pages on the web with its dramatic picture of the day as a screen saver.

THE RESPONSE TO BROADCASTING

By the mid-1920s magazines had established themselves as one of the best ways to reach consumers. They were targeted at groups, so there was little advertising wastage. Car enthusiasts read car magazines and actually welcomed car advertising. Housewives were genuinely interested in cooking and home management. The arrival of radio, which worried many newspapers, seemed almost to help magazines. Complementary print titles such as *Radio Times*, launched in the UK in 1923, became a huge success. Magazines treated radio as just another way to create an audience.

Also launched in 1923 was *Time*, which thrived on the large number of newspaper and radio outlets by promising a digest of news in a format that a busy reader would find convenient. In a triumph of design and disciplined journalism, it quickly carved out a niche by offering synthesis and clarity. Its founding editor told his journalists:

> Let all stories make sharp sense. Omit flowers. Remember you cannot be too obvious.[6]

Time did not so much compete with radio as embrace it. In 1931 the magazine's owners developed a

FORTUNE

Fortune was founded in 1930 by Henry Luce, who wanted to create a magazine of outstanding quality for a readership he called "the aristocracy of our business civilization." He specified thick cream paper, expensive inks, and a photographic reproduction process that gave an extraordinary realism to the color images. Rather than use business journalists, he hired literary writers and commissioned leading photographers to give the magazine a very strong visual signature. Even though the first edition was published just after the Wall Street Crash, it ran to 184 pages and had 30,000 paid subscribers. After the Second World War tougher economic times forced *Fortune* to abandon its ultra high-cost production values, but it remained the most influential of business magazines, giving rise to league tables like the Fortune 500.

READER'S DIGEST

In 1922 the husband-and-wife team of DeWitt and Lila Wallace launched *Reader's Digest* after years of research and experiment. The idea was to put the best of hundreds of magazines into a condensed form and to sell it as a subscription-only magazine by mail. Initially other publishers and authors were happy to see their articles reprinted without charge, but as the *Digest* became more popular they demanded significant fees or refused permission. The Wallaces came up with the novel solution of commissioning and paying for full-length articles, which they offered free to other magazines in return for the rights to condense them in their *Digest*. Aimed at Middle America, the magazine supported self-improvement and family values and was staunchly anti-communist. Its subscription marketing steadily built through word of mouth, it launched numerous non-US editions, and it grew to become the world's best-selling magazine, reaching more than 100 million readers.

highly successful radio series, *The March of Time*, and went on to do something similar with cinema newsreels.

When television came along it did kill off many of the mass-market publications and picture magazines, but at the same time it provided opportunities to create new titles based on programs and stars. Now some of the most valuable magazines in the UK and US are those based on television programs like *Top Gear*, *Gardeners' World*, and *O, The Oprah Magazine*. Magazines have become a great way to extract more money from a television format. One of the most widely read and financially successful is *People*, which features a mixture of celebrity gossip and human interest. It was only founded in the 1970s as an offshoot of the "People" page in the more venerable *Time*, but it captured the imagination of a public fascinated by Hollywood, sports personalities, and, more recently, reality television stars.

COMMUNITIES OF INTEREST

As printing and production techniques became more efficient, it was possible for magazines to be economic on very small print runs. Computer typesetting and digital photography brought down production costs. A single person armed with the right software and camera can now create a magazine working alone. All of this has allowed titles to become more and more specialized in search of narrow audiences. Magazines are in some ways the closest of the old media to the way much of the web works. They target small groups, thrive on new ideas, and keep up with popular culture by maintaining close links with their readers.

Ironically, as the number of magazine titles grows, the space for them in retail outlets reduces. The number of specialist newsagents and newsstands is declining. Big superstores like Wal-Mart and Tesco carry a smaller number of only the bestselling titles. Readers increasingly find their title of choice via a website and subscribe by post.

Electronic mobile screens, like iPads, which pose such a threat to newspapers, cannot completely replicate the physical experience of a magazine: the ease of use, the quality of photography, and the pleasure of collection. They may even offer an additional way to generate subscribers online by offering daily updates on specialist content with video and audio.

Nowadays many retailers and media owners use magazines to enhance and develop their brand

THE ECONOMIST

Founded in September 1843, *The Economist* wears its heritage on its sleeve, or at least on its contents page. It was created (as they say in the bottom-left corner of the front page) "to take part in a severe contest between intelligence, which presses forward, and an unworthy, timid ignorance obstructing all progress." Its journalists do not have bylines and it has a rigid house writing style. It is eccentric—and it is a huge success.

The Economist was founded by a Scottish hat maker, John Wilson, who became immersed in the campaign to overturn the Corn Laws, which made importing corn difficult and were seen to favor backward-looking aristocratic landowners over the new forward-thinking manufacturers and traders. It launched with the subtitle *The Free Trade Journal* and it has stuck to this positioning ever since. It is elitist and intellectual and often rather pleased with itself. This is reflected by its brilliant and popular advertising campaigns, which have made it one of the best-known media brands.

offering. It is probable that more and more magazine titles will be linked to another successful media or retail brand. They will become a way of extending the relationship for those people who want to get more involved.

However, like books and newspapers, magazines seem destined to become a more exotic and specialized medium, with many fewer titles and an even greater focus on specific interests. They will serve minority tastes without the mass audience of their heyday. Many of the most famous titles are likely to migrate to becoming a core part of the media offering on tablets, without any printed edition.

2.8 | Comics

Comic books are not just for kids. A comic has won a Pulitzer Prize and they have proven to be one of the most fertile sources of inspiration for Hollywood and video games. Comics are principally visual, so the pictures rather than the text drive the narrative. They are drawn rather than written and in some ways viewed rather than read. In the way comics work on our senses they have elements in common with cinema, but they have a grammar and style very much their own. Comics are a relatively modern phenomenon and have become one of the most innovative and creative media, where an individual artist can produce a complete end-product.

It is easy to get tied up in intellectual knots trying to define exactly what is meant by a "comic." The term, as applied to a publication with pictures, comes from a particular use of illustrations to amuse in magazines in the 1890s, and this leads to the common fallacy that comics are somehow meant to be funny. Some are, but many are not. The name deceives. It is possible to argue that comic books are just a subgenre: a specialized form of magazine or indeed book. But in practice they are a unique art form of their own.

There are several excellent books on the medium, in particular *Reading Comics* by Douglas Wolk and *Understanding Comics* by Scott McCloud. Both work through the various definitions of what comics are. For the purpose of this book they are defined as a medium in print or online that tells stories by using a sequence of images and text. A story can be presented as a self-contained comic strip of three or four panels (typically in a newspaper). It can be a dozen or more pages of frames published periodically in a magazine format—the typical comic book. Or it can be a full-length book, often now called a graphic novel. Most recently web comics have developed online.

In definitional terms it is easier to say what comics are not. They are not illustrated books where the pictures simply complement the text, and they are not one-off, single-frame cartoons. However, they are about far more than just caped superheroes and anthropomorphic animals.

The comic book or strip tells a story by using an active combination of pictures and words, of which the pictures are the most important. A magazine or newspaper may illustrate an article with a cartoon or photograph, but for a comic book the illustration is the main device by which the characters are developed and the story is carried.

Scott McCloud provides his own carefully argued and well-illustrated definition in *Understanding Comics*:

> Juxtaposed pictorial and other images in deliberate sequence, intended to convey information and/or to produce an aesthetic response in the viewer.[1]

He argues that the art form of the comic book is a rich, complex medium that has many subgenres. Douglas Wolk explains:

> Comics are not prose. Comics are not movies. They are not a text
> driven medium with added pictures; they are not the visual equivalent
> of a prose narrative or a static version of a film. They are their own
> thing.[2]

He also makes the point that one reason comics are often not recognized
as a significant medium in their own right is that their high-profile subgenres (like superheroes) wrongly color and debase people's understanding
of the overall category. Wolk defines American comics in three broad sub-
groups:

- *Mainstream*, those produced by the likes of Marvel and DC, which
  are character franchises drawn by teams of illustrators in a factory
  environment. The character copyright is normally owned by a
  corporation.
- *Art comics*, often created by single individuals, who usually retain
  the total copyright themselves. These tend to be more inventive in
  visual style, far more adventurous in subject matter, and have
  evolved into the graphic novel.
- *Manga*, which originate in Japan and have their own unique communication conventions. This style has opened up new markets
  among teenage girls and adults.

A daily comic strip is designed to be a self-contained story, even if the same
characters reappear from day to day. It is analogous to the television soap
opera. Each strip in the story has a beginning, middle, and end, and a clear
joke or message. *Peanuts*, *Andy Capp*, *Doonesbury*, and *Alex* have entertained their fans this way over many decades. Although all were later collected in albums, they were originally designed to amuse readers as a
one-off. It was comic strips collected together as supplements to Sunday
papers that were the main manifestation of what were called "comics" from
about 1900 to 1930.

A comic book is a more permanent attempt to tell a longer story than
a strip, without the need to come to a conclusion every four frames. The
original comic books were often printed by the same machine that produced the newspapers and the style of drawing was intended to work on
low-cost newsprint. They were not really books at all, but small magazines.

The French call comics "the ninth art," the first eight being music, dance, sculpture, and so on. Film is the seventh, photography the eighth.[3] This is a useful reminder that comics, as we now experience them, are a relatively new medium and that they have found favor with intellectual critics as well as the general public.

DEVELOPMENT OF COMICS AS A MEDIUM

Single-panel drawings have been used as part of other media for thousands of years. Illustrations have appeared in books and pamphlets since the invention of the woodcut, which goes back before Gutenberg. Juxtaposed, sequential images—to use Scott McCloud's definition of the comic book form—can be seen in Egyptian hieroglyphics, medieval stained-glass windows, and, perhaps most famously, in the Bayeux Tapestry, which tells the story of the Norman conquest of England. In the 1700s the English artist William Hogarth had a huge critical and commercial success with sequences of paintings that were later sold as engravings. His two best known are the morality tales of people falling from grace in *A Harlot's Progress* and *A Rake's Progress*.

The first real comic strip, as we think of them now, was made by a Swiss schoolteacher called Rodolphe Töpffer. His most famous title, *Les amours de monsieur Vieux Bois*, written in 1839 in French, was translated into English as *The Adventures of Obadiah Oldbuck*. It showed its characters in a series of panels that allowed for the depiction of changes in time and movement from place to place. It introduced much of the grammar and structure of comic books today. The strips, when collected together, became the first full-length book of the cartoon format, published in America in 1842.

The first regularly published, mass-market, illustrated story built around an eponymous hero in the UK was *Ally Sloper's Half Holiday*. The character initially appeared in a magazine called *Judy* (a rival to *Punch*) in 1867 and was first of its type to be sold as a standalone comic book, in 1884. It featured an antiheroic lowlife who "sloped" around back alleys avoiding his creditors on Saturday afternoons, which were known in working-class Victorian England as "half holidays." The magazine was a huge popular and financial success and led to many imitations. Ally Sloper is sometimes cited as the inspiration for Charlie Chaplin's tramp character.

The illustrated strip *The Yellow Kid* became a major weapon in the New York newspaper wars of the 1880s and after that cartoon strips of all styles became a feature of most popular newspapers. In the days before strict copyright enforcement these strips were often reprinted by rivals without the originators' permission.

Seeing this new market, one of the great Victorian media entrepreneurs, Alfred Harmsworth launched his own illustrated, graphic magazine in 1890, which he called *Comic Cuts*. It was this that popularized the word "comic," which then became generally applied to this type of publication. He took strips from many newspapers—hence "cuts"—and presented them in a single, slim and cheap magazine. For Harmsworth this produced a huge profit stream that allowed him to launch the *Daily Mail* and *Daily Mirror*.

THE SPEECH BUBBLE

The speech bubble, sometimes called the speech balloon, is the normal convention for showing the words, thoughts, or emotions of characters in a strip. Giving characters words coming out of their mouths in scrolls is seen in medieval woodcuts and became a popular device in the 1700s among satirical cartoonists, who needed to convey complex political messages that would not have been possible visually and would have lost the comic effect had they simply been printed as text at the base of the picture. A large number of conventions about speech bubbles and captions have developed. Different characters' bubbles are done in different colours. A sawtooth edge represents a sound heard from a radio or television, a broken line implies a whisper, and so on.

Comic strips in newspapers in both the US and the UK became big business and compilations were reprinted using four-color techniques as supplements to Sunday papers. These were the "funnies." The first stand-alone comic book was *Famous Funnies: A Carnival of Comics*, which was sold in Woolworths in 1933. To gain further income the strips were the first to appear in book form as annuals.

In the 1920s the big publishing phenomenon in America was the "pulp magazines," but by the mid-1930s the public was tiring of these and the printers needed new ways to keep their presses busy. Reprints of comic strips were popular and offered an alternative, but the US newspaper syndicate owners charged high reproduction fees. This forced printers to look for new, original, and cheap comic material. They found it, as has often been the case in America, from a new wave of immigrants in New York.

THE COMIC BOOK BOOM

In the 1930s the decline of the pulp magazine and the increased spending power of children and teenagers combined to create the conditions for a new type of specially targeted publication. The story-length comic book and the superhero character emerged from New York. Will Eisner, who was one of the founders of the comic book industry, described its early days in the 1930s in the introduction to his autobiographic graphic novel, *The Dreamer*:

> It was a very special era. Young cartoonists struggling to enter the established markets had come upon a new opportunity—the comic book medium. Here was a publishing format, actually a mutant grown out of Sunday newspaper comic sections that welcomed innovation and was open to newcomers.[4]

The romance of these comic books was as much about the competing companies and aspiring graphic artists as it was about the titles they launched. In America there was an epic battle between two New York-based publishers, DC and Marvel, which was every bit as dramatic as the conflicts of the superheroes they created.

In 1935 *New Fun: The Big Comic Magazine* was published in New York and was the first periodical to only feature originally created material. In 1937 the same company produced another title called *Detective Comics*, later changing its corporate identity to DC Comics Inc. to reflect its success. Under this name it launched the characters Superman in 1938, Batman in 1939, and The Flash in 1940. Superman was an instant hit, sell-

SUPERMAN SELLS

In March 2010 a mint-condition copy of the 1938 comic that launched Superman as a character sold at an auction in New York for $1.5 million. The original book had cost 10 cents just over 70 years earlier. Just a month before, the first Batman comic had sold in Houston for $1 million.

ing more than a million copies of each bimonthly edition within its first year. A competitor to DC was launched in 1939, with its first character The Human Torch, and in time became Marvel Comics. Reflecting public sentiment in reaction to the Second World War the company created Captain America in 1941.

The new superhero comic books were highly original, as the printers were prepared to take creative risks to find ways to use up their spare capacity. Large studios of writers and illustrators sprang up with teams of young, poorly paid artists doing separate tasks of sketching drawings in pencil, inking in lines, doing backgrounds, and adding lettering. They invented the techniques of their industry as they went along, in very much the same way that software developers and computer games designers in Silicon Valley would do 50 years later. Eisner described the office he ran as more like an Egyptian slave galley than a comic book studio.[5] The extraordinary world of the New York comic book creators is captured in the Pulitzer Prize-winning novel *The Amazing Adventures of Kavalier & Clay* by Michael Chabon.

Comic stories became hugely popular, ever more fantastic, and, in some cases, more violent and sexy. In 1954 an American psychiatrist called Dr. Fredric Wertham wrote an influential book called *Seduction of the Innocent*, in which he claimed that comic books led to juvenile delinquency because of graphic images of violence, sex, drug taking, and other antisocial behavior. He was summoned to give evidence at a Senate subcommittee on Juvenile Delinquency, which recommended that the comic industry impose some form of control to clean up their content. This led to the creation of the Comics Code Authority (CCA) by the big publishers, which acted as a self-censoring device.

The CCA Code banned stories about vampires and zombies and also the use of the words "horror" or "terror" in titles. Like the Hays Production Code in the movie industry, it was surprisingly prescriptive about content, as some direct extracts show:[6]

> Crimes shall never be presented in such a way as to create sympathy for the criminal, to promote distrust of the forces of law and justice, or to inspire others with a desire to imitate criminals.
>
> Policemen, judges, Government officials and respected institutions shall never be presented in such a way as to create disrespect for established authority.

If crime is depicted it shall be as a sordid and unpleasant activity.

In every instance good shall triumph over evil and the criminal punished for his misdeeds.

MAD

MAD started life in 1952 as a small print run, 10 cent comic book, one of a number owned by the New York-based publisher EC that was infamous for its crime and horror comics. EC was just the sort of publisher the Comics Code Authority was set up to stifle. By 1955 MAD started to specialize in satirizing the American suburban way of life. It continued to push the edges of the CCA rules, which gave it an edgy and alternative reputation. It thrived in the 1960s and 1970s at a time when television, radio, newspapers, and many magazines followed a more establishment and conservative line. Its cover character, a gap-toothed boy called Alfred E Neuman, became a worldwide icon. Features like Spy vs. Spy and Dave Berg's Lighter Side of... have run for more than 30 years.

MAD was a pioneer of satire in print, in particular parodies of other media such as films and television. It became a huge commercial and cultural success in the 1970s, selling more than 2 million copies per edition. As other media became more daring, however, MAD lost its central position as the anti-establishment voice.

Mainstream comics carried the CCA seal of approval on their cover, intended to reassure newsagents who had been encouraged to refuse to sell unapproved comic books. Most mainstream publishers signed up and their comics were, as a result, highly sanitized, bland, and formulaic. By the 1960s an underground comic movement emerged that ignored the Code and was distributed via nontraditional outlets.

By the late 1950s both big publishers realized that they needed to bring their offerings up to date to appeal to a generation who were growing up on rock and roll and the looming threat of an atomic conflict. Nevertheless, they wanted to stay inside the CCA guidelines. DC reinvented and updated several of its 1940s characters, including The Flash and Green Lantern, and in 1961 launched the Justice League of America. Marvel Comics responded by teaming up two of its employees, writer Stan Lee and artist Jack Kirby, to create The Fantastic Four, which reflected the society of the 1960s and the tensions of the Cold War. They went on to create other contemporary, complex, and troubled characters like Spider-Man (1962) and X-Men (1963). This took the American comic into a very different market from the British.

BRITISH COMICS

In the UK the long-established Scottish newspaper publisher DC Thomson launched two comics aimed at British children at the same time as Marvel and DC were going after American teenagers. These were *The Dandy* (1937) and *The Beano* (1938). The two titles were designed to dominate the preteen market and were often drawn by the same artists. Right from the start they featured strong, child-friendly, fantasy characters like Korky the Cat and Desperate Dan in *The Dandy* and Dennis the Menace and the Bash Street Kids in *The Beano*. Available on newsstands and often delivered alongside the household newspaper, these comics became a staple for generations of British children. While American kids were growing up on superheroes, the British taste, in some strange echo of empire, ran more to war stories, real-life action adventure, and sports stars. The other big comics in the 1950s were *The Eagle*, *The Valiant*, and *Roy of the Rovers*.

In continental Europe single-character comic books started as early as 1930 with Tintin the boy detective. The French strip *Astérix* came much later, in 1959. It employed sophisticated humor and contained numerous contemporary political and social references disguised in comic book style. These witty publications made comic books a respectable commuter companion in the same way that manga appealed to adults in Japan.

THE GRAPHIC NOVEL

The early comics both in the UK and the US got to market alongside, or wrapped in, newspapers. They appeared on newsstands and enjoyed the same home-delivery system. Comic strips appeared in the papers themselves and comic supplements (often printed in color) were delivered with Sunday editions.

As Marvel and DC grew stronger, they enjoyed separate distribution and their own wholesale deals. Other comic publishers found it hard to get shelf space. In the US in the 1960s, partly as a reaction against the CCA and partly to challenge Marvel and DC, "alternative" or art-house comics started to emerge with artists such as Robert Crumb (*Fritz the Cat*). However, these got almost no distribution via conventional newsstands, so a new channel of specialist shops and record stores emerged for these comics to reach their enthusiastic but small audience. The establishment of such alternative retail channels created a new market and new comic genres. Comics started to become "collectables."

In the UK it was this style of anarchic and politicized comics that inspired graphic magazines like *Oz* and later *Viz*. Although it was called the School Kids Issue, the 28th edition of *Oz* was anything but. It featured hardcore, explicit sexual content, which led to an infamous obscenity trial in 1970. The comic had become the cutting edge of counterculture.

By the 1980s the comic format was firmly established with genres that were definitely not for children and the restrictions of the CCA no longer applied. *Cerebus*, by Dave Sim, started as a pastiche of *Conan the Barbarian* and evolved into a vast story, published monthly, which explored a wide range of political, historical, and religious issues. It ran for more than 25 years. Douglas Wolk describes it as the comic equivalent of *The Birth of a Nation*.

The independent comic producers had some surprise commercial hits. The biggest was *Teenage Mutant Ninja Turtles*, which started in 1984 as a one-off black-and-white parody of other comics like *Daredevil* and *Ronin*. It turned into a publishing and merchandising goldmine and inspired many mainstream entrepreneurs to experiment with "art" comics.

A British comic book creator and occult magic fan, Alan Moore, was contracted by DC in 1984 to revitalize its horror series *Swamp Thing*, which he did with such success that DC recruited other British talent to produce a new generation of comics to compete with the art titles and to allow it to abandon completely the constraints of the CCA rules and produce comics books clearly aimed at adults.

With the publication of several long-form graphic novels, 1986 was a landmark year in taking the comic format forward. Art Spiegelman created *Maus: A Survivor's Tale*, which told the story of the Holocaust, with the Nazis depicted as cats and the Jews as mice. For DC Comics Frank Miller produced a new and much darker take on Batman with *The Dark Knight Returns*. And Alan Moore, with artist Dave Gibbons, invented the dystopian *Watchmen*, which received a rave reception. With this new wave of comic books, creators like Moore and Miller achieved the same sort of status as film directors. Spiegelman won a Pulitzer Prize for *Maus* in 1992.

Exactly what constitutes a graphic novel is open to debate. It is a comic book format but published in book form rather than as a periodical. One of the first books to use the term was *A Contract with God* by Will Eisner in 1978. Other examples include *The Snowman* (1978) and *Where the Wind Blows* (1982), both by British illustrator Raymond Briggs. Also in 1978 the Marvel duo Lee and Kirby offered a full-length version of *The Silver Surfer*.

The graphic novel was an important development as it provided a new way to package comics and opened up a different channel in book-shops. Whereas the old mainstream comics mostly sold because of the franchise of their characters, the new wave of graphic novels were sought out by customers for the identity of the author and illustrator. The most recent graphic novels feature photography and extensive digital design. Web publishing and cheap digital printing mean that almost any aspiring comic book author can now find an audience.

EMOTIONS FROM INK

Comics are cheap and easy to make, but they have developed unique communications conventions and a sort of pact with their readers. This allows comic artists to create stories that are highly absorbing and able to convey strong emotions and ideas. Using just ink on a page, these artists can conjure up powerful characters, feelings, and environments. Comics have had a significant impact on the way other media look, in particular the graphic style of animated films, many web pages, and magazines.

A key element in the emotional power of comics is the degree to which the reader has to work alongside the author to fill in the gaps in the action. And it is the reader who provides the leaps of imagination that define the movement and drama at which the two-dimensional panels hint. Comics can travel through space and time more easily than other media forms.

More than many other media, comics are a collection of fragments, a few snapshot pictures in a frame. They use a small number of words in speech bubbles and captions. They can suggest sound effects, textures, even smells and tastes. It is putting all these fragments together in the right order that tells the story. A comic hints at, rather than fully explains, a series of events.

Like newspapers and magazines comics communicate using only the sense of sight, but unlike other print they do this through the combined use of pictures, symbols, and words. A newspaper writer might tell you that the bacon roll in the picture smells wonderful. A good comic book artist can add a lot more to stimulate all your five senses by showing you context and how characters react, and by association with images and actions. A magazine can describe the sound of a rock concert. A comic book can put you in the audience—if you let it.

Comics use many of the techniques of cinema, but they have been modified for the printed page rather than the screen. The establishing wide shot, often in a double- or triple-sized frame, is used to set up a story. The close-up emphasizes an element of detail; even the movie camera zoom can be achieved by a succession of frames, each showing an ever closer image of the subject. The typical newspaper strip tends to stick to the convention of keeping the action inside a square frame and showing the characters in the same basic "shot." Too much visual activity can distract from the strip's story. However, in comic books and graphic novels many of the visual conventions are breached to provide a more stimulating result.

Many graphic artists hand draw the text in comic book captions and bubbles, and the words themselves then take on a strong visual quality through the style of the calligraphy. This further emphasizes the visual nature of the comic and its difference from other printed media. Even the language takes on an emotion-laden visual identity.

Comics are a distinct art form in their own right. *Watchmen* creator Alan Moore has frequently complained about the way film adaptations of his graphic novels are done:

> My book is a comic book. Not a movie. It has been made in a certain way, and designed to be read in a certain way: in an armchair, nice and cosy next to a fire, with a steaming cup of coffee.[7]

Comic book superstar Daniel Clowes, who was nominated for an Oscar in 2001 for his script to the film *Ghost World*, adapted from his graphic novel, also comments on the nature of the medium:

I would not pretend to think I could suddenly write a novel. Screenwriting is the closest thing to it because a comic is all about dialogue.[8]

The huge appeal of the superhero genre has been endlessly analyzed and the basic arguments of why it works are widely accepted. The appeal to teenage boys comes from the strong metaphoric and allegoric nature of the characters and their challenging circumstances, which strongly echo the trials of adolescence.

Spider-Man is about the dilemma of how to use power before having real experience. Peter Parker's career is haunted by the memory that he did not use his abilities to save his uncle from being killed by robbers. The point about duty is made very clearly by the character's creator, Jack Kirby, who finished the first episode with the quote: "With great power comes great responsibility."

Superman is the perfect being, literally the "superman" of mythology, the all-powerful avenger with a strong moral compass who can achieve any physical feat. But, as Clark Kent, he is socially gawky, shy, and nervous with girls, and he has his secret weakness in Kryptonite. He lacks confidence in his normal form.

TINTIN

The stories of the boy detective, his dog Snowy, and a cast of significantly larger-than-life characters were the brainchild of a Belgian artist, Georges Remi, who worked under the name of Hergé. Tintin first appeared in 1929 in a Brussels newspaper as a cartoon strip, but quickly the stories were presented in book form, which allowed the use of more sophisticated color printing than in a newspaper supplement. It became a worldwide bestseller.

Hergé invented, or revived, a style of drawing called ligne claire (clear line). Unlike many illustrators, he drew in lines of almost unchanging weight and thickness. He imposed the same stylized degree of detail, or lack of detail, on every character, in every box, in every panel. The result is uncluttered, almost child-like, but capable of conveying great subtlety. His second innovation was the use of plain, unshaded color. Hergé said:

The notion of shadows, of light and shade, is a convention... I prefer to stand up for single colours, which have the advantage of being simpler and more comprehensible. For a child, Tintin's jumper is blue, completely blue. Why should it be light blue on one side, and dark blue on the other? It's the same jumper.[9]

MANGA

The drawing style we call manga has been popular in Japan for hundreds of years and derives from traditional techniques in Japanese art. The term *manga*, which translates literally as "whimsical drawing," was coined by the artist Hokusai Katsushika in the late 1700s. He is best remembered for his 36 highly stylized views of Mount Fuji, which include the iconic "Great Wave of Kanagawa." However, his manga referred to the style of illustrations rather than comic books.

It was only just after the Second World War when traditional Japanese style and Western influences were combined that what we now think of as manga as a medium exploded in popularity. The main influence was an artist called Osamu Tezuka, who in 1947 created a full-length graphic novel that in English had the title *New Treasure Island* and included the character Astro Boy. This book combined traditional manga-style with American comic book structure and borrowed the techniques of cinema, including close-ups and zooms. It almost immediately led to animated films in the same style, called *anime*.

Batman seeks superhuman abilities through technology, but is driven and psychotic and, at times, as morally challenged as his enemies. He faces the dilemma of how far he should sacrifice his humanity and principles for his powers. His is confused about right and wrong.

X-Men contains perhaps the most apt storyline for the teenage audience, with its characters in a special school coming to terms with changes in their bodies and abilities and feeling alienated and rejected from society.

One of the attractions of comics is they function a bit like a private club, with the author making assumptions that readers are "comic literate" and "in on the joke." Being a reader and a fan confers a form of insider status.

WEB COMICS

In its early days the internet was very much a text-based medium, so there was no opportunity for putting any form of comic onto a website. Picture files could be sent from one computer to another, but not viewed in a casual way. In 1993 the Mosaic web browser from Netscape allowed images to be seen online, which offered cartoonists the opportunity to publish their work as web pages.

First up in September 1993 was a character called *Dr Fun* by David Farley. It was essentially a conventional single-frame cartoon posted online, similar in style to Gary Larsen's *The Far Side*. The series ran until 2006 and all postings can be still be viewed at the *Dr Fun* website. This was a classic use of the web to provide an instant and searchable archive of many years of comic frames.[10]

Many other web cartoons followed, but most were essentially conventional comic strip style, simply using the web as a distribution channel. One of the best known is *Sluggy Freelance*,[11] which uses a small cast of characters in increasingly complex and interrelated plot lines and, again, employs the archiving and search powers of the web to allow readers easily to go back to understand where a story or a joke originated.

The adaptation of manga ideas to web comics has been led by Fred Gallagher's *Megatokyo*, which started in 2000. It is hand drawn in pencil in manga style and scanned onto web pages—the most conventional of creation techniques combined with online distribution.

In 2003 Scott McCloud launched a web-based comic book that used a range of web-specific techniques, with each frame being viewed sequentially using a zoom effect. It was called *The Right Number* and was an important step in developing a unique web-based comic book approach. It also raised a problematic issue of economics, as McCloud tried to sell viewing of the comic using a micropayments approach, rather than relying on free access and advertising support. The micropayments did not catch on and most web comics are now supported by advertising, voluntary donations, promoting the sale of the comic in physical form, and merchandising.

Web comics started out simply as a way for existing comic book artists to post their work online, but new authors have now realized the potential of the technology. Stories are starting to be told not in a conventional, linear manner but in such a way as to allow users to jump around using all the abilities of the web to provide hypertext links. Authors are experimenting with combining photography and video with graphics. It is not that the web comic book is becoming an animated film, but more that the conventions of the comic, as sequential art, are taking on the capabilities of a new technology.

ANIMATED INTERACTION

Comic strips remain a popular feature of newspapers. When the creators of the British investment banker character Alex were persuaded to move from the *Independent* to the *Daily Telegraph*, they were induced by a doubling of their normal annual fee, but they took tens of thousands of readers with them.[12] The estate of Charles Schulz, creator of *Peanuts*, is said by *Forbes* magazine still to receive some $35 million a year in royalty payments. The superhero genre, taken from comics, has been one of the most fertile sources for Hollywood in recent years. Video games make extensive use of animation, which in its turn builds on a comic book heritage

Comics will remain a breeding ground of new styles and new characters, as they are cheap to create and often the inspiration of one person. They move across language and cultural barriers much more easily than other printed media, partly because they need so little actual translation. And they develop a very strong bond with their fans, because they demand a high degree of intellectual interaction to turn the visual and verbal clues into a complete narrative.

The full potential of comics created for and distributed on the web has not yet been realized. When the economics of web publishing become as good as those of conventional printing, the digital comic may become one of the most successful of all media formats.

2.9 | Telegraph

The electromagnetic telegraph, its most famous product the telegram, and its successor the teleprinter are now all, essentially, extinct, but their legacy lives on in emails and text messages, the stock "ticker" that runs across television business shows, and the language of the digital world. The telegraph was the first medium to exploit electricity and from it developed the media of recorded sound and the telephone. Author Tom Standage memorably dubbed it "the Victorian Internet."[1] The transmission of text messages from point to point without a physical delivery was a human goal since the days of the message drum, the smoke signal, and the beacon fire. The telegraph system combined electromagnetism and the use of codes to revolutionize society, industry, warfare, and communication.

The first practical long-distance telegraph system was in use 50 years before Samuel Morse sent his first electrical message. In the 1790s a French engineer called Claude Chappe came up with an exotic contraption that resembled a modified windmill, which used the same principle as semaphore flags. It had two movable arms at each end of a single bar that could be used to transmit coded messages with different configurations. It used a series of towers built about 10 miles apart, which could be viewed from each other by telescope.

People had signaled each other with sun-reflecting mirrors for centuries, but it was the breaking of the message into a code, based on semaphore, that was at the heart of Chappe's idea. It turned his towers into a viable communications medium that the French called *télégraphie*, "writing at a distance."

Chappe's first public demonstration was to local officials at his home town of Brûlon in northern France in 1791. He sent a message between a castle and a house 10 miles apart. It said (in French of course): "If you succeed [in reading this] you will soon bask in glory." The French were in the middle of their Revolution and the National Convention government was on the lookout for projects that would strengthen the newly created republic. By 1793 officials had approved the funding of an experiment to connect three telegraph towers over a 20-mile route using improved signaling devices. The experiment worked. Author Tom Standage quotes from a speech to the National Convention about the optical telegraph:

> What a brilliant destiny for the science and the arts is reserved for a Republic which, by the genius of its inhabitants, is called to become the nation to instruct Europe.[2]

The Convention paid for the construction of a full-scale telegraph line from Paris to Lille, with 15 stations spread over 130 miles. They put Chappe on a state salary and were grateful enough also to grant him the use of a government horse. When Napoleon Bonaparte seized power in France in 1799, he immediately saw the military potential of the optical telegraph and invested in a significant construction program for a country-wide network radiating out from Paris. This included plans for a link across the English Channel in preparation for his plans to invade Great Britain. That bit of the network never got built, but the system was hugely expanded across France itself and was seen as a medium of military control. In some of the lines alternate towers were staffed by deaf and mute operators, with the intention of increasing security. The role of the system in the French mind was summed up by Chappe's younger brother:

> to carry to the centre of government, at the speed of thought, all political feelings. It gives more unity of action when the government has to be ready to defend itself against attacks.[3]

The French are justifiably proud of their optical system and have created a number of websites including animated demonstrations of how it worked.[4] The British copied Chappe's ideas and created a few optical telegraph links from London to the south coast to prepare for communication in case of invasion. No trace remains of these today, except that a search on Google Maps for "Telegraph Hill" throws up several spread around southern England that mark the sites of the old optical stations. When the threat of Napoleon's invasion was over in 1816, the British secretary to the Admiralty rejected ideas for developing the telegraph network further by observing: "Telegraphs of any kind are now wholly unnecessary."[5]

America also experimented with optical telegraphs. A line connecting Martha's Vineyard to Boston gave advance notice of shipping movements and there was an optical telegraph station on Staten Island. By the 1830s the optical telegraph was a well-established technology, but was expensive and limited to daylight and good weather. People were keen to use the newly discovered electricity rather than light as a medium, although they had not been able to find a way to do it.

ELECTRICAL MAGIC

As Arthur C Clarke said, "Any sufficiently advanced technology is indistinguishable from magic." An electromagnet is simply a coil of wire wrapped around an iron core. When current passes through the wire the iron becomes magnetized. To create a telegraph system, an electromagnet is connected to a battery via a switch in a remote location. When the current goes on the magnet will attract metal near to it, which can make a bell ring or a needle move, or can be used to make dots or dashes appear on strips of paper.

The concept of an electromagnetic telegraph was understood from the early 1800s. Nevertheless, there were numerous practical problems to do with developing the right batteries, making the signal travel over a long distance of wire, and having the right type of magnet. Many separate inventors, working independently in Europe and America, all solved the same technical problems of electromagnetism at about the same time in the 1830s. However, the way actually to convey information over the wire led to two very different solutions.

The British went for a display of needles pointing to letters on a board, which was a bit like the Chappe optical method. Samuel Morse, while on a long sea voyage back to his native America, had a stroke of creative genius and invented a simple code. The Morse code is in many ways similar to the binary code that now serves all computers. In binary code everything is translated into the idea of virtual switches being "on" or "off." A combination of switches can be assigned a meaning. Thus any number or letter can be expressed in terms of a string of "0" or "1." Morse used electricity to express the letters of the alphabet as dots or dashes, the sound being created by a short burst of electricity or a long one.

He looked at the trays of type used by newspaper printers to establish which letters were the most common and made these the most simple to encode. Thus "E" is a single dot and "T" is a single dash. "S" is three dots; "O" is three dashes. Famously, "SOS" is represented in Morse code by • • • – – – • • •.

The British system needed multiple wires to control the needles; Morse needed just one to send pulses of current. Over time the Morse system would prove far cheaper and better, and when the telegraph went wireless 60 years later, it would be Morse's code that was adopted by the radio operators.

OWNERSHIP AND CONTROL

The telegraph was the first electronic medium to transmit information instantly over great distances. The way it was financed, owned, and controlled would have a profound impact on the subsequent development of other media industries. The UK and the US ended up going in radically different directions, not just in message-transmission technologies but also in how the systems were funded and operated. Both countries had what amounted to a monopoly supplier of telegraph services, with US ownership being private and UK public. Ironically, they both started from the opposite place, with initial telegraph experiments in the US being funded by Congress and those in the UK by private entrepreneurs. The decisions made about the telegraph set the mold for the ownership structure of the telephone network, radio, and television.

The UK: Post Office monopoly

In 1837 leading British scientist Charles Wheatstone and his partner William Cooke obtained a patent for an electrical telegraph that used magnetism to make a five-needle display point at different characters on a dial. The first demonstration laid six wires (one for each needle and a spare) between the railway stations of Euston and Camden Town, which were only 1½ miles apart. The machine worked first time. Wheatstone was in a small, dingy room at Euston station, but was quoted as saying at the time that he experienced:

> a tumultuous sensation all alone in the still room. I felt all the magnitude of the invention—now pronounced to be practicable beyond cavil or dispute.[6]

Two years later the Great Western Railway commissioned the Wheatstone system to run along its railway lines from Paddington to West Drayton and then ultimately on to Slough, some 20 miles away. With only two offices on the line the telegraph got off to a very slow start and to begin with was mostly used for railway messages. But by 1845 the huge potential of the technology was recognized, after a few publicity stunts described later in this chapter. A new business called the Electric Telegraph Company was formed that bought out the Wheatstone/Cooke patents. The major investors included some of the private railway companies, which saw the telegraph as complementary to their own efforts to build new lines and stations.

Dozens of competing telegraph companies started to trade. Customers included stock-broking firms, banks, government offices, and the armed services. One of the first long-distance lines connected the London Admiralty with its base in Portsmouth. The British viewed the telegraph as an important enabler of commerce not just around their own country but around the Empire. Although there was concern right from the start that it was a series of private companies building out this strategic technology, the government initially left it alone. However, the criticism became more marked by the 1860s when people pointed out that the British telegraph system was more expensive than those of America, Belgium, and Switzerland and as a result far fewer telegrams were being sent by the public.

A very unfavorable comparison was made with the mail system run by the state-owned Post Office, which was held up as a paragon of effective operation worldwide. In addition, the Post Office had its own worries that the private-sector telegraph might make its operations less viable. Egged on by ambitious Post Office officials, the government finally agreed to nationalize all the private telegraph companies in 1870. The move was, not surprisingly, opposed by the telegraph owners and railway companies, but was supported by the newspapers, which saw state control as the best way for them to get a cheap and reliable telegram service.

The private owners received very generous compensation. They had invested some £2.5 million in their networks and the taxpayer agreed to pay £12 million to take them over. What the government got was an infrastructure comprising 16,879 miles of telegraph line and 2,155 telegraph stations, with the services of 5,339 people. Much of the compensation paid to investors was put back into the submarine cable business, which remained in private hands.[7] In terms of increased usage the move to state ownership was a huge success, with telegram traffic going from 6 million a year in 1869 to more than 26 million a year a decade later. Much of the growth was stimulated by a low-cost uniform rate for a 20-word message, making a short telegram similar to the cost of a letter sent by post. The model of state control of electronic networks was thus firmly established in the British mind as the right way to do things.

The US: Western Union monopoly

Samuel Morse filed for a patent for his code and telegraph idea in 1837, almost at the same time as the British. He tried to get the US Congress interested in paying for a trial, but it was indifferent. However, it did ask for a report on the possibility of building an optical telegraph from New York to New Orleans. After years of persuasion, in 1842 Congress reluctantly agreed to invest $30,000 to fund an experimental line between

Washington and Baltimore. In 1844, after numerous technical problems, the line was completed and Morse sent his now famous first telegram over the 40-mile distance: "What hath God wrought?"

Even though it was early days, many people could see the telegraph's potential and, just as in the UK, the American newspapers lobbied for it to be taken into government ownership, particularly as the government had funded the initial experiments. However, in the US opinion was split between the northern industrial states, who rather favored government control, and the southern agricultural ones, who did not. In 1845 Congress decided to give the experimental telegraph back to Morse and his partners at no cost, and they founded the privately owned Magnetic Telegraph Company and looked for new investors.

Having a single link between Washington and Baltimore had little commercial value (the same problem as with London and Slough), but the operators could see that a connected network of major cities would open up new opportunities; particularly if they included the financial markets in New York. Private money was raised to build new lines and, in the event, the skeptical newspaper owners saw a way to get access to information, so they funded much of the expansion.

Dozens of telegraph companies sprang up in every state and thousands of miles of line were laid. The total of 2,000 miles of telegraph wires in use in 1848 jumped to 23,000 miles by 1852. The transcontinental link from New York to San Francisco was made in 1859 and by 1865 there were 39,000 miles of telegraph wire across America.[8]

Although big-city newspaper owners funded much of the initial growth of the telegraph, the railway owners also become involved, as they discovered that the new communications device was a valuable way of scheduling trains. In the US many of the long-distance railroads were laid as single tracks with passing places that required coordination, unlike in the UK where on most main lines two sets of rails ran in parallel. Exclusive deals between telegraph operators and railway companies become crucial to growing the telegraph network. However, the large number of competing companies led to many of them losing money and a process of consolidating began.

The American Civil War (1861–65) gave a big boost to the construction of telegraph lines, as generals needed to communicate with their armies. It was also a big help to Western Union, as most of its network ran east to west and was mainly in the northern states. This meant that they were not continually cut by the to-and-fro fighting, unlike their main competitor American Telegraph, which ran mostly north to south. Also, American Telegraph had been distracted into making heavy investments into transatlantic cable, which had failed. In 1866, after the war was over, Western Union was able to take over American Telegraph, giving it a virtual monopoly of the industry in the US.

This de facto private monopoly had been established just about the same time that a state monopoly was set up in Great Britain and without competition it just kept growing. By 1890 some 80 percent of all US telegraph messages were delivered by Western Union, which had nearly 20,000 offices across the country.

Critics of the resulting monopolies on both sides of the Atlantic were largely ignored, as the benefits of a standardized network were felt to outweigh those of competition, which might duplicate and waste resources. This was an argument that would resonate with the telephone network soon after, and more than 100 years later with Microsoft and Google.

In Britain the nationalized telegraph made a commitment to public accessibility. That meant opening a large number of new telegraph offices (often in existing post offices) and encouraging more use by the general public. In America, by contrast, Western Union focused on the business customer. Most new telegraph offices were opened up at railway stations, which were often located close to the business district. Rates were high and there was little attempt to be seen as a public service. By the late 1880s 87 percent of Western Union's traffic was business, 8 percent newspapers, and only 5 percent private. In the UK, by stark contrast, some 66 percent were personal messages sent at low cost.[9]

SUBMARINE CABLES

The initiative that elevated the telegraph from being a useful vehicle for commercial and personal messages into becoming the first global medium was the laying of undersea cables. At the time these were as significant as communications satellites are today. The first major submarine cable link was across the English Channel from Dover to Calais in 1851. However, the connection that really captured the pubic imagination was transatlantic. The idea of a cable to link America with Great Britain had been mooted by Morse even as he was getting his original Baltimore-to-Washington line working.

After various false starts a cable was laid in 1858, but it was too thin and it was when used with high voltages in an attempt to boost the signal, it overheated. While its opening was greeted with huge popular acclaim and marked by 100-gun salutes in both Boston and New York, it did not work at all well. A much publicized message from Queen Victoria to President Buchanan had, in fact, taken more than 16 hours to send, but, ignoring the problems, the President replied:

> May the Atlantic Telegraph, under the blessing of heaven, prove to be a bond of perpetual peace and friendship between the kindred nations, and an instrument destined by Divine Providence to diffuse religion, civilization, liberty, and law throughout the world.[10]

After less than a month the cable failed completely when the insulation burned off and there were major recriminations on both sides of the ocean. It was not until 1865 that a new and much improved cable was laid by the world's first iron ship, the *Great Eastern*. This new one worked perfectly and within a month was producing a huge income from the high volume of transatlantic traffic.[11] This success inspired the laying of cables around the world.

The pioneer of the industry was Sir John Pender, who founded 32 separate submarine cable companies with London at the hub. The spread of the cables was driven by a desire to connect the various parts of the vast British Empire and was partly funded by the compensation paid for nationalizing the local British telegraph network. India was reached in 1870, Hong Kong and Singapore in 1871,

THE GUTTA-PERCHA COMPANY

Gutta-percha is the gum of a tree native to Malaysia. It is similar to rubber and when heated it can be pressed into molds. The Gutta-Percha Company was founded in England in 1845 and the material was initially used to make chess pieces. The company discovered it had very effective electrical insulation properties and was not damaged by seawater or marine life. It became the "miracle" material that enabled submarine cables to work and, until it was replaced by synthetic insulation in the 1930s, was the key facilitator for all telegraph and telephone cables.

Australia in 1872, the West Indies in 1873, and South Africa in 1892. In 15 years Pender laid more than 22,000 miles of cable and created a single organization that controlled all of the operators and also owned the cable manufacturers, such as the Gutta-Percha Company. By 1934 this business had expanded into telephony and was renamed Cable & Wireless.

SOCIAL IMPACT

The main social manifestation of the telegraph system was the domestic telegram. It was the bringer of dramatic news, good and bad, and in the US was always associated with the Western Union courier. The slow start and then rapid growth of the telegraph provide a classic example of network effects, which would later dictate the development of telephones both fixed line and mobile, fax machines, and the internet. The greater the number of people who could send and receive telegrams, the more the utility of the network. Initially the telegraph was a crucial, if expensive, business tool and then as prices dropped it became part of people's everyday lives.

In its early days it was regarded with some skepticism. A demonstration of an early German electromagnetic telegraph so astonished Ludwig I of Bavaria in 1835 that he said to the inventors: "You are lucky to live in our days. 200 years ago, you would have been burned for performing witchcraft."[12] American Congressmen, seeing Morse's early demonstration, thought him insane. The British public and politicians showed no initial interest in the efforts of Wheatstone and Cooke. Both groups of pioneers had to build working examples to convince the skeptics, and both then had to resort to stunts to get publicity.

In Britain Cooke (who had taken over Wheatstone's commercial interests) was running out of money, so in 1844 he bought in a publicity promoter who created a public demonstration. This led to favorable press comment and in August that year the telegraph link (which ran close to Windsor Castle) was used to announce the birth of Queen Victoria's son Alfred. This was published in *The Times* long before it would normally have been possible, had the news been transmitted by messenger.

In America Morse was playing to a political audience for funding. He arranged, also in 1844, to report the news of who had been chosen as the presidential candidate by the Whig party in its convention in Baltimore. The information that it was Henry Clay arrived long before the train carrying the dispatch. Clay later lost the contest, but the speed of arrival of this news got the attention of politicians.

In 1845 the UK's nascent network was used to catch a murderer called John Tawell, when the following message was sent to the police at Paddington Station from the telegraph office in Slough:

> A murder has just been committed at Salt Hill and the suspected murderer was seen to take a first class ticket to London by the train that left Slough at 7.42pm. He is in the garb of a Kwaker with a brown great coat on which reaches his feet. He is in the last compartment of the second first-class carriage.

The word "Kwaker" was misspelled on purpose as the 20-character dial system did not support the letter "Q." Tawell was arrested in London and later convicted and hanged. The telegraph became known in popular papers as "the cords that hung John Tawell."[13]

As the price of telegrams came down, and as far more telegraph offices were opened, the public, particularly in Great Britain, started getting interested. Most telegrams were charged for by the word, so senders had every incentive to keep messages short and to the point. This had two results. First, it encouraged a use of language that produced a rather peremptory style, very different from the often verbose approach taken by most Victorian novelists and letter writers. The other feature is that telegrams became associated with important news, which continued to be the case long after the telephone was in widespread use.

By the time of the US Civil war telegrams were being used by the military on opposing sides to communicate with each other. After the bombardment of Fort Sumter, the Confederate general in Charleston sent a telegram to his Union adversary, telling him:

> Give in like a good fellow, and bring your garrison to dinner and beds afterwards. Nobody injured, I hope?[14]

In the UK the first public telegraph messages were sent in 1845 and by 1850 the term "telegram" was in common use. For the Victorians and Edwardians they became a crucial communication tool and featured heavily in novels and plays of the period. By 1913, 82 million telegrams were being sent annually.[15]

Sir Arthur Conan Doyle's stories of Sherlock Holmes are littered with telegrams arriving at 221B Baker Street. The sending of telegrams by guests unable to attend weddings started as a fashion in the 1880s. The telegram from the War Office informing of the death of a loved one became a tragic feature of the First World War.

Telegrams reached their peak popularity in the 1920s, when it was cheaper to send a telegram than to place a long-distance telephone call. People would save money by using the word "stop" instead of periods to end sentences, because punctuation cost extra while the four-character word was free.

However, by the mid-1930s the telegram operators needed to find ways to compete with the telephone. Western Union introduced the singing telegram in 1933. The UK Post Office invented the special greeting telegram in 1935. For an extra three pence it could be delivered on festive paper and put in a gold envelope. The next year it came up with a special Valentine's Day telegram, aimed particularly at those proposing marriage—50,000 people sent one, including one individual who signed off with a rhyming couplet to emphasize the high cost of his gesture:

And now I've asked you to be mine—
By gosh! It's cost me eight and nine![16]

The British tradition of the royal telegram sent to mark a 100th

GAMING THE SYSTEM

As with other media, the telegraph spurred the imagination of entrepreneurs. As messages were charged by the word, brevity was at a premium. A whole new business grew up trying to deny the telegraph companies revenue. The company charged a fixed fee for a ten-letter word, so codes were devised whereby a short word or group of letters would stand for a longer but commonly used commercial phrase. Code books were published with short forms of messages. Thus, the letters SHLELNTUE indicated the message "Ship leaving London Tuesday." To people at either end who had the same book, the longer message was clear but it would only be charged as one word. A large number of schemes encouraged people to buy these code books. In 1901, for example, the World Wide Travellers Cipher Code had bizarre made-up and foreign words to replace normal phrases. Thus, for example, Libretto meant "now in Japan" and Librillis meant "returning from Japan."[17]

birthday was started by George V in 1917. This was phased out in 1982 and replaced by a picture card sent by special delivery through the post, with an electronic facsimile of the Queen's signature. It is possible to speculate that the royal household might get fully up to date with a regal email or even a text message: Happy 100 :-). Rgrds. Liz2. It has a certain ring to it.

MEDIA IMPACT

Of all the organizations that experienced dramatic change because of the telegraph, it was another medium—newspapers—where the effect was felt most. The profession of newspaper reporter was, in effect, created by the telegraph, as was the business of news agencies. The telegraph fostered the notion of being first with the news and its language changed the argot of newspapers, bringing in "wire stories" and "wire photos." And, of course, hundreds of newspapers around the world elected to put the word "telegraph" into their name.

Prior to the existence of the telegraph network, and in particular the submarine cable, the role of a newspaper correspondent was just that. They corresponded. They wrote letters from their location, which were sent back by ship, train, or mail coach. News could be days or weeks old and, as such, it was not the most compelling element of a newspaper. With the arrival of the telegraph all that changed. News could be instant. That meant it had to be found out and reported with great speed.

At an international level, news agencies came into being to move news and business information around inside countries and across national borders using the telegraph: Havas in France (1835), Associated Press in America (1846), and Reuters in London (1854). Initially newspaper owners were suspicious of the telegraph. Some feared it would put them out of business; others felt it would help new competitors emerge. In the event, the availability of fast news from distant places helped newspapers establish new readers and a new role.

It was the Anglo-Russian Crimean War (1853–56) and the Civil War in the US that really showed what the telegraph could achieve and telegraph lines were constructed right up to the front lines of the fighting. Because this allowed newspapers to keep the conflict on the front page it was also, in effect, the beginning of politicians really having to worry about public opinion. The ordinary reader was often getting news from the battle front in the same paper that the prime minister was reading. It was in these wars that the military discovered the issues of surveillance (they constantly tried to read and intercept telegraph traffic) and censorship (they wanted to control what was being said).

The way the technology of the telegraph was used had a major impact on the structure and approach of newspapers. In both the UK and US it was clear that rival editors needed to pool resources to pay for the telegraph service, although they did it in very different ways. In the UK it was the provincial papers (which wanted to obtain national, financial, and international news) who all clubbed together to create the Press Association, which benefited from the low telegraph rates offered by the British Post Office. In the US it was the big-city papers, the founders and owners of Associated Press, which saw sharing news between themselves as a source of competitive advantage against smaller rivals. They worked hand in hand with Western Union, which offered exclusivity of carriage to members of the AP. Author Paul Starr observed:

> Nowhere is the contrast in outcomes of telegraphic development clearer than in the case of the press. While the British Post Office provided the same low rates to all newspapers and opened wire service competition, Western Union gave preferential rates to members of the AP and refused to carry other wire services. Britain's postal telegraph helped equalise power between the provincial and metropolitan press, whereas Western Union helped stronger papers dominate weaker ones.[18]

The result was that in the UK the population was far more conversant with, and enthusiastic about, the notion of Empire and world trade, while in the US the population developed a strong sense of their local identity. The fundamental characters of these two nations in the nineteenth century were supported and formed by the way they used the telegraph. The relative insularity and commercial and national focus of the US and the social subsidy policies and global ambitions of Great Britain, established in these years, have endured until the present. The telegraph has a lot to answer for.

FINANCIAL IMPACT

The most enthusiastic users of the expanding telegraph network were those in business, in particular those involved in trading. Information about stock prices, commodity trades, and foreign exchange rates were time sensitive and valuable. In the US commercial messages dominated telegraph traffic, as this huge country needed to connect its markets in terms of information, just as they had already been connected by railroad.

International trade was also growing. From the 1860s the exchange rate between the British pound and the American dollar was of vital importance and reporting it was one of the main uses of the new transatlantic cable. Foreign exchange dealers, even to this day, sometimes refer to this rate as "the cable."

Wall Street and its many stock brokerages needed rapid news of changes in stock prices, which had traditionally been carried by a runner. In 1867 a Mr. Calahan invented a machine that had a converted typewriter at one end of a telegraph line and a special printer with two wheels at the other end. This would output three letter codes for each quoted company and the latest price of that company's stock. The results were printed on a long, thin roll of paper. It was because of the noise this machine made that it became called the "ticker," hence a company's code became its "ticker" symbol, and the waste product became the "ticker-tape" parade of American legend. It is also the reason today's television business programs and some websites continue to display a crawling ticker of stock prices, with the appropriate sound effects: an unconscious echo of the early telegraph.

The Gold & Stock Telegraph Company had been set up in 1866, originally to provide dealers with an automated way to follow prices. By 1870 it had merged with the Calahan Company and diversified into various financial markets. It employed a young Thomas Edison, who developed a much improved technology and registered some 40 telegraph patents. These were bought out for $40,000, which made Edison independently wealthy. He used this to fund his own laboratories at Menlo Park, New Jersey, which developed the phonogram and the electric light bulb.[19]

The stock ticker was a major part of the business of Wall Street for many years and, as stock trading became a national obsession during the 1920s boom, the ticker was the only way for people outside of downtown Manhattan to keep up with events. By 1929, however, the speed and volume of the market became too great for the old technology to keep up with the trading activity, with the result that the printed prices received in remote offices in distant states might be an hour or more behind the real prices actually being traded. In 1929 the market started to experience huge fluctuations in values and the delays in the ticker made the uncertainty much worse. Nevertheless, the apparent reality of the established telegraph ticker in a city remote from New York was more important to people than what might actually be happening on Wall Street.

On Thursday October 24, 1929, "Black Thursday," the market crashed in the morning, but experienced a late-afternoon recovery when bankers stepped in to buy shares in a support operation. John Kenneth Galbraith described the role of the exchange telegraph in his definitive book on the Wall Street Crash:

> Across the country people were only dimly aware of the [late] improvement. By early afternoon when the market started up, the ticker was hours behind [and] continued to grind out the most dismal of news. And news on the ticker was what counted. To many, many watchers it meant they had been sold out, ruined and bankrupted. That the market, after seeming to break them, had recovered was the most chilling of comfort.[20]

TELEGRAPH HERITAGE

From the 1860s onward a series of inventions made the telegraph more effective and, in effect, automated it. This was done at first to reduce the reliance on the skills of expensive Morse operators and then to eliminate them altogether. In the UK, Wheatstone's partner Cooke invented an automatic sender/receiver that used prepunched tape. This hugely increased transmission speed and did away with the need for a real-time Morse operator for telegrams. It was used extensively in the Boer War.

However, Morse code lived on for wireless transmissions. It was Morse that the operator on the *Titanic* used in 1912 to report that his ship had hit an iceberg, and it was used extensively in both world wars. A skilled operator could easily transmit 30 words a minute. There is a fascinating example of a Morse code operator versus cellphone texting contest available on YouTube. The Morse operator wins easily.[21]

In the US Thomas Edison came up with a technique called quadruplex, which allowed four sets of telegraph messages to go down one wire. This meant a huge increase in traffic over the telegraph network and charging for telegrams moved away from price per word and toward paying by the footage of tape utilized by the message.

Early forms of teletype machine, which used keyboards like a typewriter and printed on a normal roll of paper, started to appear after 1900. The Teletype Corporation was founded in Skokie, Illinois in 1906 and the technology was adopted by Associated Press in 1914. The global Telex network, which was used to send text over the telephone system, started in 1920.

For much of its later life the telegram was sent by telephone. The desired message was read to an operator, who would convert it into a telegram to be delivered by special messenger. The cost of this process was simply added to the phone bill.

It was the internet, the natural successor to the telegraph, which finally put pay to the telegram. Email was just too fast and too cheap. The UK Post Office handed its telegram business over to a private company in 2003, and Western Union stopped its service in 2006. The telegram now only exists as a specialist service, offering a novelty style of greeting. Its role as a true communications tool has ended. Nevertheless, the style, grammar, and approach of the telegram have been preserved in the language used by email and text, and the structure of modern communications is based on the original telegraph industry.

BITS AND BAUDS

Another offshoot of the telegraph that lives on to this day as an echo of the telegraph is the Baudot Code. French inventor Emile Baudot developed a system to send messages over the telegraph network using a five-key keyboard. He called each key stroke a "bit" of information and the volume of information transfer was measured in "bauds." In today's technology, the "baud" rate is the speed at which the modern modem transmits data. It is named after Emile, who would have been proud, but probably mystified.

2.10 | Telephone

The telephone started with the modest aim of allowing two people to have a conversation when they were not in the same room. In conception it was far less ambitious than the telegraph. In the early days of the telephone other media, such as newspapers, saw it as a modest business convenience for their employees rather than as an important new invention. But as it developed, the telephone has given us the network structure and exchange technology that enabled radio and television networks to be built. And without the telephone network there would be no internet. This medium has changed society and business by making us all connected.

The telephone extends that most fundamental element of human communication, the spoken word. Its huge success as a medium reflects how much we all like talking to each other. It has created its own language of dialing, ringing, phoning, and holding on. The telephone industry was the rehearsal space for the heated debates about the pros and cons of monopoly suppliers and the true economics of networks.

A telephone call by its nature is normally a one-to-one conversation. It is a rich, personal communication but it is not a broadcast. It is not, normally, a mass medium like a newspaper or television, but it is most certainly a crucial "extension of man." In practice, it was a technical advance on the direct link of the megaphone rather than the coded smoke signal. Although some early experiments used telephones as a broadcast tool, it was as a point-to-point communications device that it found its place.

THE TALKING TELEGRAPH

By the 1870s the telegraph had been in use for more than 30 years and was the dominant commercial communications tool. Its success motivated investors, inventors, politicians, and engineers to seek ways to extend its capabilities. The holy grail of telegraph improvement was to find a way to send actual speech between two points rather than converting text into and out of Morse code. Many people joined the race to crack this problem, but the winner, just, was Alexander Graham Bell. A Scot by birth, Bell was well trained in the science of acoustics and interested in helping people with hearing problems, as his wife was deaf. This motivation combined with training in the new field of electromagnetism and a close study of the telegraph put him in an ideal position to make the breakthrough.

To make a telephone call requires a system that has three main parts: the telephone instrument itself, a microphone and a speaker that convert the human voice into electronic pulses and back again; the transmission lines that connect each telephone instrument to an exchange; and the switching mechanisms in those exchanges that can link individual telephones to each other. Over the years it is the latter two, the less visible technologies of transmission and switching, that have made the telephone the success it is. But in the early days it was all about turning the spoken word into electric signals.

Telegraph pioneers had managed to send simple electrical pulses down a wire to make clicks or print dots on a roll of paper. Bell and his rivals needed first to convert the human voice into such pulses. The key technology of the early telephone was based on the vibration of a metal membrane connected to a magnet. The sound waves from the voice caused the pressure on the membrane to vary and that, in turn, caused variations to the electric voltage generated. This variable voltage went down the telephone wire and the process was reversed at the other end. In effect, a wave of electricity goes down the line, analogous to the sound wave that created it.

In 1876 Bell was granted a patent for a telephone system, which he described as an "improvement on the telegraph." His machine started out as a one-way only instrument, in effect a remote loudspeaker. In March 1876, in Boston, he demonstrated it by sending the now famous message to his assistant "Mr. Watson—come here—I want you" over 100 feet of wire. In reality, the Bell instrument was primitive and very limited. The Bell Telephone Company was founded in July 1876 to exploit the new invention, but initially its backers were met by commercial indifference. So much so in fact that when Bell, needing money to expand, offered to sell his patents to the dominant telegraph operator, Western Union, he was turned down.

However, a few years later Western Union became worried about the threat the new telephone posed to its telegraph business and commissioned the rival inventor, Thomas Edison, to come up with technical improvements that could undermine the Bell patent. Edison did this by discovering that powdered carbon worked much better than a metal membrane in responding to pressure changes. His team developed the carbon microphone, which was a huge success and remained in most telephones until the 1970s. It could be argued that Edison rather than Bell really developed the modern telephone, but as the latter has so many other inventions to his name, it is Bell who keeps the credit.

After a few years of fruitless rivalry, Bell and Western Union/Edison did a deal to work together. This allowed them to develop the best of their combined ideas without competition. The agreement was of concern to lawmakers as it was at least cooperation, or more probably collusion. It set the model for an approach that would later become familiar to the founders of cinema, radio, and television: the attempt to create a monopoly. The enlarged Bell Company showed its flair not so much in creativity and scientific innovation, but in commercial energy, aggression, and the clever use of lawyers. In its first few years it fought and won more than 600 legal actions, mostly to do with patent rights.

The telephone came to the UK in 1878 when Bell himself demonstrated it to Queen Victoria at her home on the Isle of Wight; calls were made to Cowes, Southampton, and London. The puzzle of transmitting the human voice down a wire was solved.

The earliest telephones, like those used by Victoria, were permanently connected to each other, rather like two cans on the end of a piece of string. The world's first telephone exchange was set up in New Haven, Connecticut in 1878: 21 subscribers could be connected with each other by asking the operator to join them by plugging in cords. This was the model for more than ten years until the first automatic exchange opened in 1891. The rotary dial telephone followed in 1896.

CREATING A NETWORK

America fell in love with the telephone much more quickly than the rest of the world. It was partly the size of the country and the need for people in rural areas to be connected with vital services, and partly the fact

THE ROTARY DIAL

The first automated telephone exchange was patented in 1891 by Almon Strowger, who was an undertaker in Kansas City, Missouri. He allegedly objected to the fact that operators in the local manual exchange, possibly after being given inducements, directed calls "for the undertaker" to his competitors. He wanted to give the telephone subscriber an automatic way of reaching their desired person or business without human intervention. In his first exchange, the switch was controlled by the caller repeatedly pushing a button to indicate the desired numbers. The system was very unreliable so in 1896 Strowger's company patented the rotary dial. It sent consistent pulses of electricity that caused physical switches in the exchange to move and select the right number. In early rotary phones the pulses were sent out at the same speed that the user moved the dial, and jerky fingers often caused wrong numbers. This was improved by a spring-loaded mechanism that sent regular pulses, as the dial moved back at a steady speed under its own energy. The rotary dial was phased out by push buttons in the 1970s, but the language of "dialing" remained part of telephone etiquette long after it was gone.

that it was a nation of immigrants who found the spoken word much less daunting than written material. Europeans were much slower on the uptake; distances were less and the post and telegraph were well established. Many Europeans regarded telephones with some suspicion and clung to the established media of letters or telegrams.

In the US local telephone services were developed by hundreds of private companies. However, by far the driving force was AT&T (American Telegraph & Telephone), which was founded in 1885 to take over the combined Bell/Edison patents. Crucially, it owned the long-distance lines between cities. For local operators to provide their subscribers with national links they had to connect to the AT&T network.

The Bell patents ran out in 1894, but the size of AT&T, its long-distance lines, and the financial support of JP Morgan gave it a huge advantage over small and underfunded rivals. It acquired most of them or put them out of business and even ended up in 1909 taking control of Western Union as the telegraph business declined. This gave AT&T effective control of all aspects of the telephone industry: the local lines, the long-distance cables, and the phone equipment.

By 1907 AT&T president Theodore Vail was describing his company's approach as "one policy, one system: universal service." It was in effect a private monopoly, but it was sustained by the proposition that this was a necessary evil to encourage the huge investment in networks and to create common standards. Despite the concerns of many politicians, the 1921 Willis Graham Act recognized the monopoly as being beneficial to national development.

In the UK the numerous early, competing telephone companies were also brought into common ownership, but here they were nationalized and became part of the General Post Office, following the model of the telegraph industry. So by 1912 Britain also had a monopoly supplier, but in this case one under government control.

Both AT&T and the GPO maintained an iron grip on the technology of telephones by demanding that no equipment that was not authorized by them could be connected to their networks. Private and business subscribers were forced to lease their telephones and all instruments looked identical. It is now hard to recall that until the 1960s it was not possible to buy a telephone. Subscribers were forced to rent the type of instrument that AT&T or the GPO specified. In 1968 the Federal Communications

Commission forced AT&T to install standard jacks in people's homes so that they could buy any phone they chose. The UK government imposed similar liberalization soon after.

In 1981 the British government split the telephone network out of the Post Office and created a new company called British Telecom; at about the same time it opened up the market to allow companies to offer telephone services. Similarly, in 1984 AT&T was broken up by federal law and forced to divest itself into local companies called the Baby Bells, and to allow new competitors to use its long-distance lines. However, the 1996 Telecommunications Act in the US opened the door for telephone businesses to become consolidated once again and by 2010 many of the old Baby Bells were back under AT&T ownership.

CHANGING SOCIETY

All new media change the way society works—McLuhan's point about the "medium being the message"—but the telephone has been one of the most influential. Speech is the basic human communication tool. Writing—and its extension, printing—simply communicate and record speech in a permanent form. The telephone allows an actual conversation, at a distance. It is interactive. Questions can be asked. Arguments can be conducted. Agreements can be reached. The telephone enables families and friends to stay in touch. It allows remote businesses to trade in real time. It greatly sped up information flow for newspapers. And, of course, the technology of the physical telephone network led to the development of the internet and the web, arguably the ultimate changers of society.

The slang word "phoney" for false or untrustworthy first appeared around 1900 and it would be satisfying if it could be shown to be linked to distrust of the telephone, but no such evidence exists. It seems more likely that it came from a term for a type of confidence trick involving false, cheap rings. However, the use of the telephone by sales people and its lack of a written record led to a very poor image, even from its earliest years. In *A Social History of the Media*, Briggs and Burke quote from HG Wells, who commented in 1902: "the businessman may sit at home... and tell such lies as he dare not write."[1] As the telephone network developed so did the nuisance caller, the telephone conman, and the unwanted sales pitch. The plots of novels, films, and television series regularly revolve around characters

TELEPHONE "NEWSPAPERS"

In 1893 a Hungarian entrepreneur called Tivadar Puskás started the *Telefon Hírmondó* ("telephone herald") in Budapest. Within a few years he had signed up more than 6,000 subscribers, including the prime minister and the mayor of Budapest. It operated more than 500 kilometres of wire and employed more than 150 people. To all intents and purposes, this telephone newspaper, as it was called in contemporary accounts, functioned like a radio station with a regular program of news and financial information. On Thursday nights it transmitted live music from the local opera house. It continued broadcasting until 1925, when it converted into a radio station.

A similar service began in Paris in 1881, called the *Théâtrophone*. While it also transmitted news, it was more focused on broadcasting operas and plays. In addition to home subscribers, it had listening posts set up in cafés and hotels where people could pay 50 centimes to listen for 5 minutes. French writers Victor Hugo and Marcel Proust both describe using the *Théâtrophone* in their correspondence. Similar services were set up in the UK and Italy but, in the end, most of them converted to radio.[3]

making telephone calls; they rarely hinge on people listening to the radio or reading newspapers.

A BROADCAST MEDIUM

Making and receiving phone calls was intended as a person-to-person communication. Nevertheless, with many people able to access the network ways were found to turn the telephone into a mass medium by offering a shared experience. This happened when multiple callers were listening to the same message. This is not a classic "broadcast" where anyone with the right equipment can listen in, but in the days before radio was invented it was as close to a broadcast as was possible.

In 1892 some 60,000 people paid three pence to go to Crystal Palace to listen, for ten minutes at a time, to a play from the Lyric Theatre in London's West End being transmitted down the telephone line. In 1894 15,000 people in Chicago listened in to the results of local elections.[2] In the rural US isolated farms, on party lines, organized regular music concerts.

Once radio had arrived the telephone could not compete as a true broadcast device, but people found other ways for it to be used as a mass medium. An early example of this is the speaking clock. This was followed by automated weather and travel services, then sports information such as

THE ASCENT OF MEDIA 217

cricket and baseball scores. Later the telephone companies offered entertainment through services such as dial-a-disc to induce people to make calls.

As telephone companies worked out ways to charge premium rates for certain calls, so that the person making the call paid an extra fee as well as the normal call charge, these services expanded to enable entrepreneurs to offer paid services, including racing tips, stock prices, and, later, adult chat lines.

NONVOICE CONNECTIONS

Once the network of telephone lines was in place, people realized that they could be used for a lot more than simple conversations. Telex, fax, and modems provided ways to send text, pictures, and data over a phone line. All of these machines, in simple terms, converted information into a form in which it could be sent over a telephone wire, but most of the users were businesses rather than people at home.

The most novel nonvoice service for private subscribers was France's Minitel. France Telecom gave away millions of cheap terminals, which were simply a small, monochrome television screen and a basic keyboard. They were intended to replace the telephone listings books and allow users to look up numbers for themselves. However, the terminals quickly became used to do home shopping and could handle basic graphics. The French also invented the idea of adult chat lines, called *messageries roses* or "pink mail"; *messagerie* is now the French term for email. Because the terminals were free, and subscriptions and usage costs relatively low, the system became a huge, popular success. More than a third of the population were using it and there were terminals working in some 10 million homes by

SPEAKING CLOCK

The British Post Office offered a "speaking clock" on the telephone system starting in 1936. Users dialed 846, which spelled TIM on the rotary dial, thus giving the service its nickname. It would tell you the time for the price of a phone call and some 100 million calls a year were made at its height. Callers heard the phrase "at the third stroke the time will be X hours and Y seconds precisely." In fact, it wasn't that precise in scientific terms because of the limitations of the telephone network. A similar service began in the US in 1927. Why consumers would pay to hear the time on their telephone after the invention of digital watches remains a mystery of human behavior.

the 1990s. British Telecom had an almost identical service called Prestel, but this was much more expensive; when the BBC and ITV introduced free Teletext services using the "spare" broadcast transmission capacity on the television, the Prestel service was withdrawn. Television Teletext services such as the BBC's Ceefax and ITV's Oracle were, like Minitel and Prestel, early precursors of the web, offering screen-based information and limited interactivity.

THE CELLPHONE

Citizens' Band (CB) radio was a craze in the US in the 1970s. Starting with truckers, it became widespread in the population and demonstrated people's desire to be in touch when away from the home or the office. However, as a technology it was very limited and ineffective.

The core technology of the cellphone is the concept of the local cell. The phone handset connects to a ground station, which serves a cell using a wireless link. The cell station then connects the phone to the normal public phone network. Unlike CB radios, the phones do not connect to each other but only to the cells. As the phone user moves from cell to cell, the system software "hands over" the wireless link, so the connection is continuous even as the phone moves. Both the phone and the cells are relatively low power and have a range of about 5 miles. Thus, to cover a whole country, a large number of cell towers are required. However, this is still much cheaper than

THE MODEM

The original telephone network was designed to carry electromagnetic waves, which replicated the human voice. All elements of the system were designed with this in mind. When computers communicate they do so in digital code, so the information is transmitted at much higher frequencies than the analogue voice. Without intervention to modify this signal, much of the information would be lost over a conventional telephone line. The solution was to modify or modulate the data signal so that it would work in the lower frequency range and be able to be carried on the old-fashioned, predigital telephone network. The electronic box that does this is called a modulator/demodulator, or modem for short. The first device designed to connect home PCs to the telephone system was the Hayes modem in 1977.

installing a fixed-line system, which is why many developing countries have never bothered with a fixed-line network and have gone straight to cellphones.

The SMS (short message service) was initially created for the convenience of engineers, and by the operators to provide a way of communicating with subscribers to give service information such as notification of a stored voicemail message. The various technical committees that approved it did not see it as a medium or commercial application. They set SMS limits at 160 characters per message. The first experimental SMS were sent in 1993 and phone users, particularly the young, adopted SMS as a cool, cheap, and convenient way to reach their friends. An SMS vocabulary developed using some of the conventions of email, such as :) to indicate happy and :(to show sad. Around the world SMS became a multibillion-dollar industry, providing a near perfect example of the way human ingenuity could create a communications tool out of a new technical development that was never intended to be a medium.

Cellphones also offer many other media possibilities. Because their ringing signal is played via a microprocessor rather than a physical bell, they can make pretty much any sound people want. This produced the huge customized ringtone industry. Initially phone technology allowed so-called monotones, which meant a very simple rendition of a tune, then came polyphonic tones, which allowed a crude replication of music, and then true tones, which allowed the phone to play music, just like a radio. As with SMS, ringtones quickly became an unexpected multibillion-dollar market, which led to cellphones becoming portable music players.

Because cellphones have screens to view the numbers being dialed, the phones have a visual element. This was exploited by having the phone show pictures and later videos and, as the capacity of the mobile networks and handsets increased, the cellphone became a gateway to the internet. Smartphones take this to its logical conclusion by being a small, portable computer with internet access that also allows telephone calls.

FUTURE OF THE TELEPHONE

The telephone—in the sense of a weighty instrument connected by wire to a socket in the wall and then linked into a network—is now almost defunct. We talk to each other in any number of places, but in practice we are indifferent to the equipment we use. Digital technology has provided a large number of ways to have a remote conversation, or indeed a remote video linkup. While broadly they all use some form of digital signal, they usually have no need of the old switching gear that made the telephone companies the potent forces they once were.

The fossils of the original telephone medium crop up everywhere in the new media world: the wires of the network that bring the web into our homes, the legislation that governs much media ownership, the competition policy that reflects the tradeoffs between the benefits of monopoly to provide standardization against competition and low prices.

Technology is advancing rapidly, so soon we will all have our own unique personal code, expressed as a number or a name, which will allow us to be reached on any instrument we designate to provide a voice connection. Increasingly the machine we use to make and receive telephone calls does other things. It shows videos, takes pictures, plays music, sends and receives emails, and transmits radio broadcasts. For our convenience it is very likely that this multifunctionality will continue and increase. The humble voice call takes up so little of the vast available bandwidth that most service providers will simply throw it in as a bonus for free. It will be like getting iced water in a restaurant; they could charge you for it, but they have to have it available and every other restaurant provides it for nothing.

2.11 | Recorded Sound

The first recorded piece of music to sell a million copies was in 1907, an aria from the opera *Pagliacci* sung by Enrico Caruso. A century later, leading artists were giving their discs away and music fans were downloading digital tracks for nothing. In the nineteenth century, before recording, the only way for musicians to make money was by charging for tickets to their live performances. In the twenty-first century they are being forced to return to the same approach. From some perspectives it could be argued that the conventional record industry only lasted for about 100 years. However, selling music started long before Caruso and will remain a major media channel long after the last disc is manufactured. The nature of recording technology had a major effect not only on the distribution of music but also on the type of music that could be created.

Inventor Thomas Edison was less than pleased when his rival Alexander Graham Bell produced the first working telephone in 1876, but his response was to look for ways to improve on the instrument. One of his ideas was to create a machine that could record the human voice so that telephone calls could be answered even when the recipient was not in. He patented the phonograph or "talking machine" in 1877 and was subsequently surprised when its main use became for playing music.

Both the telephone and the radio transport sound over distance. Records preserve it over time; they make sound collectable. Recording mediates sound and allows a live speech or a musical performance to be stored. More than most other media, the development of recorded sound was driven by a series of new technologies that had a significant effect on production, distribution, and creative possibilities. The industry of recorded music has made fortunes for performers and record companies over the past century, but now its economics have been transformed, and not all for the better, by digitization.

EARLY MUSIC

The human voice was the main feature of medieval church music, which was chanted rather than played, but it achieved great range, volume, and emotion. Early forms of organ were used from about 650 AD to complement chanting.

Basic musical notation developed abut the same time as primitive writing. What appear to be directions for singing a song have been found on a clay tablet from 4,000 years ago. The ancient Greeks had crude methods to describe the sounds of music using symbols alongside text to show how a hymn should be sung.

Attempts to develop complex musical description are then not recorded until around 850 AD, when monks used symbols that we call "neumes" to show how to perform religious chants. Prior to that point we assume that harmony and pitch were communicated simply by experience. Neumes were written down using a four-line grid, the direct ancestor of today's five-line music staff.

The five-line grid is, in simple terms, a graph, with the pitch of a note on the vertical axis and the sequences of notes on the horizontal. The duration of each note is shown by the nature of the note symbol itself.

Up until about 600 AD church music developed along local lines, but then Pope Gregory I arranged to have it classified and organized into the so-called Gregorian chants, which were used systematically to accompany specific services and festivals. The music now gave structure and context to the ceremonies. It helped people understand what was happening at the event and prompted them to know how to participate and respond. Over time monks started to add clearly understandable text verses—lyrics—to the chanted melodies. These were called "tropes" and added information and meaning to the service.

In time the music became separated from the verse and more instruments were used both to complement and then to replace the human voice. From the mid-1400s musicians started to perform dance tunes at the royal courts and in noble households. Nevertheless, they would have been very small groups playing familiar melodies of the day; the equivalent of the modern string quartet. There is a persistent but unfounded myth that the tune of the English folksong *Greensleeves* was composed by Henry VIII. What is certain is that the song is referred to by Shakespeare and was performed during his time.[1] The desire by the wealthy to have music in their homes led to the development of chamber music, where a small group of professionals used stringed instruments to provide a background to dancing.

Opera as an art form emerged in Florence at the height of the Italian Renaissance. The wealthy Florentines were aware that Greek drama had included music and with a passion for reviving all things classical, they wanted to create their own musical theatre. A group of intellectuals (including the father of astronomer Galileo) formed an academy, which coined the words "opera" (Latin for work) and "melodrama" (meaning drama with music). Their first opera, *Dafne*, was presented in 1594.[2] The opera format was a hit and other composers, such as Monteverdi, invented devices like special arias written for the stars to show off their skills. From Florence the opera quickly spread across Italy, Germany, and France.

To present an opera a large group of musicians was needed and this gave rise to the orchestra as we know it today. Once orchestras existed, composers started to think about writing music that would make use of their breadth and depth of sound. The word "symphony" means sounding together. It had been used in various different ways in musical history, but it was not until the mid-1700s that the idea of the symphony orchestra was developed. The combination of many musicians led to the possibility of a new style of music that was so big and rich that it became an entertainment in itself, not merely an adjunct to singing or dancing. The availability of the orchestra—in effect a new multifaceted instrument—led to the development of concerts.

Folk or traditional music, using homemade string instruments and improvised drums alongside everyday objects like spoons and washboards, was popular in homes, but until the late 1800s professional performances were rare. This was partly because of the lack of instruments, which were expensive and partly lack of interest in the cultural activities of "ordinary people" by the patrons of orchestras and concert halls. However, as relative wealth spread and upright pianos and guitars became cheap, folk music grew far more accessible. Songs dating back to traveling minstrels were adapted and developed. Jazz was recognized as a form in the late 1800s. The music hall thrived. Blues developed from African music and provided the songs of prison work gangs and the military.

SHEET MUSIC

Before phonographs and gramophones, music could only be experienced by the audience first hand. The performance had value at one time and in one place. Composers could sell tickets, but also enjoyed income from their patrons. For instance, Mozart's patron was Emperor Joseph II. Although musical notation was being printed within a few years of Gutenberg starting his press, it was for the convenience of professional performers rather than as a source of income for the composer. The sale of musical scores was a tiny market until the 1800s when the ownership of pianos became widespread.

The Victorians developed a taste for playing music at home. By the late 1800s the piano was a feature of schools, public houses, and most middle-class homes. All these newly minted pianists needed something to play. Sheet music publishers Chappell & Co. were established in London's Bond Street in 1811 and had developed a reputation among professionals for distributing work by classical composers like Beethoven. However, it was with the rising ownership of pianos that their business really took off and they enjoyed huge success by publishing the likes of Gilbert and Sullivan.

In the US the early sheet music business was nicknamed "Tin Pan Alley," after an area in New York around 28th Street, between Fifth and

Sixth Avenues, where the growing music publishing firms congregated and aspiring song writers would go to sell their ideas. The sheet music industry in both the UK and the US lobbied politicians for increased copyright protection and by 1900 an international legal framework was established. Although originally intended to protect printed music, it was the same structure that was later used for records. To protect composers' rights as opposed to performers', organizations were created to collect royalties when their work was used. The Performing Rights Society (PRS) in the UK and the American Society of Composers, Authors, and Publishers (ASCAP) were both formed in 1914. Throughout the century of recorded sound the issue of copyright has been a constant battle and has nearly always seen the music industry at first resisting then reluctantly accepting new distribution techniques.

THE PIANO

The piano has had a huge impact on music because it is relatively easy to play and very versatile. The instrument as we now know it was developed in the early 1700s for the Medici family, as an improvement on earlier stringed instruments such as the harpsichord. Bach and Mozart were early adopters and once they had written popular works, people wanted to learn to play. Metal-framed and upright pianos emerged in the 1800s, which led to the instrument becoming a feature of many homes, clubs, and schools. The first automatic-player piano was made in 1863. Keyboards, whether used on analogue pianos or computer-based instruments, remain the most popular device for composers.

RECORDING TECHNOLOGIES

The medium of recorded sound—the cylinder, wax and vinyl record, tape, or disc—evolved through the application of a series of scientific discoveries, most of which were intended for other purposes. The recording industry has experienced dramatic booms and busts as new technologies have both enabled and undermined its ability to sell music. Science has shaped the development of all media, but its impact on recorded sound has been particularly dramatic. New technologies have changed the way people composed and performed music, as well as the way consumers have received and paid for it.

Phonographs

Edison's solution for a machine to record the human voice was reminiscent of cuneiform writing. He attached a stylus to the sharp end of a large horn, which vibrated with sound to cut a grove in a rotating cylinder covered in tin foil. His machine worked perfectly and his first recording was of himself speaking the words "Mary had a little lamb." In the early machines each cylinder record was a one-off; there was no mechanism for duplication. It was thought useful as a dictating machine, but not as a home entertainment system. However, owners of the phonographs often used them to record amateur musical performances, in particular themselves singing. Examples still exist of cylinders that were sent to friends and relatives. The early phonographs became like the audio cassette machine some 70 years later.

Gramophones

Ten years after Edison's first patent, another inventor, Emile Berliner, perfected an alternative approach, which was to make a recording on a flat wax disc. This meant that the stylus traveled at different speeds (faster at the outside of the disc and slower in the middle), but had the great advantage that one master could be used to create multiple copies. Berliner called it the "gramophone" and his discs "gramophone records." Unlike Edison, who was focused on recording speech, Berliner was interested in music from the start and he devised his machine with the specific idea of being able to make records for sale; the musical version of printing books. As with most new media, the early adopters of the gramophone were the wealthy, as both the records and the player were very expensive. Berliner realized the commercial potential of recorded music and registered in America the trademark of a dog called Nipper listening to a gramophone, which had first been used in the UK by HMV.

The bulk of the new gramophone records were devoted to classical music, but the early sound, while a great novelty, was of very low quality. As prices came down, the gramophone became a fixture in middle-class homes and many were built into exotic pieces of furniture. They occupied the space in drawing rooms and lounges that would be usurped by the radio set a generation later and the television a generation after that.

Edison reluctantly recognized that the mass-produced disc was a better solution than his cylinder and by 1912 has switched to his own, proprietary disc technology. The Edison vs. Berliner competition was an early example of the sort of Betamax vs. VHS format battle that confuses consumers and holds back industry growth.

Evolution of discs

By 1915 hundreds of recording companies had sprung up. A few continued with their own incompatible technologies of cylinders or discs, but most agreed a common technical standard, the 78 rpm (revolutions per minute) shellac record giving about three minutes of music per side. This approach was dominant for some 30 years and created conventions that prevailed long after more flexible technical solutions become available. Classical music was broken up into three-minute chunks to fit onto one side of the wax disc. Jazz was reduced from the long, improvised versions played in the clubs to a more structured, disc-friendly form. As Mark Katz reports in *Capturing Sound*, when Stravinsky composed his *Serenade for Piano* in 1925 he wrote each of the four movements to last three minutes.[3]

The "long-playing" record or LP, made of vinyl, was introduced by Columbia in 1948. Spinning at a slower 33 rpm, it provided a much higher-quality reproduction and ran for up to 30 minutes a side. The cheaper 45 rpm "single" came in at about the same time, introduced by RCA Victor. This was to become the predominant format of rock and roll and the mainstay of the jukebox. During the 1950s these new formats replaced the old 78 and by the end of the decade it

HIS MASTER'S VOICE

One of the most famous media trademarks is the dog used to promote the brand His Master's Voice or HMV. In 1889 a British artist called Francis Barraud painted a small dog of indeterminate breed called Nipper looking into the horn of an Edison phonograph. He registered the image as "Dog Looking at and Listening to a Phonograph." He hoped to exhibit it at the Royal Academy, but was turned down. He then tried to sell it to the Edison company, but was told it was not interested as "dogs do not listen to phonographs." Then he got lucky. Edison's new competitor, Berliner, said it would buy the painting, but only if the phonograph was painted over to be replaced by one of the gramophones that played the new flat discs. Barraud agreed and the modified picture, renamed "His Master's Voice," was used by the company from 1900 onward.

ALBUM COVERS

The original 78 rpm records were issued in brown-paper sleeves with a cut-out in the middle so the record label was visible. By the 1920s many people stored their records in albums made of board or leather. Rather like bookbinding before them, these were designed to fit in with the décor of the owner's home rather than to promote or distinguish the record. In 1939 artwork was used for the first time on the covers of 78s. In 1948 Columbia was the first company to employ an art director, Alex Steinweiss, to design an illustrated sleeve for the new format 33 rpm LPs. One of his first designs was for the 1949 musical hit *South Pacific*.

In the 1950s companies introduced the gatefold cover, which was made of card and allowed far more creative potential. Throughout the 1950s album covers resembled magazines, with an obvious strong influence from the likes of *Vogue* and extensive use of color photography. In the 1960s performers demanded a less conventional approach and covers began to be controversial. The Beatles in particular pushed the boundaries. Their 1966 album, *Yesterday And Today*, had to be withdrawn as the original, featuring the band dressed in butchers' smocks and surrounded by dismembered dolls, created too much protest. They then commissioned what is often cited as the greatest album cover when artist Peter Blake created the montage on *Sgt. Pepper's Lonely Hearts Club Band*. The album cover became a key selling point of some LPs, which were collected as much for their cover art as for their music.

was possible to have stereophonic sound, as each groove of the record was adapted to carry two channels of audio information. Pop music exploited the stereo capabilities.

Electrical recording

The way music was recorded had a major impact on what could be offered on disc and therefore on sales. Prior to the 1920s master records were made by a mechanical analogue process. The performer would sing or play into a large horn, which was physically connected to a needle that cut the master disc; in effect the reverse of the process by which it was played. Western Electric (the manufacturing arm of Bell Labs) had developed a range of products to manipulate sound electronically. These included microphones, amplifiers, loudspeakers, and mixer desks. By 1924 it had perfected a process of electronic recording, which provided much better sound quality. It was the same research effort that created the optical sound process that turned silent movies into "talkies." An extension of these recording techniques led to electrical instruments, particularly the electric guitar, which by the late 1950s was hugely popular as the core sound of rock and roll.

Magnetic tape

Magnetic tape was used for sound recording in Germany from the 1930s for scientific and military purposes. It was pioneered in secret by BASF as part of the German war effort. One of those who commercialized it in the 1940s was a US Army Signals engineer called Jack Mullin, who had been given captured German equipment at the end of the war. He modified it to create a commercial machine and in 1947 showed it to the singer Bing Crosby, who wanted the technology to allow him to prerecord his radio shows. This would avoid him having to perform live for the remote East Coast market so that he could spend more time on the Los Angeles golf course. Crosby arranged for $50,000 of investment to back Mullin in a California company called Ampex, which went on to develop high-quality studio-based systems. These revolutionized the recording of live events and had a major impact on the sound of rock-and-roll records, as they allowed multitracking, which led to layered sound. In 1950 Ampex went on to develop the video recorder, which in its turn revolutionized television production.

Reel-to-reel tape machines became a familiar element of recording studios and radio stations, but were expensive and bulky and had limited domestic sales. The first miniaturized audio

THE ELECTRIC GUITAR

The musical instrument that made the biggest contribution to the recorded music industry (and radio) was the electric guitar. Artificial amplification and microphones were used in traditional guitars in the 1930s to help them be heard as part of the big "swing" bands. Solid-body electric guitars appeared in the 1940s, pioneered by Les Paul and Leo Fender. Fender was a radio repair engineer who specialized in amplification. He devised the first magnetic pickup and introduced his Telecaster in 1946 and the Stratocaster in 1954.

MIDI

MIDI (musical instrument digital interface) has changed the way music is composed and has been a major influence on the sound of music. Introduced in 1982, it is a hardware and software protocol that allows a wide range of electronic instruments to be connected to and manipulated by computer. This led to single-keyboard synthesizers that can replicate almost any musical effect. MIDI allows an individual composer, who needs no classical training, to work alone and create a huge range of music.

cassette for consumer use was launched by Philips in 1964 and the first recorded music was offered on cassette in 1966. Rather like Edison's original phonograph, cassettes were initially thought of as a dictation medium and in their early form their quality was not good enough for music. It took some years for the technology to become popular with consumers, as the small tape decks were expensive.

Innovations such as Dolby noise reduction improved sound quality, and manufacturing in Asia reduced cost. People found cassettes very convenient, particularly in cars. They also realized that they could record as well as play back. When manufacturers started to produce tape decks with built-in radios, the tape format took off and widespread illegal copying of music became an industry problem for the first time.

Cassette tapes were given a huge boost by the launch of the Sony Walkman in 1979 and in the early 1980s prerecorded cassettes were outselling albums. The music industry believed that home taping was costing it billions of dollars a year.[4] By 1984 the BPI (British Phonographic Institute) was sufficiently worried to launch an antitaping campaign. This had a picture of a cassette on top of a pair of crossed bones (aping the pirates' motif) with the text "Home Taping Is Killing Music!" This was a version of what would happen 30 years later with MP3 downloads.

Compact discs

In the late 1970s both Philips and Sony were working on versions of an optical disc read by laser with digitally encoded sound. By 1980 they had jointly created their first CD and released their first experiment, music by Richard Strauss. A driving force to make the CD a fundamentally superior technology was Sony Music President Norio Ohga, who had trained to be an opera singer. He wanted a format that could accommodate all of a long classical composition like Beethoven's 75-minute 9th Symphony without having to change discs.[5] In 1982 Sony manufactured the first commercial CD player, which was launched in Japan, with the first album being Billy Joel's *52nd Street*. CDs were launched in America the following year. The first CD to sell a million copies was *Brothers in Arms* by Dire Straits. CDs quickly overtook both vinyl and tape.

Digital downloading

CDs offered digital sound, but they were initially "read-only," so in their first decade if people wanted to copy their contents they had to use an analogue tape recorder, just as they had with vinyl. This was time consuming and led to a loss of quality. Once the CD burner (a device to record your own CDs) was supplied as a normal accessory for most home computers, the ability to create pirate CDs increased dramatically. However, it was the ability to share digital audio files over the internet that really caused a revolution.

MP3 stands for "MPEG 3," or in full "Moving Pictures Experts Group Audio Layer III." In simple terms it is a commonly agreed software format that allows the compression and subsequent reproduction of audio material. It was developed by German university researchers on behalf of the film industry to handle the transport of large computer files. It, and similar types of software, enabled portable digital media players. The MP3 format was approved in 1995 and the first MP3 player on a computer was launched that year. One of the first portable players was the Rio in 1998. Apple, which uses similar software, launched its first iPod in 2001.

What turned MP3 from a technical nicety into a nightmare for the record industry was peer-to-peer file sharing. Up until the late 1990s most computers were linked in what was called a client/server structure, where files and software on a remote PC (the client) were accessed by a link to the master computer, the server. Peer-to-peer (P2P) allowed any computer connected to the internet to share files with any other. Thus if an enthusiast had stored hundreds of their favorite music tracks on their hard drive, they could use P2P to make all these tracks available to other people instantly and without charge. In effect it was the same action as lending your albums to a friend, but now you could simultaneously lend them to 100,000 people who could make their own instant copies.

Internet sites such as Napster, launched in 1999, allowed computer users to share music tracks and provided a way of indexing and labeling them. People wanting music could find it on any connected machine and it could then be copied across to portable digital players or burned to a CD. The music industry saw this as stealing. Lars Ulrich, the drummer in heavy metal band Metallica, commented about Napster:

> This is something that's clearly illegal. If people want to steal our music, why don't they go into Tower Records and put the album under their shirts instead of hiding behind their computers.[6]

Napster's legal flaw was that it used a centralized server that could be identified and attacked by the legal system, and legal action closed it down in 2001. Since then many hundreds of other file-sharing programs have developed that cannot be easily policed as they have no central element.

The Apple iTunes store and the associated iPod (and the later iPhone and iPad) offered a legal way to distribute and pay for digital music tracks. Apple has sold some 200 million iPods and the iTunes store has sold more than 5 billion tracks; within five years it became a bigger retailer of music in America than Wal-Mart. The product has been successful because it offers a very effective way to store, catalogue, share, and play music. Apple has the enthusiastic support of the record industry. Other online services have developed, such as Spotify (which also has the music industry's blessing) that allows streaming of music tracks in return for listening to advertising; in effect, a music-only radio service over the web.

THE RECORDED MUSIC INDUSTRY

The music industry is now dominated by four major organizations: Universal Music, Sony BMG, Warner Music, and EMI. Nevertheless, some 25 percent of records are still released by smaller, independent companies, which are attractive to new artists. The history of the industry is one of booms and slumps. In the booms—such as the 1910s when low-priced gramophones arrived; the 1950s with the introduction of vinyl LPs; the 1960s when rock and roll came of age; and the 1980s after the introduction of the CD—new companies emerge to offer new artists an independent alternative. In the slumps—the 1930s because of the rise of radio and the Great Depression; the late 1970s reflecting home taping; and the late 2000s because of digital downloading—there is significant consolidation, with the independents being bought out by the majors.

A musical performer has four ways to make an income. They can persuade an audience to pay to listen (the concert); use their performance to attract an audience and then sell them something else (the traveling minstrel); sell a recording of their performance (the record business); or sell the rights to the music they have created (royalties for copyright). The complex music industry of record labels, publishers, record stores, concert promoters, and online downloading has built up to exploit these opportunities.

It would be simple, although inaccurate, to assume that the music

AUDIO BOOKS

The idea of recording books dates back to the 1930s, when charitable foundations commissioned "sound books" for blind people. Listening Books was founded in the UK in 1959. By the 1970s audio books had become a popular format on the newly developed tape cassettes and stories read by actors became a welcome distraction for children on long car journeys. The BBC produces a large number of titles and in the US producers have created a trade body, the APA (Audio Publishers Association), which estimates that more than 25 percent of American adults have listened to an audio book. Titles are also now available for digital download. It has become a $1 billion a year industry, although it remains small in comparison with recorded music. The offer of speech as part of a Kindle book may end this as a separate business.

available simply reflects changing public taste. In fact recording technology, copyright law, and the interplay with film, radio, and television have also been major influences. Early records were mostly of vocalists, as the recording and playback technology of the first gramophones could not handle most instruments. Violins were almost inaudible. Drums could often not be used because the percussion caused the recording needle to jump. Double basses simply did not register.

The first great recording star was Italian opera singer Enrico Caruso, who ultimately made some 500 discs. In a rather satisfying example of media circularity, there is a YouTube video showing his original recording of *Vesti la giubba* being played on an early gramophone. You can hear the recording of 100 years ago via the web even though it has long ceased to be available on disc.

The first recorded music boom roughly coincided with the so-called Jazz Age (1918–29). Jazz was widely played, popular, and cheap to produce and jazz records started to be made in large numbers from 1917. The best known exponent was the Original Dixieland Jass Band, a multiracial group from New Orleans who later changed their spelling to the more familiar form. They had the first million-selling jazz title with "Livery Stable Blues."

The film studios realized that music was a vital part of the cinema experience even before the "talkies" came along and as early as 1914 studios employed their own composers. In theatres pianists, organists, and even a small orchestra were provided to play along with the silent movie. As the technology improved, cinemas played specially made records to accompany a film.

After electronic recording came in a much wider range of music could be captured, including dance bands and light orchestras. Nevertheless, a combination of the growth of radio, which in effect offered free music, and the weak economics of the Great Depression significantly cut record sales. In 1927 104 million discs and 987,000 players were sold. By 1932 sales had dramatically dropped to 6 million discs and 40,000 players.[7] A number of the original companies went bankrupt (including Columbia in the US, which ended up being purchased by its British subsidiary). The lack of retail sales meant that during the 1930s the jukebox in clubs became a very significant market for record companies.

The success of synchronized sound in motion pictures, a revival of interest in musicals, and the end of the Depression helped revitalize record sales. Improved recording quality and better domestic playback machines made big-band music popular. This led to the "Swing Era" of 1935–46, which featured band leaders like Benny Goodman and Glenn Miller. In 1939, *Time* magazine reported: "Of the 12 to 24 discs in each of today's U.S. jukeboxes, from two to six are usually Glenn Miller's."[8] Crooners like Bing Crosby and Perry Como also found new fans; this style of singing would have been impossible before microphones, as the performer would have been inaudible against the orchestra.

The blues

In 1941 ASCAP had a major dispute with radio broadcasters over royalties; as a result, all records administered by the Society were withdrawn from airplay in the US. This meant that composers such as Irving Berlin, Cole Porter, and George Gershwin as well as Glenn Miller were off the air. This led to stations playing more rhythm and blues and jazz and what was called at the time "race music," featuring black artists like Bessie Smith and Louis Armstrong. These artists and their record labels, who were not ASCAP members, were happy to sign deals much less generous than those demanded by the established stars. Although the dispute was resolved after 10 months, it gave the public a taste for new styles of music and after the Second World War a much wider range of genres was played on radio and sold in record stores. The introduction of vinyl long-playing discs plus on-location tape recording freed artists from the constraints of the three-minute studio track and allowed long, improvised jazz sets and live concert performances to be recorded and sold.

COLUMBIA RECORDS

Columbia started life in 1888 selling Edison phonographs and cylinders in Washington, DC, the district from which it took its name. It was always an innovative company: it pioneered flat-disc records in 1901, and introduced the black wax disc in 1903 and the double-sided record in 1908. In 1925 it was the first company to move to electronic recording, in 1938 the first to hire an art director to design record sleeves, and in 1948 it introduced the 33 rpm long-playing record. One of its first albums in the new format was by Frank Sinatra. Columbia did well with folk rock and its artists included Bob Dylan, Simon and Garfunkel, and Janis Joplin.

Records, radio, and rock and roll

The development of radio had been a setback for the record business in the 1930s, but in the 1950s the arrival of television undermined the popularity of radio. US radio broadcasters abandoned their mixed speech and music formats because the variety shows and soap operas had moved to television. They started to play records to save money. The profession of "disk jockey" had arrived and rock and roll turned out to be the salvation of both the radio stations and the record industry. It was the music style that gave radio a new, young audience and the popularity of top 40 countdown shows led to an explosion of record sales in the new 45 rpm format. This laid the ground for the rock music of the 1960s, which for a period made recorded music the most valuable of all consumer media. The fascinating question is where rock and roll came from and why.

In 1951 a DJ in Cleveland Ohio called Alan Freed (on-air nickname Moondog) started to play rhythm and blues on his show and described it as "rock and roll" (the term had been around for some years in the African-American music community). In 1952 he organized the Moondog Coronation Ball in Cleveland, Ohio. The event was a sellout but was shut down after just one number when a fight broke out in the audience; a fitting start for this kind of music. The first big hits were Elvis Presley in 1954 with "That's Alright (Mama)" and Bill Haley and the Comets in 1955 with "Rock Around the Clock."

In Britain's clubs skiffle music and jazz had become popular, as had rhythm and blues. The first British rock-and-roll record was "Move It" by Cliff Richard in 1958. The rock group formula of two electric guitars, a bass guitar, and drums had the great merit of being cheap and the music lent itself to the three-minute tracks demanded by radio

JUKEBOX

Soon after Edison invented the phonogram, by 1889 there were coin-operated machines in public places that let people listen to two minutes of recorded music. The quality was poor and in the days before electric loudspeakers people had to hear the music using listening tubes. Nevertheless, the novelty was huge and the first nickel-in-the-slot phonograph in San Francisco took $1,000 in six months. The first real jukebox (the word jook is African–American slang for a dance) was manufactured in 1927 by the Automated Music Industry Company. It played standard 78 rpm records using amplification and electric speakers.

In the Prohibition era jukeboxes became a fixture in speakeasies. When alcohol sales were legalized in 1933 and normal bars opened again, they wanted music but could not afford live bands. In the Depression years home sales of records had collapsed, but by 1938 there were some 500,000 jukeboxes in America and a staggering 40 percent of all records sold were for use on this public medium.[9] By the 1950s the 45 rpm single was in widespread use and jukeboxes had the familiar automatic changers, which required the middle of vinyl singles to be punched out.

and the 45 rpm disc. Although the UK did not have commercial radio, offshore pirate stations and Radio Luxembourg emerged to fill the gap in promoting the new music. The huge demand for rock and roll was the backdrop to the formation of groups like The Beatles, The Rolling Stones and The Beach Boys.

The 1960s and 1970s were an extraordinarily successful period for recorded music. New small groups were constantly forming. The latest tracks were featured in radio top 40 shows and were sold as singles. Successful artists collected their hits together and sold them again as albums. While live performance was seen as a way to boost record sales, it was not normally a profitable activity in itself.

Beyond original rock and roll

The record boom encouraged many new groups to be formed covering a wide range of musical styles. Folk rock (Pentangle, Fairport Convention) offered a melodic alternative to heavy metal (Led Zeppelin, Black Sabbath), which focused on volume and aggression, and progressive rock (Pink Floyd, Yes), which featured a complex technical mixture of electronic effects. Garage rock (Patti Smith, The Ramones) was a return to more basic rock and roll.

The large number of new groups were served by an equally large number of newly formed independent music labels. Record shops opened new branches. Radio stations started to specialize in just one type of music to segment the audience.

MOTOWN

Motown Records was founded in Detroit in 1959, the first recording company to be owned by African-Americans and feature African-American music. The name is a contraction of Motor Town, the nickname for Detroit. The company's first hit band was Smokey Robinson and the Miracles. Over the next ten years it launched a huge number of acts, including The Four Tops, The Jackson 5, Marvin Gaye, Diana Ross & The Supremes, and Stevie Wonder. Motown had a very distinct sound and many of the early songs were written and produced by the brothers Brian and Eddie Holland and Lamont Dozier. Their hits include "Stop! In the Name of Love" and "Reach Out I'll Be There." After moving from Detroit to Los Angeles, Motown was eventually acquired by a major label and is now part of Universal.

Mechanical music

By the 1960s performers were using tape recording to create effects that could never happen in live performance. The Beatles' "Strawberry Fields Forever" is famous for being created from two separate takes in different keys and tempos, which were merged by changing the speed of the tape during playback.

By the 1980s a great deal of music was being artificially created, either by electronic effects in the studio or by club DJs manipulating discs on turntables. Digital sampling and sound processing made it possible to create hit records without any conventional instruments. Music also became a crucial element of television, which commissioned large volumes of original work, much of which was produced by synthesizers rather than conventional composers and musicians. However, despite the immense popularity of music, sales of vinyl albums and singles started to decline.

Impact of the CD

By the 1980s record sales were sliding badly as people made more use of home taping and listened to high-quality FM radio. The record business was saved, for a period at least, by the development of the compact disc, one of the most rapidly adopted consumer electronic products. Easy-to-store CDs overtook both vinyl and cassettes as the medium of choice and they encouraged people to replace their old album collections with the same music in the new very high-quality digital format. CDs brought significant benefits to record companies and retailers, but had a limited stimulus on the creation of music. While digitization of sound made the CD possible, it would be digitization that would fundamentally change the economics of the music industry.

Digital sound

Making a taped copy of analogue sound always resulted in a slight loss of quality. A copy of a copy lost more. Copying was also time consuming. However, once music was digital it was possible to make unlimited perfect copies—clones, in fact—almost instantly. As the personal computer revolution got underway and the internet became ubiquitous, it was easy to send audio files from machine to machine.

The role of the traditional record company as promoter was called into question by British group Arctic Monkeys. In 2003 they were an unknown band from Sheffield, but at local concerts they made demonstration CDs and gave these away. Fans started to burn their own CDs of the music and passed them on to others. The fans—not the band—also started a Myspace website that allowed their music to be heard. The result was that without conventional promotion the group had sellout concerts. When they did finally sign a record deal in 2005, their first single, "I Bet You Look Good on the Dancefloor," went straight to number 1.

In 2007 rockers Radiohead questioned the conventional record company's role in physical distribution. They made their new album *In Rainbows* available on their own website for download at whatever price a fan chose to pay, or even for nothing. Although they did not make the results public, it was reported that six out of ten fans did not pay anything. The stunt gained huge publicity and when the album was made available as a conventional CD three months later, it went to the number one position in both the UK and US, suggesting that all the free publicity and the free downloads did not harm sales.[10] Radiohead guitarist Ed O'Brien expressed dissatisfaction with the traditional record industry when commenting on the band's decision to break its links with EMI following the latter's acquisition by private equity firm Terra Firma:

> It's been taken over by someone who's never owned a record company before... and they don't realise what they are dealing with. It was really sad to leave but they wouldn't give us what we wanted. They don't understand the record industry.[11]

And in 2011 rock band Kaiser Chiefs came up with a further innovation in an attempt to add more value to digital music. They offered fans the opportunity to put together their own album compilation from 20 new tracks and to choose their own unique artwork for an album cover. The result could then be downloaded for £7.50. In addition, if fans sold their version of the album to friends via Facebook and other sites, those fans were rewarded with £1, making them part of the retail sales process. The site plays the tracks while the fan works and the whole thing has the feel of an immersive video game. The band's lead singer Ricky Wilson explained:

> You've got to embrace being digital but the only problem is it is not very tactile... there's no ownership. [With this idea] it's not just that

you get your own artwork and tracklisting. It's the experience of making your own album does make the intangible tangible.[12]

THE FUTURE OF RECORDED SOUND

We now listen to more music than at any time in history. iPods, cellphones, radio, and web services make it universally available. Its use in films, television programs, commercials, ringtones, and increasingly behind web pages makes it omnipresent. A few generations ago our forebears had to make a special trip to a church or a concert hall to experience a musical performance; now we all have it, everywhere, all the time.

The way we hear and make music seems to hold a key to understanding the way our minds work. A previous chapter recalled the cliché of one picture being worth a thousand words, but with music the emotional impact can be even more dramatic. Can anyone really say that they hear the opening few bars of a national anthem or the start of one of the great rock songs without experiencing a strong reaction?

There is no reason to assume that recorded music (and speech) will not continue to be an extremely popular part of people's lives, be it listening for pleasure, as part of a film, or as a complement to some other activity. But the question is how we will receive it and pay for it. For a century the traditional delivery method has been the disc or tape. This was purchased, like any other retail item, from a shop. The retailer, the record publisher, and the artist all got their share and a huge industry developed. However, with digital music the model has changed; and there is no going back.

Musicians will continue to compose and perform, partly for the love of the art and partly because they will always be able to make money from live events. But traditional record companies and record stores have already experienced drastic changes. In addition, music copyright was often sold to publishers and record companies at an early stage of a musician's career. In effect, they became employees or at least contractors to a record label. That is likely to change as artists retain their copyright and distribute their music more directly.

Radio, both broadcast and via the web, will be an important shop window for new music. And we seem happy to pay to see that music performed. 2008 was the first year when receipts from live concerts in the UK (£1.28 billion) was greater than the income from selling records (£1.24 billion). When releasing this statistic the Performing Rights Society noted that album sales for 2008 had dropped back to the same level as in 1986. The trend away from paying for recorded music will continued to accelerate.

People will still buy some CDs for convenience, but they may well be burned to order; analogous to books being printed in store. Mass production in advance of sale no longer makes sense. Vinyl will survive as a collector's art form much as hardback, illustrated books will continue. Access to a vast musical library will be a normal feature of every computer, telephone, and home entertainment system. The vast bulk of music will be in digital form and the search and indexing capabilities of the web will mean that the accessible range of music on offer will be more extensive than at any time previously.

It may be that the salvation of the industry will be a return to quality. Most digital music is heard on relatively cheap equipment and some digital music files lose sound quality in the compression process. Veteran music producer Jimmy Iovine (whose artists include Bruce Springsteen and Lady Gaga) argued in the *Financial Times* that the answer to piracy is for music to insist on high quality standards, analogous to 3D in cinema and HD in television.[13] True fans would then pay for the extra audio quality that pirated material could not offer.

The recorded music industry was the first to experience the transformation of digital technology on both creation and distribution. And it was the first to see the disintermediation effect of the web, which allows consumers and creators direct access to one anther. Fred Goodman's *Fortune's Fool* describes it as "the canary in the internet coalmine."[13] The lessons from music are now resonating in all other media.

2.12 | Radio

Radio takes the magic of the campfire story, the message of the market-place orator, and the thrill of the live performance out from a live audience and into the home. It created global personalities who became household names but who, unlike the movie icons, seemed real and accessible. It produced great media institutions such as NBC, CBS, and the BBC and enjoyed a dot-com-type boom when it launched. It was the first battleground for electronic copyright and redefined the practice of politics and advertising. From the 1920s to the 1950s radio dominated the media landscape.

The differences between radio in the UK and the US are striking and continue to this day. The two broadcasting systems provide a fascinating insight into the divergent social and commercial attitudes of these two English-speaking nations, and into the structure and ownership of their rest of the electronic media industries.

For a child who grew up in England in the 1960s, radio had two distinct personalities: the authority and paternalism of the BBC and, in stark contrast, the clandestine, beneath-the-blankets conspiracy of Radio Luxembourg and Radio Caroline, the "pirates" with American accents (real or adopted) who beamed in the latest in music and attitude. For an American of the same generation the essence of radio consists in the irreverent spinning of discs, bringing music and excitement to kids in their cars.

Those who were adults between the two world wars remember radio as the medium that brought into their homes drama, variety, comedy, news, and politics. It was radio that hosted FDR's weekly address and Winston Churchill's great speeches. It broadcast the British King's Christmas message and the Mayor of New York City's children's stories. The radio was the center of the living room and the source of all entertainment. Families gathered around to hear Arthur Askey and Tommy Handley in Britain and Jack Benny and George Burns in America.

The pioneers of radio took performers from the music hall and ideas from newspapers, but for the most part, they made it up as they went along. For the digital natives of the internet generation the importance of broadcast radio is hard to fathom, as audio entertainment is now available in such abundance through so many different channels. We still spend more time with audio than any other medium, but the way we get it is so diverse that as an industry with power, profits, and influence, radio's glory days are over.

DEVELOPMENT OF RADIO TECHNOLOGY

Radio began as an alternative to the copper wire that linked telegraph machines. At its outset it was intended simply as a two-way, point-to-point medium. Radio links were used as an alternative to the cables of the telegraph. That's why the pioneers called it the "wireless."

Spark generators

The telegraph worked by sending an electrical impulse down a wire that made a receiver at the other end click—the dots and dashes of Morse code. The wireless telegraph worked by sending out an electromagnetic wave from a spark generator. This was detected by a receiver that could turn the wave back into clicks or, with some further refinement, into speech and music.

In 1894 British scientist Sir Oliver Lodge used radio waves to send Morse code blips, thus creating wireless "telegraphy," and in 1900 Canadian inventor Reginald Fessenden sent the first voice transmission, creating wireless "telephony." But it was Guglielmo Marconi who pulled all the technical elements together and made the technology a commercial success. His objective was to allow communication with ships at sea or between fast-moving armies on the ground. The first commercial operator of radio was his organization, the Marconi Wireless Telegraph Company, based in the UK. As Marconi reported when accepting his Nobel Prize:

> I commenced early in 1885 to carry out tests with the object of determining whether it would be possible by means of [electromagnetic] waves to transmit to a distance without the aid of connecting wires. My first tests were carried out with an ordinary spark oscillator. With such apparatus I was able to telegraph up to a distance of about half a mile.[1]

By 1901 Marconi had managed to send Morse code right the way across the Atlantic. The use of invisible waves that radiated out from a transmitter in all directions led to the name "radio-telegraphy" and it became a feature of all ship-to-shore communication. This signal from a single transmitter was intended for a single listener, but could be picked up by anyone with a receiver. Early amateurs built their own "cat's whiskers" receivers that moved a wire, like a cat's whisker, across a crystal to resonate on the right frequency. They took great delight in eavesdropping on maritime communications. The fact that wireless transmissions could be heard by anyone with a homemade receiver was seen by most operators and governments as a distinct disadvantage, as it made them less secure.

Similarly to the fixed-line telegraph, it was events that made radio telegraphy a popular sensation. In 1904 infamous murderer Dr. Crippen was fleeing from England to Canada but was captured when his crimes were reported to his ship at sea by wireless telegraph. In 1912 wireless telegraphy had its most famous application when the Morse code message from the SS *Titanic*, saying it had struck an iceberg, was picked up by shore-based stations and the news went around the world.

An employee of the Marconi Company, who was alleged to have been one of the recipients of that message, was a young telegraph operator in Philadelphia called David Sarnoff. In 1916 he was to write a seminal memorandum to a vice-president in Marconi arguing that radio could do a lot more than simply be a wireless telegraph. It was later known as the "radio music box" memo:

> I have in mind a plan of development which would make radio a "household utility" in the same sense as the piano or phonograph... the idea is to bring music into the home by wireless...The receiver can be designed in the form of a simple "Radio Music Box" and arranged for several different wavelengths which should be changeable with the pressing of a single button. If only one million families thought well of the idea it would yield considerable revenue.[2]

Sarnoff's idea did not find favor with Marconi, who saw broadcasting as a distraction to wireless telegraphy. However, Sarnoff would go on to prove himself right by founding NBC and RCA.

AM: A broadcasting revolution

By the 1920s the introduction of the vacuum tube in America, or "valve" as it was called in the UK, made spark generators obsolete and created the much superior broadcasting technology we now call AM radio. This stands for amplitude modulation and means that the length of the radio wave is varied depending on the sound being carried. In effect, a voice or music changes the shape of the wave. It needs a lot of electrical energy to transmit AM, but the signal travels a long way. AM technology supports three separate bands of radio services: long wave, which is used rarely but has great range; medium wave, which is what the vast majority of commercial stations use; and short wave, which bounces off the ionosphere and can be used to provide a low-quality sound service over a great distance from the transmitter.

THE "REAL" FATHER OF RADIO

Marconi pioneered the technology of radio, but it is less clear who really started broadcasting as commercial entertainment. His supporters place the credit with Charles Herrold, who ran a radio station called FN from San Jose, California between 1909 and 1917. He used a spark-generator transmitter, which allowed him to broadcast music and speech to a local audience of enthusiasts who had homemade radios. At the time, most radio transmissions were commercial and in Morse code, so using radio as an entertainment medium was a daring innovation. Herrold is also credited with coining the term "broadcasting," as he came from a farming background and was used to the idea of broadcasting seeds, meaning throwing them in all directions as opposed to narrow casting them into a furrow. In 1917 Herrold's licence was canceled because of the war, and by peacetime his technology had been superseded by the vacuum tube and his station declined. In old age he became penniless and ended up working as a floor sweeper in a shipyard.

Medium-wave AM radio signals normally only travel a few hundred miles in daylight, but after sunset they have a property similar to short wave, which means they go much further. To avoid interference at night many stations reduce their power outputs, although a small number of broadcasters in America are granted "clear channel" status, which means they are allowed to keep their power up and thus be audible over much of the country in hours of darkness. It is from this old term that the US radio giant Clear Channel Communications took its name.

While short wave has limited commercial value, the BBC World Service uses hundreds of frequencies to broadcast to audiences many thousands of miles from London. Long wave has been used to communicate with submarines as it penetrates water and the BBC still uses it to broadcast Radio 4 all over Europe.

AM was the dominant radio technology from 1920 right through until the 1970s, when it was overtaken by the superior sound of FM.

FM: Better quality, more stations

FM means frequency modulation and here the frequency of the waves (the time gap between the arrival of the peak of each wave) is varied to carry the signal. This gives a crisper, cleaner sound and requires much less power, but does not range as far. FM technology was patented in 1933 by electrical engineer Edwin Armstrong, but its commercial development was hampered for many years by the vested interests in RCA, which used AM and saw FM as a threat. This led to a lengthy legal battle over the patent, which is thought to have contributed to Armstrong's suicide in 1954.

In the 1960s FM started to be used in America by upmarket classical music stations, attracted by its superior sound quality, although it took 20 years to overtake AM in popularity. In the UK the BBC experimented with FM from the 1950s, but it was not until the creation of commercial radio on the FM band in 1973 that it became the major force. Because FM is more precise and goes for much less distance than AM, it allows a huge increase in the number of stations that can coexist without interference.

Transistors: Making radios portable

The world's first transistor radio was unveiled at a trade fair in Germany in 1953. The devices were small and portable but very expensive, costing more than $300 in today's money. However, when manufacturing moved to Hong Kong prices fell dramatically. "Transistors," as they became known, replaced the heavy, mains-powered valve radios and took the medium out of the living room so that it was truly mobile.

Just as it looked as if radio might be rendered obsolete by television in the 1960s, the portable and cheap transistor gave it a new lease of life. Radio could be in the car, the bathroom, the garden, on the beach, and in the office.

Satellite radio

At first distributing radio to sets by satellite may seem unnecessary when the conventional land-based tower does the job so well. Nevertheless, for America in particular it has two potential advantages. One signal can cover the whole country and encoding technology means that listeners can be asked to pay for the service. Two rivals launched in the early 2000s. Both XM and Sirius invested hundreds of millions in creating competing networks and program lineups. Both charged around $10 a month for a subscription and offered hundreds of channels, some without advertising. The services proved a surprise hit with audiences, but because of the huge cost the two companies were forced to merge in 2008 in an attempt to create a single, viable broadcaster.

Digital: Unlimited capacity

Digital broadcasting simply means that instead of using radio waves to carry a program by variations in either wavelength or frequency, the signal is broken up into binary computer code, which is then transmitted by radio or over the internet. Instead of having radio transmitters and receivers, there is simply a computer at either end to encode and decode the stream of information. Once audio content is in digital form it can break free from conventional radio broadcasting.

Digital streams can be broadcast either over existing wavelengths, which is the American way and is called IBOC (in-band on-channel); or by using different radio wavelengths, which is the method chosen in Europe, called DAB (digital audio broadcasting). There are numerous other digital distribution methods. Services that stream over the internet like Spotify or Last.fm, MP3 players, the iPod and iPad, cable television, satellite systems, and cellphones mean most people can now choose from thousands of audio channels that are not traditional radio broadcasters.

THE VOICE OF THE NATION

Radio has experienced distinct eras. It started as an experiment, became the dominant mass medium, evolved into a showcase for recorded music, and later became a soapbox for (mostly right-wing) polemicists. However, right from its early days governments wanted to control it.

Radio control

Radio was initially adopted by enthusiastic amateurs—radio "hams"—who usually built their own equipment. They mostly communicated with each other, although a few experimented with more general transmissions to a wider audience. Once it was clear that radio broadcasting could be an entertainment medium rather than just a communications tool, it became obvious that there was big business to be had in ready-made receivers. And the companies that made these radio sets had a strong vested interest in ensuring there was attractive content to induce people to purchase their machines.

Governments decided early on that radio broadcasting needed to be controlled. The British saw the new technology as a natural extension of the telegraph and passed the Wireless Telegraphy Act of 1904, which said that all transmitters and receivers would have to have a Post Office license. In the US the Radio Act of 1912 accepted that there were already thousands of "hams" in action and let them operate their existing radio stations while restricting them to a narrow band of wavelengths, reserving most of the spectrum for the military. Initially there was little control and how they paid for broadcasting was up to them. This early difference of approach would lead to radically different industry structures.

Commercial pioneers in the US

As Charles Herrold was experimenting with his spark generator in California, a more commercially successful pioneer was Lee De Forest, who used the superior vacuum tube. His radio station 2XG broadcast speech and music out of Harlem, New York. In 1910 he put on a live Enrico Caruso concert from the New York Met and during the 1916 Presidential election 2XG broadcast the results to an audience of some 7,000.

During the First World War the technology of radio was jealously guarded by the military. However, come peacetime vacuum tubes were in widespread civilian use and the potential of radio as an entertainment medium became obvious. The American government wanted to ensure the US led the global development and encouraged the creation of RCA.

Hundreds of local radio stations sprung up across the US, launched by telephone companies, schools, department stores, and enthusiastic amateurs. These stations broadcast to a small geographic area, limited by the technology of their transmitters. They were known by their four call sign letters, which normally started with a *K* or a *W*. One of the first on air was KDKA Pittsburgh in 1920, which generated income by promoting records for sale in a local shop.

By 1922 the Department of Commerce had granted more than 300 broadcasting licenses. The number of radio sets in use in homes in America went from 5,000 in 1920 to 2.5 million in 1924. During this period the whole range of radio formats was developed and the "wireless" transmission of point-to-point telegraphy had become the "radio" of mass consumer entertainment. The first true radio advertisement appeared in 1922, in the same year as the phone giant AT&T tried, unsuccessfully, to claim it had a patent on the concept of advertising on radio. Advertising was a contentious issue from the start, with Commerce Secretary Herbert Hoover (a future US President) saying in 1922:

RCA: THE FIRST INTERNET STOCK

The Radio Corporation of America (RCA) was formed in 1919 as a mechanism to monopolize the technology of radio in America. It forcibly took over the US assets of the British Marconi company and, under its charter from the government, had to be American controlled. When commercial broadcasting started RCA came to the notice of the stock market. It had numerous radio patents, owned the NBC network, made most of the radio sets sold, and in 1929 it became the world's largest producer of gramophones as well as owning record producer RCA Victor. RCA was the "hot stock" of the 1920s boom. Investors were mesmerized by the potential of radio in exactly the same way as they were by the internet some 80 years later. The stock price went from $1 in 1921 to over $110 in 1929, and then back down to below $10 in 1931 after the Wall Street Crash. RCA never paid a dividend and at its height had a price/earnings ratio of 72:1. For most of its corporate life RCA was led by David Sarnoff (the author of the Radio Music Box memo) and in 1986 it was sold to General Electric, which had been one of the original shareholders in the 1920s.

It is inconceivable that we should allow [radio] so great a possibility for service, news and entertainment and education... to be drowned in advertising chatter.[4]

Nevertheless, his concerns were ignored and advertising and sponsorship become the driving economic force of American broadcasting. RCA encouraged many new stations to open in order to sell their listeners more equipment. The local station owners quickly realized that there were great economic advantages in linking together to create networks. Programming costs could be shared; big stars could be lured from music hall; and by combining sales efforts, advertising could be offered on the basis of a much greater audience.

The National Broadcasting Company (NBC), owned by RCA, was the first radio network and began regular shows in 1926. It networked its output by using the long-distance telephone links of AT&T, an RCA shareholder. These joined stations between New York and other eastern cities. It quickly became the dominant radio operator, splitting into Red and Blue networks to allow it to serve competing local stations in the same cities. A rival network, the Columbia Broadcasting System (CBS), began in 1927, but did not thrive until 1928 when it was bought by cigar manufacturer William S Paley.

Early radio in the US was chaotic, with many stations using the same frequencies and little or no control over content. The Federal Radio Act of 1927 created what became the Federal Communications Commission (FCC) with the clear intention of regulating broadcasting in technical terms, but leaving it as a diverse, commercial model, with no government editorial interference.

The birth of the BBC

The British did things very differently and the UK government clung to the idea that radio's function was as a point-to-point rather than a broadcast medium. Amateurs were not encouraged or licensed. Local stations did not spring up. But under pressure from manufacturers, who wanted to sell radio sets, and the public, who wanted to hear programs, the Post Office allowed the Marconi Company to experiment with radio broadcasting from Chelmsford in Essex.

FIRST RADIO ADVERTISING

The first true broadcast advertisement was probably on a radio station called WEAF in New York late in the afternoon of August 28, 1922. At the time listeners were hearing a learned talk about the nineteenth-century novelist Nathaniel Hawthorne. Toward the end the speaker explained that what Hawthorne considered to be "a good home" was "removed from the congested part of the city, right at the boundaries of God's great outdoors." There was then a very specific message that the Queensboro Corporation had been so inspired by this thought that it had constructed a new apartment complex in green and leafy Jackson Heights with the name Hawthorne Court and apartments were now on sale. Queensboro had paid $100 for the plug and was later rewarded with tens of thousands in sales. A few weeks later American Express and Tidewater Oil also bought mentions on WEAF and the commercial radio industry was underway.[4]

In 1920 Marconi engineers offered a half-hour program of records and experimented with the first radio play, *Cyrano de Bergerac*. Other early programs included live readings from Bradshaw's railway timetable, so it is not a surprise that early British radio was not a popular success. On June 15, 1920 one of the UK's great press barons, Lord Northcliffe, came up with the idea of broadcasting opera superstar Dame Nellie Melba live from Chelmsford and promoting the event in his *Daily Mail* newspaper. The hit achieved by Dame Nellie and

CALL SIGNS

From the early days of the telegraph each station along a railway line was designated its own unique call letters to identify the location where it transmitted. When wireless telegraphy came along this convention was extended to all transmitters, both on shore and on ships. To provide clarity official call letters or numbers were assigned to all countries at an international conference in 1912. The UK got, among others, the number 2; hence 2LO, the first station of the BBC. America got the letters K and W and by convention dating from the 1930s American radio stations west of the Mississippi use a four-letter identifier starting with K and those to the east start with a W. One of the very few exceptions to this was the first on air, KDKA Pittsburgh.

the news filtering through of the success of radio in America led to the creation of other stations, which were licensed to commercial operators on an experimental basis. 2LO operated from the roof of the Selfridges department store in London's Oxford Street, 5IT in Birmingham was run by Western Electric, and 2ZY by Vickers in Manchester.

By 1922 the British government decided to copy the RCA model and created a consortium of radio manufacturers to collectively owned the British Broadcasting Company, which was given a monopoly of radio broadcasting. It was funded by a levy on the sale of radio sets and by an annual license fee for radio use, collected by the Post Office.

The job of running the BBC was given to John Reith, an austere Scot with a strong sense of public duty and ironclad moral values. He took over all the small local stations to create regions and set them to developing a series of culturally acceptable and educational programs. Reith favored classical music and created a children's hour of "improving material" and uplifting talks. News was not allowed until after 7 pm, following pressure from newspaper publishers who feared for their sales. By 1925 Reith decided to move away from the regions and most of the national output originated from London at a newly constructed studio in Savoy Hill.

Reith felt that broadcasting was too important to be subject to commercial interests, so he lobbied against carrying advertising and sought to be freed from the ownership of the radio manufacturers. He wanted the private BBC to become a state-owned entity financed solely by the license fee. In 1926, as his ideas were being considered, Britain suffered a traumatic

General Strike, which shut the country down for 10 days. This presented the BBC with a huge dilemma. The strike closed most newspapers and because of this the BBC was given permission to broadcast news all day. If it had reported the strike from a pro-government perspective (which was the strong desire of the then Home Secretary Winston Churchill), it risked the strikers shutting down the BBC by force. However, if it seemed to support the strikers, the government, which controlled the transmitters, could have stopped it broadcasting. Under Reith's leadership the BBC managed to remain impartial and thus was seen as a service to the population as a whole, rather than as an arm of the state.

Strengthened by the strike, Reith got his way and at the end of 1926 the BBC was nationalized and the British Broadcasting Corporation was created. This was a government-owned body but independent of all commercial and political interests and supported by a 10-shilling annual radio license on all sets in use. In 1923 just 80,000 licenses had been issued, but by 1927 this had grown to 2 million. By 1928 more popular programs reached an audience of some 15 million people. This was a huge percentage of the population.

Home entertainment: The golden age

From the late 1920s onward most families in the UK and the US owned a radio set. By the time of the Second World War most people had radios in several rooms and some in their cars. Once the transistor arrived in the 1950s, there were more radios than people. The early radio receivers had been technically complex, crystal sets that required considerable skill and patience to operate and were listened to through headphones. These appealed to young male hobbyists, rather like the early days of the internet. By the late 1920s the valve and the loudspeaker had transformed radios into desirable home furnishings, which can be seen in contemporary photographs playing a central role in the life of the family, with members gathered around, all listening intently. These large domestic "radio sets" had particular appeal to stay-at-home housewives and daytime radio programming quickly evolved to reflect this large domestic audience.

Both in America and Britain, radio became a major social force. Networks in both countries were hybrid, full-service entertainment and information providers. Each channel tried to be all things to all listeners. The huge importance of radio was demonstrated by the architecture of its premises. The Radio City Music Hall in New York, which opened in 1932, was the world's largest indoor theatre and was located next to the studios of NBC. In the same year the BBC opened its spectacular and much admired Art Deco-style Broadcasting House in London, which housed 22 soundproof studios. Radio City was famous for its high-kicking dancing girls, the Rockettes, and Broadcasting House for its classical sculptures of Ariel and Prospero, derived from Shakespeare's *The Tempest*. The contrast must have pleased John Reith and exemplified the differences in the British and American approaches.

Producers started to create material specifically for the new medium. The nightly comedy program *Amos 'n' Andy*, which ran from 1928 to 1955 in the US, was the model for hundreds of subsequent situation comedies or "sitcoms." Producers of one-off dramas realized that radio, with its use of sound effects and the imagination of the audience, allowed ambitious experimentation. The first BBC drama specially written for radio aired in 1924. It was called *A Comedy of Danger* and was set in a coal mine after the lighting had failed; an early example of a playwright showing he appreciated the unique nature of sound broadcasting.

During the 1930s and 1940s all three national networks in the US enjoyed growing audiences and rising advertising. NBC was deemed so successful that it was forced to sell off its Blue network, which became ABC radio in 1945. The three networks grew to cover the whole country and developed the model of wholly owned stations (called O&O, "owned and operated") and affiliated stations that became the blueprint for the organization of television in America.

In the UK, without the stimulus of commercial competition, the BBC adopted a more conservative and patrician approach, staying true to the values laid down by its founding Director-General John Reith to inform, educate, and entertain—in that order. It decided to offer two country-wide program services, the National and the Regional. The desires of the British audience were deemed less important than the need to have high-quality, public-service programs. Reith argued his case for high ideals in his book *Broadcast over Britain* in 1924, writing:

> It is occasionally indicated to us that we are apparently setting out
> to give the public what we think they need—and not what they want...
> but few know what they want, and very few what they need.[5]

Reith's highbrow formula included live performances of classical music. The BBC started sponsoring and broadcasting the annual Promenade Concerts in 1927 and began its own orchestra in 1930. American jazz was frowned on and only a much watered-down British style was allowed on air. Recorded music was used vary sparingly, partly because the music companies (who held the copyright) objected to their records being played and demanded very high performing rights. Drama and light entertainment were based on getting theatre and music hall stars to perform on radio. Reith's influence was particularly strong on Sundays when he mandated that programs would not start until the afternoon and would feature a strict schedule of religious services and classical music. This clashed with the weekend audience's desire for entertainment and left a gap for foreign operators like Radio Normandie and Radio Luxembourg, which captured up to 80 percent of the available audience on Sundays in the mid-

SOAP OPERAS

Radio stations needed to get listeners to tune in day after day and they wanted to stop people changing channels. Programmers found the best solution was to tell a good story in short episodes, with engaging characters and cliffhanger endings. Most great works of literature, novels and plays, had a clear beginning, middle, and end. What radio needed was a saga that just kept on going.

In 1930 three university friends suggested to the Chicago radio station WGN that they perform a 15-minute program featuring light-hearted domestic stories. Initially they did it for nothing and called it *Clara, Lu, and Em*. This was later sponsored by Colgate and taken up by NBC. Also in 1930 the same Chicago station commissioned a 15-minute serial drama aimed at housewives, written by Irna Phillips. This was *Painted Dreams*, which started in October and claimed to be the first "soap opera." Ms. Phillips invented many of the soap conventions that are still familiar. In 1937 she went onto create *The Guiding Light*, the longest-running soap, which only finished in 2009 having transferred to television in 1952. She also developed *As the World Turns* and *Days of Our Lives*.

The BBC had less need to retain audiences as it enjoyed a broadcasting monopoly, but in 1950 it launched what has become the longest-running British soap, *The Archers*, dubbed "an everyday story of country folk." It copied all the American techniques (except for sponsorship) and remains a hugely popular program.

WAR OF THE WORLDS

The power of radio drama was dramatically illustrated by Orson Welles' Mercury Theatre production of *War of the Worlds*, a dramatization of the HG Wells novel broadcast on CBS on Halloween 1938. The original book was about the effects of a Martian invasion of England. Welles changed the location to Grover's Mill, New Jersey and told the story in a series of simulated radio news reports. The program was sufficiently novel and realistic that many listeners were fooled and panic ensued. The following day the *New York Times* ran a front-page feature about the broadcast and in the following month more than 12,500 newspaper stories mentioned it. Even Adolf Hitler cited the controversy as proof of "the decadence and corrupt condition of democracy."[6] The panic was probably helped by public paranoia in the run-up to the Second World War. Nevertheless, in the post mortem CBS agreed never again to allow fictional use of the phrase "We interrupt this program to bring you..."

1930s. Fortunately for the BBC both were closed down by the outbreak of war.

The war was good to the BBC in other ways. The developing technology of television was halted and the public's desire for instant live news gave radio a huge advantage over newspapers, which suffered from rationing of paper and ink. Radio was also the medium of choice of all four of the key war leaders—Roosevelt, Stalin, Churchill, and Hitler—who used it to make regular broadcasts. The BBC also decided to reconfigure its output radically. Its agreements with newspapers not to broadcast news in the daytime were scrapped. It launched two channels, each with clear objectives. The Home Service was the old BBC, serious and high minded, aimed at the domestic audience, while the Forces Network was a lighter, more popular mixture of music and comedy designed to motivate and entertain the troops in France. After a few years the domestic audience seemed to prefer the Forces Network, which sounded more like an American channel. And indeed, American radio came to Britain in the shape of AFN (American Forces Network), broadcast to US bases in the UK but audible to the domestic audience.

The war—and Reith's departure in 1938, when some say he was forced out—led the BBC's approach to be far more popular in tone. Its most famous product was a comedy show using sound effects and multiple characters called *ITMA*, which stood for *It's That Man Again*, a popular catchphrase referring to Adolf Hitler. *ITMA* was fresh and revolutionary, it satirized the establishment and made fun of authority. The listeners loved it and it regularly got audiences of 15 million. It was the inspiration for numerous other anarchic formats. The old guard at the BBC accepted defeat. By 1944 it started to syndicate popular American variety shows with personalities like Jack Benny, Bing Crosby, and Bob Hope. And in 1945 the Home Service was relaunched for a peacetime audience. The Forces Network became the Light Programme and to keep the remaining Reithians happy, a new highbrow channel called the Third Programme was created.

Liberated by the success of shows like *ITMA*, the BBC launched dozens of new formats in the 1950s, including many that are still familiar, like *Hancock's Half Hour*, *Any Questions?*, and *Gardeners' Question Time*.

REINVENTION: ROCK AND ROLL AND RABBLE ROUSING

The Second World War was the high water mark for radio. When peace was declared in 1945 there was renewed interest in promoting television. The big-name stars, the most successful program formats, the advertisers, and the audiences migrated to the new visual wonder.

In both the UK and the US it was the organizations that ran radio that were given the new television licenses. In the UK

ED MURROW

Edward R Murrow was the most famous American radio journalist. He joined CBS in 1935 and became head of operations in Europe in 1937, living just a few streets away from the BBC's Broadcasting House. In the run-up to the Second World War he presented *European News Roundup*, which pioneered the technique of live reports on location from different places. From 1939 Murrow reported at first hand on the Blitz and adopted his catchphrase "This is London." With the emphasis on "this" it became a trademark for all CBS correspondents for years afterward. It was also in London that Murrow started to end his reports with "Good night and good luck," a phrase he borrowed from a broadcast by the then Princess Elizabeth and then used as the title of his film biography. After the war Murrow went back to America and transferred to television, where he famously battled against Senator Joe McCarthy.

ADOLF HITLER, RADIO STAR

Adolf Hitler was made Chancellor of Germany on January 30, 1933 and the very next day gave his first national radio broadcast. Many more would follow, as Hitler saw in this medium the ideal way to lead a new political movement. He was far ahead of politicians in Britain, and even America, who were more focused on newspapers. The Nazi party was very aware of the importance of radio. It set up a special Ministry of Propaganda under Joseph Goebbels, who made these comments in a speech in August 1933:

Napoleon spoke of the press as the seventh great power. Its significance became politically visible with the beginning of the French Revolution, and maintained its position for the entirety of the nineteenth century. The century's politics were largely determined by the press. One can hardly imagine or explain the major historical events between 1800 and 1900 without considering the powerful influence of print journalism.

The radio will be for the twentieth century what the press was for the nineteenth. With the appropriate change, one can apply Napoleon's phrase to our age, speaking of the radio as the eighth great power. Its discovery and application are of truly revolutionary significance for contemporary community life. Future generations may conclude that the radio had as great an intellectual and spiritual impact on the masses as the printing press had before the beginning of the Reformation.[7]

television was treated with suspicion by the leaders of the BBC, who regarded it as a second-class service. But in the USA the best and the brightest moved enthusiastically to the new medium.

By the mid-1950s American radio was in trouble. The most obvious feature was the collapse of the radio network model. In 1946 more than 80 percent of all US radio stations were network affiliates and, as such, received most of their quality programming from network production. By 1952 nearly 50 percent of stations were no longer affiliates. Ed Sullivan moved to television in 1948. In 1951, Ed Murrow moved *Hear It Now* from radio to become *See It Now* on CBS Television. The last radio soap opera in America was broadcast in 1960. And as the advertising dollars moved to television, radio executives were forced to slash costs. This meant the end of any sort of expensive variety, drama, news, or factual programming; faced with a slump in revenues, local station owners relied on their own staff playing records.

Nevertheless, technology came to the rescue. The arrival of the transistor made radio a totally mobile medium. By 1960 only 6 percent of American radio income came from network advertising spots and the medium had become local once again, with individual stations wholly focused on specific types of popular music.

In Britain BBC radio fared better in the face of television, if only because the BBC had a monopoly of both. Tradition and inertia kept spending on sound broadcasting high. However, with the arrival of commercial television in the UK in 1955 and the radio pirates of the 1960s, BBC radio saw its audiences shrink dramatically. The pirates showed that there was a huge demand for rock and roll and in the end the BBC acknowledged this by scrapping its old hybrid approach and following the American model of more formatted channels. In 1970 in came Radio 1 for pop music, Radio 2 for light music, Radio 3 for classical music, and Radio 4 for news and speech.

RADIO LUXEMBOURG

Luxembourg is a tiny, rich country on the borders of Belgium, France, and Germany that is mostly famous for its secretive banking laws. In 1933 its government decided to launch an advertising-supported English-language radio station, aimed at the British audience, using long-wave frequencies legally assigned to Luxembourg. Among the British who at the time were only allowed to listen to the austere BBC, Luxembourg's more light-hearted programming was an immediate success. After the war the station started to transmit on the 208 wavelength on the medium wave and became hugely popular with British listeners in the 1950s and 1960s.

The huge increase in availability of FM frequencies in America in the 1970s made it possible for many more radio signals to be heard in each market. A new breed of producers and presenters started to focus more narrowly on single types of music: classical, jazz, soft rock, hard rock, classic rock. All had their own stations, which pleased advertisers and listeners by delivering more targeted audiences.

In the UK the new FM band launched commercial radio in 1973 to provide competition to the BBC. Thus the first advertising on UK radio was heard more than 50 years after it started in America. UK commercial radio was designed along US lines, with most big towns and cities being granted a franchise. However, unlike America, the creation of networks was not allowed, which put the new stations at a distinct disadvantage. They struggled to sell national campaigns and many ran into financial problems.

Disc jockeys

Arguably the world's first disc jockey was Christopher Stone, who played recorded music on the BBC starting in 1927, although he was simply described as an "announcer." The first use of the term "disc jockey" was for American Martin Block in 1935, who was so described by fellow broadcaster Walter Winchell, meaning, in a rather derogatory way, someone who plays discs by operating machinery. Block presented a show called *Make Believe Ballroom* in which he pretended that listeners were hearing the country's greatest dance bands perform live, when in fact he simply played records.

As 45 rpm records became big business, the record companies decided that far from airplay being a problem, radio was now their most important marketing channel. "Payola" is the practice of record companies paying disc jockeys an "inducement" to play their tracks on air. It was widespread in American radio but in 1960 it was made illegal and Alan Freed, the "inventor" of rock and roll, was unlucky enough to be the first person convicted of the offense. His career was ruined by the bad publicity and he died in 1965, aged 42, of alcoholism.

Casey Kasem hosted the weekly US top 40 countdown shows for much of the 1970s and 1980s. *Casey's Countdown* combined the novelty of new music with the uncertainty of a quiz show. It laid the ground for the *American Idol* type of talent show 40 years later.

As FM radios became common in homes and cars, listeners and broadcasters came to see the technical limitations of the AM band, on which the signal was crackly and indistinct. By the 1980s AM was in rapid decline. One use became sports stations, which did not need high-fidelity sound and were able to offer far more live commentary than was available on television. However, the real salvation of what could have become a redundant technology was the telephone and the sound of the human voice.

Shock jocks

Talk radio as a format in the US had been around since 1945 when a presenter called Barry Gray had invited listeners to "phone in," but it was not until 1960 that a few big stations adopted the format. The phone-in soon became the staple of AM radio. Talk radio changed from a monologue to a dialogue, from a broadcast to a discussion. What made the fictional Frasier Crane and the hundreds of real-life radio talk-show hosts so popular was that the audience were listening to themselves. The phone-in host was acting as a catalyst for conversation; social networking long before Facebook. A constant problem of phone-ins was felt to be that the callers often expressed extreme views that the host had to moderate. But far from being a negative, this was going to become a major attraction.

In 1987 the FCC repealed its so-called fairness doctrine under which any station that broadcast controversial comment had to provide free airtime for the opponents to make their case. This had made opinionated speech unattractive to station owners, who were faced with giving away free airtime to what often proved to be boring amateur politicians. When the rule was dropped it opened the way for political pundits to broadcast their own trenchant views without forced balance. This led to a huge increase in the popularity of talk radio in America in the 1990s.

Broadcasters used their shows as soapboxes for their own robust political sentiments and encouraged their callers to do likewise. For some years the single most popular radio talk-show host in the US has been Rush Limbaugh. Since he started his unashamedly right-wing rants in 1987, Limbaugh has been consistently conservative and antiliberal. During the Clinton Administration he was called "the leader of the opposition" and since the victory of Barack Obama he has been characterized as "the real leader of the Republican Party." His show is syndicated in almost all major US radio markets and regularly achieves 13 million plus listeners; he is paid some $30 million a year.

However, the best-paid radio star ever is Howard Stern, who developed an anarchic mixture of (often obscene) talk and rock music and is regarded as the first real "shock jock." In 2004 he signed a five-year contract with satellite radio operator Sirius that was then worth some $500 million.[8] He is also the most heavily fined of any radio performer, having had numerous conflicts with the FCC since he started in the 1980s. He was heavily criticized for on-air comments about oral sex, anal sex, masturbation, and racism. An arrest warrant was issued after some of the racial comments. Despite all this, his morning show on New York's K-Rock was hugely popular and widely syndicated.

By comparison, British shock jocks are a mild bunch. In 2009 Jonathan Ross and Russell Brand were taken off the air by BBC Radio 2 for broadcasting themselves leaving obscene messages on the answering

NATIONAL PUBLIC RADIO

America has never been wholly comfortable with its commercial broadcasting approach. Numerous politicians criticized the lack of cultural breadth that results from a commercial model. In 1967 President Lyndon B Johnson signed the Public Broadcasting Act and commented:

It announces to the world that our Nation wants more than just material wealth; our Nation wants more than a "chicken in every pot." We in America have an appetite for excellence, too. While we work every day to produce new goods and to create new wealth, we want most of all to enrich man's spirit.

The Act led to the creation of both National Public Radio (NPR) and the Public Broadcasting Service (PBS). NPR stations are mostly paid for by charitable foundations, private donations, government grants, and, to a limited degree, corporate sponsorship, which is restricted to scripted messages rather than traditional commercials. NPR enjoys great success but with a relatively narrow audience. Its morning and evening drive-time shows are its most popular programs.

machine of a retired television actor. Lord Reith would not have been pleased, but Howard Stern would have been baffled by the fuss.

BORDER BLASTERS AND PIRATES

Although radio waves do not respect national boundaries, most governments, for political, social or economic reasons, are very keen to control what their citizens can listen to. Stopping radio being beamed in from outside a country's borders has been a constant battle. Various international conventions have agreed an allocation of radio frequencies to try to avoid adjacent stations interfering with one another and to seek an equitable allocation of natural broadcasting resources. But this throws up strange anomalies. Nations as small as the Isle of Man are given rights to broadcast a signal that may be audible many hundreds of miles beyond their borders to a much bigger audience in other countries. Or a relatively poor nation, like Mexico, has stations that, while intended for domestic consumption, have far more commercial value across the border in the US.

Mexican stations start with an X and hence high-power transmitters like XERB became known as "border blasters" or "X-Radio." A pioneer in border blasting was XER, which was established in 1932 by an American doctor called John R Brinkley who had not been allowed to broadcast his eccentric medical services (which included implanting goats' testicles in humans to improve fertility) in the US. The station transmitted at 500,000 watts, 10 times the power of licensed US stations. Numerous other border stations followed advertising patent medicines and religious preachers. They shared something with today's Viagra spam emails. With their huge power output they could be heard across the whole of America. The US Congress passed the Brinkley Act of 1934 to prevent US-based studios being used to supply programs to Mexican-based transmitters.

The most famous border blaster personality was Wolfman Jack, who played rock and roll in the early 1960s from XERF, a direct descendant of XER. His show was hugely popular in California and features in George Lucas's cult film *American Grafitti*, in which the Wolfman (whose real name was Bob Smith) played a cameo role as himself.

The British version of the border blaster was the so-called pirate radio, whose originator was the improbably named

RADIO CAROLINE

By the early 1960s the music and youth revolution was well underway in the UK. The Beatles were getting famous but British radio was still lost in the past. The BBC was staid and conservative. Popular music was all but ignored. The only major station playing pop was based in Luxembourg. An Irish entrepreneur called Ronan O'Rahilly found a way around UK laws by equipping a ship as a radio station and mooring it in international waters in the North Sea. He named it Radio Caroline after the daughter of President Kennedy and "hijacked" an unused frequency of 199 meters in the medium wave. It started broadcasting at Easter 1964 and its first track was a version of "Not Fade Away" by the Rolling Stones. Caroline was a "pirate" station, which gave it an irresistible popular appeal.

Over the next ten years many others followed, using ships and even old forts located out to sea. The UK government made numerous attempts to shut the pirates down, but in the end the only solution was to give listeners a legal alternative. The BBC responded with the new "youth" station of Radio 1 in 1970 and UK commercial radio stations were created in 1973. Although Caroline and some other pirates tried to continue, most of their audience and many of their star DJs migrated to legal, land-based stations and the golden age of marine pirate radio was over.[9]

Captain Leonard Plugge, a British Conservative MP who founded the International Broadcasting Company that launched Radio Normandie in 1931, based in France. This broadcast into the UK in English a selection of American dance band music and advertising. It was followed by Radio Luxembourg, which adopted a similar formula. Both these land-based services were closed down by the Second World War, but Luxembourg opened again with great success in the 1950s, becoming the UK's main popular music station.

More extreme than the land-based extra-national stations were the true pirates, like Caroline and Radio London, which operated from international waters in the North Sea. The pirates were outlawed by the 1964 Marine Broadcasting Act, but many found ways around this, and as late as 1984 the ship-based station Laser 558 was getting audiences of up to 5 million. Listening to Radios Luxembourg or Caroline was technically a criminal offense, which was a thrilling thought for its millions of teenage fans although no one was ever prosecuted.

UBIQUITOUS AUDIO

When you are learning how to be a radio broadcaster, one of the first things you are told (at least if you learn at the BBC) is to imagine you have an audience of one. You are sitting in a soundproof box and in front of you is a microphone. Do not, they say, try to imagine 6 million listeners out there, imagine just one person. Radio is a dialogue, a one-to-one conversation. It is a very personal medium, which is what makes audio communication, both speech and music, very compelling. However, this does not ensure a bright future for the traditional industry of radio, only for the medium of sound.

In the 1990s commercial radio on both sides of the Atlantic enjoyed a temporary boom. Narrow-format music stations and shock jocks proved popular and advertising spend grew. Small, independent stations were acquired by broadcasting conglomerates like Clear Channel and Viacom in America and Capital and GWR in the UK. Consolidation reduced operating costs. The 1990s were more profitable and there were more listening hours than at any time in radio's history, but it was not to last.

What killed radio in economic terms, in both the UK and the US, was the superabundance of stations and digital technology. Since the 1960s, in response to a clamor for more choice, politicians on both sides of the Atlantic issued increasing numbers of licenses, until the audience and income were spread so thin that many stations were no longer viable businesses. In addition, the arrival of the iPod, other MP3 players, cellphones, and online streaming sites made a huge range of music available outside of conventional radio.

All of these developments will make radio broadcasting towers and traditional receivers seem as quaint as the telegraph line and the Morse key. Listeners will still want people to act as cultural guides, to introduce new music and new ideas and to entertain and inform us. But the next generation of Ed Murrows, Howard Sterns, Rush Limbaughs, and Alan Freeds are likely to be talking to us on very different channels from conventional broadcast radio.

2.13 | Cinema

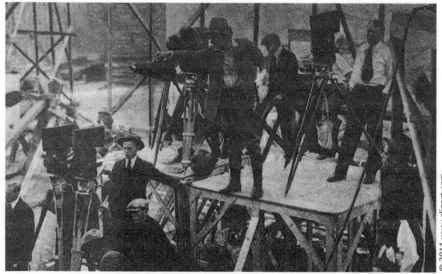

In the late 1940s, after the deprivations of the Second World War and before the development of television, nearly 100 million Americans, almost 70 percent of the population, went to the movies every week.[1] By the first decade of the twenty-first century, weekly attendance had dropped to only 10 percent. What had been the dominant public entertainment medium had evolved into a niche pursuit. So did this mean that the industry sometimes known just as "Hollywood" was in fundamental decline? Far from it! The economics of the overall film industry are bigger than ever, but only about 20 percent of the money comes from selling seats in cinemas. The bulk stems from DVDs, television broadcasts, pay TV, books, games, and merchandising. The new Hollywood is about creating entertainment franchises that dip their fingers into consumers' pockets in many different ways.

Cinema is a complex and highly technical medium, originally combining the chemistry of photographic film with the mechanics of creating an optical illusion. Over a 100-year period it has moved from fairground novelty to fine art and high finance by way of the studio system, the power of the stars, and a ruthless business approach. It was the proving ground for many of the economic models of the modern media industry.

AN INAUSPICIOUS START

Just after Christmas 1895, a group of 33 people agreed, somewhat reluctantly, to pay 1 franc each to see the first public demonstration of the new technology of *cinématographie* at the Grand Café in the Boulevard des Capucines near L'Opéra in Paris. The presentation was mounted by a French entrepreneur and photographer from Lyon called Auguste Lumière. He had adapted the mechanics of a sewing machine to create a camera that could take a series of still photographs on a roll of celluloid. The same technology, plus a bright lamp, was then used in reverse to project the images from the developed film onto a screen rapidly one after the other, to create the illusion of movement.

Lumière's first audience was highly skeptical, and in a room laid out for more than 100, most were friends and employees who had been invited to make up the numbers. They had no idea what to expect, but when they saw a horse and cart trundle across a flickering screen and a crowd of factory workers leave a gate, they were mesmerized. A few weeks later 2,500 people a day were queuing for hours to see the new novelty. Fights broke out and the police were called. Moving pictures had arrived in the public consciousness, but they had been in development for some time.[2]

The first attempts to turn still pictures into moving images had been made in 1877 by a British photographer at the request of the Governor of California, Leland Stanford, who wanted to understand how a horse looked when at full gallop. This was the same Stanford who founded the university near San Francisco that bears his name and has become the fountainhead of computer science, the internet, and the web.

Prolific inventor Thomas Edison—having created the phonograph in the same year Stanford was photographing the horse—wanted to be able to complement recorded sound with moving pictures. He set his laboratory the task of making a suitable camera and in 1893 patented a machine called

THE GALLOPING HORSE

Leland Stanford had made his fortune in railroads and was keen on breeding racehorses. He wagered that when at full gallop a horse had all four legs off the ground. In 1877 he hired pioneer photographer Eadweard Muybridge to prove it. The solution was to mount 12 cameras along the side of a racetrack in Sacramento and have a series of trip wires to work the shutters, such that as a horse went past at full speed, 12 pictures were taken in quick succession. When later processed and mounted on a revolving drum, they could be viewed through a peephole and showed the horse in motion and fully airborne. This established the principle of motion pictures, but lacked the mechanical camera and projector needed to make it a viable medium.

a Kinetograph, which used the mechanism of a clock to run film with sprocket holes in front of a lens at a precise speed that coordinated with the shutter. The resulting film was then played back through another machine, called a Kinetoscope, which reversed the process. This showed a primitive moving picture viewed by looking through a lens into a large dark box—what we might describe as a "peep show" or "What the Butler Saw" machine. These machines became very popular as arcade novelties that people paid a nickel a time to watch. Edison constructed a small studio with lighting for his large, complex, battery-operated camera. Vaudeville stars, magicians and circus acts were brought to the studio to be captured on film, to be seen later on Kinetoscopes in hotel foyers, railway stations, and penny arcades. However, Edison's machines were designed for the individual to experience moving pictures in private, not for a public display.

In France, Lumière had followed a different route. His lightweight camera was cranked by hand, which let him go on location. Also, his film was viewed by shining light through it using a simple, portable projector. His pictures were shown on a screen and gave a shared experience to the audience. He used the camera as an observer to record real events. Lumière's technology became a sensation throughout Europe and India and cameras were sent to exotic locations to bring many images of far-flung places to the cinema audiences.

While Europe brought the audiences into the newly created cinema theatres, America stuck with Edison's technology and his films were mostly used by traveling carnivals and fairground operators in peep-show booths.

They were often called "animated photography," were very short—a minute or two—and featured novelties with titles like *Boxing Cats*.

Even in France, early film projectors were often used by magicians to enhance their acts as they traveled from town to town. Lumière's brother Louis, who had done much to make the new technology work, didn't really see its full potential, commenting:

> The cinema is an invention without any commercial future... it's more of a fairground job. It may last six months, a year perhaps.[3]

It took a combination of developments around the turn of the twentieth century to create the motion picture industry we recognize today. Edison saw the obvious benefits of projection and launched his own display machine, which he called the Vitascope. He had a competitor in the Biograph, invented by a company founded by William Kennedy Dickson who had been employed by Edison's laboratory. Between the two, they encouraged a large number of itinerant film exhibitors who toured the country to show off their new machines. This led in turn to a demand for a lot more new films.

All the very early films, on both sides of the Atlantic, used a single static camera to film a single scene, which was replayed without editing or any changes of angle or focus. It was a small snippet of real life recorded as it happened—pure observation. A full reel of film ran for just a few minutes. A French magician called Georges Méliès experimented with stop-action photography and editing, going far beyond the original "point-and-watch" approach. In 1902 he produced a long feature based on the Jules Verne novel *From the Earth to the Moon*. It ran for 14 minutes and used 825 feet of film with scenes edited together. Although revolutionary at the time, this movie still resembled a conventional theatre production captured on film. The camera was rooted to the spot and the action was seen from one angle. Nevertheless, it was a sensation and everyone started to copy this "narrative" approach to film making.

Méliès' main American disciple was a film projectionist called Edwin Porter, who improved on the French technique to make one of the first long US features, *The Great Train Robbery*, on a Western theme. It was the first movie to feature back projection and camera movement. The era of the film as a small-scale novelty was ending and film as a dramatic storytelling medium was underway.

Charles Pathé had made his fortune by taking one of Thomas Edison's phonographs around local fairs in France and charging people to listen to recorded music. He then started to sell Edison's Kinetoscopes to the same showmen, but found business tough as the novelty of the short animated picture began to wear off. He managed to get financial backing from a French industrialist and started a film production business that focused on quantity over quality. He saw film production as an industrial challenge rather than an art form. Another French pioneer was Léon Gaumont, whose financial backers included Gustave Eiffel, the builder of the eponymous tower. In 1905 Gaumont started making movies with stories and characters rather than following the documentary, "observational" approach. The French pioneers changed how film was used but it was the Americans who changed the way it was watched.

American film exhibitors grew tired of the challenge of touring their projection equipment around to carnivals and converted halls. They began to set up permanent screens in empty buildings. These exhibitors were serviced by distributors, who bought finished films from the producers and rented them to the exhibitors. When one exhibitor had satisfied local demand, the distributor would get the print back and rent it to another exhibitor in another town. This was the basis of the theatre circuit system.

In the same year Gaumont set up his production business in France, a vaudeville tycoon from Pittsburgh called Harry Davis set up the first "nickelodeon" cinema. For just 5 cents (a nickel), audiences got to sit on cheap wooden chairs in a disused shop on a city street. The idea caught on in a spectacular way among the newly arrived American working class, many of whom spoke little or no English, and by 1907 there were some 5,000 nickelodeons across the country. These new cinemas demanded longer and more entertaining films.

MONOPOLY PART I: THE STAR IS BORN

In the first decade of the twentieth century the majority of movies seen in America were imported from Europe. Pathé, Gaumont, and a Danish production company called Nordisk Film were the world leaders. Pathé in particular approached films as factory items and produced them in huge numbers. Although there were American studios, mostly in New York, in the early years of film this was a cottage industry and could not offer the range of stories and subjects that came out of Europe.

In a move that would later be echoed in an attempt to control the technology of radio, the main American film companies got together in 1908 to form a cartel that they called the Motion Picture Patent Company or MPPC. Its objective was to create a total monopoly over the ownership of cameras, film, and creative talent and to issue licenses to allow only local American companies, and perhaps a few selected others, to make and distribute movies in the US. They invited Pathé to join, which he did, as access to the American market was too attractive to pass up. The smaller US independent film makers and other Europeans were excluded and tried to fight what they characterized as a monopolists' "trust," but they lacked resources and political influence.

One of the tactics of the cartel was to keep its actors anonymous for fear that fame would lead to demands for higher wages. Thus leading ladies in companies that were stalwart MPPC members, such as Biograph and Vitagraph, were not known by their own names but simply as the Biograph Girl or the Vitagraph Girl. A leading independent film producer, IMP, challenged this by luring one of the anonymous Biograph leading ladies to work for it. Her name was Florence Lawrence. Through a series of publicity stunts IMP made her famous in her own right and the public flocked to see her films. She later revealed after the promotional campaign that she had received more than 3,000 proposals of marriage. Another Biograph girl to achieve similar fame by promoting herself in her own right was Mary Pickford. Actors' wages did rise, as the trust members had feared, but the films with recognized names did spectacular business and the star system was established.

MPPC members had mostly made short films, often just 10 minutes long, which were shown in groups of five or six to provide an hour of entertainment for a nickel. The European films were much longer and were shown by themselves, perhaps supported by a "short" at the beginning. Independent theatre owners and more educated audiences preferred the longer format and by 1910 the days of the nickelodeon were numbered.

THE MOVIES GO TO HOLLYWOOD

The second decade of the twentieth century saw the foundation of the Hollywood we now recognize, both literally and geographically. The clear distinction between production, distribution, and exhibition developed further in these years, with each part of the industry having its own separate character. The division between the "producer" who organized the film and the "director" who was responsible for the creative content was also established. The distributor moved film prints around the various American states and the exhibitor owned the cinemas. These were the early days of the "studio system," with actors and directors being under contract to a studio that controlled their careers. It was at this time that the practice of preselling a film or often a package of films to a distributor began as one of the key sources of finance.

The First World War starved European film producers of resources and stopped most of their local film making. This handed a huge opportunity to the American industry. The power and influence of the MPPC had declined rapidly after the Federal Government started an antitrust action against it in 1912. The public had also tired of cheap "shorts." There was a huge boom in local American long-form film production and high-quality cinema construction. Independent producers started to copy the Europeans and experimented with more radical film ideas. Leading among this new breed, who saw film as a medium for the epic narrative story rather than a documentary feature or an amusing novelty, was Adolph Zukor, who had been an early pioneer of penny arcades, which he had constructed on a grand scale. He developed the idea of having a luxury cinema above his rooms full of peep-show machines, which he called the Crystal Hall.

Zukor decided to import longer, multi-reel European films, which he dubbed "main features," and he started producing home-grown American films with the same artistic objectives and approach. He arranged for these to be shown in his lavish venues and did much to overturn the image of the "fleapit" nickelodeon. He made motion pictures culturally acceptable to the educated middle classes and made going to the cinema a more upscale experience.

Many of the new, longer films were made in Los Angeles, as the climate was far more predictable than on the east coast, the long distance from New York made it easier for early filmmakers to avoid the restrictions placed on them by the MPPC, and Los Angeles had the advantage of not having any unionized labor, which made production much cheaper. One of the first big investors in what would become Hollywood was IMP, which by 1914 had changed its name to Universal. It made a bold declaration of confidence by building a 250-acre studio complex in Hollywood called Universal City.

In an attempt to clean up the messy and very localized distribution system of film prints to local theatres, a group of distributors came together to create a major national network called Paramount. Pioneer producer Adolph Zukor saw this as a threat to his production business so he engineered a takeover in 1914, thus creating the first vertically integrated motion picture giant. He named it Paramount Pictures and listed it on the New York stock exchange—the first use of Wall Street money. It was during this period that most of the big Hollywood studio names were founded, including Fox, MGM, and Warner Brothers. Columbia and RKO followed in the 1920s.

Production, distribution, and exhibition were now in common ownership. The new studios had access to funds via Wall Street. Hollywood was home to the biggest movie-making business in the world. This model of vertical integration and corporate ownership was to be the defining structure of the industry for the next 30 years. These companies and their founders were outsiders, first- or second-generation Eastern European émigrés, who had broken the power of the MPPC and wanted true American films to fill up the theatres they owned. By 1915 Hollywood employed more than 15,000 people.

THE BIRTH OF A NATION

DW (David Wark) Griffith was an actor turned director who did more than any other early pioneer to invent the techniques of camera movement, editing, lighting, and scripting that came to define motion pictures. He was also the first to experiment with the big-budget epic, the first and most famous of which was *The Birth of a Nation* in 1915. Griffith realized that the camera was not just a passive observer of a scene but an active participant, and that camera angles and movements such as pans, zooms, and tracking shots all imparted a dramatic mood of their own. He found ways to get emotion into motion pictures by the use of uniquely cinematographic techniques. His masterpiece was based on a play called *The Clansman*, about the role of the Ku Klux Klan in the American Civil War. It turned out to be highly controversial as well as wildly popular. Griffith continued working into the 1930s and made an early sound movie called *Abraham Lincoln*, although he never reproduced the commercial success of his epic.

APPLIANCE OF SCIENCE: SOUND AND COLOR

From the earliest days of the film industry people had experimented with sound and color and in the 1920s both became common features. There were numerous ways of marrying a film with an audio track. Many silent movies came with instructions to ensure that, when exhibited, the action was accompanied by a pianist or even a full orchestra. Warner Brothers, one of the smaller studios, had one of the best technical solutions and in 1927 it released *The Jazz Singer*, in which Al Jolson was heard to sing some numbers. This was not revolutionary, as the audience had become used to a gramophone record of mimed song being played in the cinema, but he also turned to camera and spoke synchronized dialogue, which caused a sensation.

Between 1927 and 1929 all the major studios switched from mostly silent to mostly sound production. At first this created many problems as microphones were primitive, which meant that actors had to stand on the spot and talk into strategically placed stage props concealing the recording equipment. The movement of the camera was also severely curtailed; cameras were noisy and the early microphones picked this up. The solution was to place cameras in large containers, sarcastically called "ice boxes" by the operators as they were hot and airless. These had glass fronts but they were far less mobile than before. However, when these early technical problems were overcome, sound changed the nature of film.

The hugely popular slapstick silent comedies that relied on visual gags declined. Actors who did not speak well or who could not remember lines were dropped. Musicals became hugely popular, as did films of well-known stage dramas that needed complex dialogue. In an example of art imitating life, the story of the 1952 film *Singing in the Rain* features a fading female star of the silent movie era who uses an unknown actress to dub over her vocals and songs in an attempt to prolong her career.

Studios experimented with crude forms of color from 1914 when the Technicolor Company was formed, but it was an expensive and complex process and audiences seemed happy with black and white. By the 1930s a three-color process had been perfected and Disney won an Oscar in 1931 for its color cartoon *Flowers and Trees*. In 1939 *The Wizard of Oz* mixed color and sepia, and from then on nearly all films were made in color unless the director had strong artistic reasons for wanting a monochrome effect.

Converting all the exhibition theatres to sound, building sound stages, and installing the new, quieter color cameras was an expensive gamble. The big studios turned to the financiers of the east coast for money.

MONOPOLY PART II: THE STUDIO SYSTEM

From the start of synchronized sound until they were broken up by the Federal Government in 1948, Hollywood was dominated by five major studios, each of which was a vertically integrated giant along the lines originally defined by Paramount Pictures. They owned the cameras and the studios, they had long-term contracts with actors and directors, they owned the regional distributors, and they owned the cinemas. Small, independent producers found it all but impossible to get their films distributed except through one of the majors. The monopoly that had been attempted 30 years earlier by the MPPC had now come about in practice through commercial aggression. Directors, producers, and stars—the power players of the modern movie industry—were kept under the thumb of the all-controlling studios with onerous, long contracts. The studio bosses, the movie moguls, controlled everything.

The powerful studios demanded that exhibitors contract to take blocks of films, so that if they wanted the big stars and major hits they also had to pay for a wide range of secondary "B" pictures. This produced a guaranteed up-front source of income. The US Justice Department did not like the structure one bit and as early as 1938 took legal action accusing the studios of a conspiracy to restrain trade, but the many attempts at legislation and "trust busting" were circumvented by lawyers and lobbyists. With such a high level of vertical integration and control, each of the studios developed its own recognizable style of film making.

Paramount, with its European heritage, was the most sophisticated and emphasized its stars, which included Mae West, Marlene Dietrich, and the Marx Brothers. It also made the Bing Crosby/Bob Hope "Road" pictures and branched out into cartoons with *Popeye*. MGM had the most lavish production values and made more early color films than other studios. It was famous for *Gone with the Wind* and *The Wizard of Oz*. Warner Brothers, which had led the sound revolution, was still smaller than the others and focused on cheaper productions, often with a lot of location filming. It became known for gritty gangster dramas featuring its main star,

SOVIET CINEMA

When the Bolsheviks took over Russia following the revolution in 1915, one of their main problems was how to unite a sprawling country of more than 150 million people. With diverse languages and culture, they decided that cinema was their most important medium. The industry was nationalized in 1919 and was initially controlled by Lenin's wife Nadezhda Krupskaya. Considerable state resources were put into film, which was used as a propaganda tool. Sergei Eisenstein, who made *Battleship Potemkin* in 1925, was the most famous of the early Soviet directors. His sequence in that film called "The Odessa Steps," in which a camera follows a baby carriage as it bounces down the stairs, has been reproduced in numerous subsequent movies.

James Cagney. It also employed Humphrey Bogart in *The Maltese Falcon* and *Casablanca*. Fox (which later merged with the smaller Twentieth Century Pictures) was more fixed on owning its theatre chains than on creating unique movies. It was an early pioneer of sound and produced the Movietone newsreels. The last of the "big five" was RKO, a studio created by RCA, which wanted to ensure that its proprietary sound equipment was used for making "talkies." From its opening RKO specialized in films with synchronized soundtracks. It took more creative risks than some others, for example making *King Kong* and *Citizen Kane*.

After some 20 years of unrivaled dominance, two events brought the Hollywood studio system to an end. In 1948, 10 years after the case started, the US Supreme Court ruled that it was no longer legal for the studios to own chains of cinemas and they were forced to sell them. Then, a couple of years later, the star James Stewart, represented by the powerful talent agency MCA, cut a deal with Universal under which he got a share of profits from a film. This marked the end of the downtrodden and undervalued star and the rise of the agent and "points" system, which prevails to this day. The monopoly was over and the studio heads bemoaned their fate. Then along came television to make it all seem so much worse.

SMALL-SCREEN SALVATION

In true Hollywood tradition the studios saw the arrival of TV as a threat and they did everything they could to hamper its development. They regarded the television pioneers as annoying and dangerous upstarts. Many studio bosses refused to sell their films to the newly emerging television networks. Some refused to allow television sets to appear in movies and banned their talent from doing TV shows. The ostrich-like moguls had their heads firmly planted in the old media sand.

The studios were afraid that a television in every living room would undermine the movie-going habit. They were right, but much more of a factor was the postwar exodus to the suburbs and the decline of the city centers, the traditional home of the movie theatre. The new suburban lifestyle revolved around the shopping mall. Young families preferred to stay at home rather than trek into the increasingly rundown and dangerous inner city.

Despite themselves, the studios got lucky. Television needed to fill many hours in the daytime schedules and old films were the perfect solution. The original negatives had languished in the studio vaults virtually forgotten, but now they had a new lease of life. A critical part of 1950s technology, the telecine machine, allowed films to be shown on television. Royalties started to roll in. Suddenly the studios were rich again and for a few years everything looked rosy. But after a while the increasingly

HAYS OFFICE AND PRODUCTION CODE

The cinema industry has always been aware of the huge public impact of its products; and keen to avoid external controls. Its solution has been to offer to be self-policing. In 1922 the US industry hired Will H Hays, former Postmaster General, to run an advisory body to administer the Purity Code for films to avoid provocative, violent, or sexually suggestive scenes.

By 1934 the powerful studios decided to go further when faced with threats from the Catholic Legion of Decency, which sought aggressive censorship. They adopted the Production Code, which was written by a Jesuit priest and set out what was morally acceptable in film. It prohibited scenes of passion, swearing, and nudity. It required that any criminal activity should be shown to be punished by the end of the film. It even banned the showing of double beds lest they hint at sexual activity. Scripts had to be submitted to the Production Code Office in advance for assessment, after which they would receive a seal of approval, without which they could not be distributed. Non-compliance resulted in a fine. The code continued to be followed well into the 1950s.

powerful television networks decided they could make films for themselves. This bid up the price of talent and established stars were paid huge appearance fees to participate in "made-for-TV" movies.

The studios started to struggle again. Not only was their distribution channel under threat but, still hampered by the prudish Hays Production Code, they were making the wrong sort of film for a changed market. They had simply lost touch with a new generation who were preoccupied by rock music, the Vietnam War, and hippy, anti-establishment culture.

SMALL SCREEN SALVATION: THE SEQUEL

In the 1970s the traditional distinction between the "aristocracy" of Hollywood and the "peasantry" of television began to blur. The US government also forced the TV networks to buy some of their shows from third parties—the so-called Fin-Syn rules. The traditional studios were among the best equipped to become suppliers and many changed their focus to making for TV. Big-name stars and directors moved between media and the foundations were constructed for what we experience today, where a major television series is just as important as a major film.

Without their original distribution chains, the film studios were relatively small businesses and became targets for the new breed of corporate raiders in search of Hollywood glamor. In 1966 Paramount still had the 93-year-old Adolph Zukor as its chairman. It was sold to conglomerate Gulf+Western and started to focus far more on making television series, notably *Star Trek*. In 1968 MGM was sold to a consortium focused on real estate and gambling, and the MGM name was used for hotels. The MGM film studio then acquired United Artists and its film library was later sold to Ted Turner, founder of cable news network CNN. MGM's television series included *The Man from U.N.C.L.E.* By 2010 it was owned by a private equity consortium and despite operating the evergreen James Bond franchise, it was flirting with bankruptcy.

Also in 1968 Warner Brothers was sold to a group that had made its money out of car parking and funeral parlors. Despite its unlikely ownership, it continued to focus on making star-led movies and developed both Batman and Superman series. In 1989 it was merged with the publishing giant Time and in the 1990s went on to build the Harry Potter film franchise. It remains one of the most successful studios.

During the 1970s Universal concentrated mostly on making for television, with *Law & Order*, *Miami Vice*, and *Northern Exposure* among its output, but it also had major film hits, including the Steven Spielberg films *Jaws*, *ET*, and *Jurassic Park*. Universal was taken over by talent agency MCA in 1962. Japanese electronics group Matsushita then took a stake. Subsequently French water utility Vivendi took control, only to pass it on to NBC, part of General Electric. In 2010 cable company Comcast became the majority owner.

Twentieth Century Fox was one of the most successful studios, making *The Longest Day*, *The Sound of Music*, and *Star Wars*. In 1978 it was acquired by two financial investors, one of whom later had to flee the country to avoid tax-evasion charges. It ended up being owned by Rupert Murdoch's News Corporation, which developed is own television network, also called Fox.

FROM FILM TO MULTIMEDIA

By the 1990s it was clear that owning a film studio was a glamorous but not very profitable exercise. Most of the corporate raiders had drowned in debt. The corporate ownership of the studios became impossibly complex, but most of them ended up part of, or closely associated with, diversified media conglomerates. The original film companies had been vertically integrated organizations, making moving pictures to fill their theatres. Now the model had switched to horizontal integration, with owners having interests in the associated and less risky media of television, publishing, music, and telephony. To make profits films needed to be exploited across a multimedia platform.

With the arrival of videocassettes in the 1980s, Edison's vision of moving pictures as a private medium was realized, albeit 90 years later. The VCR (video cassette recorder) proved to be one of the most rapidly adopted of all consumer electronic devices and the sale and rental of tapes provided Hollywood with a huge new source of income. As the big studios no longer owned cinemas, this new technology did not frighten them and rather than worrying about the cannibalization of traditional channels, they embraced the VCR and later DVD, which they saw as an extension of selling theatre tickets.

Studios now increasingly relied on the income from discrete "windows" after the initial theatrical release. Films could make money from a sequence of timed exposures, each of which addressed a different market. Airlines and hotel rooms paid a premium for early access; cable TV shared subscription revenues; cassettes and DVDs produced cash from sell-through and rental income; first-run national commercial television shared advertising costs, as did syndicated repeats on local stations. A film could fail at the box office and still be a profitable venture. All this meant the skills of film studios moved toward ever greater reliance on agents, lawyers, and deal-makers. The game became to find 360-degree exploitation of the product. And the master of this was Michael Eisner of Disney.

The Walt Disney Company had been founded in 1923 as a small animation studio making cartoons to be distributed by other major players. Building on the characters it created, it expanded into theme parks, radio and television networks, shops, sports teams, cruise liners, musicals, and merchandise. It is now, by some definitions, the world's largest media company. Michael Eisner took over as CEO in 1984, when the business was in trouble, and then gave a near two-decade long masterclass in multimedia exploitation. In 1995, in a move symbolic of the new approach, Eisner appointed the famous and powerful talent agent Michael Ovitz as president of Disney, but Ovitz clashed with the corporate culture and left after 14 months with a severance deal worth more than $100 million. Eisner himself left some eight years later, but Disney has continued as the model of a diversified entertainment conglomerate.

With the wide range of money-making opportunities, and without the need to own theatres, many new independent studios opened up; as they became successful they were absorbed into the majors, who needed to show they could acquire growth. Miramax, set up by the Weinstein brothers in New York, made *Pulp Fiction* and *Shakespeare in Love*. It was acquired by Disney, but the relationship was uncomfortable and in 2010 it was sold again to private investors. New Line, also from New York, became famous for *Nightmare on Elm Street*. Over the years it prospered and grew to make the *Lord of the Rings* trilogy. It is now part of Time Warner. DreamWorks SKG, established by Steven Spielberg, made *Saving Private Ryan* and *Gladiator* among others, but is now owned by Viacom.

BOLLYWOOD

More feature films are now made in Bombay, India than in Hollywood, California, hence the "Bollywood" nickname for the Indian industry. These productions, usually in the Hindi language, follow the traditional model of numerous song-and-dance numbers worked into a plot that almost always involves "boy meets girl and boy triumphs over adversity." The sheer scale of the Indian industry has now brought it to the attention of America, but India has always been a major film producer in its own right.

India was one of the first countries to experiment with film making, starting in the late 1890s. One of the original pioneers, Dadasaheb Phalke, made an Indian epic movie called *Raja Harishchandra* in 1912 when Hollywood was still making novelty shorts. The 90-minute film was based on Indian mythology and features the first screen appearance of the god Shiva.

From that point on the Indian film industry remained based on a very strong, homegrown culture. One of the most famous films is *Devdas*, first made as a silent feature in 1928 and then remade as a "talkie" in 1935. It has since been remade more than a dozen times in various local languages. It tells the story of a doomed love affair between a rich landlord's son and a poor woman in rural Bengal and is based on a classic Indian novel. The star of the 1935 version, Kundan Lal Saigal, suffered a throat infection toward the end of the filming and when it came time to record his songs he had to do it in a quiet, soft style like that of an American "crooner." This proved hugely popular and set the model for many Bollywood singers to follow.[4]

In the early days of Indian film the performers usually sang their own songs, but from the 1940s onward the trend developed for using actors who looked good to act and singers who sounded good to sing. There was no attempt to hide this from the audience and the practice of what Bollywood called "playback singing" became the norm. Both singers and actors got star billing on the film and the songs were often released ahead of the movie to become hits in their own right.

Unlike Hollywood, the Indian industry has not been vertically integrated and has not had access to corporate funding. Most films are financed by money from friends and family. Also unlike Hollywood, the key factor is not getting a script greenlighted by a studio executive, it is finding a willing leading actor. Mihir Bose explains in his book *Bollywood: A History*:

> Bollywood completely reverses the procedure. The script is almost the last thing written... the starting point is the telling of the story to the male star whose agreement will make or break the film.[5]

The global success of the multi-Oscar-winning British film *Slumdog Millionaire*, set in India and with references to Bollywood-style movie making, demonstrated the full potential for the Indian industry.

HOLLYWOOD-ON-THAMES

The movie industry in Britain has produced films of extraordinary quality and appeal but it has never been a steady and consistent industry like Hollywood. The story in Britain is of individual production companies that grow, have great success, and then either collapse because they overreach themselves or decline when key talent gets lured away to America. The UK has been the birthplace of more successful producers, directors, and actors than any other country apart from the US, but many of them end up living and working in Hollywood. The UK's problem has been that its home market is simply too small to support significant domestic industry and its cinema audiences are very culturally happy with US products. Nevertheless, the skills of the UK's technical experts and its studios are still in constant demand.

The very early British films from 1900 to the 1920s were mostly factual and educational, or short dramatic adaptations of classic stories from Dickens and Shakespeare. The first Sherlock Holmes movie *A Study in Scarlet* was made in 1914. In the 1920s the two main film makers in the UK were Gainsborough Pictures, which had studios in the East End of London, and Gaumont British, at Lime Grove in the West, a location ultimately taken over by the BBC. In 1927 another UK company was founded called BIP, which owned 500 cinemas. It made the first British sound film, *Blackmail*, directed by Alfred Hitchcock in 1929.

The imposition of a British government quota on imported films in 1927 led to a huge boom in domestic production. Much of it was low quality and some of the best movies were not dramas at all. British film-maker John Grierson coined the term "documentary" in the 1920s and was a leading exponent of the form. In 1936 he narrated the now justly famous *Night Mail* about the train from London to Edinburgh, which used a specially written poem by WH Auden and music by Benjamin Britten.

Grierson was clear about his motives, saying: "I look on cinema as a pulpit, and use it as a propagandist."[6]

During the Second World War American films were hard to get and the British factual tradition resulted in many documentary-style, quasi-propaganda movies such as *In Which We Serve* starring Noël Coward and Richard Attenborough. These wartime films created a large pool of technical, acting, and directing talent that shaped a flourishing cinema industry in the late 1940s. This was dominated by the Rank Organisation, founded in 1937, which, like a Hollywood operation, owned all five major British film studios, including Pinewood, Ealing, and Lime Grove, and more than 600 Odeon cinemas.

The late 1940s and 1950s produced world-class movies like *The Third Man*, *Brief Encounter*, *Great Expectations*, *The Dam Busters*, and *The Cruel Sea*. It also saw the first British film to win an Oscar: *Hamlet*, starring Laurence Olivier in 1948. Ealing Studios specialized in comedies such as *Whisky Galore!* and *The Lavender Hill Mob*. The industry was extremely successful but mostly middle brow and populist.

In the 1960s Britain led the world in music, London was a swinging city, and the film industry benefited from a new wave of adventurous producers. The James Bond franchise started in 1962 with *Dr No*. Michael Caine starred in a series of spy thrillers, beginning with *The Ipcress File* in 1965. And films like *Alfie* and *Women in Love* pushed the boundaries of public moral

QUOTA QUICKIES

In 1927 the British government tried to rescue its domestic film industry. In the previous year, of some 700 films shown in the UK more than 600 came from America and only about 30 from the UK. The government passed the Cinematographic Film Act, which forced distributors and exhibitors to show a minimum quota of British-made films. While this did lead to some additional domestic production, its main impetus was to cause the American-owned distributors to set up shop in the UK to make ultra-cheap "B" films to be shown alongside American-made hits. By making locally they were able to meet the quota without having to spend big money.

A few quota films had reasonable budgets, like *Goodbye, Mr. Chips* and *The 39 Steps*, both starring Robert Donat, but the target was typically to make films for "£1 a foot" and shoot a 60-minute movie over a 10-day period. Critics at the time denounced the "quota quickies" as rubbish, but some have survived and won subsequent praise.[7]

acceptance. This success allowed the financing and production of epics like *Lawrence of Arabia*, which won seven Academy Awards.

The 1970s saw a British slump, but by the 1980s a new local company called Goldcrest was formed and fresh talent was emerging. Hugh Hudson and David Puttnam—both from the advertising industry—teamed up to make *Chariots of Fire*, which won four Academy Awards. Goldcrest also made *Gandhi*, *The Killing Fields*, and *Local Hero* before it collapsed, having also invested in a number of expensive and spectacular failures.

By the 1990s British companies such as Merchant Ivory (*Howards End* and *Remains of the Day*), Working Title (*Four Weddings and a Funeral*, *Notting Hill*, and *Bridget Jones's Diary*) were winning global audiences for the characteristic British style and subjects, although mostly with American money. More recently the Harry Potter franchise has kept the UK at the top of the film-making league, albeit again with significant US investment.

THE ENGINE OF ENTERTAINMENT

Going to a movie remains one of the most intense entertainment experiences, but the income from movie tickets is now a relatively small part of the income for film. Arguably, cinema no longer exists as a standalone medium. It has become film-based multimedia. If the creative ideas that originate in the theatre, books, and comics are the iron ore of entertainment, cinema is the steelworks that converts them into the girders and plates that are used to build the entertainment industry.

Studios are increasingly focused not just on making a film but on creating sustainable character franchises. The granddaddy of them all is James Bond, but others like Spider-Man, Harry Potter, and Jason Bourne have followed the same path. A franchise creates audience familiarity and greatly cuts down on marketing costs. Word of mouth, web-based chatter, and anticipation make sequels hugely profitable. The practice of shooting several films in the same franchise at the same time was taken to the extreme by the three-part *The Lord of the Rings*.

The film industry watched in horror as colleagues in the recorded music business were undermined by digital piracy and cheap file sharing. Initially the reaction was to try to establish legal and technical barriers, but faced with the experience of music the movie studios have embraced alternative methods of web-based distribution. In the US most studios support Netflix, which has signed up some 15 million subscribers who receive DVDs by mail, cutting out traditional outlets such as Blockbuster. Netflix (and a very similar service in the UK called Lovefilm) then moved on to video streaming to make films available on PCs, internet-enabled televisions, and tablet computers like the iPad. It reports that more than 60 percent of customers have now tried this way of watching.[8] Other web streaming services such as Hulu, YouTube, and BBC iPlayer also offer a viable and legal online outlet for studios. Like television, VCRs, and DVDs before it, digital media may well be another boom for film makers if they are prepared to innovate. But the bonanza of the DVD is ending and new digital charging mechanisms must be found.

And despite the huge expansion in other media, physical cinema attendance is actually growing again. 2009 was the first year US box office receipts exceeded $10 billion, which reflected rising ticket prices, but with 1.4 billion visits made the actual number of tickets was also up on previous years. The UK experienced similar trends. This reflects the greatly improved experience of a cinema visit in terms of quality of seating and catering.

It also reflects the spread of digital projection, which offers better picture and sound, and the experience of "big" films like the 3D *Avatar*, which offers an entertainment package that cannot be replicated at home. While the golden age of cinema is certainly past, movies are nevertheless thriving in the multimedia environment and remain the engine of much of the entertainment industry.

2.14 | Television

For many people born in the Western world since the 1940s, leisure time has been dominated by the box in the corner of their living room. Writers like George Orwell, from a generation before television, were shocked by the impact they saw the new medium have on society. Television has been around for about 70 years and has undergone extraordinary changes in technology, organization, and content. It experienced more rapid growth than any other medium until the web. A newspaper or magazine publisher today runs a business that would be broadly familiar to Benjamin Franklin and his contemporaries, but to a pioneer of television what we now experience would be unrecognizable.

If this book had been written in the 1990s this chapter would have begun by describing television as the most powerful medium of all time. In that decade the free-to-air broadcast television networks were still the undisputed media kings. But since digital technology has become widely available, conventional broadcast TV has lost its crown and is beginning to experience the decline and reinvention familiar to its older cousins of print, cinema, and radio.

There used to be three distinct technical elements of television: production (cameras, editing, and recording machines), transmission (broadcasting towers and cables), and viewing (cathode ray tubes). These old, analogue technologies have all been overtaken by superior digital alternatives, which offer better, cheaper and quicker ways of making, distributing, and accessing programs. This has taken away the monopoly power of the original TV network operators.

When we talk about newspapers or books or magazines we tend to mean the physical media themselves, the things we touch. We do not think of booksellers or news stands as the medium, simply as the retail outlets. With television, however, it is the whole system we describe and it is the names of the big broadcasters—BBC, ITV, ABC, CBS, and NBC—that have defined the industry.

In the digital, multichannel, mobile world the old way of thinking about the medium of television is increasingly redundant. It is now more usefully thought of as a combination of sound and moving pictures, viewed on a variety of screens rather than on the box in the corner of the living room controlled by a broadcasting organization that scheduled your evening for you. Ben Silverman, co-chairman of NBC Entertainment, observed: "If you ask me what business I am in, I say the video business as opposed to just television."[1]

The origins of television, technically, creatively, economically, and managerially, are to be found in radio. In both the US and the UK the established institutions that dominated radio were, rightly or wrongly, handed the keys to TV by their respective governments. And it is attempts by governments to keep control of the broadcast spectrum that have so influenced the institutions that have run the television industry.

TV TECHNOLOGY

The development of television has been driven by technology, but it had a complex and protracted start. Unlike the invention of radio, which can be traced to a small number of people with clear objectives, television is the result of the efforts of many individuals over a long period, in different countries.

Television works because it fools the human eye. Images on the screen, made up of hundreds of lines of bright dots, change so rapidly that the eye and the brain "see" them as representing continuous movement. It is a similar illusion to the one produced by film going through a projector. But unlike film, which is a physical process of shining a light through a series of still photographs, the transmission of TV requires a lot more electronics. The original image must be scanned in some way to turn it into electronic information. This information must be transmitted over radio waves or a wire, and then it must be turned back into an image at the receiving end using some sort of projection.

The basic principle is similar to that of the telephone microphone, which worked because of the variable resistance of carbon to electric current. The resistance altered when a sound wave hit the carbon and changed the pressure acting on it. As long ago as the 1870s it was found that the metal selenium behaved in a similar way, but in its case it was light rather than sound that caused its resistance to vary. In 1884 a German engineer, Paul Nipkow, patented the theory of a selenium-based system using spinning discs with holes in them to break up an image into individual snapshots. It did not work in practice, but his theory was correct.

In the formative years of television no one was quite sure what the transmitted images might be used for. As a result, there was little commercial or governmental interest, so it was left to a host of inventors to experiment. The word "tele-vision"—viewing at a distance—was coined in a patent application in 1900, long before the medium became a reality. Then over a 30-year period numerous small technical advances produced improvements in all the three parts of the television system.

Mechanical or electronic

Nipkow's scanning concept was taken forward in the UK by a Scottish inventor, John Logie Baird, and in the US by Charles Francis Jenkins. Both captured the imagination of the newspapers but neither built a business.

Baird first demonstrated an image of a human face in 1926; Jenkins showed off his "radiovisor" a few months later. In 1928 he opened the world's first television station, W3XK, in Washington, DC. Baird formed his own company and by 1929 he was making experimental broadcasts for the BBC. However, mechanically scanned pictures flickered badly and others sought an electronic alternative.

In 1908 another Scot, Alan Campbell-Swinton, described the theory by which streams of electrons could be manipulated by magnetic fields to create a picture on a luminescent screen. He called these streams "cathode rays," but he never built a working machine. A Russian student called Vladimir Zworykin had worked on cathode ray tubes in Moscow. In 1923, he emigrated to the US where he patented an all-electronic television system and by 1929 he had developed a functioning projector. Another American, Philo T Farnsworth, developed an electronic camera he called the "Image Dissector."

The technologies of Zworykin and Farnsworth were combined by RCA in America, while in England another team working for EMI found ways to make the picture clearer. Both broke the picture up into a series of fine lines, which was much superior to the flicking effect of the mechanical spinning disc.

The winning formula

In 1936 the BBC decided to have a contest to select the superior solution. It experimented by broadcasting, in alternate weeks, the Baird system with a mechanical camera and the EMI/RCA system, which was all electronic. The electronic approach won hands down and regular British television commenced in 1937 with the standard of 405 lines per screen.

In America the first commercial broadcasts, also using the EMI/RCA technology, started in 1939 and were unveiled with a great public fanfare by David Sarnoff of RCA, who claimed that his company had invented television. With BBC TV closed for the duration of the war, all the development efforts occurred in the US.

In the early 1940s the American National Television Standards Committee decided to regulate all US television on the technical model of 525 lines—what we now call NTSC—which then was considered superior to the UK approach. In 1960 the UK abandoned its standard and joined most of Europe, using 625 lines, called PAL (phase alternating line). The

French decided to go down yet another route with 819 lines, called SECAM. Thus were born three incompatible video systems that have driven generations of VCR and DVD owners to despair ever since.

When color came to television there were, inevitably, two competing systems in Europe and America. The US government finally decided on the three "gun" approach championed by RCA. So once again its favorite domestic technology company was the winner and its broadcast network, NBC, started to offer the world's first color broadcasts in 1956. The UK, suffering postwar economic problems, would have to wait until 1967.

In television's early years it was hard to show projected films, until the invention of the telecine machine, which turned film output into a usable TV signal. The BBC did not install its first telecine until 1950, which is why the bulk of its early output was live. The same was true for NBC and CBS. In contrast, by the time ITV arrived in the UK in 1955 the telecine was ubiquitous, so early ITV schedules featured a huge amount of prefilmed programs, often imported from the US.

At first the only way to keep a permanent recording of live television was to film the picture on a monitor, which resulted in very low-quality copies. However, after the arrival of videotape in 1956, programs had a longer shelf life with high-quality, low-cost reproduction, which created a market for repeats, syndicated shows, and exports. Videotape also allowed action replays, which revolutionized the nature of sports coverage.

By the early 1960s in both the US and the UK television service was available to nearly 80 percent of the population and receivers had been installed in more than 50 percent of homes. Television was by then the main mass medium.

The end of scarcity

New technologies such as videotape and lightweight cameras had a significant impact on the nature of programming in the 1960s and 1970s, but government restrictions on broadcast franchises maintained the near monopoly of the networks. What finally opened up television in the 1980s was more choice brought about by cable and satellite channels. This allowed television to serve niche audiences in a way that had previously only been done in print by magazines.

Cable TV had started in America in the 1950s, as a way for remote communities, or people in the middle of cities, to get service where their normal domestic aerials were inadequate. Large commercial antennas were constructed on hills or high buildings and the signal from this "head end" was distributed to homes by a wire. Entrepreneurs worked out that this cable could deliver more than just the existing broadcast channels. However, the local cable systems were isolated and could not afford to develop their own quality content.

The arrival of satellites in the late 1970s allowed diverse cable companies to create networks to rival the traditional free-to-air broadcasters. By the 1980s another, and very different, use of satellite was to reach consumers directly in their homes. Because the so-called geostationary satellite sat above the equator in a fixed position, a receiving dish did not need to move to track it. The reception dishes could be much smaller and cheaper and this paved the way for direct-to-home (DTH) stations. Like cable, these were capable of delivering hundreds of channels and were able to charge subscriptions, as the signals were encoded.

On tape and disc and on demand

Video cassettes of magnetic tape started to become available for domestic use in the 1970s and saw another classic, incompatible technology shoot-out: JVC's Video Home System (VHS) versus Sony's Betamax. As is often the case, the Betamax was technically superior but consumers found the VHS easier to use, so it won. Recording machines became a feature of most households and by 1985 some 50 percent of all homes in the UK and US had one. The magnetic tape of

THE SATELLITE

If there is a single technology that transformed the industry of television, it is the satellite. It has done this in three different guises: international program sharing, cable distribution, and direct-to-home broadcasts. In 1962 the Telstar satellite allowed program sharing across the Atlantic; in simple terms, it replaced the undersea cable. The Mexico Olympics and the 1969 Moon landings were worldwide television events, thanks to satellite transmissions. Satellites made TV the viewers' "window on the world."

From the 1970s the second use of satellite was to enable local cable companies in the US to create alternative national networks. It was this that allowed Ted Turner to take WTBS national and to launch CNN. The final application was the direct-to-home broadcast, of which the most successful examples are Sky TV in the UK and DirecTV in the US.

VHS was overtaken by the digital encoding of DVDs (digital versatile discs) using optical lasers, the video version of the audio CD.

VHS and then DVD became so popular that they developed as a distribution medium in their own right, with movies and television series being sold and rented as an alternative to watching them on television or going to the cinema. This was a positive for the program makers, in that they offered another route to market that enabled television shows to be sold like music albums. Home recording combined with wireless remote control devices had a further, negative effect on the networks. Channels could now be "surfed," programs "time-shifted," and commercials avoided by "zapping" (changing channels) and "zipping" (speeding through advertising breaks).

Digital diversity

By 2005 most television broadcasts in Britain and America were distributed in a digital format rather than the original analogue signal, and once a television program existed as a digital file, the conventional networks essentially lost control of it. VHS and DVD players were replaced by harddisc personal video recorders (PVRs), which were really just computers with names like TiVO and Sky+. Many homes controlled their viewing through an on-screen electronic program guide (EPG), which made channel surfing and prerecording that much easier. The internet had been developed to share computer files, which meant it was ideally suited to a host of special-interest digital television channels. Over an internet link a video file can be viewed (streamed) and transferred from one machine to another (downloaded). Every conceivable variation of service started to be offered, from YouTube with short clips of amateur content to the BBC's iPlayer, which allowed viewing of the previous week's programs. Video material was now available to anyone, anywhere, at any time, which held profound implications for the economics of the traditional television industry.

A STATE-SPONSORED OLIGOPOLY

Evolving technology shaped television, but government action determined the structure of the industry. In both the US and the UK the broadcast spectrum was jealously guarded by politicians. Regulators created television franchises and handed them out for the most part to the same people and organizations that had been running radio. This led to an initial period of domination by the BBC in the UK and by NBC and CBS in the US.

However, although they both created near monopolies, Britain and America managed their television systems in very different ways. The UK opted for the public service ethos of the BBC. The US's commercial radio giants, NBC and CBS, lobbied to grab control of television—if only to slow down its development. The commercial versus public service issues that divided the two nations in radio were magnified and extended into what would become the more powerful visual medium.

In the UK the BBC looked on television as a natural extension of its public service activities. BBC radio professionals hated what they saw as the tawdry commercial "dumbing-down" of the radio medium in the US. They went out of their way to insist that British television ran no risk of following the American lead of being advertising funded. In the US, in stark contrast, where commercial radio was accepted and popular, TV was seen as an important part of the postwar economic stimulus and advertising on television was regarded as a crucial part of building demand for consumer goods to generate new jobs. Thus, the commercial nature of US television was not just tolerated but encouraged.

Government interference

The history of broadcasting is littered with government initiatives. The British in particular love their public inquiries.

The 1951 Beveridge Report supported the BBC enjoying a monopoly and was highly critical of television in America. The Labour Government accepted the Beveridge Report's findings, but a subsequent Conservative administration decided that commercial broadcasting was a good thing in any case, which led to the start of ITV. In 1963 the Pilkington Report adopted a rather patrician view of the new ITV service and demanded that it clean up its downmarket act and put more emphasis on quality journalism.

The Annan Report in 1977 took exactly the opposite view and felt that television must become less exclusive and more reflective of all elements of society. It said that the ethos of public service should be about pluralism and access, rather than providing moral leadership. This also led to the creation of the iconoclastic Channel 4. Annan said in a direct repudiation of the approach of Lord Reith: "We do not accept that it is part of the broadcaster's function to act as arbiter of morals and set themselves up as social engineers."[2]

Yet another committee in the 1980s decided that Channel 4 was still not enough. It led to the Broadcasting Act of 1990, which opened the way for a fifth national television channel. The Communications Act of 2003 recognized the convergence of television, the internet, and telecommunications and set up a new body called OFCOM (Office of Communications) to oversee a new set of regulations for a multichannel, digital world.

In America the government was less involved in tinkering and left most of the control to the FCC (the Federal Communications Commission). It was always intended to have a light touch compared to the British system. Television in the US is fundamentally a local service and it is at a local level that licenses are awarded and operated. However, the economics of television favor national networks and much of the FCC's time has been spent trying to balance the tensions between local and national concerns.

The FCC had little control over networks, but they could dictate who owned the local broadcasters. So, for example, in the 1940s they prevented CBS and NBC owning more than one station in each major market, which led directly to the establishment of the third network, ABC. However the FCC did not always approve of what it controlled. In 1961 the chairman, Newton Minow, gave a landmark speech called "Television and the Public Interest" in which he issued a challenge:

> When television is good, nothing—not the theatre, not the magazines or newspapers—nothing is better. But when television is bad, nothing is worse. I invite you to sit down in front of your television set when your station goes on the air and stay there without a book, magazine, newspaper, profit-and-loss sheet or rating book to distract you—and keep your eyes glued to that set until the station signs off. I can assure you that you will observe a vast wasteland.

His "vast wasteland" phrase was widely picked up by media and politicians and was a major influence of the 1967 Public Broadcasting Act, which set up federal funding for what became the Public Broadcasting Service (PBS), an American attempt to replicate the high-minded ideals of the BBC. Another FCC initiative was to try to curb the power of networks by preventing them from both owning and distributing programs. The Fin-Syn rules

THE FIN-SYN RULES

In the 1960s the three US television networks (ABC, CBS, and NBC) enjoyed an extremely powerful position. They had replicated old-fashioned Hollywood. They made the programs, owned and ran the networks, and sold all national advertising. Hollywood and Madison Avenue felt that the networks were getting too strong and persuaded politicians to share their concerns. They argued that vertically integrated networks had too much control, which, they said, led to a lack of diversity in television programming. In the 1940s the Supreme Court had forced Hollywood to cede ownership of its cinema outlets; now Hollywood wanted television to take the same medicine. And movie bosses could be very persuasive, as the *Hollywood Reporter* pointed out:

The studios could get a starlet to go to Washington and sit on a congressman's desk and he could get his picture taken. That was a powerful incentive.[3]

The result, in 1970, was the Financial Interest and Syndication Rules (Fin-Syn), which prevented the television networks from owning an interest in the production companies that made network shows. This led to a boom for the traditional film studios and an explosion of independent producers. The Fin-Syn rules were abolished in 1995, which, once more, led to rapid consolidation. Disney (a studio) acquired ABC (a network). NBC (a network) acquired Universal (a studio). CBS merged with Paramount. Warner and Fox (both studios) ended up launching their own TV networks.

did much to create a new industry of independent television producers and proved a lifeline for struggling Hollywood studios. In its mission to create diversity, in 1986 the FCC approved the creation of a fourth network, Fox.

In recent years the FCC has turned its attention more to content than industry structure and has been gently ridiculed for issuing fines to broadcasters that defy regulations about maintaining public good taste. When singer Janet Jackson exposed a breast during the live Super Bowl broadcast in 2004, the FCC was the butt of much humor when it fined the broadcaster CBS $550,000 for what singer Justin Timberlake described as a "wardrobe malfunction."

BBC: The "establishment" voice of the nation

On May 12, 1937, BBC television broadcast the coronation of George VI, which was a sensation in the newspapers even though only about 10,000 people watched. May 1937 also saw the first live broadcast of Wimbledon tennis and in 1938 the BBC broadcast the Oxford vs. Cambridge Boat Race. Early BBC programs were presented by public school educated announcers in formal dinner jackets and became a novelty for about 20,000 upper middle-class households who could afford the very expensive receivers, which cost the same as a small car. However, development was abruptly halted by the outbreak of the Second World War when BBC TV was declared "closed by Government order." Transmission simply stopped in the middle of a Mickey Mouse cartoon on September 1, 1939. It came back in June 1946 with the same cartoon and just in time to do a live outside broadcast of the Victory Parade.

The television habit was slow to catch on in the UK partly because postwar shortages made it very difficult to manufacture enough sets. Even by 1947 television broadcasts could be received only in London and only close to the transmission site at Alexandra Palace. The BBC broadcast for just a few hours a day and the news bulletins were read with somber authority and no pictures; in effect like watching radio. Television was seen by most established media professionals in Britain (including the BBC's own radio people) as an undesirable new threat. Racecourse owners, football clubs, and the British Board of Boxing Control initially refused permission for live outside broadcasts on the grounds that they would reduce the number of paid admissions. But by the 1950s transmission towers were being built outside London, the price of sets came down, the quality of the programs improved, and TV viewing started to grow dramatically.

In 1953 the Coronation of Elizabeth II was the key inflection point in British broadcasting when television asserted its dominance. The broadcast drew an audience of some 20 million—more than half the adult population—many of whom watched in pubs, clubs, and cinemas. It was the first real "water-cooler moment" for the UK and it led to an explosion of television ownership.

ITV: A UK commercial upstart

The huge success of the BBC led to demands that its monopoly be broken and hence the Conservative Party introduced the 1954 Television Act, which created an independent television service. When the legislation was debated in the House of Lords, the BBC's original leader, Lord Reith, was not keen, to say the least. He said commercial television was "akin to the introduction into Britain of smallpox, the Black Death and the bubonic plague."[4]

Despite his protests ITV went on air in 1955. It had a couple of difficult years when it was only available in London and advertisers were skeptical, but as additional regional franchises were created, the channel took off. So much so, that by 1957 when Scottish Television was launched, its then owner, Canadian Roy Thomson, felt able to describe his business as "a license to print money."

ITV established itself as more attuned to popular culture than the BBC, but also made a significant contribution to innovation in news and drama. It competed head on with the BBC for audience, but was handed a monopoly to sell television advertising. British worries about the American way meant that single-program sponsors were not allowed. The first UK advertisement was for toothpaste and in its early days the commercials on ITV attracted more comment than its programs.

By the 1960s it was clear that the competition with ITV had led the BBC to go far more downmarket than many of its staff and viewers wanted. So the UK government gave the BBC another national channel, BBC2, with the remit of getting more culture on air and generally raising the tone of broadcasting. This was followed 20 years later by another commercial service, Channel 4, which was told to cater for minorities and demonstrate innovation.

US networks: A powerful cartel

US government policy held that American television broadcasting would be a local service reflecting local needs, but in practice the economics overwhelmingly favored a national network model. Local stations, which were not actually owned outright by NBC or CBS (or later ABC), were normally affiliated to one of them, as the programs available were far better than anything they could make for themselves. The networks, as had been the case in radio, enjoyed huge, centralized power in the commissioning and scheduling of programs and the sale of sponsorship and advertising. The fact that the radio giants NBC and CBS were awarded the first television licenses should come as no surprise. What is perhaps surprising is that they managed to hang on to their comfortable and valuable oligopoly for so long.

In its early days TV was heavily subsidized by the near monopoly profits of radio. Although regular broadcasting started in 1939, American television was slow to take off. In 1946 only 8,000 households had television sets and by 1948 there were still only 108 licensed TV stations, mostly in larger cities. Most of these early stations lost money and there was significant interference between adjacent signals. In the face of chaos, the FCC imposed a four-year freeze on the issuing of new licenses, a huge boost for the established cartel. However, by 1960 TV reached nearly 90 percent of the US population and the big three were set for a golden age of profits and power.

The end of oligopoly

Over a 30-year period from 1955, the major television broadcasters in the US and UK enjoyed an extraordinary status as the main cultural and information channels. It was new technology that opened up the airwaves. HBO (Home Box Office) was one of the first premium pay cable channels, starting in New York in 1972. By 1975 it was available nationally by satellite and one of its first big events was the Mohammad Ali vs. Joe Frazier boxing match, the so-called Thrilla in Manila.

In 1976 a small local station in Atlanta, WTBS, rented time on a satellite and made its local broadcast available to cable systems across the continent. It was able to show its local baseball games in other markets. It instantly became a challenger to the established TV networks. TBS stood for Turner Broadcasting Systems and it was owned by Ted Turner, called the "mouth from the South." Inspired by the success of WTBS, in 1980 he went on to create CNN, Cable News Network. In the UK cable was slow to develop. Neither the government nor the population saw any real need for it. This left a gap for satellite services.

In 1988, after years of deliberation, the UK government granted a direct-to-home satellite license to a grand consortium of establishment media owners called British Satellite Broadcasting (BSB), which was due to launch in September 1989. However, newspaper baron Rupert Murdoch had beaten it to the punch by acquiring what amounted to a pirate station based in Luxembourg using the pre-existing, low-cost Astra satellite. In effect it was a television version of Radio Luxembourg. His Sky TV, launched in February 1989, proudly chose to have a simple and technically inferior distribution system using small, off-the-shelf satellite dishes and worked on the existing PAL equipment. It showed cheap American imports and located itself in an industrial estate in West London.

BSB, by contrast, did everything in a Rolls-Royce manner. It built its own satellites at a cost of some £200 million (Sky's rental bill for ten years of satellite use was only about £50 million). BSB had its own unique, sophisticated aerial system called a "squarial"—which did not work properly. It had its own luxury studios by the River Thames. It commissioned original and expensive programming. And it was all so complex, it did not get on air until March 1990, by which time Sky had an uncatchable audience lead.

However, the public were confused by the two incompatible systems. BSB was better in theory, but in practice Murdoch's Sky was better at marketing. With both services losing millions of pounds a week, in October 1990 BSB collapsed and it was announced that it would "merge" with Sky, simply a smokescreen for a takeover. With a monopoly of British commercial satellite broadcasting in place and without any government regulation or control, Sky went on to become one of the most successful satellite broadcasters in the world.

EVOLUTION OF PROGRAMS

The first two sections of this chapter described the technical and political forces that have shaped the television industry. For most of us as viewers it is what we watch that really interests us, not the background plumbing that delivers it. It is the content not the corporate structure that gets our attention.

Broadcasters tend to be motivated by professional fulfillment, by having fun, and by seeking the admiration of their peers, as much as by making money for their corporation. This inherent tension between program makers and business managers has been a feature of the medium since it began. The nature of the programs that get made at any one time depends on who is winning the argument.

The other tension is between broadcasters and politicians. In practice, licensees have often made decisions designed to preserve their franchises rather than to make the "best" television. While program makers often seek to challenge the political establishment and push the envelope on moral and social issues, the license holders are frequently far more cautious.

The style and nature of programs are influenced by a range of factors. Technology has had a huge impact, with inventions like the telecine machine, videotape, and electronic news gathering making a major contribution. Economics, the availability of advertising, and the huge increase in the number of channels have led to the development of new formats such as reality television and home shopping. Social changes, like attitudes toward violence and bad language, have affected program content too.

Although the US and UK have many differences in programming, they both broadly fit into three eras:

- Experimental—1935 to 1955
- Network—1955 to 1985
- Multichannel competition—1985 onward

EXPERIMENTS IN TELEVISION: 1935–55

The early operators of television were not sure what to do with their new toys. Many of them had worked in radio, which relied on the human voice and music. Others came from music hall, theatre, and cinema. The movie industry in Hollywood and Pinewood had developed its own ways of telling stories, but early television was mostly live and had little money. Not only did the TV pioneers see no point in making movies; being mostly "radio guys," they did not have the skills. And the movie studios saw no point in making product for television, which had a far smaller audience than cinemas and which, in any case, lacked the technology to broadcast films effectively or charge for them.

Thus, early TV really was "radio with pictures," viewing at a distance. The cameras were simply pointed at events rather then seeking to create new content. In film the camera is part of the action, almost one of the performers. It moves and interacts, and scenes can be cut and edited. In television, at least in its early days, it was an unblinking observer, often forced to be rooted to the spot with an umbilical cord connecting the camera, via broadcast towers, to the cathode ray display technology in the home.

Very early television was about events, like Franklin D Roosevelt's Presidential address from the 1939 World's Fair. TV in the 1940s was about seeing existing radio personalities, variety shows, and highly staged and rehearsed interviews with politicians and sports stars.

By the early 1950s the television pioneers were enjoying enormous freedom. For the most part the broadcast organizations lost money, but they knew they were establishing a powerful new medium so they could take risks and make things up as they went along. When broadcaster Ed Murrow transferred the format of his radio show *Hear It Now* to TV in 1951 he called it *See It Now*, and introduced it by saying: "Here is an old team trying to learn some new tricks."

A few of the early big hits broke new ground by using the technology in novel ways. *I Love Lucy*, normally listed as one of the most popular television shows ever, ran from 1951–57 on CBS. It created the concepts of independent producers, reruns, and syndication. Lucille Ball, the show's star, was already a successful radio comedienne. She and her husband Desi Arnaz decided they could make *I Love Lucy* with their own production company, Desilu. They also did not want to move to New York and insisted on working in Los Angeles.

To avoid the big east coast markets having to show a poor-quality copy, *I Love Lucy* was shot on three 35 mm cameras in front of a studio audience. This mimicked the multiple cameras of television but resulted in a very high-quality original print. This was expensive, so Desilu agreed to foot the bill and in return CBS allowed it to keep the rights to the shows. *I Love Lucy* was shown repeatedly on CBS affiliates and was sold to other broadcasters, including Britain's ITV. The show made a fortune and the company went on to make television history with programs including *Mission Impossible*, *The Untouchables*, and *Star Trek*.

In a sign of the times, *I Love Lucy* was sponsored by cigarette manufacturers Philip Morris and the opening credits showed a cartoon version of Lucy and Desi climbing down a Philip Morris carton. They and other characters smoked branded cigarettes throughout the program.

Dragnet, which launched the idea of serial drama, was invented by a radio announcer called Jack Webb. It started on radio in 1949 and moved to television in 1951. It was, arguably, the inspiration for most subsequent police shows. Early episodes always started with the announcer proclaiming "The story you are about to hear is true. Only the names have been changed to protect the innocent." The premise was that each episode was based on a real police case. Webb played Detective Sergeant Joe Friday, badge 714 of the Los Angeles Police Department, and audiences found it all so convincing that reality and fantasy became confused. When Webb died the LAPD mounted an honor guard and officially retired his fictitious badge number. The show, which was initially sponsored by Chesterfield cigarettes, ran simultaneously on television and radio and was the early model for developing a complete franchise. An extract from a 1953 magazine article gives a fascinating insight:

> In slightly more than four years, *Dragnet* has burgeoned from no more than an idea to a vast business enterprise. The Sunday radio version is on the full NBC network, and the Thursday TV presentation appears on 80 stations. *Dragnet* has a comic strip running in 35 papers, and its producers are thinking of a full-length movie as well as foreign syndication. Friday guns, badges, fingerprint kits and police games may be licensed for sale on the juvenile market if they are authentic and in good taste.[5]

The Quatermass Experiment was the first science-fiction production by the BBC and one of the first shows specially written for TV. Performed live in six half-hour episodes starting in 1953, it featured a fictional British space mission that goes wrong and brings a sinister alien presence back to Earth. The show was shot with primitive, fixed electric cameras in black and white. It was done in what seems to us now a clunky and amateurish style with an obviously fake studio set, but it was a national sensation. The last episode reached 5 million people, representing a 90 percent share of the potential audience. Because videotape had not been invented, the program was recorded by filming the output of a television monitor in the studio. One recorded scene shows a fly crawling slowly across the image—not a creepy special effect, simply an errant insect that got between the film camera and the TV screen.

By the mid-1950s the majority of the public in the US and the UK had access to a television, and the networks and governments had invested in building a national system of transmission towers. TV now became a mass medium rather than a novelty and with that it started to develop its own creative ideas and its own syntax. The biggest names in entertainment both on and behind the screen now wanted to work for it. Advertisers began to regard it as an important commercial channel.

THE NETWORK ERA: 1955–85

Grouping the next 30 years of television into one period does not suggest that the medium stayed the same for that length of time. There were great changes, but on both sides of the Atlantic the structure of a cosy network oligopoly remained in place. Programs evolved in response to competition between broadcasters, because of shifts in public taste, and the adoption of new production techniques with the huge resources of the networks. The sorcerer's apprentices of television came out from under the shadow of radio and turned into wizards of their own medium.

What changed most over the 30 years was society itself and

THE TELECINE MACHINE

Films depict motion because of an optical illusion. As the 24 frames per second pass through the projector, our brains are tricked into seeing continuous action. Television is a similar, electrical, optical illusion but at about 30 frames a second. In its early days television could not easily show films. Focusing an early TV camera onto the film screen produced unacceptable flickering. The solution, in very simple terms, is to speed up the film to make the frame rate the same as television, but it is done using a "pull down" technique that generates additional "fake" frames. The opposite process was used to store a live television transmission on film in the days before video tape. Telecine machines came into use in the 1950s, which meant that film sequences could be used in TV shows and entire films shown on TV if the studios agreed.

television reflected this. In the 1950s shows were based around safe, conservative, and comfortable values. The medium reflected the loving, unstressed, nuclear middle-class family, often grouped around its television set in a well-appointed suburban living room. By the end of the era television had brought into that same living room sex, violence, war, poverty, and conflict. It moved from a mirror of middle-class values to a window on a complex and disturbing world. In doing so, it established its credentials as a medium of extraordinary power and importance.

Over the period a more realistic and challenging approach evolved. Younger program makers, who had not come from a radio or cinema background, took far more cultural risks than the pioneers who were just fascinated by the technology. The new breed wanted to experiment with their medium and make it reflect what they saw happening in their own lives. This was television moving from supporting the status quo to challenging it.

In the network era American material seemed more prominent in the UK because the US had the resources and large home market to create expensive drama such as *Hill Street Blues*. The UK did much better with the intellectual capital of low-cost situation comedy, game-show formats, and documentaries.

There are endless lists of the most popular TV shows. Some reflect audience size, some critics' opinions, some are based on opinion polls, and others sales of DVDs. There is no single, accepted authority. The two lists opposite are an amalgam of various sources, including *TV Guide*, *Time* magazine, and the British Film Institute. They are not intended to be exhaustive; they simply represent shows that were, in their own way, television landmarks.

Interestingly, the only name to appear on both sides (*Brideshead Revisited*) originated in the UK. However, the documentary *The Family* is a UK remake of *The American Family*. Going in the other direction, the US comedy *All in the Family* is a remake of the UK's *Till Death Us Do Part*. It is also noteworthy that two talk show hosts (Letterman and Parkinson) switched networks: David Letterman moved from NBC when he did not get Johnny Carson's old spot on *Tonight* and Michael Parkinson switched to ITV after a dispute about scheduling with the BBC. The American list is dominated by variety, talk shows, and situation comedies. The British has more dramas and documentaries; it has a majority of BBC shows but with a strong performance by ITV, which thrived in the network era.

News and current affairs

Many broadcasters saw reporting the news as their most socially important function. This was much encouraged by politicians (who like seeing themselves on television). It thus became an important and, in some cases, a required element of ensuring that a broadcast license was renewed.

In the US news programs were dominated by trusted and experienced journalists and personality news presenters were the norm. CBS had *Douglas Edwards with the News* and NBC *The Huntley-Brinkley Report*.

SIGNIFICANT NETWORK ERA SHOWS

US	UK
Today, NBC, 1952–	*Panorama*, BBC, 1953–
The Ed Sullivan Show, CBS, 1955–71	*Hancock's Half Hour*, BBC, 1956–61
The Twilight Zone, CBS, 1959–64	*Tonight*, BBC, 1957–65
The Andy Griffith Show, CBS, 1960–68	*Blue Peter*, BBC, 1958–
The Dick van Dyke Show, CBS, 1961–66	*TW3*, BBC, 1962–63
The Tonight Show, NBC, 1962–92	*Dr Who*, BBC, 1963–
Star Trek, NBC, 1966–69	*World in Action*, ITV, 1963–98
The Carol Burnett Show, CBS, 1967–78	*Cathy Come Home*, BBC, 1966
60 Minutes, CBS, 1968–	*Monty Python's Flying Circus*, BBC, 1969–74
Sesame Street, PBS, 1969–	
The Mary Tyler Moore Show, CBS, 1970–77	*Till Death Us Do Part*, BBC, 1966–75
	News at Ten, ITV, 1967–
The American Family, PBS, 1971	*Parkinson*, BBC/ITV, 1971–2007
M*A*S*H, CBS, 1972–83	*The Family*, BBC, 1974
Saturday Night Live, NBC, 1975–	*World at War*, ITV, 1973–74
All in the Family, CBS, 1971–83	*The Naked Civil Servant*, ITV, 1975
Brideshead Revisited, ITV, 1981	*Fawlty Towers*, BBC, 1975–79
Hill Street Blues, NBC, 1981–87	*Boys from the Blackstuff*, BBC, 1982
Late Show/Late Night with David Letterman, NBC/CBS, 1982–	*Brideshead Revisited*, ITV, 1981
St. Elsewhere, NBC, 1982–88	*The Jewel in the Crown*, ITV, 1984
Cheers, NBC, 1983–93	*Yes Minister*, BBC, 1980–88

The combination of filmed reports, on-location correspondents, and live interviews drew large audiences and the news divisions of the various networks became very profitable. In 1962 Walter Cronkite took over at CBS and started a long tradition of star news anchors that would lead to the likes of Dan Rather and Peter Jennings.

In the UK the arrival of ITV and its impact on news presentation is a classic example of the benefits of competition. From the mid-1940s until 1954 the BBC had treated television news as simply an extension of radio. The nightly BBC television news consisted of a radio script without film, read over a still picture of Big Ben. The feeling was that pictures would spoil the authority of the broadcast.

The ITV network created its own news service called ITN, run by a new breed of journalists who had none of the BBC's sense of history and self-importance. They decided from the start to have on-screen personalities and called them newscasters to emphasize that they were more than just readers. They used all the new technologies of telecine and video tape to create lively bulletins that borrowed heavily from American techniques and were soon getting 80 percent of the news audience.

It now seems almost inconceivable, but up until 1957 both BBC and ITV agreed to shut down all programming between 6 pm and 7 pm for the so called "toddlers' truce." Children's programs finished at 6 pm to help parents get their offspring to do homework or prepare for bed. Even at the time this was considered bizarre by many people. The government minister responsible for broadcasting, Lord Hill (later to become both chairman of ITV's supervising body and chairman of the BBC), observed in 1956:

> This restriction seemed to me absurd. It was the responsibility of parents, not the state, to put their children to bed at the right time... I invited the BBC and ITV to agree to its abolition.

Nevertheless, the BBC dragged its feet and the truce sustained until 1957 when the gap was filled by *Tonight*, the makers of which enjoyed the role of television revolutionaries. Led by Cliff Michelmore, they wanted to experiment with new formats, mixing light entertainment with live interviews and filmed reports. The program won numerous awards and was described as "informal, irreverent and modern," words not normally associated with the BBC at the time. The DNA of *Tonight* is now detectable in current affairs programs around the world and it provided the environment for the ground-breaking *That Was the Week That Was* ("TW3"), which launched the career of David Frost.

Chat shows

The chat-show format was built around the smooth and articulate celebrity host who brought on entertainers, authors, and musicians with something to sell. The originator was Ed Sullivan, whose first show, *Toast of the Town*, started in 1948 but was iconically renamed *The Ed Sullivan Show* in 1955.

It ran every Sunday night at 8 pm and dominated the schedules for many years. It was the principal vehicle for new stars to be seen. Elvis Presley was launched on it in 1956 and The Beatles made their first appearance in 1963. Critics names this broadcast the start of the "British Invasion" of American music.

Entertainment: Soap operas and series

Soaps were a big hit in the 1950s and audiences have been hooked on them ever since. *As the World Turns* on CBS started in 1956. *General Hospital*, the longest running US soap opera on ABC, began in 1963. And *Days of our Lives* on NBC started in 1965.

In the UK the soaps were, initially, much more the natural preserve of ITV than the BBC. *Coronation Street*, which first aired in 1960, was a reflection both of the desire by the mass UK audience to see programs about "themselves" and also of the regional nature of the ITV companies. It was made by Granada in the north west and set in a fictional street in Manchester. A few years later the Midlands franchise holder ATV came up with *Crossroads*, set in a motel near Birmingham.

Soaps tended not to be experimental but were designed to be cheap and often ran every day. Serial drama, much of which was light comedy. could afford to be more ambitious. *The Mary Tyler Moore Show* was an early example of social realism. Mary was a single, working woman with a sex life; a very long way removed from the suburban mother who was the target of much of the advertising. *M*A*S*H* (mobile army service hospital) was a TV version of a Robert Altman film, but with a half-hour format and a great reliance on tight scripting and

WALTER CRONKITE

Walter Cronkite was the frontman of the CBS Evening News for nearly 20 years (1962–81). He was voted "the most trusted man in America" and was the inspiration of generations of broadcasters. When covering the Democratic and Republican Conventions in 1952, he was the first reporter to be described as a "news anchor," to indicate he was holding all the fast-moving coverage in place. In 1962 he was the main face of the Cuban Missile crisis, the first big news event to be played out live on TV, and he was in the studio as the tragedy of President Kennedy's assassination unfolded in Dallas. Later, reporting from Vietnam, he observed that he felt the war was unwinnable. President Lyndon B Johnston commented: "If I have lost Cronkite I have lost Middle America."

SPAGHETTI TREES

In 1957 *Panorama*, the serious and respected flagship of BBC current affairs, broadcast what has subsequently been called the biggest television hoax in history. It ran a three-minute film, on April Fool's Day, reporting in a factual and strait-laced fashion, that the spaghetti harvest in Switzerland was enjoying a bumper year because of a mild winter and the non appearance of the "spaghetti weevil." The film, which showed spaghetti growing on trees, was voiced by the BBC's most respected journalist, Richard Dimbleby, and seen by some 8 million viewers. Pasta was not a well-known dish in Britain at the time and many called in the next day asking for instructions for how to grow spaghetti. They were told to put a piece into a can of tomato sauce and hope for it to sprout. The hoax (which can still be seen on the BBC website) is a salutary reminder that the program makers in the 1950s took themselves far less seriously than did their administrators and the government.

character development. Running for much of its time during the Vietnam War, it hid its criticism behind the disguise of being set in the Korean conflict.

Cop shows and westerns

The early success of shows like *Dragnet* showed the audience's appetite for cop shows. Towards the end of this period came *Hill Street Blues*, which had an ensemble cast, with multiple storylines combining dark humor with drama. It was one of the first to use handheld cameras to create a sense of movement. In addition, television exploited the success that Hollywood had already achieved with the western. *Gunsmoke* was on CBS from 1955 to 1975 and in its early years was the number one show on television, competing with similar series like *Bonanza* and *The Lone Ranger*. Made on film and running for an hour, it was easy to export these programs to other markets and all became popular in Britain.

Children

Children's program *Blue Peter* was launched in 1958 with worthy aims. Despite being a BBC product, it was consciously less educational than the multi-award-winning *Sesame Street*, which overtly introduced children in the US to mathematical and language skills. *Blue Peter* relied on wholesome presenters who represented non-threatening role models and made interesting things with old detergent bottles. *Sesame Street* introduced the iconic and iconoclastic Muppets mixed in with live actors and animation. It also used all the most advanced techniques of program research to understand what worked with its young audience.

Game shows

Studio-based game shows may have been cheap, but they became a crucial element of television. Cash prize quizzes were a feature of American radio and were a central part of the schedule when they moved to television. In 1954 the US Supreme Court ruled that the shows were not considered gambling and the size of the prizes immediately rocketed. The radio show *The $64 Question* became *The $64,000 Question* on television. When quiz shows returned after the 1959 scandal, they faced a raft of restrictions. *Jeopardy* started with small prizes in 1964, *The Price Is Right* followed in 1972, and *Wheel of Fortune* in 1975.

In the UK the BBC was uncomfortable with the game-show format, which in the 1950s and 1960s left the way open for ITV to enjoy huge success with *Take Your Pick* and *Double Your Money*. The game show format would later play a big part—perhaps the central part—in the multi-channel era when it morphed into reality television.

THE QUIZ SHOW SCANDALS

Big-money prizes for television game shows were a staple of the American networks in the 1950s. The uncertain outcome and instant cash proved compelling to viewers. Sponsors like Geritol (an iron supplement), which owned the quiz *Twenty One*, were heavily involved with the shows' producers who were keen to keep their ratings up. This led to popular, audience-friendly contestants being "helped" to get the right answers. By 1958 unhappy ex-contestants gave evidence that far from being fair, the shows were scripted and fixed. A huge public scandal resulted and, following a Congressional investigation in 1959, quiz shows almost disappeared from American TV. The network owners blamed the influence of single sponsors. They used the affair as an excuse to have more control of content and moved to the sale of advertising time in fixed spots, in order, they claimed, to reduce commercial influence.

MULTICHANNEL: THE AUDIENCE TAKES CHARGE

After the mid-1980s what had been a scarcity of broadcast channels suddenly became an abundance of choice. The notion of the happy family

THE WAR GAME

For the British, who like to think of their media as being part of an open democracy, the story of *The War Game* is shocking. In 1965 documentary maker Peter Watkins made a 50-minute film of what he said would be the aftermath of a nuclear attack on the UK. It showed the potential destruction and misery experienced by the civilian population, but did so in a documentary style that made it feel like a news program. It was due to be broadcast on the anniversary of Hiroshima, but the BBC, after some still unexplained discussions with the government, banned the program. It said at the time: "the effect of the film has been judged by the BBC to be too horrifying for the medium of broadcasting." After much lobbying the film was given restricted cinema access and went on to win the Academy Award for Best Documentary Feature in 1966. After two decades of pressure the BBC finally allowed it to be broadcast in 1985.

grouped around their television became a nostalgic memory. Each niche and demographic now had its own channel. In many homes each person now had their own TV.

Technology allowed control of television to move away from the network executive and into the hands of the viewer. People at home could channel switch, pause live broadcasts, time shift, and multitask. Just observe any teenager surfing websites, making phone calls, and doing homework, all while "watching" TV. In the UK the multichannel environment started to be available in 1982, but the concepts of multichannel programming were invented in America.

In their early years most cable channels in the US simply recycled old programming, but by the mid-1980s operators were able to invest in high-quality original material and audience figures started to improve dramatically. By 2000 most homes had more than 500 channels to choose from.

To make things more difficult for the establishment, new free-to-air networks were created by grouping together independent television stations and recruiting existing affiliates away from the big three. Fox started in 1986; WB (Warner Brothers) and UPN (United Paramount Network) followed in 1995. All three benefited from being owned by a major film studio and all focused on a particular audience niche, which forced NBC, CBS, and ABC to rethink the way they did business. In 1980 the original three networks had enjoyed an over 95 percent share of audience; by 1990 this had dropped to 60 percent and by 2000 to below 50 percent. Getting attention in the multichannel world demanded a different type of program.

Rolling news

The arrival of extra channels meant that news broadcasts were no longer confined to fixed times but could happen at all hours, in the same way that real news did. Satellites also allowed journalists to feed live pictures back to their studio from anywhere in the world. The 24-hour rolling news format was pioneered by CNN (Cable News Network), which launched in 1980. Initially derided as the "Chicken Noodle Network," it took a long time to become an essential part of people's viewing. However, by the first Gulf War in 1991 CNN, with its instant and constant news from the front, was beating the traditional network news hands down. That success spawned many imitators.

Special-interest channels

MTV had launched in 1981 as a video jukebox aimed at teenagers and with repeated showings of Michael Jackson's music video for "Thriller," it started to capture a big audience. The culture channel A&E launched in 1984. It featured original stand-up comedy with *An Evening at the Improv* and imported significant amounts of BBC programming. Lifetime (1984) was aimed at women and featured sex therapist Dr. Ruth. Nickelodeon (1981) made original shows for children.

Independent drama franchises

Whilst the rise of multichannel was bad news for the networks, it was a huge opportunity for independent program makers. Popular franchises now had considerable value in syndication. The networks needed to invest in the best original drama to try to keep their primetime audience. Programs were designed not just to be ephemeral, domestic broadcast events but to have a long life on multiple international channels and as boxed sets.

Hospital drama *ER*, created by bestselling author Michael Crichton and director Steven Spielberg, offered a pace and excitement not seen before. It took the concept of multiple story lines, an ensemble, and a constantly moving camera even further than *Hill Street Blues*.

The West Wing (NBC, 1999–2006) took the multiple story structures and camera techniques of *ER* but added a highly literate and demanding

FOX: THE FOURTH NETWORK

Fox was launched in 1986 in the face of derision and disbelief from established television operators. It was created by media baron Rupert Murdoch acquiring six stations from Metromedia and then signing up a further 90 affiliates. This gave access to 80 percent of the US audience. Fox was built on the concept of providing "tabloid" programming targeted at 18 to 34 year olds, at a time when the big three networks still tried to be all things to all men. Two early successes were *Married... with Children* and *The Tracey Ullman Show*.

Married... with Children challenged sitcom convention by displaying the dysfunctional Bundy family using bad language, involved raunchy plot lines, and saw the cast failing in almost every practical and moral way. *The Tracey Ullman Show* featured a British comedienne in traditional comedy format but with many new ideas, the most enduring of which was a short cartoon, called *The Simpsons*, which went on to become one of TV's biggest hits.

Until 1993 Fox was a distant number four network, but then, in a signature Murdoch strategy, it acquired the exclusive rights to the NFL. It went on to commission other original material aimed at its young target audience, such as *Beverly Hills, 90210*, *The X-Files*, *24*, *House*, and more recently *American Idol*. By 2005 Fox in had become the top-rated network for reaching young adults.

script and, unusually for US television, had a single author for most episodes—the creator of the show, Aaron Sorkin. Multiple Emmy award-winning *Mad Men*, commissioned by the AMC cable channel, was also driven by a single individual, Matthew Weiner, and exhibited production values normally associated with big-budget movies.

Law & Order has been made by Dick Wolf for NBC since 1990 and *CSI*, made by Jerry Bruckheimer for CBS, started in 2000. Both have spawned numerous spin-off shows and both franchises are valued in the billions of dollars, with extensive sales in syndicated and many markets around the world.

It was a similar story for comedy. The multichannel era needed the production values, strong characters, and rich storylines that ensured they would survive multiple showings without boring the audience. *Seinfeld* (NBC, 1989–98) holds the title of the most popular American TV show. *Friends*, *Frasier*, and *Will and Grace* are typical long-running comedies that started life as audience builders on specific networks, but have found a huge fan base in global syndication.

Live sport

It is ironic that in the early days of television the cameras were banned from many sporting events on the grounds that they would reduce the live audience. With multichannel, the broadcasters became the principal source of funds for major teams and pumped in so much cash that the economics of professional sports were radically changed. Baseball, American football, soccer, tennis, and others were transformed by the value of their television rights. And because live sport does not lend itself to time shifting, it became one of the main drivers of primetime TV. NBC paid more than $2 billion for the television rights to the Olympics. Sky paid £1 billion for four years of rights to UK Premier League soccer.

Reality television

The concept of "fly-on-the-wall" documentaries following "real" people has been around for decades, a famous British example being the *Up* series, which started in 1964 with *Seven Up!* featuring a group of 7 year olds. It has returned to them every seven years since to film their real lives unfolding. *The American Family*, made in 1971 by PBS, took cameras into a real home in California. *The Family* did the same thing in Britain in 1974. Both were a success with the audience but they were conventional, professional television.

BIG BROTHER

One program that epitomizes success in the multichannel era is *Big Brother*. The format is simple: a group of unknowns ("ordinary" people, who are much cheaper than stars) are collected together in a locked house and made to carry out various tasks. Hidden cameras watch and each week the audience is asked to vote for which of the "housemates" should be removed. The show can run live 24 hours a day on one channel and be shown for half-hour periods on another, while edited highlights appear on a third. The eviction of contestants continues until there is a winner. The audience votes by telephone or text using premium-rate lines that bring in extra income. The whole format, including website templates, camera positions, graphics, and production notes, is sold to broadcasters around the world as a franchise.

Producers of "BB" have gone out of their way to create conflict and titillation by peopling their house with attractive, sexually active, and sometimes dysfunctional contestants and making them do tasks involving few clothes and lots of alcohol. The program was developed in the Netherlands in 1999 and by 2010 was running in more than 100 countries.

As cable and satellite eroded the economics of the networks broadcasters needed to find cheap shows that had a sense of being an event. Reality television takes the medium back to its roots by pointing a camera at "real," allegedly unscripted events and letting the audience watch, and indeed participate, as the action unfolds. It is voyeuristic and intrusive—perhaps just what television was meant to be?

Big Brother is often cited as the archetypal reality show, but there are dozens of others. Talent shows like *American Idol*, *The X Factor*, *The Apprentice*, and *Survivor* all share the format of contestants who get knocked out as the show progresses.

Mega-format fantasy

Audiences in the 1960s and 1970s would have struggled to comprehend action/fantasy series like *24*, *Lost*, and *Heroes*. In any event, the economics of the television industry at the time would never have supported them. Their development needed a generation of viewers who had been led into multiple story lines and lurching time shifts by shows like *ER*. On top of that, they needed exposure to comic books, computer games, and websites to get a feel for storylines that left so much unexplained. Also, at many millions of dollars an episode, these shows needed all the skill of Hollywood packaging, with guaranteed world markets, to even begin to make their economics make sense. A visit to the NBC store in New York demonstrates the importance of hats, shirts, and other memorabilia in recouping the cost of their hit shows like *Heroes*.

THE END OF TELEVISION AS WE KNOW IT?

The industry of network television is nearing the end of a 60-year period of dominance. Many of the heritage stations will end up as part of a broader media business. By contrast, the medium of video is thriving and is available on a huge array of screens, both large and small, static and mobile.

Television, as a free-to-air broadcast medium, is returning to its roots. When it started it was a way of bringing live events into people's homes, and increasingly that is what it will be again. The technologies of the telecine machine, video tape, and satellites allowed networks to become distributors for a wide range of premade programs and, while they were the only channel for this, they thrived. They forced viewers to watch what the broadcasters selected. But now consumers have myriad ways of obtaining video entertainment at a time, place, and price that suit us. The old, linear model of scheduled television programs that controlled our living-room habits is gone. The genie of video-on-demand has got out of the bottle and cannot be put back.

Television used to be "seeing at a distance." It allowed people to look at coronations, inaugurations, speeches, sports, wars, and stage performances even if they could not attend the event itself. That is now its main role once again. We can be part of the audience for *American Idol* and *The X Factor*. We can vote, we can participate. We can watch the World Cup or the Super Bowl live and from 20 angles at once.

In the digital world we can control video material to fit in with our lives rather than fitting our lives around it. Video can now be stored and searched. It is an artifact, not an ephemeral image. Using our keyboard and mouse we can cut and paste video with the same ease that an earlier generation could tear out and share a newspaper story.

Television broadcasting is not going to be replaced by the web but it will be greatly modified. The next generation will be enthralled by their own versions of *Blue Planet*, *Lost*, *Desperate Housewives*, and *House*. But these will not packaged in prime time by a channel like CBS, NBC, or ITV. As the head of Time Warner Cable Glenn Britt has observed, "There's no such thing as a TV anymore. There's a video display device."[6]

Ironically, the one institution that may thrive in all this is the BBC. When commercial television first arrived the BBC was pushed into the shade as the Niagara of advertising money allowed the independent sector to grab all the best talent. But now free-to-air commercial television is stumbling, the state-funded BBC is one of the few organizations that can afford to make high-quality programs, although ultimately it may choose to do offer them over the internet rather than by conventional broadcasting.

2.15 | Video Games

Video games have become, in some ways, the most popular and valuable medium and their influence on all other media has been huge. By combining text, audio, and video and involving players in an intense and interactive experience, games are proving to be the key transition between the media's analogue past and its digital future.

The degree to which video games have become a rich narrative experience was emphasized by the extensive background research and huge production budget for *Call of Duty*. In the run-up to Christmas 2010, *Call of Duty: Black Ops* became the fastest-selling video game ever, notching up nearly $360 million in sales on its first day.[1] No Hollywood blockbuster or hit album has ever made so much money so quickly. It was treated like a major movie project, with the emphasis on story as much as game play. Mark Lamia, the studio head who produced it, comments:

> The story is being told from the moment you put in your disc to the end of the campaign... It is so immersive; the story is tied to everything you are doing.[2]

Social gaming company Zynga was only created in 2007. It offers simple and basic games like *Farmville*, accessed on Facebook, which allows players to operate their own farm by growing crops and raising animals. Within three years of its foundation Zynga had more than 300 million active users for its games and was valued at over $10 billion. Part of its huge success is selling players, for real cash, virtual goods like plows and tractors. Zynga founder Mark Pincus says:

> When you go and see a movie, what do you leave with? Nothing physical—just the experience of the film. Well, this is the same. It's entertainment—people are buying into the game in a bid to be more entertained.[3]

The Nintendo game *Super Mario Bros.* celebrated its 25th anniversary at the end of 2010 and had, by then, sold more than 240 million units across all the various games platforms.[4] Along with associated feature films, comic books, and character merchandise, Mario has become a hugely valuable global multimedia franchise.

When Marshall McLuhan was writing *Understanding Media* in 1964, video games were unknown outside of computer laboratories. He was commenting on the communications role of group activities like baseball, ice hockey, and poker, but he certainly foresaw what multiplayer video games might become:

> Like our vernacular tongues all games are media of interpersonal communication... That games are extensions, not of our private but of our social selves and that they are a media of communication, should now be plain... Games are situations contrived to permit simultaneous participation of many people.[5]

Video games started as student hobbies on university mainframes and then moved into arcades, replacing traditional electromechanical machines. Basic home consoles like Atari took those arcade games into the living room, and then personal computers allowed a huge range of games into the bedroom and office. Handheld machines like the Game Boy made them mobile and advanced consoles like the Xbox enable online multiplayer interaction, which creates huge communities playing against each other, indifferent to geographic location or time zones. Video games are now a central part of the media ecology and a familiar feature of most households. A typical family spends far more on games than on cinema tickets or recorded music and devotes more of their time to them.

The industry has been dominated by companies like Atari, Activision, Electronic Arts, Nintendo, Sega, and Sony, but it is the big titles that captured the public imagination: the basic two-player tennis of *Pong*, the man-vs.-computer interaction of *Space Invaders*, the Japanese quirkiness of *Donkey Kong* and *Super Mario Bros*, the antics of *Tomb Raider*, the glamorized vice of *Grand Theft Auto*, and the mythical fantasy of *World of Warcraft*. These and all the rest have entertained and, the critics would say, addicted a generation.

The influence of video games on other media and society has been immense. Some argue that they have corrupted young minds and advanced violent and antisocial behavior. Their champions believe that they represent a radical new way of communicating and can have a major and positive role in education, as well as providing entertainment and promoting social cohesion. There is certainly far more to them than just "games" and increasingly the term "interactive media" might be more appropriate, because unlike the media types before them, video games really do provide a two-way experience. The player is an active participant, not simply a consumer.

GAME TYPES

There are now many thousands of video games titles and almost as many ways to classify them. Because video games are relatively new and designers so innovative, there is no agreed classification by type. There has been a clear progression of the various technical platforms and the same games often appear in arcades, and on home consoles, PCs, and handheld devices. But it is the game that is more relevant to consumers than the technology that delivers it. Broadly speaking, video games fall into the groups described below.

Action

This is the format where video games started. These simulate actions like shooting, racing, and jumping—the translation of a physical skill onto a screen, the imitation of activity that in real life requires coordination and gets the adrenalin flowing. These games tend to be played in a short session and there is a clear way of winning. The player achieves his or her (nearly always his) goals by competing with the machine and its programmer. These are ideal for arcades, which is one reason they were the earliest form to develop. They start with the very first screen-based game in 1961, the missile-firing *Spacewar!*, which had no public sales, and then *Pong* (1972), *Space Invaders* (1978), and later *Sonic the Hedgehog* (1991). Much later a huge range of driving, racing, and so-called first person shooters arrived in the "action" category. Many of the most popular recent games such as *Halo* and *Call of Duty* have a significant action element, but they combine elements of simulations, platform, and narrative games described below.

Action games often play better with special input devices like light guns, joysticks, and steering wheels. These devices were central to the design of the early arcade versions and then were offered as peripherals for home games machines and personal computers. The now very familiar game controllers such as the Xbox, PlayStation, and Wii developed out of the need for devices that allowed for more control than a keyboard for games that had a significant physical element. The hugely popular music participation formats like *Guitar Hero* and active sports like *Wii Tennis* owe much to the early action titles as they offered an immersive video simulation of real-life action.

Narrative

These are adventure games that allow the player to take part in and control a story. They were relatively late in arrival as they did not have an arcade heritage and needed the power of a computer, not just a circuit board. The first was *Colossal Cave Adventure*, developed by Will Crowther in 1976. It was a purely text-based game written in 700 lines of code in FORTRAN and told a story of going into a series of caves and having encounters with elves and trolls. Crowther was a keen caver and the game exhibits strong influences from Tolkien's stories. Players are offered various options for movement and their responses set the direction of the game. The original source code is now available on a website.[6] Even more than 30 years on, in simple black-and-white text, it is strangely compulsive to play. Type in "go north" and the machine will respond "you are on an open road in a forest"; typing "go east" gets you "you are in a valley with a tumbling stream." Type "blast" and the program tells you "blasting needs dynamite."

The game was sent around the world to computer departments and it was two players at the University of Essex, Roy Trubshaw and Richard Bartle, who took the idea to the next level by creating an environment in which more than one player could participate by using computers linked using a very early version of the internet. They called the idea *MUD*, for Multi-User Dungeon. Borrowing from the pencil-and-paper game "Dungeons & Dragons," later versions of *MUD* allowed players to adopt a fantasy persona and to progress to ever higher levels and obtain better weapons by solving puzzles and winning battles. This set the base for a huge range of role-playing games (RPGs) that have come to dominate the industry today.

Early screen-based games used crude animation. Later backgrounds became available to create two-dimensional worlds, and then advances in software enabled 3D graphics, and greater computing power allowed full-motion video. But right from the start the player became part of the game and could influence the outcome of the story. Solving sequential puzzles and controlling the action in *Myst* made it one of the early big hits. A strong storyline was also a selling point of the hugely successful *Grand Theft Auto* action game franchise.

Strategy

These games include the subgenres sometimes called "sandbox" or "real-time strategy," which require the player to make decisions and use resources over a large number of game moves over a long time. The challenge is intellectual more than physical. The early ones were ideally suited to home PCs as they benefited from, rather than were restricted by, the use of a keyboard as an input device.

One of the first was *M.U.L.E.* (Multiple Use Labor Elements), launched in 1983 for an early Atari home computer. It was a mixture of strategy and economics set on a fictional planet called Irata (which is Atari spelled backward). Four players take turns to both compete and collaborate to build a colony by harvesting raw materials. War games like *Red Alert* from 1996 built on this heritage. They made full use of the graphics and sound capabilities of a new generation of home computers and while they had a military theme, they were far more to do with problem solving than shooting and rapid action.

A variant of strategy titles are sometimes called "God games" or simulations, where the player creates and develops a society. In the US designer Will Wright created *Sim City* and at about the same time UK video game pioneer Peter Molyneux was working on *Populus*. Both were released in 1989 and both became international hits, unusually for Anglo-Saxon titles also in Japan. Building

AVATARS

Many video games invite us to adopt a virtual personality and play the game through that character. In something as basic as *Space Invaders* we are the missile launcher; in *Pong* we are the bat. In more sophisticated games we control Mario or Lara Croft. In virtual worlds like Second Life we participate by being a character whom we can design in terms of body shape, clothing, gender, and ethnicity. It is this ability to place ourselves into the game that is a huge part of the attraction.

The word *avatar* comes from the Hindu religion and describes the persona adopted by a deity when he or she descends from Heaven to appear on earth. At some point in the mid-1980s it started being used for characters in video games. The first use was probably in the game *Habitat* in 1985. It was explicitly used in the sense of being a virtual character in the novel *Snow Crash* by Neal Stephenson in 1992. As we are all encouraged, almost forced, to have an online presence that mirrors or substitutes for our real life identity, the use of an avatar is likely to become more widespread.

MARIO

In the late 1970s the Japanese playing card firm Nintendo was failing to get a foothold in the American market for its traditional arcade games. At its HQ in Kyoto it had hired a young industrial designer called Shigeru Miyamoto, who brought together his fascination with King Kong, the conventions of manga, and the whimsy of Japanese fantasy to come up with the story of a carpenter called Jumpman whose pet gorilla abducted his girlfriend. The game was to make Jumpman climb scaffolding on a building site to rescue the girl while the gorilla threw objects. The name of the game in Japanese roughly translated as "stubborn gorilla." Miyamoto used an English dictionary to translate this more literally as *Donkey Kong* for the US consumer.

Nintendo's American landlord, who had been generous about late rent payments, was called Mario and in his honor Jumpman was renamed *Mario* for the US market. In 1983 Miyamoto invented a brother for Mario called Luigi and in 1985 Nintendo launched a fully updated version called *Super Mario Bros.*, which let players progress to different levels in a fantasy world and fight various "super boss" enemies to define the format of what we now call a platform game It become the most popular video game for two decades, with more than 40 million units sold.

on the genre came one of the most popular of the simulations, *Civilization*, launched in 1991. As its name suggests, the player is able to develop a primitive tribe through all the historical layers of human development.

In 2002 Wright released *The Sims*, which built on the idea of *Sim City* but let players control the look, character, and lives of virtual people. It proved a big hit with women, who had not been traditional gamers, and quickly became the biggest-selling game of all time. In total the franchise has shipped more than 100 million units. A recent variant is *Spore*, where players start with a microorganism and develop it though numerous stages to become an advanced life form.

Platform and virtual worlds

The most famous of this type of game is probably *Super Mario Bros.*, which dates from 1985. Here a large and complex virtual world is created that can be explored by the characters in pursuit of a quest—in the case of Mario, to rescue a princess. They were particularly suited to the early home consoles where the input device made jumping and throwing easy to control. As game technology allowed the use of full-motion video and studio-created 3D graphics, the nature of the platform became far more sophisticated and the once basic scrolling backgrounds developed into full virtual worlds.

These games let the player loose in a fantasy environment. The creator of *Mario*, Shigeru Miyamoto, is often quoted as saying that in his fantasy worlds of *Mario* and *The Legend of Zelda* he wanted to recreate the wonder he felt as a child roaming the rural Japanese countryside.[7] Rather than just showing a single screen for action, the platform game offers an unfolding adventure world where city-bound children and adults can go to play. It is the digital realization of the emotional appeal of *Alice's Adventures in Wonderland*.

The early Mario was constrained by moving in a linear fashion through a cartoon landscape, which scrolled across the screen as the action progressed. As software improved the player could be given more freedom to go where they chose. This required vastly more computing power and a huge increase in production budgets to create the virtual world. But the greater the degree of freedom the players enjoyed, the more compelling and popular games became. *Grand Theft Auto III* is set in a fully realized three-dimensional city where the player can take the role of a criminal experiencing all the dark things a city has to offer: car chases, violence, sex, and drug culture. Players have to make moral decisions as well as controlling action sequences.

Multiplayer

The internet allows players in remote locations to participate in the same game by linking their machines. As far back as the late 1970s it was common for students on different continents to play virtual games of chess and noughts and crosses by taking turns over an electronic link.

One of the most successful arcade games to fight back against the home computer boom was *Gauntlet* in 1985, which allowed four players to compete against one another, each with their own in-game character controlled by a joystick. It created a social dynamic of group participation in mall games, which had been traditional solo activities.

With high-speed broadband now a common feature of many homes, some games have developed into the so-called Massively Multiplayer Online format (MMO), which allow people to compete not against the machine or by taking turns but against other players in real time. Some of these are first-person shooters, others require players to adopt characters and play roles as in *World of Warcraft*, in which players adopt an avatar and over hundreds, and possibly thousands, of hours of game play build up skills and resources, join guilds, and participate in complex group quests.

Coalescence

The most popular games often now bring together aspects of the once distinct formats of action, narrative, strategy, virtual worlds, and multiplayer social interaction. A major new game now rivals a big movie in terms of production values and launch budget. In fact a game is even more a "work of art" than a film in the sense of being wholly artificial. Everything in a game has been created by human imagination. Every aspect has been drawn and then rendered by animation software. All the character traits have been invented. All the sound has been added. The techniques of other media like film, television, and comics have been adopted and then something exceptionally powerful has been added—interaction. The audience is no long passive, it participates. Leading games scriptwriter Rhianna Pratchett is quoted in the book *Fun Inc.* talking about the nature of video games:

> They're not always good art and they occupy a different definition of "art" than we've previously been used to. They embody the art of the journey: interactivity, exploration, adventure—a kind of high-octane theatre with a shattered fourth wall.[8]

The phenomenon of Second Life is a virtual world in which all the action is created by the players themselves. People can buy land and build houses. The game has its own virtual currency, the Linden Dollar, but players use real money to buy credits to acquire virtual goods. It has more than 400,000 regular users.

Most of the big, popular games are now coalescences. In Microsoft's *Halo* you play a character called the Master Chief on a mission to save humanity that involves driving vehicles, shooting weapons, developing skills, and moving through a beautifully rendered virtual world. *Call of Duty* requires players to fight their way through Cold War locations. The *Grand Theft Auto* series lets players live out a fictional life in places like

Liberty City, modeled on the real New York. *Red Dead Redemption* has a similar approach set in the old West. The original ideas of these games can still clearly be traced to *Spacewar*, *M.U.L.E.*, and *MUD*, but the scale and impact must astound the medium's founding fathers.

Social and casual games

Not all games are complex, multimedia productions. The arrival of social networks like Facebook and Myspace provided a new platform for simple games that could also be played through web browsers and portals like Yahoo and iGoogle. These do not need the technology of the console or high-end graphics and sound to provide pleasure and engagement. They can be accessed from any internet-connected computer or enabled mobile device and offer simple game play, often allowing contests with friends. Games like *Restaurant City* from Playfish and *Farmville* from Zynga can be downloaded at no cost and have millions of players. The allure is being part of the contest rather than visiting a virtual world.

WAVES OF TECHNOLOGY

The type of game available over time has been driven by successive waves of technical innovation. The nature of input devices—how we control a game, the speed of computer processing, graphics, sound, and storage devices—has improved beyond all recognition in the 50 or so years since games began. As each new advance came along innovative designers found ways to make use of it.

Playing with mainframes: 1960s

The Festival of Britain in 1951 was meant to celebrate all that was new and technically advanced. A star exhibit was a computer called Nimrod, which had been specifically designed to let visitors play an electronic version of an ancient game called Nim, based on picking up sticks. It caused a sensation but had no practical value as a medium or as a consumer game. A year later IBM showed off a program that could play the board game checkers on an IBM 701. By 1955 the program was able to learn from its mistakes and when this was made public the IBM share price went up by 15 points.[9] Three years after that a US government research scientist in New York decided to make the public open days at his laboratory more interesting by programming an oscilloscope screen to simulate a tennis game he called *Tennis for Two*—the first real video game.

In the late 1950s most university mainframes used punch cards for input and paper printing or tickertape for output. Inventive minds used them to simulate games like chess, but the time between moves was slow and the game play boring. In 1961 the Massachusetts Institute of Technology (MIT) took delivery of a leading-edge mainframe computer called a DEC PDP-1, which was controlled by a keyboard and used a cathode ray screen display. It was the size of a car, but was an early and huge version of what would become a desktop PC. A group of students, much to the initial disgust of their professors, devised a game called *Spacewar!*. This used the computer screen to stimulate an interstellar battle between two players who were able to shoot missiles from rocket ships. The game won enthusiastic student supporters, who improved on its functionality to the extent that it was adopted as a teaching aid. It became so popular that DEC engineers gave away copies to help sell more machines.

Taking over arcades: 1970s

A Stanford University student called Bill Pitts was the first to try to turn these mainframe hobby games into a business. In 1971 he obtained a small computer and launched a coin-operated version of *Spacewar!*, which he called *Galaxy Game*. He set it up in the Stanford student union and charged 10 cents a turn—far too little ever to recoup the cost of the complex computing equipment inside the machine, but it can claim to be the first computer-based arcade game.

The breakthrough to make electronic games a commercial proposition came from Nolan Bushnell, who had played *Spacewar* at the University of Utah. After graduation he went to work for Ampex, a company that boasted Bing Crosby as an early investor and had pioneered audio and video tape. Bushnell had knowledge of electrical engineering and connections in the amusement arcade and pinball business. He realized that if he could find a way to get cheaper computing power, he could create a viable coin-in-the-slot arcade game. He did this by having the various elements of the game served by specific low-cost computer boards. He launched his company, which he called Atari, in 1972, and its first major game was *Pong*, which allowed two people to play a digital version of table tennis.

Pong was an instant success and a typical machine was taking in $200 a week in coins when a classic pinball machine was only taking $50. It created a new market of family-friendly arcade games that replaced the rather seedy image of traditional games machines, which were thought to have links to organized crime.

A desire to turn *Pong* into a single-player game led to the development in 1976 of *Breakout*, in which a bouncing ball destroyed bricks. In an attempt to reduce the cost of making the game, Atari employed a youthful Steve Jobs to simplify the design to use fewer transistors. He in turn recruited his friend Steve Wozniak. The work they did on *Breakout* is credited by Wozniak as having a major influence on the way he went onto design the Apple II computer with the specific intention of having the video and sound capabilities to be a games-playing machine.

The Japanese had always had a strong arcade tradition and in 1974 the playing card company Nintendo opened a video games business. In 1978

ATARI

In 1972 Nolan Bushnell believed that the future of arcade games would be electronic not mechanical, so he launched a company to make them. He called it Atari, the name of a position in the Japanese game Go, roughly equivalent to "check" in chess. His first employee was an engineer who perfected the technique of using a television screen to display a table tennis game, which would become *Pong*. Earlier attempts at computer-based arcade games had failed because they were too complex, but *Pong* had simple paddle controls and only one instruction: "avoid missing ball for high score."

The company went on to develop a hugely successful home games console and an early home computer. In 1976 it was running out of cash to fund its new microprocessor-based machine, the VCS, and so it sold itself to media giant Warner Brothers.

Atari had been one of the most freewheeling of the new Bay Area technology businesses, with a hippie culture, wild parties, and accusations of drug taking. It did not thrive under corporate ownership and despite heavy investment, it virtually collapsed in the face of new competition from Nintendo and Sega. By 1983 the company had expanded into dozens of separate divisions spread over 50 locations in Silicon Valley. First its corporate owners cut the workforce by two-thirds, then faced with closure they sold the video game business to the founder of Commodore Computer, Jack Tramiel.

RALPH BAER

Arguably, the title of "father of home video games" should go to Ralph Baer, a television engineer who, in 1968, patented the concept of a games machine attached to a TV set that allowed the screen to display two paddles that appeared to act like ping-pong bats. He had the original idea sitting at bus station in New York in 1966. Baer turned his concept into a so-called brown box machine that could be hooked up to a domestic television. TV maker Magnavox supported Baer's prototype and launched the first home games machine, the Magnavox Odyssey.

Baer had demonstrated a home tennis game before Bushnell launched *Pong*, but Atari proved to be much superior at marketing. After a long legal dispute, Atari agreed to pay Magnavox a license fee. Baer was a true pioneer: as early as 1966 he described the concepts of racing and shooting games, and for Magnavox he developed the first light gun to control a target on a television screen. In 2006 he was awarded the National Medal of Technology.

another Japanese company launched *Space Invaders*. It sold more than 100,000 machines and demand was so great that the country's supply of 100 yen coins was consumed for a time, stopping people using phone boxes and buying transit tickets. It was just as successful in America and was followed by *Asteroids* from Atari and *Pac-Man* from yet another Japanese company.

Into the living room: 1970s

The first attempt to bring games to the family television was the Magnavox Odyssey in 1972. Magnavox was a major TV manufacturer and saw the games machine as a natural add-on. It insisted that it was sold only through its existing retail network and also that it provided a range of conventional games, such as poker, and was packaged with playing cards and gambling chips. It was a modest success, although not a sensation. Ralph Baer had hoped that his game would sell for less than $20 and was most unimpressed with the way it was taken to market by Magnavox. He said:

Magnavox did a really lousy job. They over-engineered the machine. They upped the price phenomenally [with extras] so that the damn thing sold for $100. Then in their advertising they showed it hooked up to a Magnavox TV sets and gave everyone the impression that this thing only worked on Magnavox.[10]

By 1975 Atari had its own *Pong* home machine ready. It used the newly available microchips, which were more expensive than circuit boards but technically much superior. Despite the huge sales of the arcade game it had little initial success with home *Pong*, as toy retailers would not carry it. Then the huge department store Sears decided to sell the game through its sporting goods department and it became a smash hit.

The first novelty was for people who had seen *Pong* in arcades to be able to play it at home. But Atari also provided other games via special cartridges. It offered its machine cheaply and the cartridges at a high price. The logic was similar to that famously adopted by razor manufacturers: that the razor (the home console) was sold at a loss, with the plan to make all the profit on the blades (the games). The Atari VCS defined the home gaming industry and by 1982 was selling some 8 million units a year.

Crash stop: 1983

By the early 1980s video games in arcades and front rooms were delighting millions of teenagers and worrying millions of parents and politicians. Amusement arcades were mushrooming in towns all over the world and machines playing *Space Invaders* were appearing in almost every pub, club, and café. Many millions of homes boasted an Atari console.

However, in a frenzy of "get rich quick" too many arcade machines had been installed using borrowed money. When the novelty wore off and with the same games available at home, the cash take was spread across too many operators. The companies' big debts could not be serviced and many of them went bankrupt.

In the home, a massive rush of poorly designed and low-cost games swamped the market. Atari had no exclusivity on the technology of its game cartridges, so anyone could make games and they did, often on the cheap and with little creative merit. A glut of game cartridges led retailers to offer big discounts, making them cheaper still. To make things worse two new technologies, the VCR and the home computer, started to become available and consumers decided the home games console was something they could do without. In 1983 the annual home video game market was worth $3.2 billion; by 1986 this had collapsed to $100 million a year.[11] Over the same period thousands of arcades closed and machines were scrapped. The video game industry was in ruins.

NINTENDO

In Japanese Nintendo means "leave luck to heaven," an appropriate motto for a playing card manufacturer founded in 1889. In 1974 it acquired the Japanese license for the US home video machine the Magnavox Odyssey, and then started making its own arcade games and later home consoles. It has been an innovator in both software and hardware, launching *Donkey Kong* in 1981 and *Super Mario Bros.* in 1985, the NES (Nintendo Entertainment System) in 1983, the Game Boy handheld in 1989, the GameCube in 2001, and the Wii in 2006. The company is now one of the most valuable in Japan.

Into the bedroom via the PC: 1980s

As the arcade and console businesses were declining, the winner was the personal computer located at home. Models like the Apple II and Commodore 64 were much desired household purchases, but people were unsure what to do with them. They were talked of as glorified calculators, sophisticated typewriters, or electronic filing cabinets. In fact, the most popular software for home use turned out to be games. As they evolved each generation of machine came with better graphics and sound and users wanted to make full use of these features.

Console games had relied on programs built into microchips in cartridges, which appealed to the mass market but were a closed professional system. Early home PC games were nonanarchic, written by amateur hobbyists on floppy discs and sold to fellow fans in plastic bags. Computers were controlled through the keyboard and mouse and often watched through a dedicated desktop monitor. This all led to a different type of gaming experience. While it was possible to replicate console and arcade games with peripherals such as joysticks, the real originality came from exploring the processing power of the PC.

A key development in making PC games successful was the founding of the company Electronic Arts in 1983 by Harvard graduate Trip Hawkins, who had worked for Apple and saw that there was an opportunity to make stars of game designers and to package and promote titles with devices like album covers. EA went on to publish some of the most successful titles.

By the early 1990s PCs had increasingly sophisticated sound and graphics capabilities and users wanted to show off their new multimedia devices. Launched in 1993, the puzzle-solving game *Myst* was set on a surreal island with extensive use of graphics and music. It was a huge hit when released on the Apple Mac and PC, as it let users work their way through complex scenarios in their own time in the privacy of their own home. In contrast it sold poorly on consoles, which normally offered more active racing or shooting, arcade-type experiences. Another huge hit was *Doom*, a first-person shooter, which made extensive use of the high speed of the new generation of 3D graphics cards.

Console wars

After the shock of the 1983 collapse, the industry realized that it had to reinvent the home console market. Having seen the success of the home computer, companies set about designing computers, disguised as home consoles, which could outdo the PCs at their own game. This was the start of a long home console "arms race," which was initially between Nintendo and Sega with battle later joined by Sony and Microsoft. Each generation of consoles was more sophisticated than the previous one, with better graphics and sound and more memory storage. After the collapse of Atari the fight was largely between Japanese companies, as they had a huge home market for arcades but also saw games as a new medium in their own right.

The first console was the Nintendo Entertainment System or NES, which was launched in the US in 1985 having been pioneered in Japan a couple of years earlier under the name Famicom, standing for Family Computer. It used primitive 8-bit chips and had a bespoke controller rather than a keyboard. *Super Mario Bros.* drove sales of the NES. Sega fought back with a racing game featured a superfast hedgehog, Sonic.

SONIC THE HEDGEHOG

In 1990 the Sega Company was trailing Nintendo and desperately needed a hit game to sell its new Genesis console. It consciously wanted to go one better that *Mario*, so designed a scrolling racing game to exploit the relative speed of its new machine and developed a character with more teenage appeal and "attitude." This was a blue hedgehog wearing running shoes called Sonic. Designer Yuji Naka became famous for his total control of the whole user experience, which grew to be the norm for many of the best game designers. He said of *Sonic*:

I am really careful about everything... it's the overall flow of the program. In my mind it's handling all aspects of the game including the music, graphics, picture and everything.[12]

In the early 1990s Nintendo and Sony had joint plans to launch an advanced console incorporating a CD-Rom, but Nintendo pulled out of the partnership, enraging Sony and motivating it to develop its own platform. The result was the 32-bit Sony PlayStation, which was launched for Christmas 1994 featuring three-dimensional graphics and a CD-Rom, which allowed much larger and more complex games to be played. The next big leap forward was the Xbox from Microsoft in 2001, which featured a built-in hard drive to store games, a better solution than memory cards and cartridges.

The use of CD-Roms encouraged game designers to start using video sequences, which made games more and more complex. It was not unusual to find that a game needed five or six CDs to play. These video-rich games moved away from simple action and puzzles, but were unwieldy. Often the player simply became a viewer, watching a premade movie sequence rather than interacting with a game. A new generation of designers learned how to use 3D computer rendering of backgrounds and characters, which was felt to be more in keeping with gaming than the movie sequences. Games such as *Tomb Raider* made full use of polygonal graphics rather than trying to incorporate video.

Handheld: 1990s

While home consoles were getting more complex, another area of video games was retuning to its basic roots. Handheld electronic games like chess and checkers started appearing in the 1970s as simple one-game novelties using primitive screen displays. In 1989 Nintendo came up with the Game

Year	Maker	Model	Key feature
1983	Nintendo	NES	Extensive software library
1988	Sega	MegaDrive	Advanced graphics
1994	Sony	PlayStation	CD-Rom
1994	Sega	Saturn	CD-Rom
1996	Nintendo	64	Joystick controller
1999	Sega	Dreamcast	Modem
2000	Sony	PS2	DVD compatibility
2001	Nintendo	GameCube	Unique Nintendo games
2001	Microsoft	Xbox	Broadband modem

Boy and lunched it bundled with the game *Tetris*, which was particularly well adapted to a small handheld device. It was a sensation, selling more than a million units in a few weeks. Nearly a decade layer the Game Boy Color was launched along with the virtual monsters game *Pokémon*. By linking machines together players could battle each other's monsters and swap characters to build their collection. It was an early indicator of the power of social networks.

In 2004 Nintendo extended its dominance of the handheld market with the DS, which had two screens allowing for a different type of game play and had a wireless connection to greatly improve contests between players. In technical terms it was basic—certainly much less powerful than Sony's rival PSP—but as is so often the case in media, great marketing and an inspired choice of games proved more effective than better technology. The DS went on to sell more than 125 million units, partly because it appealed to a much broader audience than children as it carried a range of adult puzzle games, such as *Brain Age* which taught mental agility. The *Pokémon* and Game Boy franchises would prove vital to Nintendo, which lost out badly to Sony and Microsoft in the conventional home console market.

TETRIS

Russian mathematician Alexey Pajitnov created the computer code for *Tetris* while working for the Soviet Academy of Sciences in Moscow. A tetromino is a shape made up from four squares in the same way that a domino is made up of two. Pajitnov based his game on five four-block shapes and named it as a combination of tetromino and tennis. The software created shapes in a random order and the player had to manipulate them to build a solid wall. It was simple, but addictive. In 1984 Pajitnov released it for use on PCs and it became a craze among computer workers. By 1988 he had signed the copyright to the game over to the Soviet government, but it was already in widespread use and at least six companies claimed that they had already purchased the rights, including both Atari and Nintendo. Critically, Nintendo wanted *Tetris* for its new handheld Game Boy and in the end was able to negotiate an agreement. Having the game bundled with the Game Boy helped sell more than 40 million machines and was the making of the handheld format. In 1996 the rights transferred back to Pajitnov, who moved to America and went to work for Microsoft.

Connected consoles

In 2005 Microsoft launched the Xbox 360, which let players download games over a broadband connection and made multiplayer games straightforward. Sony's PlayStation 3 and the Nintendo Wii followed in 2006. This "seventh generation" of consoles had far more computing power than the typical office PC and was part of a plan to "own" the living room by being the device that could deliver internet access and television to a family home. It was a dramatic demonstration of the way games had become a key medium in a digital world.

Nintendo in particular had decided to compete not so much on computing power, but by designing the most effective interface between player and machine. Its motion-sensitive wand made the Wii particularly attractive to families wanting to play simulated sports. Xbox countered in 2010 with the Kinect, which used a camera to detect body motion and actions to allow machine control by gestures.

Games as apps

While many games were becoming multimillion-dollar productions, others were returning to their roots as simple but compulsive diversions. The development of web browsers, social networks, and mobile devices allowed a new games platform to develop where the game became a simple application embedded in another computer program. Quick and easy to download, these could be played alone or against other social network members.

MACHINIMA

In the 1993 first-person shooter game *Doom*, it was possible to record short sequences of animated game play onto a hard disc to let players relive complex sequences or show off their victories to others. The successor to *Doom* was *Quake*, which had a more sophisticated replay facility. In 1996 a group of gamers used this capability to create a short film called *Death of a Camper*, which featured a simple sequence of scripted screenplay orchestrating the actions of a number of characters who were all in on the act. This was the first of what were called *Quake* movies, which later were given the name machinima (machine + cinema).

Games designers realized that encouraging players to design their own stories and create their own characters made the game even more immersive. In 2003 filmmakers based in Texas used the capabilities of the Xbox game *Halo* to create a series of comic shorts called *Red vs. Blue* in which *Halo* characters are seen to interact using digital puppetry with comedy voiceover scripts.

Initially some game companies tried to stop machinima creators using their characters and settings, but most came to the conclusion that the extra creations provided positive marketing opportunities and have licensed game characters to so-called machinimators for noncommercial use. The convergence of games, animation, and film making has encouraged a generation of skilled creative people whose influence is now being seem in all forms of digital media. It seems inevitable that machinima techniques will play an increasing part in traditional media for education, information, and entertainment.

SHIGERU MIYAMOTO

Most video games are written by computer engineers, experienced with coding and technology. But the originator of some of the most popular trained as an industrial designer. Shigeru Miyamoto is the creative force behind *Donkey Kong, The Legend of Zelda*, and *Super Mario Bros*. With a background in Japans manga comics and the traditional arcade business, he says he is trying to create games for families.

ARE VIDEO GAMES DANGEROUS?

Most new forms of media receive trenchant criticism from the established order. Plato distrusted the written word, seeing speech as a superior medium. Theatre, cinema, comics, and television have all been condemned as corrupters of public morals. Nevertheless, video games have engendered particularly harsh censure, both for being addictive and for leading to violent acts. In the years when they first flourished in arcades, video games were seen as preferable to the machines that had gone before. The early console makers like Nintendo exercised self-censorship in terms of game content to ensure that titles were family friendly.

However, by the early 1990s consoles were in many family homes and game makers were competing for new audiences. Two-player "beat-'em-up" games had been popular in arcades and in 1993 a particularly violent and graphic title, *Mortal Kombat*, was converted for home use in the

US, which brought it to the attention of Senator Joe Lieberman, who initiated a full-blown Congressional inquiry into video game violence. The cause of games was not helped by the release of the big-budget and sexually suggestive *Night Trap*, where the gamer had to "rescue" teenage girls in nightdresses from vampires at a slumber party.

Like other new media before them, the games manufacturers suddenly realized the risk of legislative controls and outright bans. They formed their own trade association and created their own self-imposed rating system, the ESRB (Entertainment Software Rating Board), which set its own standards just like Hollywood and comic books before it. Games started to come with an approved age rating and warnings about violence and sex. A similar approach was taken in the UK. However, unlike movies, where producers would often try to avoid an 18+ rating as it reduced the audience, many game makers actively sought out such a classification in the knowledge that it boosted sales. Parents often ignored the labels and teenagers were able to buy the games without any problem at all. Some games became, if anything, more violent and graphic.

There is an unresolved debate as to whether video games actually cause violent behavior. The perpetrators of the Columbine school massacre in 1999 were allegedly obsessed with the game *Doom*,[13] and in more than one court case defense attorneys have argued that video games inspired their clients' criminal sprees. More concerning is the broader issue of becoming addicted to playing. In 2009 a three-month-old Korean child died of malnutrition while her parents played a video game in a local café, based, of all subjects, around bringing up a virtual infant.[14] The irony was not lost on journalists, who made it a worldwide story.

There is no doubt that many people spend huge amounts of time playing video games and in many cases game play is overtly designed to be "addictive," at least in the sense of having devices like new levels and bonus points that make the player want to keep going. Alcohol, tobacco, and opiates have proven physically addictive properties; gambling has been shown to get people mentally hooked; but in their own way so do television, gossip magazines, crosswords, and Sudoku. Numerous academic studies have looked to find some sort of physical addition linked to games, although the evidence is inconclusive.

What is clear is that the interactive nature of games does make them an exceptionally powerful medium and thus for those individuals who have addictive personalities, they represent a particular risk. But given the billions of hours devoted to games by hundreds of millions of players, the incidence of problems stemming from abuse seems remarkably small.

THE FUTURE OF VIDEO GAMES

As a medium of communication the video game is a long way from realizing its full potential. Not only will games themselves evolve to be an even richer entertainment experience, they are influencing other forms of media, bringing new levels of interaction and involvement. TV formats like *Big Brother* and *The X Factor* owe much to the consumer's gaming experience. Using an iPad to access an online newspaper or magazine has a game-like feel to it. In surveys, one of the jobs most coveted by western teenagers is games designer. The medium is a magnet for technology, money, and talent, which gives it huge momentum for further development.

Right from their very early days the nature of video games showed them to be different from traditional media. And that difference was user control. Part of the attraction of *Pong* was that it enabled people to interact with their TV sets, whereas television viewing had traditionally been a "sit back and watch" experience. The marketing of *Pong* was also done in the sporting goods department. It was a participative activity. From the basic monochrome *Spacewar*, to the cartoon jumping of *Super Mario Bros.* and the full 3D intensity of *Call of Duty*, games take players into a parallel world where they decide what happens next. A little imagination and the screen becomes a real place, the characters real people, and the tasks real challenges.

The increasing popularity of games can be partly explained by the increasing sophistication and intensity of the way we interact with them. Consoles came with ergonomically satisfying controllers. Nintendo's Wii offered its motion detector and Microsoft's Kinect a smart camera system to recognize gestures. New generations of game controllers are now approaching a natural user interface (the NUI), which will make games more even realistic and become a model for the way we interact with all forms of machine.

The value of games beyond pure entertainment is now widely recognized. The military use sophisticated war games to simulate real-life combat situations. Hospitals have experimented with game software to teach triage decision making and surgical procedures; and there seems to be a huge opportunity in education to use games to supplement or even replace conventional textbooks and video as teaching aids. The power of video games is explained by author Tom Chatfield:

> The best analogy is not film but architecture. Video games are spaces within which things happen. These spaces may now look stunningly realistic but at their heart lies a function that has changed little since *Space Invaders*: the creation of miniature worlds which players experience actively, learning as they progress, mastering tasks and challenges.[15]

Indeed, games may be changing the way we interact with and view society. In one way of thinking Facebook is a giant game where our avatar is a likeness of ourselves and we project him or her into society not by going out, but by logging on.

Video games are playing an extremely important role in the development of digital media. They have been the active laboratory for many innovations in terms of the use of graphics and sound and also in the creation of news ways of telling stories. The experience of game play in virtual worlds has made a new generation think about reality in a different way. It has made people demand more of their other media experiences.

The games industry is ambitious for its own future. One of the leading designers, Peter Molyneux, comments:

> The games industry... has this dream that one day it's going to be real. We're going to have real life. We're going to have real characters. We're going to have real drama. We're going to change the world and entertain in a way that nothing else has ever before.[16]

Games have taught us the power of active involvement and two-way communication. In this they have been the backdrop to the development the most immersive medium yet invented, the web.

2.16 | Web

The web is the most powerful medium in history. In terms of size of audience, hours spent with it, and advertising revenues generated, it is growing faster than any traditional form. This is partly because of the great breadth of what it offers and the ease and low cost of getting access. The web is available on a huge range of screens, from a 2 inch phone to a 60 inch plasma. It is ubiquitous. It is changing the way society functions—and it is only just getting started.

What has made the web particularly potent is that has become a carriage channel for most of the traditional media. Almost every existing media brand has its own website, but in addition we have web television (YouTube), web radio (Last.fm), web text (Huffington Post), web games (Farmville), and web telephony (Skype). It is truly the über-medium because it is the means by which digital files can be shared. In addition the web is a medium in its own right, with new services like Facebook, Twitter, and Wikipedia that could not have existed in a pre-internet age.

Unlike its media forebears it is the users of the web, rather than the producers of content, who decide when and where to consume what. And the users are able to participate in creating content to a much greater degree than ever before. The web is making media more democratic and accessible, but in so doing it has undermined the economics of traditional media providers. Looking back through the lens of media history, it is clear that the web is still at an adolescent stage—it is a "work in progress."

ORIGINS OF THE WEB

The ideas behind the web go back far earlier than the development of the internet technology it now uses. In July 1945 the US Presidential science adviser, Vannevar Bush, reflected on what science had to contribute to humanity after the Second World War was over. He wrote an article in *The Atlantic Monthly* called "As We May Think" and argued that the next challenge was to organize and access information. The magazine introduced his ideas by saying: "if properly developed [science] will give man access to, and command over, the inherited knowledge of the ages."

Bush had a notion about a mechanical library he called a "memex," combining microfilm and mechanical reading devices, which would allow information to be organized, accessed, and interconnected. He described the concepts of hypertext links and search, but, as digital data was unknown, saw them in the context of sheets of chemical film and physical storage drawers. In 1945 he wrote:

> The world has arrived at an age of cheap complex devices of great reliability; and something is bound to come of it.... Wholly new forms of encyclopaedias will appear, ready made with a mesh of links running through them... The lawyer has at his touch the associated

opinions and decisions of his whole experience, and of the experience of friends and authorities. The patent attorney has on call the millions of issued patents... The physician, puzzled by a patient's reactions [can study] earlier similar cases... The chemist, struggling with the synthesis of an organic compound, has all the chemical literature before him in his laboratory... The historian has a vast chronological account of a people.[1]

A fascinating book, *Lost in Cyburbia* by James Harkin, traces some of the ideas that underpin the web back to the science of cybernetics in the 1940s, and the attempts to break down conventional editorial structures by publications like the *Whole Earth Catalogue* in the hippie days of San Francisco in the 1960s.

Cybernetics is about the interplay between man and machine and in particular the beneficial effects of a feedback loop of information. The pioneers of the science were trying to make anti-aircraft guns more effective, but their underlying ideas were about how a constant flow of information and immediate feedback lead to incremental changes and improvements in performance. This was a forerunner of the notion of a peer-to-peer network, where people interact not through a traditional mediated hierarchy but directly with each other—the idea behind services like Wikipedia.

The *Whole Earth Catalogue* (WEC) was a publishing phenomenon of the early 1970s that encouraged readers to make their own contributions about ideas, equipment, and information sources that they thought other readers might find useful. One of the WEC editors explained how it grew out of the mood of its time:

> The beatniks had a negative, existential vibe. They weren't into sharing. But the hippies came along and wanted to share everything. Whatever they discovered, they just wanted to broadcast. The WEC was the very best example of this.[2]

James Harkin sees it as a forerunner of social networking:

> The *Whole Earth Catalogue* rapidly became a self-sustaining enterprise aimed at encouraging the direct and spontaneous swapping of

WHOLE EARTH CATALOGUE

The *Whole Earth Catalogue* was only in regular production for four years, from 1968–72. It was a large-format book that looked a bit like a conventional product catalogue and featured a highly eclectic mixture of product reviews, ideas, and synopses of other publications. It started out with a particular focus on reviews of useful tools and, indeed, was subtitled "access to tools," but it started to define "tools" very widely, including intellectual instruments such as books, maps, and pamphlets. By the early 1970s it was selling more than a million copies an edition and was available by mail order throughout the world.

information among wildly different groups of people who could meet as peers in its pages.[3]

And Apple founder Steve Jobs, in a speech at Stanford University, compared WEC to a search engine:

[WEC] was before personal computers and desktop publishing, so it was all made with typewriters, scissors, and Polaroid cameras. It was sort of like Google in paperback form, 35 years before Google came along: it was idealistic and overflowing with neat tools and great notions.[4]

It would be the children of the WEC's creators and readers, from the same part of northern California, who would pioneer the web a generation later. And it was the approach of that publication that colors the web's philosophy today.

FROM INTERNET TO WEB

The web is an application that sits on top of the electronic network we call the internet. The words "web" and "internet" are not interchangeable, although many people use them as if they are. The internet is a technology, a network of networks. The web, email, video streaming, and social networks are examples of applications that use it. The internet is simply the mechanism by which individual computers are connected to one another. The web allows easy access and manipulation of data on those machines.

The ARPANET (Advanced Research Projects Agency Network) was created by Vannevar Bush and others to allow computer systems at American universities to communicate with one another as part of making the US defense research program more effective. The first link was established in late 1969 between Stanford University in San Francisco and the University of California, Los Angeles. This was extended to other universities and the first email was sent in 1971.

In 1974 Vint Cerf, often called one of the fathers of the internet, developed the Internet Protocol or IP, which allowed every computer anywhere in the world to have its own unique location number or IP address. It started out with a nine-digit code, which gave a total possible number of addresses of some 4 billion. With the explosive growth of internet-linked devices, many, many more addresses are now required. As Vint Cerf himself expressed on a now famous T-shirt, "IP on everything" is the new internet motto.[6] The latest address system, called IPv6, will offer 3.4×10^{38} addresses, which is an unimaginably large number.

By the 1980s most universities and government operations had their computers connected by networks, which allowed early forms of file sharing and email. In subsequent years more and more computers were added to these networks, but the internet remained the province of academics and expert users. The concept of domain names was introduced in the 1980s and the first .com was registered in 1985 by a computer company called Symbolics. At this stage machines could communicate with each

THE START OF @

In 1965 computer scientists at MIT devised a program to allow users of big mainframes to leave electronic messages for each other on the same machine. It was analogous to pinning notes to a board. In 1971 a company called BBN in Boston was working for the US government helping to build the ARPANET and it wanted to find a way to allow members of its team, who were using different computers in different places, to swap information electronically over telephone lines. One of their engineers, Ray Tomlinson, wrote a program to do just that and realized that, as with conventional mail, people would need unique addresses that combined their name with where they could be located. He was "Tomlinson," he worked at BBN, and he used an operating system called Tenex. His primitive computer keyboard had limited punctuation keys, so he chose the "@" symbol to connect his name with his computer's address. He became tomlinson@bbn-tenexa and sent his first email, machine to machine, using the system in October 1971.[6]

other, but the data on them was often incompatible, in various formats and different structures.

EARLY MEDIA ON THE INTERNET

In the first days of the internet academic and military computers used the new network to share information but not much more. The growing army of home PC owners were also offered the opportunity to get connected, but not so much with each other as with centralized service providers. The internet would have emerged as a major carriage network for a wide range of digital media even if the web had never happened.

In the late 1970s services like CompuServe and The Source offered dial-up services that allowed people to connect their new computers to central resources. The Source described itself as an "information utility" and used the slogan "It's not hardware. It's not software. But it can take your personal computer anywhere in the world."[7] For a monthly fee it allowed subscribers to use a modem to dial up to access services like news, weather and sports results.

America Online, which would become AOL, was founded under a different name in 1983 to provide access to dial-up games for users of Atari home games machines. It went on to build a broad offering, including chat rooms and a range of entertainment services. all based on people paying to dial in and get access.

AOL and its rivals were "walled gardens," providers of services that were only available to their subscribers. For more than a decade they were the main way PC users could access online media and they offered a huge range of information and entertainment. At the time computer and transmission technology would not have allowed for streaming audio and video, but had it done so the internet, and the likes of AOL, would have become a clear alternative to broadcasting and cable TV. As it was, AOL was mainly seen as an alternative to newspapers and magazines.

In the event, after the web was invented subscribers to AOL and others started to use them as an "on ramp," a way to access the much broader offerings available on the "open" web. The limited, closed services of AOL looked like very poor value for money compared to thousands of free websites. Telephone companies and cable operators started to offer direct web access, calling into question the whole notion of the walled garden. In 2000

AOL merged with Time Warner in a $180 billion deal that would prove to be a disaster for both companies.

WEAVING THE WEB

The notion of hypertext was first demonstrated in 1968 when a rudimentary mouse-type pointing device was used to allow people to jump between documents to follow up references. However, it was not turned into a practical tool.

In 1991 the CERN laboratory in Switzerland made public work by a scientist called Tim Berners-Lee, who had developed improved ways of displaying and sharing information stored on different computer systems. It was initially intended to help the global high-energy physics research community work more closely together.

Berners-Lee found a way to overcome the problems of multiple computer formats and different encoding schemes that hampered file sharing. His solution was to develop what we now call Universal Resource Locators, which in effect gave each "page" of data on any computer a unique address. Hypertext Transfer Protocol was a way of allowing data to be accessed from machine to machine and software system to software system, irrespective of coding differences. The whole thing was called the World Wide Web. These initials URL, HTTP, and WWW are now eerily familiar aspects of everyday life.

The CERN web was designed to make the internet more user-friendly and to facilitate cooperative research. It was not intended as a commercial tool. It was a few years later in 1994 that an electronics entrepreneur, Jim Clark, backed a student, Marc Andreessen, to launch a commercial web browser called Mosaic and then Netscape Navigator, which incorporated graphics, sound, and video clips. This allowed users to see images on remote sites without having to wait to download them. It made web pages fun and easy to get, and the web as a medium was ready to take off. Andreessen is quoted as saying that his innovation did not initially please the web's inventor:

> Berners-Lee didn't welcome the change. He felt images cheapened his academic medium. Tim bawled me out in the summer of '93 for adding images to the thing.[8]

TIM BERNERS-LEE AND //

After receiving a first-class degree in Physics from Oxford University, Tim Berners-Lee was working for the nuclear research organization CERN in Switzerland. In 1989 he wrote a paper called "Information Management: A Proposal." This was to make the sharing of computer files more straightforward using hypertext to search and link documents. CERN funded a project to develop the core concepts and create a practical software solution. The first website, put up by CERN in 1991, used a NeXT computer (developed by Steve Jobs) as a server and it contained what they called a web browser, which they named the WorldWideWeb. The logo with three *W*s was designed by Berners-Lee's colleague at CERN, Robert Cailliau. Berners-Lee has subsequently said that putting the two forward slashes—//—into web addresses seemed like a good idea at the time, but was an unnecessary complication.[9]

The early graphic web was used by semiprofessional enthusiasts, but as the number of home computers grew, broadband links multiplied and with the development of internet cafés, the web moved from being a novelty for geeks to a mass medium for home and office users. As more and more media was created and stored in digital form, the web became the ideal way to use the internet to provide low-cost, global distribution. The digital media era was under way.

WEB ERAS

The web is simply too new to be seen in much of a historical context, but in broad terms there are three clear eras of development. The early web is now often called Web 1.0, reflecting the nomenclature used for the first version of software releases. This period began with Netscape Navigator and was, at its most basic, a huge collection of pages that could be accessed via a browser. The existence of the web encouraged organizations, commercial companies, and individuals to create websites, which acted like brochures or broadcast devices to make their material available to anyone who visited them. They presented facts and opinions that people could access via a search. The bulk of sites were text with a few pictures. As the 1990s progressed, various software developments allowed for the streaming of audio and video. This first phase overlapped with the period that most online activity was being conducted via services such as CompuServe and AOL.

By the early 2000s software was being written that allowed far more interaction between websites and web users. People were writing weblogs—blogs—which invited and recorded comment. The techniques of RSS (Really Simple Syndication) allowed bloggers to offer other web users the ability to subscribe to a feed to a page, so whenever the publisher put up something new it would automatically appear on the subscriber's own portal. Wikipedia was launched in January 2001 to allow web users to collaborate on encyclopaedia entries. Friendster, one of the earliest social networking sites, started in 2002.

The term Web 2.0 to describe this era of increased interactivity was coined, as a theoretical notion, as early as 1999. It was used widely by 2002 and in 2004 a conference was held with the title Web 2.0, which explored the idea of the web as a platform for collaboration. There is no significant technical difference between the 1.0 and 2.0 eras, and it could be argued that this is a slightly artificial distinction, but there is no doubt that the nature of the web by 2005 was very different from 1995. It had emerged as a truly two-way experience rather than just a shop window for information.

The web's originator, Tim Berners-Lee, has talked about the next phase being the semantic web,

BROWSER WARS

The protocols of the web had been developed to allow sharing of information by the research community rather than the general public, but that changed when Marc Andreessen, a student at the University of Illinois, co-wrote a more user-friendly graphical browser for general use, called Mosaic. In 1994 he teamed up with businessman Jim Clark to launch the commercial version, Netscape Navigator, which was initially a huge success.

Software giant Microsoft realized, a little late, the importance of the browser and licensed the original Mosaic software to create its own solution: Internet Explorer. With Microsoft money and marketing skills, IE became market leader. A revamped Navigator was called Mozilla (which had been the project's original codename) and this has now morphed into Mozilla Firefox, an open-source, free browser which became the biggest competitor to IE. In 2009 Google released its own browser, Chrome, which had a huge budget. Before the web, whoever supplied the operating systems (it was mostly Microsoft Windows) controlled the industry. Once web use became near universal, that crown moved to the most popular browser.

which some people call Web 3.0. The idea here is that the web becomes an environment in which machines can make intelligent judgments in response to search questions. In the Web 2.0 world a search engine like Google or Bing can find a group of words or a name, but cannot answer a plain-language question directly. One of the ideas of the semantic web is that documents and images can be tagged with a description and classification; in internet terms "metadata," or data that describes data. This information would provide guidance to both the content and context of a data file, making the search process far more precise.

To make the point, a photograph of a sunset over a beach in the Bahamas taken on January 1, 2011 might be tagged "sunset," "beach," "Bahamas," "New Year's Day," 1/1/11, etc. The idea is that if large numbers of web users are invited to supply appropriate tags, then some intelligent but automatic analysis of data can be done that goes far beyond its raw contents. This concept gives the web even more potential as a medium, as much of the experiment and development will be done by a vast army of web users, not merely a few professionals employed by a media owner.

TRADITIONAL MEDIA ON THE WEB

In the first decade of the new millennium web use grew at huge speed and traditional media stared to experiment with it as a distribution channel. On the web you can access a newspaper page from almost any place from almost any time—and you can do it with extraordinary speed. Within seconds of a journalist completing his or her story and pressing "publish," you can read it, whether it originated in Sydney, Singapore, or San Francisco. And that information then exists in searchable cyberspace for all time.

When you buy a newspaper, what you want is news, information, ideas, and entertainment. You get this, but you also pay for paper making, printing, transport, wholesalers, retailers, and sometimes delivery. In addition, your money is subsidizing waste, in that many of the copies printed will not be sold because of ineffective distribution. On a website the links between you and the originating journalists and photographers are much more direct and, indeed, can be interactive. If printed newspapers did not exist we would not invent them now.

On the web you can watch television programs or films when it suits you. You can find any music track you want; whether or not you pay for it is another matter. All this all leads to huge consumer benefits, but also to the biggest challenge of the web as a distribution channel: how to make its economics work. In most cases traditional media owners spent far more creating content than they could ever get back from distributing it online.

The web also allowed the sharing of digital files between individuals. In the analogue world people paid for a copy of a magazine or a CD or a DVD because it was the simplest and most cost-effective way to obtain the content. However, once that content was available as a digital file, it was very difficult for the original owner to collect any additional payment.

In the web's early days many media owners made their content available without charge in the hope that visitors to their site would be attractive to advertisers. This led to the bizarre situation that with consumer media such as newspapers and magazines, people came to expect to get web content for nothing, while they were happy to pay for the same material delivered in a traditional printed package.

Commercial radio and television started out as "free-to-air" media supported solely by advertising, as there was no technology to collect fees. However, the broadcast pioneers also made money from selling the reception hardware. Once the market for buying radios and televisions was saturated, broadcasters were able to rely on advertising income, as they enjoyed a near monopoly of the scarce broadcast spectrum. The web has no such constraints, so the limited pool of advertising could never be enough to support the vast number of media offerings. It is instructive that many of the most successful providers of traditional media online are supported by tax revenues (the BBC) or charitable trusts (*The Guardian* newspaper).

The least successful examples of traditional media on the web arise when the original content is simply displayed on a screen and no attempt is made to employ unique web features. The exact look and layout of a magazine or newspaper can be reproduced on a website, even the sound of pages being turned. But why would anyone want this? If you are receiving the media via a screen, it seems pointless to deprive yourself of available screen-based features such as synchronized sound and moving pictures. The most successful traditional sites are those that tailor their content to utilise the web's full capabilities.

The lessons of history are that as each new medium became available, its most successful practitioners were a new generation of creative workers and managers who were not rooted in the past. This was true of the transitions from books to newspapers to radio and to television. There is no reason to believe that the web will be any different. The most successful will be those who see it as a medium in its own right.

THE MEDIUM OF THE WEB

The web is a two-way street where users have a huge amount of power over what they consume. All media before have been controlled by editors, schedulers, and programmers; the web is different. Marshall McLuhan would certainly have recognized the web as a medium—a classic extension of man. The web is the realization of his global village and it absolutely proves his point that the medium is the message, as its very existence has changed society and behavior. There are five key characteristics that make the web exceptionally powerful as a medium:

- *Multiformat*: Audio, video, and text are delivered simultaneously, which makes for rich content. Smell, taste, and touch will come in time.
- *Storable*: Everything ever created as a web page can be stored indefinitely; the ultimate archive.
- *Searchable*: Because web pages can be tagged, the required text or images can be looked for; the ultimate card index.
- *Collaborative*: The web can act like a giant conference call so people feel involved. It creates teams and communities.
- *On demand*: All the content sits on a server somewhere ready to be viewed or downloaded as the user decides. There are no schedulers or editors. The medium does not have linear constraints.

The ways of using the web as a medium are still in an exploratory stage. The biggest current challenge is not so much how to create content, but how to get people to pay for it or how to generate revenue.

Professional content creators have tended to continue to focus on traditional media, which pay better, and have seen the web more as a marketing tool or a distribution channel, rather than a new form in its own right. Much of the most compelling early content was created by users themselves on social networking sites like Myspace, Facebook, and YouTube and via collaborative activities such as Wikipedia.

SEARCH: THE ROAD TO GOOGLE

From the web's very early days the sheer volume of material meant that the ability to search sites easily was one of the key challenges. A medium is of limited value if you cannot find what you are looking for; imagine 5 million channels of television with no program guide. Early web search techniques used conventional library-type systems. The first was Archie, developed in the pre-web era in 1990 at McGill University in Canada, to access archived files. Yahoo! started in 1994 as a catalogue of web pages that the founders liked personally. Others, like Excite, did a similar job on a bigger scale. But as the web grew exponentially, directories became impossible to maintain and automated software spiders or robots were used to look at and catalogue pages. One of the first was Webcrawler in 1994. In 1997 Ask Jeeves was launched to provide natural-language search and by then numerous alternatives were available, including Lycos and AltaVista. The problem for all of them was how to make money.

Google was founded in 1998 on the innovative idea that the relevance and value of a web page could be measured by the number of other pages that linked to it. This was the online equivalent of academic citations, where the most valuable papers receive the largest number of mentions by others. Nevertheless, Google also struggled with income until it hit on the idea that people would pay to have search results promoting their business displayed on the same page as the answers thrown up by the natural search process. The outcome has been a multibillion-dollar business, which claims its mission is to "organize the world's information and make it universally accessible and useful."

Newspapers and magazines have traditionally created their own communities. Newspapers were differentiated from each other based on types of information and sometimes political stance; magazines focused on different but common interests. Being a reader of the *Wall Street Journal* or a subscriber to *Vogue* says a lot about you, your pursuits, and your peer group. The web also creates communities, but allows much smaller and more geographically spread groups to be viable and effective.

The web has blurred the definition of what constitutes a media experience. Playing sport or going shopping competes with television as

WIKIPEDIA: A TRUE WEB MEDIUM

Wikipedia was founded in 2001 with the object of creating an encyclopedia that could be edited by the public. The name is a combination of *wiki*, the Hawaiian word for quick, and encyclopedia. It is built on software that allows articles to be created by any user and for all subsequent edits and additions to be compared with earlier versions. The idea is that errors or facts or analysis will be exposed to public review and will be corrected by Wikipedia participants who are better informed than the previous contributor.

Despite huge controversy and skepticism from the academic community, the premise seems to be broadly correct. Entries often contain text, graphics, audio, and video. For example, enter the name of a common bird like "blue jay" and you get detailed ornithological information and also photographs, video, and audio of the bird song and animated maps of migration patterns. It is a rich media experience that could not have happened before the web. The venerable Oxford University Press has stopped publishing illustrated reference books, as it feels that Wikipedia has taken that market away.[10]

alternative uses of time and cash, but they are not competing media. However, when someone uses a website to buy groceries or garden furniture or to play an online game, they are, in some ways, denying their time to various other web offerings. Home shopping can be just as entertaining as watching streaming videos and, unlike the "real" world, does not require getting into a car. The alternative is just a click away. Time online can equally be used to view media (sites that mediate content) or to do an activity (buying groceries).

Search engines allow users to locate and obtain relevant information, which is analogous to flicking through an encyclopaedia or dictionary. Auction sites like eBay let us participate in a buying and selling process that offers us the chance to make transactions, but also makes us players in a sort of game. Much online retailing such as Amazon has significant media characteristics: it is like a home shopping catalogue, but far more than just that, as shoppers can write reviews and find out what our peers are buying. Net-a-Porter is an amalgam of an online fashion magazine and a store. Netflix is a source of expert opinion on the latest movies as well as a way to buy them. Retailing online has become a rich media experience.

WHAT NEXT?

In the 1890s the pioneers of cinema had no clear idea of what their medium would become. The same was true in the 1920s for radio and in the 1940s for television. The web is but one use of the technology of the internet; there are many others. It is too early for us to say with confidence what sort of media the internet will enable.

In 2010 Chris Anderson, the editor-in-chief of *Wired*, wrote an article entitled "The web is dead,"[11] pointing out that less that half of internet traffic was web related and that the growth was in areas like video streaming and social networking. A key observation was that traditional media practices such as charging for content and restricting access were becoming established once again on the internet. The walled garden was back, most notably in the offers from Apple in the iPod and iPad.

Sharing digital files is an excellent way of providing mediated content. Most media is now created, or at least stored, in digital form. The internet can get this into the hands of the consumer almost instantly at almost no cost. The consumer can then decide how to enjoy it. They can use a big screen, small screen, speakers, ear buds, printed versions (color and black

YOUTUBE

YouTube was created in 2005 by three ex-employees of PayPal who wanted to find a way to share short-form home videos on the internet. It was the classic web medium as its content was created by its own users, called up on demand, and ranked by the users to enable others to find the most popular items quickly. Just over a year later lonelygirl15, who purported to be a 16-year-old video-blogger called Bree, became a huge hit by uploading videos that revealed the angst of being a teenager. After three months it was revealed that it was a commercial ruse and that Bree was actually a 20-year-old actress called Jessica Rose. By the time "Bree" stopped webcasting in 2008, she had had more than 100 million hits.

The ruse annoyed internet purists, but showed the media world that short-form video on the web had huge potential. YouTube was purchased by Google for over £1 billion. It was quickly seen by the commercial world as an ideal way to get video clips available to all. By 2010 there were more than 1 billion videos available on it and at an average of 3 minutes each, it would take someone more than 5,000 years to watch them all. By definition, it has become a medium with little editorial control as no single editor can possible see everything.

and white). They can use it at home, in the office, or on the move. The choice is endless: it depends on the consumer's needs, what devices they like using, and how much they are prepared to pay. In the early days of the web they had many opportunities to pay nothing, but that is unlikely to continue.

There is an active debate about the idea of net neutrality. The belief that all packets on information flowing over the internet should be treated equally is well established and well supported. The point is that internet operators, or governments, should not be able to discriminate between various information flows in terms of access or charging. However, this is sometimes extended into the notion that it is somehow wrong for a media owner to offer services over the internet for which they ask their customers to pay a premium. In fact, this is just an agreed transaction between creator and consumer. It is what we do each time we purchase a song from iTunes or buy an app from the App Store. It is also what we do when we log onto Facebook, which is a walled garden where Google cannot search and only members and approved applications can get access.

A medium connects the originators of content with a consumer, which is exactly the role of a social networking site. According to a senior executive of Facebook, the largest such site: "We want to be the pipes that you use to share information with your friends, no matter where you are."[12] Social networks now consume as much user attention as professionally created web pages and traditional media. In effect, each user's site is a small media outlet devoted to the activities and recommendations of that person—it is "The Daily Me." The network uses the internet to connect its users, but is not usually accessible via the open web. People log on to record their activities and to discover what their contacts are up to.

SixDegrees was probably the first social network, in 1997; Ryze, aimed at business users, arrived in 2001. Myspace, begun in 2003 focused on sharing music selections; in 2005 Facebook moved from the exclusivity of Harvard University to American high schools. If people want to use the web to be entertained or to locate entertainment or to get recommendations for things to buy and do, social networks can be a powerful, and possibly superior, solution to search.

The web now consists of billions of pages and the success of Google is that it helps us find the digital needle in a massive and fast-growing haystack. Nevertheless, the realization is growing that rather than starting with a global pile of virtual hay, it might be easier to go directly to the service we want. This is the world of apps. An app—short for application software—does something specific. Traditional examples are the Microsoft programs Word, which processes text, or PowerPoint, which creates presentations.

However, the term is more often used in relation to apps on smartphones and websites. You can get apps that give you a weather forecast, convert inches to centimeters, provide traffic information, or make restaurant bookings. Amazon's Kindle software is available on the Kindle itself, as an app for the iPhone and iPad, and for a PC or Mac, allowing you to read ebooks purchased from the site on the device of your choice, picking up at the point you stopped reading before. In practice, an online subscription to *The Times* or the *Wall Street Journal* is an app that delivers an edited package of news and comment that meets your needs. The tradeoff between the open web and an app is usually convenience and exclusivity. Music lovers buy songs from iTunes because of the range and ease of use. Given time and effort they could probably build the same music library from free sites, but, leaving aside the moral and legal issues, they pay the money for the convenience of service.

The next phase of internet media is likely to be defined by further technical breakthroughs. The tabloid format gave a new lease of life to newspapers; the paperback did it for books; and the transistor for radio. Early signs are that the iPad and similar tablets will do the same for the internet.

So in terms of the ascent of media the web is not the "end of history". It is the most powerful communications medium so far, but progress will continue. The future is digital media in the round, and the final section of this book speculates on how old and new media are likely to develop alongside each other.

The web is dead. Long live the internet.
Chris Anderson, Editor of *Wired*, 2010

Key Events in Media

Part Two showed that three forces—politics, economics, and technology—have shaped the media industry. The main events or product launches in each of these three areas are shown below.

POLITICAL

399 BC	Socrates made to drink poison
1393	Richard II makes inn signs a legal requirement
1516	Henry VIII establishes Royal Mail
1557	Establishment of Stationers' Company in UK
1559	Pope publishes Index of Prohibited Books
1624	Statute of Monopolies, start of patents and copyright
1643	Licensing Order, UK, Stationers' Company given monopoly
1660	Charles II establishes General Post Office
1688	Glorious Revolution in UK
1695	Abolition of Stationers' monopoly
1710	Statute of Anne, first copyright law UK
1712	Stamp Duty, UK and colonies
1737	Benjamin Franklin appointed postmaster of Philadelphia
1765	Stamp Duty Act, UK and America
1776	Declaration of Independence, US
1790	Patent Act, US
1792	Libel Act, UK
1792	Post Office Act, US
1798	Sedition Act, US
1843	Theatre Regulation Act, UK
1850	Public Libraries Act, UK
1853	Advertising tax abolished, UK
1853	Hackney Carriage Act, UK
1855	Stamp Duty on newspapers removed, UK
1868	Telegraph Act, UK
1889	Copyright Act, US
1904	Wireless Telegraphy Act, UK
1912	Radio Act, US
1921	Willis Graham Act, US
1927	Cinematographic Film Act, UK
1927	Federal Radio Act, US
1930	Motion Picture Production Code, US
1934	Federal Communications Commission (FCC), US
1950	European Broadcasting Union formed
1951	Beveridge Committee, UK

1954	Comics Code Authority, USA
1954	Television Act, UK, establishes ITV
1962	Pilkington Report on future of TV in UK
1965	Highway Beautification Act, US
1967	Public Broadcasting Act, US, creates PBS and NPR
1970	Financial Interest and Syndication Rules (Fin-Syn), in US
1973	Commercial radio starts in UK
1977	Annan Report, UK, leads to Channel 4 and Sky TV
1995	Fin-Syn rules abolished
1996	Telecommunications Act, US
1997	Net Book Agreement abolished, UK
2003	Communications Act, UK, establishes Ofcom

ECONOMIC (AND SOCIAL)

c 1200 BC	*Epic of Gilgamesh*, first written story in cuneiform
534 BC	Athenian government pays for drama contests, Thespis as actor
380 BC	Plato's *The Republic*
350 BC	Aristotle's *Politics*
230 BC	Great Library of Alexandria founded
103 BC	Roman Senate publishes *acta diurna*
79	Public notices (posters) in Pompeii
c 800	*Book of Kells*
c 850	Start of musical notation
1452	Gutenberg prints the bible
1476	William Caxton sets up first English printing press
1490	Thurn und Taxis granted mail monopoly by Austrian Empire
1576	First theatre in London
1594	*Dafne*, first opera
1599	Globe Theatre opens in London
1605	Cervantes writes *Don Quixote*
1622	*Corante: Weekly News*, first regular newsletter in England
1623	Shakespeare's First Folio printed
1665	*Philosophical Transactions of Royal Society* first published
1665	*Oxford Gazette*, first official newspaper in England
1690	*Worcester Postman*, first regular newspaper in England
1702	*Daily Courant*, first daily newspaper in England
1704	Daniel Defoe's *Review*, first magazine in England
1719	Daniel Defoe's *Robinson Crusoe*
1731	*The Gentleman's Magazine*
1755	Dr Johnson's *Dictionary*
1788	*The Times*
1792	WH Smith retail newsagents founded, UK
1799	Rosetta stone discovered

1806	Noah Webster's *Dictionary*
1817	*The Scotsman*
1839	*Obidiah Oldbuck*, first comic book
1840	Penny Black stamp
1842	*Illustrated London News*
1843	*The Economist*
1844	Samuel Morse sends first telegram
1845	Magnetic Telegraph Company formed, US
1845	Electric Telegraph Company formed, UK
1852	First pillarboxes for letter collection, UK
1860	Pony Express starts
1861	First prestamped postcard, USA
1868	Paris authorized Morris Column for posters
1878	J Walter Thompson opens advertising agency
1885	Yellow Kid, first comic strip
1885	Marconi demonstrates wireless telegraph
1886	Coca-Cola brand registered
1892	*Vogue*
1893	*Telephone Herald*, Budapest
1896	*Argosy*, "pulp fiction"
1896	*Daily Mail*
1898	Columbia records founded
1902	*A Journey to the Moon*, first feature film
1905	First nickelodeon opened
1908	Motion Picture Patent Company
1909	FN San Jose Radio
1912	Universal Studios founded
1914	Paramount Pictures founded
1915	DW Griffiths' *The Birth of a Nation*
1917	First royal telegram from George v
1917	Barnes & Noble opens in New York
1919	RCA founded
1920	KDKA radio, Pittsburgh
1922	FM radio advertising, WEAF New York
1922	BBC founded
1923	*Time*
1923	Claude neon sign company founded
1926	NBC founded
1927	*The Jazz Singer*
1927	CBS founded
1930	FM soap opera, WGN Chicago
1930	Hergé's *Tintin*

1930	*Fortune*
1933	Radio Luxembourg launched
1935	Penguin paperbacks launched
1937	BBC TV starts
1938	*Superman*
1938	*War of the Worlds*, CBS Radio
1939	*Batman*
1939	NBC TV starts
1945	ABC founded (forced sale of part of NBC)
1946	Jukeboxes go into mass production
1950	*The Archers*, BBC Radio
1951	*I Love Lucy*
1952	*Checkers* game on IBM 710
1958	*Tennis for Two* game
1961	*Spacewar* game on DEC PDP1
1961	*Private Eye*
1963	ZIP codes, US
1964	Radio Caroline launched
1964	BBC 2 starts
1971	*Galaxy Game*, first arcade video game
1972	*Pong* launched by Atari
1973	Commercial radio starts, UK
1976	*Colossal Cave Adventure*, text-based computer game
1978	*Space Invaders*
1979	WTBS Superstation goes national from Atlanta
1980	*Multi-User Dungeon*
1981	British Telecom created
1982	USA Today launched via satellite printing
1982	Channel 4 starts, UK
1984	Sky TV starts, UK
1984	AT&T broken up
1985	*Super Mario Bros.*
1986	Wapping dispute
1986	Fox network starts, US
1990	British Satellite Broadcasting launched
1991	*Sonic the Hedgehog*
1993	*Mortal Kombat*
1993	*Dr Fun*, first web comic
1996	*Tomb Raider*
1998	Google founded
2006	Last telegram sent by Western Union

TECHNOLOGY

50,000 BC	Great Leap Forward/first language
35,000 BC	Flutes made from bone in Germany
15,000 BC	Earliest sophisticated cave drawings
3500 BC	Harrapan, earliest writing
3000 BC	Musical instruments in widespread use
2600 BC	Papyrus used for documents
2000 BC	Development of phonetic alphabet
1000 BC	Movable type used in China
500 BC	Parchment developed
100	Paper invented in China
1415	Brunelleschi demonstrates perspective
1447	Invention of the printing press, Gutenberg
1791	Optical telegraph, Chappe
1796	Lithography, Senefelder
1814	Steam-driven printing press
1825	Electromagnet, Sturgeon
1837	Electronic telegraph patent, Wheatstone
1839	Daguerreotype photography
1841	Fox Talbot photographic patent
1840	Paper mass produced from wood pulp
1843	Rotary printing press, Hoe
1851	Telegraph cable under English Channel
1858	Transatlantic telegraph cable
1860s	Newsprint comes in rolls made from wood pulp
1867	Sholes and Glidden typewriter
1876	Telephone patent, Bell
1877	Galloping horse pictures, Muybridge
1877	Phonogram patent, Edison
1878	Halftone printing by *New York Daily Graphic*
1885	Marconi demonstrates wireless telegraph (radio)
1886	Automated typesetting Linotype ("hot metal")
1888	Kodak camera patented, Eastman
1891	Telephone exchanges
1993	Kinetoscope, Edison
1895	Cinématographie demonstrated by Lumière
1896	Rotary dial telephone
1906	Teletype Corporation founded
1912	First neon sign
1920	Radio valve (called vacuum tube in US)
1920	Telex network founded
1926	Television—mechanical imaging (Baird)
1927	First jukeboxes, AMI

1928	Magnetic tape data storage
1929	Television—electronic imaging, RCA/EMI
1935	Kodachrome color film
1947	Telecine machine
1947	Transistor, Bell Labs
1948	33 rpm long-playing record, Columbia
1948	45 rpm vinyl single record, RCA
1951	Nimrod games computer
1956	Videotape first used
1956	Hard-drive data storage
1957	Sputnik, first satellite
1962	Telstar, first communications satellite
1963	Hypertext, Ted Nelson
1963	Computer mouse, Douglas Engelbart
1966	Audio cassettes
1968	Magnavox Odyssey games machine
1971	ARPANET opens
1976	CD data storage
1977	Hayes modem
1977	Atari 2600 VCS
1979	Sony Walkman
1982	Musical Instrument Digital Interface (MIDI)
1982	Photocomposition replaces "hot metal" type
1982	CD players and discs
1985	Nintendo Entertainment System (NES)
1988	First digital camera, Fuji
1989	Nintendo Game Boy
1991	First web browser, CERN
1993	WorldWideWeb, Tim Berners-Lee
1993	Netscape Navigator
1994	Sony PlayStation
1995	DVD data storage
1995	MP3 audio file format approved
1998	Rio, early portable MP3 player
1999	Napster, audio file sharing
1999	TiVo, digital video recorder
2001	iPod, Apple
2001	Xbox, Microsoft
2005	Sony e-book
2007	iPhone, Apple
2007	Kindle, Amazon
2010	iPad, Apple
2010	Kinect, Microsoft

PART THREE
Future | Everything that went before... and more

The vast range of media we now enjoy is a cocktail of different formats resulting from many centuries of the interplay of politics, economics, and technology. Old media are not simply replaced by the new—they are modified and add to the rich mixture available. The choice is only going to get richer still and will do so with increasing speed. And the impact of media on the way society functions is going to get greater.

Digital technology is enabling new forms of creation, production, distribution, and consumption of content that are modifying existing media and offering new communication opportunities and problems. We are entering a new era of superabundance of media, much of which will be delivered by screens. This is producing a huge challenge for consumers, drowning in choice, of how to find what they really want to read, listen, and watch amidst all the noise, and for media professionals of how to fund their activities as the established models of advertising and subscription break down.

Traditional formats like books, newspapers, radio, or television were separate and discrete channels; each used technology in its own way. In the digital era these distinctions are vanishing and the same internet-linked, screen-based devices will be used to offer an almost unlimited amount of content, with the user, not the distributor, deciding exactly what, where, and when they read, listen, or watch.

The media landscape that surrounds us today started to form in the London coffee shops around the year 1700. It was then that what had been the exclusive and expensive fifteenth-century technology of printing was first adapted to create mass communications. The relaxation of English government control in the wake of the Glorious Revolution of 1688, improved distribution by new roads and postal systems, better printing machines, and the rise of an educated merchant class led to the emergence of newspapers. In 1710 Queen Anne gave legal force to the idea of copyright, which provided the economic structure that led to novels, magazines, comics, sheet music, and the professions of journalist, author, and composer.

The invention of the telegraph in the 1840s made information transfer instant and, once submarine cables were laid, international. In the 1920s broadcasting made live events accessible to the audience at home and led to the notion of mass media. The growth of radio and later television fundamentally changed the nature of society, commerce, and the political process. The internet and the web have made communications two way and truly worldwide. The profound impact of this is not yet clear, but it is likely to lead to the use of English as a common global language and greater awareness of and action to solve complex world issues such as climate change.

It would be simple but wrong to assume that the ascent of media has been a logical and linear progression, driven by a succession of new technologies. The reality is far more complex. Innovations have gone in fits and starts and rates of change vary in different political systems. Even similar nations like the US and UK show marked differences in the development of their media. Sometimes the shape of a new medium is driven by economics, as with magazines and advertising. At other times it has been politics, for instance restrictions on early newspapers. Others are mostly defined by technology, for example the telegraph or radio.

The future of the media is vital to all of us because it shapes our society. In the 1950s Canadian economist Harold Innis[1] was one of the first to study the impact of media on the process of civilization in his *Empire and Communications*. He described the role that writing played in creating early empires like Assyria, Egypt, and Rome. His academic successor in Toronto, Marshall McLuhan,[2] argued in the 1960s that the mere existence of a new medium acted to change the way we live. Asa Briggs and Peter Burke,[3] publishing first in 2002, showed how the emergence of media has been intertwined with the development of society itself. By 2010 Tim Wu[4] was warning that we must not take for granted the open and accessible nature of the internet given the past history of monopolies forming in cinema, telephony, radio, and television.

Wolfgang Riepl, editor-in-chief of the *Nürnberger Zeitung* in Germany, studied the evolution of media going back to ancient history. In 1913, in the very early days of radio, cinema, and recorded music, he proposed a "law" that newly invented media do not replace old ones but simply converge with them, so the traditional forms become used in different ways. If there is an overall theme to this book it would be to argue that 100 years of subsequent development have shown that Riepl's law remains valid, with the qualification that the old media also often develop a new lease of life as forms of art. As such they happily coexist with new media but are no longer dominant means of mass communication.[5]

The media is a huge part of our lives. People spend nearly half their waking hours consuming mediated content and increasing amounts of this time are taken up by multitasking as we interact with several media types simultaneously.[6] The media as a whole has become a trillion-dollar global industry and the influence of mediated content is growing. Politicians are judged more than ever on their media performance. The impact of the web in Obama's 2008 campaign in the US and the dramatic upsets of the first televised general election debates in the UK in 2010 showed the media's growing influence on politics. In the commercial sphere, the increased importance of brands and peer-group recommendations in conditioning our buying behavior as well as the role that mediated content plays in creating opinion on social networks demonstrate that media is more embedded in the fabric of society than ever before. What we buy, wear, eat, drink, and think are all now informed by media experiences.

However, while media plays an ever larger role in our work and leisure, traditional media companies have been struggling to come to terms with the new economic structures. The web is delivering text, audio, and video in forms that we can store and share and indeed, in many cases create for ourselves. All the accepted wisdom about cover prices, subscriptions, advertising, copyright, censorship, privacy, and professionally created content is now being called into question. The traditional media will survive, but they will transform and shrink to serve an increasingly niche audience.

Consumers are in control and can access the content they want, in the format they like, by using software to dictate the output of their media tablet, rather than having to choose between a book, a magazine, or television. We are no longer limited to being described as readers or viewers or listeners. We are now simply users of multimedia; "tableteers," perhaps.

This final section of the book assesses the lessons of history, but it is, inevitably, influenced by my own experience of having worked in media for some 30 years. During this time I have seen dramatic and painful changes at first hand and this has conditioned my own thinking. To reflect the personal nature of the analysis, and to accept full responsibility for it, I am telling this final part of the story in the first person.

THE CHALLENGE OF CHANGE

When I first worked in television, for the BBC in the late 1970s, journalists still used typewriters to prepare scripts and news cuttings libraries were just that, physical bits of cut-up newspaper stored in little envelopes. The telephone was the key information tool; it had a mechanical dial and was plugged into the wall. Television news stories were made by a six-person crew using 16 mm color film that had to go through a two-hour chemical process before being physically cut into strips and then stuck back in the desired order using clear tape. The resulting three-minute report was broadcast to people who received it through a roof-top aerial and watched it via a cathode ray tube in their television receiver. To a twentysomething at the time it was all cutting-edge technology. Thirty years on it looks as archaic as smoke signals.

At that time in the UK the only channels were the BBC and ITV. If people got bored with television they could listen to BBC radio or they could put a vinyl record on the stereo. The experience in America was similar, dominated by network television and radio. The list of media then not available is a long one: CD, DVD, VHS, PVR, MP3 player, digital radio, cellphone, satellite TV, plasma screen, LCD, personal computer, iPod, iPhone, iPad, and of course the internet itself.

Television now is fully digitized, so a video reporter can do the whole process of making a three-minute news film by him- or herself in about an hour. Pictures are captured on a disc, edited by computer, transmitted over satellite, stored on a hard drive, and watched, as part of a 500-channel offering, at a time and place that suits the viewer. It is quicker, cheaper, and far more abundant.

In 1970 British TV presenter Joan Bakewell wrote a book called *The New Priesthood*[7] about the small elite of television professionals and the exotic and technically complex world they inhabited, which gave them access to powerful communication tools denied to the man in the street. Television then was a mass medium, but control and creation were in the hands of a tiny minority. Now most of those barriers have been broken down. As a result of digital tools, media is more democratic and accessible than at any time in history.

The rate of change in media is greater than ever before. It took 71 years from launch for a half of households in America to have a fixed-line telephone in the 1900s. As noted in Part Two, it took just 14 years for the cellphone to have a similar uptake in the 1990s. The evidence suggests that tablet computers like the iPad will hit the 50 percent access level in less than five years. It is this rate of acceleration that makes running a media business so challenging and exciting.

SHAPING THE FUTURE

Prediction is a risky task, particularly in fast-moving media. When I joined Thames TV as a reporter in 1980 I was given a then recently published book called *Television: Here is the News*. The final chapter was "The Future."

Here is an extract:

> British television must not present its own opinions as a newspaper
> does and is never likely to be allowed to until there are as many alter-
> native news channels as there are newspapers, which is not a fore-
> seeable event. From time to time a "news only" channel has been
> mooted. Its likelihood is small... Not much can be done to increase
> the number of channels.[8]

Just two years later Channel 4 was created and a satellite television station
was launched. In 1984 that satellite station was purchased by Rupert
Murdoch, who renamed it Sky. At last count I had more than 30 news
channels on my Sky+ box and some 500 separate TV offerings. Things
change faster than we can imagine. The future of the media will continue
to be an unpredictable collision of new technologies and human
ingenuity.

In 1500, 50 years after Gutenberg printed his first bible, you would
have been hard pressed to predict the coming world of novels, newspapers,
and magazines, since the concepts did not exist. While the technology was
there, the economics were still to emerge. Church control was strict and
copyright had not yet been invented. We are only two decades into digital
media and the elements of politics, economics, and technology remain in
flux. While exact predictions are difficult, there are three factors that are
clearly shaping the future of the media: screen-based devices, user control,
and unlimited capacity.

Screen-based devices

Screens of all sizes will become the predominant way in which we receive
information and entertainment. Different formats will meet various needs.
Computer monitors are merging with televisions. Smartphones are merging with tablets. Some of the screens will be as thin as card and will roll up
just like an ancient scroll. All will be connected to the internet, all the time.
These tablet devices will serve multiple purposes: at times for reading text,
at others for watching video, and sometimes to listen to audio.

This does not mean that printed paper will vanish, but it will become
a premium-priced, niche format for the enthusiast and collector. And as
output becomes screen based, it will increasingly be controlled by touch

Media's Future

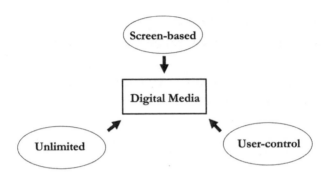

and voice command. The technology of the NUI (natural user interface) allows us to use gestures and voice to control our media devices. Soon using a physical keyboard will be a minority activity, rather like writing with a fountain pen.

A magazine is already a fusion of words, photographs, and images. Some include advertisements impregnated with scent. It is not unknown to have a sound chip that speaks a message or plays a tune when the page is turned. Once it is screen based the magazine will feature video and audio without the need for any printer's gimmicks.

We are used to conversations along the lines of: "What are you watching on TV?" "I'm watching a film/documentary/quiz show." In future, using any of the screen-based media devices, the dialogue will go: "What are you using it for now?" "At the moment it's *The Economist/New York Times*/Jazz Radio/Food Channel."

In addition to media converging into screen-based distribution, we are increasingly using multiple media simultaneously. Reading a magazine while listening to music is hardly a new phenomenon, but we now consume multiple inputs on a huge scale. It is common to watch television with a laptop open, messaging friends while checking out restaurant reviews and shopping online. The practice of so-called media stacking or "second screening" is monitored by ratings agencies and regulators like the UK's OFCOM, as it calls into question the impact and value of advertising when multiple media channels are being used at the same time.

The concept of transmedia storytelling is becoming common in advertising and will extend more generally to entertainment and information. To get a full understanding of the characters, plot, and message the audience needs to access a range of media over a period of time, often combining comics, video games, recorded sound, long-form video (television), and short-form video (web streaming). The story builds and characters develop through multiple touch points. This has been pioneered by television series such as *Heroes* and *Doctor Who*.[9] If a teenage boy talks today on the phone about *Spider-Man*, do you assume he means the comic, the book, the film, the game, the YouTube video, or the magazine?

User control

Media consumers are becoming creators and editors in their own right. Digital technology allows anyone to make content. Prize-winning movies can be made for less than $1,000 and uploaded to sites like YouTube for nothing. A couple of friends in a garage can produce a viable online newspaper. Local people commenting on local issues are able to generate material of great interest to their community. The same holds true for narrow-focus hobbies and minority sports.

The dramatic rise of blogs and services like Twitter adds to the available content, but does not replace professional products. Many, indeed most, media outlets will incorporate citizen journalists in the same way that newspapers have always had a letters page. Those media that make this "amateur" content accessible and entertaining through careful editing and packaging will be the ones that thrive.

Early video games offered contests but did not transmit content or allow a narrative. However, more recent offerings such as *Halo* and *Call of Duty* involve players in creating their own characters, defining their own playing fields, and constructing their own stories. The outcome of the game is a collaborative effort between the designer and the players. Virtual worlds such as Second Life have most of their content created by their own users. Multiplayer games like *World of Warcraft* are rich media experiences, with the excitement created by other players. And on television, hit shows like *American Idol* need the participation of real people in the role of contestants as well as acting as judges.

It is not only in making content that users are taking control, it is in constructing the media menu. We are on the way to all being the owners and operators of "my medium"; the traditional role of editors and schedulers who dictated our diet of entertainment and information is fast disappearing. Media consumption now happens where and when we choose it, the "Martini media" phenomenon: available anywhere, any place, any time.

Media history is littered with attempts to control content for the "public good": The Index of Prohibited Books, the Stationers' Company, the Hays Office for movies, the Comics Code, the FCC, and the games industry code. But now it seems likely that we, the users, will have to supply our own ratings and control. We will suggest what people see and avoid through recommendation and comment rather than censorship.

Moral censorship evolved mostly to protect children; we accept that adults must take their chances on what they see and hear. Before the digital age the policy in the western world was that restricted and paid-for media such as theatre, cinema, and books could do what they liked as long as they warned their audience. Publicly open and free media such as television, radio, and posters had to exercise far more self-restraint. But once content is digital, conventional censorship techniques fail to work and the only sensible answer seems to be to limit access to media devices rather than to attempt to control their content.

Unlimited capacity

Digital production and distribution allow for an almost limitless amount of content. It may be good and bad, balanced and biased, inspired, or awful, but there is certainly a vast volume of it. While the amount of time we have available to consume media cannot increase much more, the total of media available will continue to grow exponentially. Some 30 hours of video material are uploaded to YouTube every minute[10] and there are more than 100 million active blogs. Seeing more than a tiny fraction of all this would be impossible, so people will be drawn to those items that are recommended by trusted sources and that get to the top of social media hit lists.

The traditional role of media professionals as content creators will change, with more of them becoming curators of the vast pool of material developed by people and organizations outside of the conventional mainstream media organizations. Nevertheless, the guarantee of quality and editorial balance will remain with the leading media brands. Just because vast amounts of the output will be mindless rubbish does not mean that the media as a whole become any less reliable or lower quality.

The access to obscure content enabled by the internet was described by Chris Anderson in *The Long Tail*,[11] where he showed how the search capabilities of the web make niche titles accessible to a widely spread minority audience. This gives new economic life to minority tastes, but in fact it appears the gap between blockbuster hits and niche products is widening. There is just too much to browse at will and the speed of communication helps the winners to win bigger than ever. Major films and books like Harry Potter get a huge following. TV shows like *American Idol* and *The X Factor* defy the trend of audience fragmentation by creating "must see" live events that are widely covered in other media.

ARISTOTLE'S *AGORA* GOES GLOBAL

Aristotle suggested that the size of a workable society was limited by the media available to allow the citizens to communicate with each other.[12] On that basis, recent media developments should allow society to be a truly global structure.

The *agora* was the open area in ancient Greek cities where people gathered. It translates as "place of assembly." (The fear of being in such public spaces gives us the modern term "agoraphobia.") Community communication and social organization started with the orator in the *agora*. The content was the speech. It was not mediated, it was immediate and direct. All the audience could hear the message at the same time in the same location. This created a cohesive group.

Plato, he of the cave analogy, had very fixed views on the ideal society: he calculated that the perfect size was 5,040 citizen farmers. Beyond this he suggested that the group was too big to be manageable. Aristotle was more optimistic. In his *Politics* he appears to suggest that the maximum size of a functioning, democratic society was some tens of thousands, the number of people who could crowd into the *agora* and simultaneously hear the orator's voice. In his time documents were scarce and speech was the medium that connected people.

Manuscript, papyrus, parchment, and paper extended the size of the audience and thus a society, but it was still limited by the effort and cost to make and distribute copies. Printing, when combined with postal systems, greatly increased the reach of communication and had the additional effect of fixing the spelling and grammar of a language, thus leading to the concepts of nationalism and nation states. Printing also enabled the dissemination of knowledge, which was the basis of the Renaissance. Once extended to pamphlets and then newspapers, printing allowed the development of political movements and thus the Reformation in religion and the revolutionary shift of political power away from monarchies and aristocracies.

The telegraph enabled the control of much larger empires, both commercial and political. Broadcasting produced mass audiences and a common experience. Coronations, presidential inaugurations, sports events, even wars became available live, via radio and then television, to huge numbers sitting at home, who also become customers for the soap powders and packaged foods that paid for it all. Broadcasting let society listen to and look at itself at a distance and on a much greater scale. It made us all more aware of our world, but is often described as a "lean-back" medium. It encouraged us to be observers rather than participants.

Then we developed the internet, which is like broadcasting but more powerful because it is two way and always on. In its early days the internet's reach was less than the mass media of radio and television, but in most developed countries the web is now a near universal channel. The internet is Aristotle's *agora* on a worldwide scale.

This is more than the global village envisaged by Marshall McLuhan, which recognized that people would all access the same mass media and have common experiences but did not anticipate the full interactive crowd effect. The internet is a "lean-forward" medium and has created a global city square in which the assembled can participate, contribute, debate, and question.

STEVE JOBS AND MOSES

In addition to its revolutionary role as a connector of people, the internet also acts as a traditional distribution channel; in effect, an alternative to radio waves, postal routes, and printing presses. For delivering content (text, audio, and video) the internet will grow in importance and the traditional channels of bookshops, newsagents, cinemas, and broadcasting networks will have to adapt to survive. For us as consumers, the nature of the content delivered will not radically change, but the way it reaches us will.

For communicating his ten commandments Moses allegedly used stone tablets, the most durable and reliable medium of the time. Roll on two millennia and he would have used a printed page. Today it would be an iPad app. New media do not, as some critics lament, mean the end of serious content, independent journalism, good writing, or quality drama. The form of communication is changing, but the fundamentals of information, education, or entertainment will remain.

The new devices and apps will do for digital media what the codex format did for the book. They will deliver a more convenient consumer experience, which will make them the medium of choice for the next generation of Shakespeares and Spielbergs; or indeed Moseses. Some of these apps will come to us "free," subsidized by advertising, others we will happily pay for as we will value their combination of content and packaging.

The role of Apple and Steve Jobs in all this is particularly interesting. Apple's innovations—the iPod, iTunes, iPhone, and iPad—are in effect a complete media package, a marriage of hardware, software, and content that is strangely similar to the early walled-garden days of the cinema, the phonograph, and radio.

Ironically, the sheer volume of material now available might make it attractive to have a single organization that does much of the selection and organization for us. One solution to superabundance might be to hand control to a gatekeeper—to let Apple, for example, choose our media diet.

BILL GATES AND ADAM SMITH

Despite the web's early love affair with the notion of free access for everything, paying for content will become more widespread. There will be more use of subscriptions, micro-payments, and pay-per-view. Ultimately, professional content creators have to be rewarded, and that means someone has to pay. The volume of advertising is limited—if only by the size of the consumer economy—so effective ways of charging for digital content must emerge. The conundrum of audience and income was highlighted by Microsoft founder Bill Gates as long ago as 1996 when he wrote:

> Some content companies are experimenting with subscriptions... It's tricky, though, because as soon as an electronic community charges... the number of people who visit the site drops dramatically,

reducing the value proposition to advertisers. But within a year the mechanisms will be in place that allow content providers to charge just a few cents for information.[13]

Gates was right about the problem, but wrong about the speed of a solution. More than a decade on it has not yet been solved, although it will be.

In the early days of the web when people argued that "eyeballs would lead to income," NBC Chief Executive Jeff Zucker was credited with observing that moving traditional media advertising onto the internet was "exchanging analogue dollars for digital pennies." By 2010 he had a more optimistic view, updating the quote to "digital dimes."[14] Sensible business models of payment are now emerging—the day of the true digital dollar being charged is coming.

Rupert Murdoch has pioneered subscription on satellite television and is experimenting with paywalls for newspapers. The initiative was met with skepticism, but some form of charging for digital content is inevitable, as advertising alone will not be enough. The technology of the internet will allow a mixed economy. The free web will be like the town square or London's Speaker's Corner, where people can make their ideas and creations available to all at no charge. Alongside this will, inevitably, develop digital services that are only available if paid for.

Economist Adam Smith famously argued that the "invisible hand" of the market shaped industries. He was writing in the early boom years of newspapers in the 1770s. Much of the discontinuity in media is that digital production and distribution are simply significantly less costly than their analogue predecessors. By trying to maintain historical pricing structures for services like music, games, and news media, companies created the environment for piracy. We the consumer have an inherent sense of the "right" value and as the price of digital media moves to more closely reflect the real cost, a more realistic mix of advertising and subscription will probably come into balance.

A NEW STATUTE OF ANNE

However, whatever the balance of income from advertising subscription and direct payment, it is only if we can find ways to reward creative endeavor and prevent the making and distribution of illegal copies of digital content that we can guarantee the media's future in terms of quality. In the analogue world there was a cost to making and distributing copies that acted as a natural barrier to piracy. In the digital age we make clones that, for all practical purposes, are the original.

The original copyright laws stimulated an explosion of creativity and investment. We must be careful not to move backward. We have to find ways to protect intellectual property without making the consumer feel constrained or cheated. Suing teenagers for downloading music is clearly not part of the solution.

Daniel Defoe was one of the first to enjoy the new copyright protection laws, both as a novelist and as a magazine publisher in the early 1700s. He had experience of real pirates, depicted in his works of fiction, and had very clear views on the theft of intellectual property by unscrupulous printers:

> To print another Man's copy is much worse than robbing him on the Highway; for the Thief takes only what he finds about him, but the Pyrate Printer takes away his inheritance... not of the Author only, but of his Family and Children.[15]

If a shop customer puts a magazine into their bag and walks out without paying, it is clearly an act of theft. The shop does everything it can to deter this or it will lose revenue. On the internet, the act of distributing a digital file of that same magazine without payment is equally stealing, but in most cases the site offering it makes its income in other ways and did not pay for the creation of the magazine, and is thus indifferent to the loss of value to the original content owner.

Digital files can be easily hallmarked, watermarked, or tagged. Google-style search algorithms can quickly locate those sites that have legitimate copyright authority and those that do not. So the problem is not one of technology but of jurisdiction and enforcement. And that will come down to monitoring and controlling what travels over the internet.

It makes no sense if a new technology turns us all into potential lawbreakers. Copying a CD from one's own computer onto one's own phone is a legitimate convenience but may be seen as illegal. Using a tablet computer among friends to show a picture, glance at a page of a book, listen to a piece of music, or watch a video clip should not be seen as copyright infringement—it is simply sharing. But the moment some-one seeks to charge, and make a profit from, intellectual property that they did not create, a transaction occurs and value has been pirated. This is a simple principle that must, somehow, become enshrined in a new, global version of the Statute of Anne, without becoming a barrier to creative endeavor.

WHO OWNS THE INTERNET?

In simple terms no one owns the internet, as it is a network of standalone networks. A data file goes from one user to another in packets of information that can travel over an almost unlimited number of pathways. A service provider like a telecoms company or a cable TV operator probably owns the wires that link any one computer to the system, but the internet itself remains public property. It is common land or open sea.

The idea of network neutrality has been around since the development of postal systems and in particular the telegraph in the 1850s, when the principle that all messages would be treated equally was enshrined in legislation.[16] The exact meaning of "net neutrality" is actively debated, but the broad sense is that any user should be allowed access for any legal traffic. However, to take this further and argue that all traffic must be treated equally in terms of speed and volume flies in the face of history and common sense. It cannot be right that content providers wishing to provide free streaming video of dancing cats should be allowed to use so much capacity that phone calls or emails linked to medical diagnoses are disrupted or delayed. The internet is not a completely "free good." If someone from the 1700s wanted to graze a huge number of their sheep on the common land, they would be expected to compensate the rest of the village for the loss of amenity. First- and second-class post is a well-established principle to allow people and businesses to pay more to obtain superior service. The internet will need to establish similar principles.

LESSONS OF HISTORY

Although the technology employed by media advances continuously, the same issues of ownership, control, and organization keep recurring. There is no reason to believe that the digital era will be any different.

In the 1500s attempts by the King of France to take charge of domestic publishing were frustrated by a thriving and unregulated French-language printing industry in the adjacent Netherlands. Attempts to shackle the web by various governments face similar challenges today.

Shakespeare captured the maximum value from his intellectual property by selling tickets to his plays rather than publishing completed scripts. Author JK Rowling has retained her digital rights to Harry Potter and is now operating her own direct sale website; rock band Kaiser Chiefs allowed fans to create and buy their own albums. All avoided going through the media marketplaces owned by others.

Early magazines and newspapers were hampered by government licenses and stamp taxes, but the rise of London coffee houses in the late 1600s provided a forum for the quasi-public reading of restricted texts that were not conventionally published. Blogs offer a similar mechanism for discussing material not made available in a traditional way.

Low-cost paper and printing enabled chapbooks in the 1600s. Steam presses, wood pulp newsprint, and railways enabled the dime novel in the 1800s. Both radically reduced the cost of publication and opened the market to new genres of popular fiction—often much to the chagrin of the literary establishment. The same is happening again with the 99 cent digital novel on the Kindle.

In the 1800s a profusion of British pamphleteers were able to defy government attempts to silence them as small low-cost printing presses had become common items of equipment in all towns and it was impossible to control their output. In a same way, the ubiquity of services like Twitter mean that the law courts (in Britain using the much-derided super-injunctions) are unable to control what amounts to gossip between people.

The English copyright laws of 1710 were demanded by writers and publishers and intended to stimulate creativity to overcome the stultifying monopoly of licensed printers. Now in both America and the UK, the laws of intellectual property are felt to have become dysfunctional as they hinder innovation. There are, once again, calls for a new copyright regime.

In the 1890s the arrival of high-speed rotary presses and the rapid growth in advertising encouraged huge competition between newspapers in America, which led them to push moral and ethical boundaries and resulted in the lurid and sensational approach we now call "yellow journalism." This defined a new low point in media behavior. In an echo of that time, the intense competition from the internet and falling advertising has led some papers to indulge in previously unseen levels of obsession with celebrity and intrusion of privacy to sell more copies, evidenced in the UK by the tabloid phone hacking scandals.

Networks, like those of the telegraph and the telephone, started out as hundreds of competing companies, which proved chaotic. "Natural" national monopolies evolved like the privately owned American Telegraph & Telephone or the state-controlled British GPO. These organizations provided users with a good service but, on principle, governments sought to break them up, resulting in structures like the Baby Bells and the separation of the Royal Mail from British Telecom and O2. Now internet giants like Facebook and Google benefit from exactly the same network effects and exhibit "winner-takes-all" results. A rerun of government intervention seems inevitable.

The start of many new media in the 1900s often led to vertically integrated monopolies driven by swashbuckling tycoons like Adolph Zukor (Paramount Pictures) and David Sarnoff (RCA), who dominated their markets by owning the total system of production and distribution and justified it as they were able to deliver the consumer a simple, quality product. It now seems that Steve Jobs (Apple) and Jeff Bezos (Amazon) are on a similar mission, offering the total package of software and hardware. In the past competitors lobbied regulators to take action. That is happening again.

History also shows that the chaotic early days of a new medium are no clear guide to its likely final shape. The initial use is frequently frivolous, even demeaning. As author Clay Shirky has pointed out, some of the early printers applied their skills to very low-brow objectives:

> When the printing press came along something very similar to the internet happened. We got erotic stories in the 1400s but didn't get scientific journals for another 150 years. You always get the stuff that caters for the most basic human desires first.[17]

It takes time for a new medium to mature. The early newspapers of the 1700s simply made things up or relied on letters from far-flung, unpaid correspondents; professional journalism came more than 100 years later. Cinema started with titillating "what the butler saw" clips shown as fairground amusements; it took 40 years to make *Citizen Kane*. Radio was, at first, a hobbyists' novelty until it became a vehicle for variety shows; disc jockeys were 30 years in the making. The gramophone was designed for office dictation; in early machines the poor quality of music recordings made them almost unusable. Television was originally intended simply to bring pictures of live events into people's homes; scripted drama and all the rest waited for the invention of the telecine machine.

WHAT COMES NEXT?

As explained in the Preface, the idea for this book started in Palo Alto just a few years ago, at a time when the prospects for the traditional media industry looked grim. Advertising was in a slump and the army of new web-based start-ups had undermined the economics of conventional players without developing robust business models of their own. The audience for digital media was expanding fast, huge sums of venture capital money were going in, but not much cash and precious little quality content seemed to be coming out.

Now things are looking much more positive. The chaotic early period—the Wild West phase of the internet—is behind us and people are finding ways to create quality content and make digital media pay. At the same time, traditional media have reduced their cost base, reengineered their products, and are experimenting with new sources of revenue.

The rallying cry remains that "content is king." The traditional monopoly power that went with owning a printing press, a cinema, a record store, or a broadcast tower and license has been eroded by digital code. What you produce is now far more important than how you distribute it. How you get paid for it is still unclear, but cool devices like the iPad offer a rich media experience and a simple payment mechanism. The demand for new, mediated content can only increase. Nevertheless, it has to be offered with the right packaging, pricing, and protection if it is to succeed.

As media consumers, we are much more interested in the story we are told than the technology that brings it to us. We want the experience to be easy, fun, and value for money, and increasingly we demand a good return for the hours we invest. In the face of huge media proliferation, consumer time will be a scarcer resource than money. We will pay for services that make our media time more productive and enjoyable.

It is this scarcity of time and the need for a professional curator that will sustain a reinvented role for the editor and scheduler, informed more by constant public feedback than professional gut instinct. They will also fashion the future of outlets like bookshops, cinemas, and theatres, which will need to enhance the cultural experience of media consumption with ambiance and expertise rather than merely acting as neutral distribution outlets.

Heritage media companies can no longer rely on their traditional content to be successful in the emerging channels. Web-specific and, more broadly, digital-specific material will develop, as it did for other new media like cinema, radio, and television. Pointing film cameras at plays, having radio announcers reading out newspapers, and television bulletins presented by studio-bound newsreaders without pictures did not succeed. The exponents of new forms of transmedia storytelling will reap the rewards denied to those who simply recycle the conventional. The questions for the future are: Where will these people come from? What will they create? And how will they be rewarded?

Now that the first couple of decades of breathless digital development are behind us, it is hard to pin down any single location as the hub of digital media. Theatre started in Greece, printing on the banks of the river Rhine, cinema in Hollywood, radio in New York, and television in London's Alexandra Palace. While Palo Alto provided much of the early digital infrastructure, content is emerging from everywhere. Mostly in English but in no fixed location, it encompasses games, films, websites, music, and information. Digital media is dynamic, democratic, and diffuse.

In terms of industry structure, the main impact of the internet will be on physical distribution rather than creation. Postal services have already surrendered basic letters to email and instant messaging. Broadcast towers are being replaced by YouTube. Radio masts are becoming redundant in the face of music services like Pandora and Spotify. Newsagents and magazine kiosks are giving ground to tablet computers—comic books and magazines are already among the most downloaded apps. Content creators are striving to find the right routes to markets and the best economic models, but all the indications are that they will emerge successful in the digital environment, while some distribution businesses will vanish altogether.

The media are entering an exciting era. We are just beginning to see the full range of ways in which the digital technology can be used and how old media can respond. Experiments with free web pages, advertising-supported streaming, paywalls, micropayments, subscriptions, metering, and all the rest have been dizzying. Video games and the two-way nature of the internet have left us demanding much more from our media experiences. Over the past 20 years, the dot-com boom and the credit crunch crisis have led to such hectic activity that it has been almost impossible to see the digital wood for the virtual trees. However, things are settling down and we can recognize the internet for what it is: a vast electronic pipe down which all forms of digital content can be delivered, both free and paid for. Digital media, if properly packaged and protected, can be a huge opportunity for content creators to prosper and consumers to be informed and entertained.

One of the clearest lessons of history has been that each successive media era tends to start its golden age only when the politics and economics come into line with the new technology. This was true of books, newspapers, telegraph, telephone, cinema, radio, and television. Digital has opened up extraordinary creative opportunities, but we are only in the early days of evolving the right legal and commercial framework. There are issues that must be resolved:

- There is simply not enough advertising to pay for quality content, so simple and friction-free charging mechanisms must be developed.
- Digital files can be exactly reproduced at no cost, so a robust new copyright regime must be found to protect intellectual property without stifling creative endeavor.
- The volume of content is unmanageable, so we have to create filter mechanisms to help us find what we want. We need curators.
- The powers of search and archiving mean that privacy can be easily compromised. We must find the right balance to protect ourselves.
- Access to the internet should not be restricted, but usage and service quality has to be differentially priced, as bandwidth is not wholly free.

FROM TABULAE TO TABLETS VIA TABLOIDS

In 1726, as the leaders of the Age of Enlightenment were laying the economic and political foundations of the modern media industry, the young Benjamin Franklin, visiting London for the first time, decided to jump into the Thames to demonstrate a range of elegant swimming strokes he had invented. It must have been a bizarre spectacle as he made his way from Chelsea to Blackfriars and it was one that could well have been watched from the north bank of the river by Daniel Defoe.[18]

Franklin was yet to make his name as a writer, newspaper publisher, pioneer of the post office, public library founder, and investigator of electricity as well as an American revolutionary. Defoe was near the end of his career, but still basking in the glory of having been a leading pamphleteer, the inventor of the magazine format, lobbyist for the introduction of copyright, and the first English novelist with *Robinson Crusoe*. The men had homes close to each other in London. They may or may not have met in 1726, but they both recognized in their writings that they were living in a heady time of advancement in science, art, and democratic institutions. Progress was driven, informed, and supported by the rapidly growing medium of print in its many guises. We are privileged now to be living through an equally exciting time as digital media is enabling great social and creative change.

Although modern media started in the coffee shops of Georgian London's Fleet Street, the fundamental media issues go back far beyond the 1700s. When Roman writers inscribed their poems and essays onto their wax tabulae, they were already running into questions about censorship, copyright, piracy, privacy, payment methods, and freedom of information. As new technologies developed and media become more powerful, the same problems keep recurring in new ways.

Earlier media critics such as Diderot and Voltaire complained about the superabundance of books. Their experience of excessive output was nothing to what we have today. Because of this we, as consumers, have always welcomed some form of expert curator to organize and recommend our media menu. And now we need it more than ever. The discriminating role traditionally fell to the publisher, bookseller, and editor. Pioneer disc jockeys like Alan Freed in the US and John Peel in the UK were trusted sources of musical guidance. It is no accident that some of the biggest-selling magazines are guides to what is on TV. The internet has bought recommendation engines like that of Amazon and, perhaps most significantly, social network tools like Facebook that allow us to eavesdrop on the taste of others as a guide to finding what we might enjoy. We need help. The bewildering range of digital media on offer today might not quite be a "vast wasteland," as FCC commissioner Newton Minow described US television in the 1960s, but it is certainly a greatly oversupplied market.

Social media evangelist Clay Shirky has coined the phrase "cognitive surplus,"[19] recognizing the huge volume of output and the two-way nature of the internet, which allows us all to be not just consumers but creators and publishers of content. The challenge this poses is the same as that highlighted in the 1471 letter quoted earlier: How do you discriminate the good material from the vast flood? Faced with superabundance, we are rediscovering the role of the content curator, but in the new media such people's authority comes from being trusted by their record and sought out for their views rather than from their ownership of a means of distribution.

The internet replicates, on a huge scale, the social structure of the eighteenth-century coffee shops where Defoe and Franklin would have passed their time. Then, as now, people communicated in two directions. Content is not simply transmitted via print or broadcast where it can be filtered by media owners or politicians. It is shared by a community that needs to make its own rules about privacy and access. There is increasing acceptance of the idea that the legion of bloggers, tweeters, video uploaders, and social network users are becoming a "fifth estate," building on Edmund Burke's notion of the then newly powerful press. The combined efforts of citizen journalists, who are not employed by an established media owner, are now a major factor in shaping government policy and public taste.

The traditional media have enjoyed financial structures that created forced subsidies for content and services that otherwise might not have been economic. The Net Book Agreement in the UK ensured that there was no discounting of titles by retailers. This maintained high margins that kept a lot of small bookshops and publishers in business when unrestrained price discounting might have led to their closure. The abolition of the agreement in 1997 and the rise of online booksellers have fundamentally changed that industry. Local newspapers were for many years the only viable channel for highly profitable classified advertising that enabled them to fund local news coverage. Classified websites have undermined that by separating the lucrative local marketplace from expensive journalism. Broadcasters in radio and television enjoyed effective monopolies as governments issued a restricted number of licenses creating "false" scarcity. Satellite and cable distribution and now broadband links have ended that and profit margins of traditional operators have fallen.

Nevertheless, media organizations adapt. Bookshops are reinventing themselves, returning to their roots, by offering an enjoyable experience of authorship, reading, collection, and gift giving in a retail environment rather than treating books as simply consumer goods. The more forward-looking local papers are emerging as local web and video providers and once again regaining the classified marketplace. Magazine publishers are serving their niche audiences with specialized tablet apps and video channels. The independent producers of television programs who sell to global markets are booming. Cinema can now offer a luxury night out—reflecting the original ambitions of the crystal halls.

The impact of digital technology on the media has yet to be fully realized. From as early as the 1980s digital *production* was an unalloyed positive. Television was revolutionized by electronic news gathering, film by special effects, and newspapers (as famously evidenced by Rupert Murdoch's move to Wapping) by greatly reduced costs. Even posters enjoyed a new lease on life through electronic displays and computerized printing. It was a one-way street of benefits reflected in rising share prices and the increasing value of media mergers.

However, up until the mid-1990s many media professionals had not begun to realize that the economic effects of digital *distribution*—the internet—would be far more mixed. Digital files were cheap (almost free) to both copy and transmit. People realized that the conventional media bundle—the album, the magazine, the newspaper, and the TV channel—enjoyed what had become an artificial price mechanism, forcing consumers to pay for a package of material they did not always want or need. It was this that created the conditions for piracy, unbundling, and disintermediation. And it was this technology that also opened the door for entirely new and hugely disruptive media models to arrive. The likes of Google, Twitter, and Facebook had no traditional media encumbrances.

The old distinction of media by physical form will blur, but the underlying intellectual structure of traditional formats will surely live on. We still talk of *films* today when in practice many of the products we watch are wholly digital in both production and distribution. We *dial* a telephone (when in fact we push buttons), buy a *video* (which is actually a disc), and make a mix *tape* (which is actually on a hard drive). Some books will continue as preprinted paper and ink, while many others will come as a print-on-demand product or as a screen-based file. However, the product we enjoy will still be a book in the sense of being an intellectual experience rather than an object. The magazine will remain—as envisaged when the term was first coined in 1731—a store of useful information. But it will, in most cases, provide this service on screen rather than on a page. And most newspaper readers will not touch any paper at all but will get their customary diet of information, opinions, and ideas on their tablet.

From tabulae of clay and wax through tabloids of wood pulp and now tablets of silicon chips, media has embraced new technologies to move content to an ever larger audience in ever greater amounts and at an ever increasing speed.

In the early days of a communications revolution it is easy to be bewitched by the latest novel application and bedazzled by the newest shiny gadget. But in the long term the media are shaped by social change and enabled by economic models that prove robust. As in the previous great advances of printing, telegraphy, and broadcasting, the digital era will modify the nature of media, which in turn will change the way society functions. We are all getting more interconnected and involved and the ascent of media seems unstoppable.

Acknowledgments

In a digital media world moving rapidly toward a screen-based consumer interface, the writing of a book remains one of the few media formats that allows an individual to control the whole process. That does not mean, however, that an author, certainly of nonfiction, can ever claim to have been without help. Over a career in many media organizations I have had many thousands of discussions with work colleagues, competitors, analysts, and commentators about where the media is going and where it came from. Each of these conversations will have had some impact on my thinking.

Inspiration came from strange places. For giving me a fascination with early printing, I must thank John Wolfson for his hugely generous gift of a leaf from *The Golden Legend*, printed in 1498 in Westminster by Wynkyn de Worde on paper made by John Tate in Hertfordshire. It is framed on my wall and I never cease to marvel at how fresh and crisp it looks after 500 years.

Despite having worked in media my whole life, I first became interested in its history when I read Marshall McLuhan's *Understanding Media*. Then in an odd coincidence I discovered that McLuhan's colleague Harold Innis had taught economics to my Canadian father-in-law. Visiting Toronto I realized that there was a lot more to media than at first appeared, but that there was little written on its history. I must thank my Canadian family for their forbearance; most of this book was written in their various houses while on vacation, making me an antisocial guest.

To list everybody whose brains I have picked or work I have read would be impossible, but thank you particularly to Chris Anderson (*Wired*), Chris Anderson (TED), Amanda Andrews, James Ashton, Nikesh Arora, Sly Bailey, Emily Bell, Nick Bertolotti, Neil Blackley, Tim Bowdler, Simon Buckingham, Andrew Edgecliffe-Johnson, Claire Enders, Richard Eyre, Ivan Fallon, Ben Fenton, Rupert Gavin, Tom Goddard, Jonnie Goodwin, Paul Gooden, Al Gottesman, Stephen Grabiner, Roy Greenslade, Jonathan Helliwell, Richard Hooper, Brendan Hopkins, Rupert Howell, Jeremy Hunt, Greg Ingham, Nick Jones, Lucy Küng, Guy Lamming, Jeremy Male, Mark Mays, Coline McConville, Mervyn Metcalf, Roger Mosey, Archie Norman, James Palumbo, Wayne Pitout, David Puttnam, Peter

Reid, Paul Richards, James Robinson, Jonathan Rothermere, Dan Sabbagh, Peter Scott, Stephan Shakespeare, Nick Shott, Stevie Spring, Tom Standage, John Tate, Mark Thompson, Lorna Tilbian, Ed Vaizey, Richard Wheatly, Robin Wight, Nadhim Zahawi, and Paul Zwillenberg.

I am particularly grateful to those who were kind enough to read parts of the manuscript to put me right on errors in their areas of expertise: Jean-François Decaux, Dominic Dromgoole, David Mansfield, Guy Michlemore, Tony Mott, Graham Stewart, and Russell Taylor, and to Peter Bazalgette for educating me about Wolfgang Riepl, whose "law" seems validated by recent media history.

Nick Brealey and his team took my rough-and-ready text and polished it into what, I hope, is something nearer to a gemstone than I might have achieved. Thank you to Sally Lansdell for editorial assistance, Andrew Menniss for sales support, and Tom Viney for publicity.

For constant support, helping with research, creating exhibits, proofreading, organizing material, and greatly improving the whole manuscript, my great thanks go to my long-time media colleague Zarina Khan.

Roger Parry
Paradise Island, Bahamas, 2011

Sources

The Ascent of Media is not intended to be an academic textbook. It has set out to explain how the main media types have become they way they are and to illustrate the story with anecdotes and case studies. Although not an academic work, I have gone to great trouble to try to ensure accuracy and thus have given sources for the key facts used. Perhaps appropriately for a book, the most valuable and reliable sources have been other books.

The subject of media has attracted a great deal of interest from academics and commentators. However, many have taken a rather disapproving approach based on a Marxist analysis or a general mistrust of the motives of the media "barons." Authors are often looking for the hidden hand of malevolent media manipulation by government and corporations. As a working media professional, I would dispute that this analysis reflects how the vast numbers of media workers really behave; most have no hidden agenda.

In writing *The Ascent of Media* I have accessed a large number of documents. Where they relate to a specific point in the text this is recoded in the Notes. The books and websites in this section are the ones I found most useful and enjoyable.

Anderson, Chris (2006) *The Long Tail*, London: Random House. Economic analysis of what happens to consumer behavior when there is almost unlimited choice accessed via the search capabilities of the internet.

Bakewell, Joan (1970) with Nicholas Garnham, *The New Priesthood*, London: Allen Lane. A series of interviews with the leaders of the television industry of the 1970s.

Battelle, John (2005) *The Search: How Google and Its Rivals Rewrote the Rules of Business*, London: Nicholas Brealey Publishing. John Battelle is a co-founding editor of *Wired* and founder of the *Industry Standard*. He tells the story of Google through the eyes of a Californian insider. It is particularly valuable in explaining the business story behind the company.

Bernstein, David (1974) *Creative Advertising*, London: Longman Group. A biographical book written before the media explosion of the 1980s, which gives an insight into the way advertising worked in a much simpler media environment. It recalls that creative originality was valued more than media planning and buying skills.

Bissell, Tom (2010) *Extra Lives: Why Video Games Matter*, New York: Pantheon Books. A beautifully written account of what it is like to play video games, which gives an insight into their role in media history.

Bodanis, David (2005) *Electric Universe*, New York: Little, Brown. A scientific insight into the way electricity changed the world and enabled broadcasting.

Bose, Mihir (2006) *Bollywood: A History*, London: Tempus Publishing. The definitive book on Indian cinema, with a strong section on the general history of film.

Boyer, Peter (1998) *Who Killed CBS?: The Undoing of America's Number One News Network*, New York: Random House. CBS News has been called the "Tiffany Network" in reference to the high quality of its programming. The book tells the story of the relative decline of the news division from its early glory days under founder William Paley and provides a good feel for the inherent tensions between corporate profits and the production of television news.

Briggs, Asa & Burke, Peter (2005) *A Social History of The Media: From Gutenberg to the Internet*, Cambridge: Polity Press. This is one of the leading academic texts on media history. It provides a huge amount of detail on the social and cultural context within which media developed. For serious students of the history of media this is a "must read." The authors argue that the development of new media isn't simply a function of technology.

Chapman, Jane (2005) *Comparative Media History*, London: Polity Press. Describes the development of media since 1789 and compares the situation in five countries (UK, US, France, Germany, and Japan). The comparative approach produces interesting case studies. This is an extremely detailed academic textbook designed for undergraduate courses in media studies. It covers similar ground to Briggs and Burke.

Chatfield, Tom (2010) *Fun Inc.*, London: Virgin Books. An excellent read that puts games into the context of other media and wider social issues, and explains the economics, creative allure, and underlying philosophy of games. Very good on the impact of social and casual games.

Chester, Lewis & Fenby, Jonathan (1979) *The Fall of the House of Beaverbrook*, London: André Deutsch. Tells how Canadian businessman Max Aitkin (later Lord Beaverbrook) built a publishing empire around the *Daily Express*.

Chippindale, Peter & Franks, Suzanne (1991) *Dished! The Rise and Fall of British Satellite Broadcasting*, London: Simon & Schuster. Containing a lot of inside information, this is the story of how Sky came to dominate satellite broadcasting in the UK. Interesting to read before the Horsman book described later.

Crisell, Andrew (1997) *An Introductory History of British Broadcasting*, London: Routledge. Andrew Crisell is a professor of broadcasting studies who describes in great detail the history of British broadcasting, mostly focusing on events at the BBC.

Darnton, Robert, *The Case for Books*, New York: PublicAffairs. A collection of essays that mostly focus on the impact of Google Book Search and digital distribution via Amazon and Apple. It raises many issues about the role of copyright law. Darnton is director of the Harvard University Library and the essays reflect a rigorous academic approach.

Derrick, Robin & Muir, Robin (2007) *Vogue Covers*, London: Little, Brown. A collection of Vogue cover art going back over nearly 100 years. A useful insight into how new printing and photography techniques allowed photographs to replace graphic art and into the importance of the cover in selling magazines.

Dennis, Felix (2006) *How to Get Rich*, London: Ebury Press. Biography of the eccentric founder of a magazine empire that is huge fun to read, with insights into the entrepreneurial nature of publishing.

Deutscher, Guy (2006) *The Unfolding of Language*, London: Arrow Books. A ground breaking book that seeks to explain where language came from. A major source for the building block section of this book.

Donovan, Tristan (2010) *Replay: The History of Video Games*, Hove: Yellow Ant. Probably the most comprehensive of the various video games histories. Lots of anecdotes much based on firsthand interviews.

Eisner, Will (1986) *The Dreamer*, New York: WW Norton. This is a semi-autobiographical story of Will Eisner's participation in the birth of the comic book industry in New York in the 1930s. Drawn in Eisner's distinctive style, it provides the factual basis for Michael Chabon's Pulitzer Prize-winning novel *Kavalier and Clay*.

Evans, Harold (1978) *Pictures on a Page*, London: William Heinemann. Written by the then editor of the *Sunday Times*, this is a detailed description of the way photographs and graphics are used in newspapers and magazines. It is particularly useful on all the various techniques that are employed to grab attention and, in particular, on the ways picture editors can use techniques to give misleading impressions.

Fallon, Ivan (1988) *The Brothers: The Rise and Rise of Saatchi & Saatchi*, London: Hutchinson. The early history of the world's most famous advertising agency.

Farr, Michael (2001) *Tintin: The Complete Companion*, London: John Murray. Explains the background to the Tintin books. It describes the evolution of Hergé's drawing style and the huge amount of research that he did on the background of the stories.

Feather, John (2006) *A History of British Publishing*, 2nd edn, London: Routledge. An authoritative and meticulously researched history of book publishing in the UK. A core text for anyone looking for detailed information and reference notes.

Galbraith, John Kenneth (2007) *The Great Crash, 1929*, London: Allan Lane. Reprint of Professor Galbraith's classic analysis of the Great Depression, published originally in 1954. It is particularly useful for understanding the role that the stock exchange ticker played in spreading the panic about falling stock prices.

Goodman, Fred (2010) *Fortune's Fool*, New York: Simon & Schuster. The story of Edgar Bronfman, Jr.'s career, focusing on his controversial purchase of Warner Music Group. It provides insight and numerous case studies from all the music majors into the rapidly changing economics of the music industry in the face of digital technology.

Groensteen, Thierry (2007) *The System of Comics*, Jackson, MS: University Press of Mississippi. Originally published in French in 1999, this is an academic analysis of the way comics work. It is a far more academic work and more difficult to read than the books of Scott McCloud.

Harkin, James (2009) *Lost in Cyburbia*, Toronto: Alfred A Knopf. Describes the background to the development of the web, but focuses more on social and scientific influences rather than technology. Harkin describes the science of cybernetics and looks at the way in which the counterculture movement in San Francisco in the 1960s led to early forms of social networking.

Hartnoll, Phyllis (2006) *The Theatre: A Concise History*, London: Thames & Hudson. Has established itself as the definitive history of the theatre. Richly illustrated, it covers all aspects, starting from Greek drama through to Tom Stoppard and Alan Ayckbourn. Particularly useful in explaining the importance of actor/managers like David Garrick.

Hilmes, Michele (2005) *The Television History Book*, London, bfi. A series of essays from industry insiders with lots of case studies.

Hitchings, Henry (2005) *Dr Johnson's Dictionary: The Extraordinary Story of the Book that Defined the World*, London, John Murray. This is the story of how Samuel Johnson came to write his dictionary. Interesting to get a feel for what London was like in the

1700s and the challenges facing a pioneer wanting to provide precise definitions of words.

Horsman, Mathew (1997) *Sky High: The Inside Story of BSkyB*, London: Orion Business Books. Written by a journalist who had a particular insight into Sky television when it was taken over by Rupert Murdoch. A good, racy read.

Innis, Harold (2007) *Empire and Communications*, Toronto: Dundurn Press. Harold Innis taught political economy at the University of Toronto and made a major study of the impact of communications technology on the shape of society. This book marks the beginning of the academic discipline of media studies and certainly Innis was a significant influence on Marshall McLuhan. The book, based on a series of lectures at Oxford University, was first published in 1950. Innis was the first author to argue that papyrus played an important role in the development of the Roman Empire.

Johns, Adrian (1998) *The Nature of the Book*, Chicago: Chicago University Press. A multiple prize-winning analysis of the development of printing and books. A hugely detailed academic study of the early history, which explores the role of print culture.

Katz, Mark (2005) *Capturing Sound: The Technology that Has Changed Music*, Los Angeles: University of California Press. Katz is the Chair of Musicology at Johns Hopkins University. The book describes the impact that recording technology has had on music, starting with the invention of Edison's phonograph and running through to MP3s and digital file sharing. It is particularly valuable in understanding how technology influenced changes in the way music was composed and played. Fittingly, the book comes with a CD, making it a multimedia production.

Kent, Steven L (2001) *The Ultimate History of Video Games*, New York: Three Rivers Press. The most comprehensive of the early histories based on some 500 interviews but published in 2001, so it predates the Xbox 360 and the Nintendo Wii.

Knee, Jonathan with Greenwald, Bruce & Seave, Ava (2009) *The Curse of the Mogul: What's Wrong with the World's Leading Media Companies?* New York: Portfolio. This is one of the best and most up-to-date analyses of the economics of media companies. It points out that media conglomerates have been consistent underperformers in terms of return to shareholders and calculates that most acquisitions have been failures. It is a particularly useful book for understanding network effects and other aspects of media economics. It is also one of the best accounts of the mega-mergers of the 1990s.

Kuritz, Paul (1988) *The Making of Theatre History*, Upper Saddle River, NJ: Prentice Hall. Useful factual background with high level of detail.

Levinson, Paul (1997) *The Soft Edge*, New York: Routledge. Written in 1997, this predicts what was then felt to be the likely impact of the internet. Levinson is extraordinarily prescient and reading the book in the context of what actually happened is a fascinating experience. It is particularly useful in explaining the theories of Marshall McLuhan.

Levinson, Paul (2004) *Cellphone: The Story of the World's Most Mobile Medium and How It Has Transformed Everything!* New York: Palgrave Macmillan. Discusses the social impact of the cellphone, but goes quite a way beyond that and has some interesting ideas about how all types of media really work.

Lewis, Michael (2000) *The New New Thing: A Silicon Valley Story*, New York: WW Norton. Describes the background to the development of Netscape and shows how the economics of the early internet were intimately linked to the existence of the venture capital industry in and around Stanford University.

Lewis, Michael (2001) *The Future Just Happened*, London: Hodder Headline. A collection of case studies showing the web at work and demonstrating the way it has changed the economics of media and retailing.

Loxley, Simon (2006) *Type: The Secret History of Letters*, London: IB Tauris. Detailed story of the people and companies who created typefaces. It is written by a graphic designer who clearly both loves and understands his industry. It helps explain the mysteries of serifs and sans serifs and gives the human stories behind the names of typefaces.

Malseed, Mark & Vise, David (2005) *The Google Story*, New York: Bantam Dell. This book, by a Pulitzer Prize winner, is mostly a biography of Larry Page and Sergey Brin and the company they created. It revels in the human details about their first office in a Menlo Park garage and the menus offered by Google's in-house chef.

McCloud, Scott (1993) *Understanding Comics: The Invisible Art*, New York: Harper. Explains how comics work by using comic strip format. It includes a particularly interesting section on the comic format going back to the Bayeux Tapestry. It is the seminal work on the comic medium.

McCloud, Scott (2005) *Making Comics*, New York: Harper. A follow-up to *Understanding Comics* that goes into practical detail about the exact mechanics of how comics work.

McCrum, Robert (2010) *Globish*, Toronto: Doubleday. Traces the origins of the English language back to the Anglo-Saxons and shows how its flexibility and its way of adapting words from other languages is setting it on the path to becoming the world's common language.

McLuhan, Marshall (1962) *The Gutenberg Galaxy*, Toronto: University of Toronto Press. This was McLuhan's first major book and talks about the evolution of what he calls "scribal man" (people before the advent of movable type and printing) into "typographic man." He also argues that the arrival of photography then converted typographic man into "graphic man." It is the book in which he coins his famous phrase "the global village."

McLuhan, Marshall (1964) *Understanding Media*, New York: McGraw-Hill. This has to be the most discussed and most influential book on the media. It gave us the gnomic and rather mysterious phrase "the medium is the message." McLuhan was a philosopher and historian. The book is a collection of short essays full of big ideas, puns, and allegories. Its extraordinary fame is based on its perfect timing at the start of the counterculture revolution of the 1960s. It is one of those books that is far more talked about than read.

Mercer, David (2006) *The Telephone: The Life Story of a Technology*, London: Greenward Publishing Group. Traces the history of the telephone from its origins in telegraph technology through to the cellphones of today.

Mezrich, Ben (2010) *The Accidental Billionaires: The Founding of Facebook*, New York: Anchor Books. A highly anecdotal and entertaining account of how the founders of Facebook came to meet each other at Harvard University and how they subsequently fell out.

Monaco, James (2000) *How to Read a Film*, 3rd edn, Oxford: Oxford University Press. Detailed and extensively illustrated book that goes far beyond its title. It tells the history of film by genre, but also describes the way different media work on our senses.

Munk, Nina (2004) *Fools Rush In*, New York: HarperBusiness. The story of the $163 billion takeover of Time Warner by America Online, in particular the doomed relationship between Steve Case of AOL and Jerry Levin of Time Warner.

Nasaw, David (2000) *The Chief: The Life of William Randolph Hearst*, New York: Houghton Mifflin. A huge and hugely detailed biography.

Ogilvy, David (1983) *Ogilvy on Advertising*, London: Pan Books. In 1963 David Ogilvy published *Confessions of an Advertising Man*, which talked about advertising techniques. This subsequent book updated these ideas on how advertising actually works. In David Ogilvy's own words on the first page, "I do not regard advertising as an entertainment or an art form but as a medium of information. When I write an advertisement, I don't want you to tell me that you find it 'creative'. I want you to find it so interesting that you buy the product."

Packard, Vance (1955) *The Hidden Persuaders*, New York: David McKay. Written by a cynical journalist, the first major attack on the profession of advertising. Very influential at the time.

Page, Bruce (2003) *The Murdoch Archipelago*, London: Simon & Schuster. Biography of Rupert Murdoch and News Corporation.

Puttnam, David (1997) *Movies and Money*, London: Vintage Books. Written by a highly successful film producer, this is one of the best guides to how the film industry works. Very useful for understanding the impact of technologies such as sound and television on the film business.

Reidelbach, Maria (1991) *Completely MAD*, New York: Little, Brown. A detailed history of the comic book phenomenon *MAD*.

Robinson, Andrew (1995) *The Story of Writing*, London: Thames & Hudson. Goes back to the origins of written scripts, with detailed sections on cuneiform, hieroglyphics, and the development of the phonetic alphabet. It is also particularly strong on the role of the Rosetta Stone in deciphering ancient Egyptian.

Rosenkrantz, Linda (2003) *Telegram!* New York: Henry Holt. A collection of hundreds of famous, funny, and unusual telegrams from the first half of the twentieth century.

Smith, Anthony (1976) *The Shadow in the Cave*, London: Quartet. A description of the history of broadcasting and the relationship between broadcasters, the audience, and politicians.

Sontag, Susan (1977) *On Photography*, London: Penguin. One of the most influential commentaries on the role of photography, a collection of seven essays that first appeared in the *New York Review of Books*. She writes at length about the interaction between photography and fine art. In particular, the essays raise questions about whether photographs really represent reality or are distortions.

Standage, Tom (1998) *The Victorian Internet*, New York: Walker. This is a great source for the history of the telegraph and the way it can be compared to the modern internet. The author is a working journalist and tells the story in an extremely entertaining way.

Starr, Paul (2004) *The Creation of the Media: Political Origins of Modern Communication*, New York: Perseus Books. Starr is a Pulitzer Prize-winning author and this is a *tour de force* analysis of the development of media in the US. It particularly focuses on political and legislative developments to show why American newspapers, magazines, and, in particular, radio and television developed the way they have. It highlights the importance of the news media in the American War of Independence and the Civil War. In some ways it is the US equivalent of Briggs & Burke.

Sterling, Christopher with Kittross, John (2002) *Stay Tuned: A History of American Broadcasting*, Englewood Cliffs, NJ: Lawrence Erlbaum. At nearly 1,000 pages long the definitive history of the US. Hugely detailed and aimed at students.

Stross, Randall (2007) *The Wizard of Menlo Park: How Thomas Alva Edison Invented the Modern World*, New York: Three Rivers Press. A major biography. It provides considerable detail on the invention of the phonograph. Also features well-researched information on Edison's involvement with the telegraph, the stock exchange ticker, the telephone, and, of course, the light bulb.

Walker, Alexander (2003) *Icons in the Fire: The Decline and Fall of Almost Everybody in the British Film Industry, 1882–2000*, London: Orion. Written by the film critic of the *Evening Standard*, this explains why the UK fails to have a profitable film industry.

Whittemore, Hank (1990) *CNN: The Inside Story*, New York: Little, Brown. A very detailed, blow-by-blow account of the personalities and events that created CNN. Written before the first Gulf War (which was the event that really put CNN onto a global stage), it is an insight into the minds of pioneers and, in particular, into the approach of CNN's founder, Ted Turner.

Wolff, Michael (2008) *The Man Who Owns the News: Inside the Secret World of Rupert Murdoch*, London: Bodley Head. Probably *the* definitive biography of Rupert Murdoch. Wolff is both admiring and critical. Much of the book is devoted to Murdoch's successful purchase of the *Wall Street Journal*, but interweaved with this are a lot of biographical details of his early life and the way his family is central to the running of News Corporation.

Wolk, Douglas (2007) *Reading Comics: How Graphic Novels Work and What They Mean*, Cambridge, MA: Da Capo Press. Both a history of modern comics and a detailed analysis of the way they work. Insight into the growth of the graphic novel.

Wu, Tim (2010) *The Master Switch: The Rise and Fall of Information Empires*, New York: Knopf. An analysis of the growth of media in the twentieth century, with a focus on the way in which industries like cinema, radio, and telephony have tended to become monopolies. It contains detailed backgrounds of people behind the major American groups like Theodore Vail (AT&T), Adolph Zukor (Paramount), and David Sarnoff (NBC). Wu promotes the idea of "the Cycle," in which media start as a hobby, based on a new technology, and trend toward a monopoly. Written by a law professor who invented the idea of "net neutrality."

Wyatt, Will (2003) *The Fun Factory: A Life in the BBC*, London: Aurum Press. Wyatt describes 35 years of his life working at the BBC. He rose from being a producer on *Late Night Line Up* to being Deputy Director-General.

Zyman, Sergio (2002) *The End of Advertising as We Know It*, New York: John Wiley & Sons. Zyman was chief marketing officer of Coca-Cola. The book talks about the challenges of using advertising in a fragmented media environment and the early impact of the internet on advertising.

WEBSITES

Much of the information available on media, or indeed any topic today, is now most easily accessed by looking at websites. Inevitably the online encyclopaedia Wikipedia emerges in the top ten listing for almost any subject searched. I found it of great use to get basic facts; however, wherever possible I have tried to verify all Wikipedia entries from other printed sources. Wikipedia is a wonderful resource but at times some of its anonymous contributors make mistakes and are prone to simply cut and paste from other websites, so any error generated in the first place is simply reproduced.

The main other websites I have used in researching this book are:

www.atlantic-cable.com. Detailed and extensive site devoted to the history of transatlantic submarine cables, starting in 1857 and running up to the modern day. It contains a large number of contemporary documents, pictures, and photographs.

www.distantwriting.co.uk. Dedicated to the history of the telegraph companies that grew up in Britain between 1838 and 1868. It works as a complement to atlantic-cable.com, but is dedicated to the onshore telegraph companies in the UK rather than submarine cables. It has a large number of original documents and pictures.

www.paperbarn.com. This is the website of the Hyde Park Book Store, a bookshop in Boise, Idaho. It has a well-researched section on the history of the paperback book.

www.retro-gram.com. The website of a commercial service offering facsimile telegrams, but it contains a useful history section that gives a lot of anecdotal information about the development and use of the telegraph and telegram. It is particularly good on cipher codes.

www.stocktickercompany.com. A comprehensive guide with extensive photography of the original stock ticker technology.

www.telegramsonline.co.uk. This is a commercial service that took over the creation of telegrams from British Telecom. It contains a history section that gives some useful facts and dates.

www.visite.artsetmetiers.free.fr. This website celebrates French inventions and features the Chappe telegraph. There is another good French site at www.chappe.ec-lyon.fr, which details 196 different signals.

Notes

Preface

1   Andrew Edgecliffe-Johnson, E-books overtake print sales, *Financial Times*, April 14, 2011.

Part One: Media's Building Blocks

1   John Gapper, Consumers gain from the media industry's pain, *FT Magazine*, November 14, 2009, p10.
2   Ofcom. Annual Communications Marker Report, August 19, 2010.
3   Ian Brown, *Financial Times*, Digital Business, November 3, 2009, p1.
4   David Sarno, *Los Angeles Times*, December 2, 2009.
5   bbc.co.uk, May 14, 2003.
6   *Times*, June 22, 2004.
7   Guy Deutscher, *The Unfolding of Language*, 2006, p9.
8   Forbes audio interview with Noam Chomsky, October 3, 2005.
9   Africa said to be mother of all human language, www.cbsnews.com, April 15, 2011.
10 *Daily Telegraph*, May 1, 2007.
11 Deutscher, *op. cit*, p11.
12 Robin Lane Fox, *The Classical World*, London: Allen Lane, 2005, p73.
13 Asa Briggs & Peter Burke, *A Social History of the Media*, 2010, p24.
14 BBC News, June 25, 2009.
15 Philip Ball, *New Scientist*, May 8, 2010, p32.
16 Diana Deutsch, Scientific American Mind, July/August 2010, pp36–43.
17 BBC News, May 4, 1999, news.bbc.co.uk.
18 Andrew George, *Epic of Gilgamesh*, London: Penguin, 1999.
19 Richard Hooker, *World Civilizations*, Washington State University, www.wsu.edu.
20 Lane Fox, *op. cit.*, p259.
21 Robert McCrum, *Globish*, 2010, p18.
22 Daisuke Wakabayashi, *Wall Street Journal*, August 6, 2010, p31.
23 Marketing Society, *Market Leader*, Q1 2009, p20.

Part Two: The Media Journey

1   Aristotle, *Politics*, Book VII, Chapter 4. Translation by Benjamin Jowett says: "all cities which have a reputation for good government have a limit of population... when too many it is not a state, being almost incapable of constitutional government. For who can be the general of such a vast multitude, or who the herald, unless he have the voice of a Stentor?... If the citizens of a state are to judge and to distribute offices according to merit, then they must know each other's characters; clearly then the best limit of the population of a state is the largest number which... can be taken in at a single view."
2   Chris Anderson, *The Long Tail*, New York: Random House, 2006.
3   A Short History of Coffee Advertising, www.web-books.com.
4   Paul Starr, *The Creation of the Media*, 2005, p86.
5   Adam Thierer, On measuring technology diffusion rates, May 28, 2009, http://tech-liberation.com/author/adamthierer (citing *Forbes* magazine and Census Bureau).

6   ABC News reporting *China Daily*, March 30, 2005; www.abc.net.au.
7   The accidental title of *The Medium is the Massage* is explained on the website maintained by the McLuhan Estate, www.marshallmcluhan.com.
8   Marshall McLuhan, *Understanding Media*, New York: Routledge Classics, 2003, p9.
9   James Harkin, *Lost in Cyburbia*, Toronto: Alfred A Knopf, 2009, p54.

2.1 Theatre

1   Phyllis Hartnoll, *The Theatre: A Concise History*, 2006 p11.
2   www.chestermysteryplays.com/chester-guilds.html.
3   Jonathan Bate, The Mirror of Life, *Harpers Magazine*, April 2007, pp37–46.
4   George Rowell & Anthony Jackson, *The Repertory Movement: A History of Repertory Theatre: I Britain*, Cambridge: Cambridge University Press, 1984.

2.2 Books

1   Books in Print, bowker.com, May 20, 2011.
2   Harold Innis, *Empire and Communications*, 1972, p114.
3   www.paperonline.org/history.
4   *Ibid.*
5   British Association of Paper Historians, www.baph.org.uk.
6   Hyde Park Books, www.paperbarn.com.
7   Kevin Hayes, *Poe and the Printed Word*, Cambridge University Press, 2009, p88.
8   Jeremy Lewis, *Life and Times of Allen Lane*, Penguin, 2005, p117.
9   Robert Darnton, The case for books, *Public Affairs*, 2009, pxiv.
10 Jeff Bezos speaking on BBC *Newsnight*, May 6, 2009.

2.3 Pictures

1   Marshall McLuhan, *The Gutenberg Galaxy*, 1962, p78.
2   Jenny Uglow, *Words and Pictures*, London: Faber & Faber, 2008, p3.
3   Colm Tóibín, The Art of War, *Guardian*, April 29, 2006.
4   Susan Sontag, *On Photography*, 1979, p88.
5   *Ibid.*, p18.
6   Life and Arts, *Financial Times*, January 17, 2009, p13.
7   Harold Evans, *Pictures on a Page*, 1978, Introduction.
8   George Orwell, As I Please, *Tribune Magazine*, February 11, 1944.
9   JB Harley, *The New Nature of Maps*, John Hopkins University Press, 2001, p44, 57.
10 *The Beauty of Maps*, BBC Four, April 23, 2010.
11 *The Economist*, December 22, 2007, p76.
12 Adam Bernstein, Odile Crick, *Washington Post*, July 21, 2007.

2.4 Posters

1   Alison Cooley, *Pompeii: A Sourcebook*, London: Routledge, 2004, p118.
2   www.fordham.edu/halsall/ancient/pompeii-inscriptions.html.
3   David Bernstein, *Advertising Outdoors*, London: Phaidon Press, 2004, p179.
4   www.urban75.org/london/billboards.html.
5   *Ibid.*
6   Ogden Nash, *The Face Is Familiar*, Garden City Publishing, 1941, p21.
7   David Ogilvy, *Ogilvy on Advertising*, London: Prion, 1983, p217.

2.5 Postal Systems

1 Sherlock Holmes, *Stamp & Postal History News*, July 8-21, 1981, p24.
2 Briggs & Burke, *op. cit.*, p21.
3 British Postal Museum.
4 Briggs & Burke, *op. cit.*, p107.
5 Edwardians discovered "Twitter" first, *Daily Telegraph*, September 3, 2009.
6 www.uh.edu/engines.
7 JD Hayhurst, *The Pigeon Post into Paris 1870–1871*, www.cix.co.uk/mhayhurst.
8 Alvin Toffler, *The Third Wave*, New York: William Morrow, 1980, p50.

2.6 Newspapers

1 Speech by HRH Price of Wales, St Brides Church, March 11, 2002.
2 Thomas Jefferson, letter to Edward Carrington, 1800.
3 Starr, *op. cit.*, p131.
4 *Ibid.*, p39.
5 Martin S Fridson, *It Was a Very Good Year: Extraordinary Moments in Stock Market History*, John Wiley and Sons, 1998.
6 Roy Greenslade, *Press Gang*, London: Pan, 2004, p68.
7 *Ibid.*, p7.
8 Starr, *op. cit.*, p248.
9 http://econsultancy.com/blog/412-the-100th-birthday-of-the-press-release.
10 History of The Observer, www.guardian.co.uk.

2.7 Magazines

1 www.pickeringandchatto.com.
2 www.bodley.ox.ac.uk.
3 James Greenwood, The Seven Curses of London, 1869, www.victorianlondon.org.
4 Caroline Seebohm, *The Man Who Was Vogue*, Weidenfeld and Nicolson, 1992, p50.
5 Robin Derrick, *Vogue Covers*, Boston, MA: Little, Brown, 2007, p49.
6 Mark Tungate, *Media Monoliths*, London: Kogan Page, 2005, p186.

2.8 Comics

1 Scott McCloud, *Understanding Comics*, 1994.
2 Douglas Wolk, *Reading Comics*, 2007, p14.
3 Thierry Groensteen, *The System of Comics*, 2008.
4 Will Eisner, *The Dreamer*, Amherst, MA: Kitchen Sink Press, pvii.
5 *Ibid.*, p23.
6 Code of the Comics Magazine Association of America, Inc., adopted October 26, 1954.
7 Watchmen review, *Daily Telegraph*, March 6, 2009, p27.
8 The New Review, *The Observer*, June 13, 2010, p40.
9 John Lichfield, *Independent*, December 27, 2006.
10 www.ibiblio.org/Dave/drfun.
11 www.sluggy.com.
12 Email to author from "Alex," July 2010.

2.9 Telegraph

1 Tom Standage, *The Victorian Internet*, New York: Walker, 2007, Preface.
2 *Ibid.*, p12.

3   David Mercer, *The Telephone*, 2006, p3.
4   www.visite.artsetmetiers.free.fr.
5   Starr, *op. cit.*, p157.
6   Briggs & Burke, *op. cit.*, p112.
7   www.distantwriting.co.uk.
8   Starr, op. cit., p171; Briggs & Burke, *op. cit.*, p115.
9   Starr, *op. cit.*, p183.
10 www.atlantic-cable.com.
11 Bern Dibner, *The Atlantic Cable*, Huntington, CT: Burndey Library, 1959.
12 www.statemaster.com/encyclopedia/Electrical_telegraph.
13 Standage, *op. cit.*, p50.
14 Julian Borger, *Guardian*, February 3, 2006.
15 www.telegramsonline.co.uk.
16 Anthony Waldstock on www.storyoflondon.com.
17 www.retro-gram.com.
18 Starr, *op. cit.*, p183.
19 stocktickercompany.com.
20 J Kenneth Galbraith, *The Great Crash, 1929*, 2007, pp125, 126.
21 Morse code beats text messaging, www.youtube.com/watch?v=t041g4X-aM0.

2.10 Telephone
1   Briggs & Burke, *op. cit.*, p122.
2   Anthony Smith, *The Shadow in the Cave*, London: Quartet Books, 1976, p11.
3   Thomas Denison, The Telephone Newspaper, *World's Work*, April 1901, pp640–43.

2.11 Recorded Sound
1   In *The Merry Wives of Windsor*.
2   Paul Kuritz, *The Making of Theatre History*, Englewood Cliffs, NJ: Prentice-Hall, 1988.
3   Fred Goodman, *Fortune's Fool*, 2010, p133.
4   BBC News, June 17, 2005.
5   Norio Ohga, bbc.co.uk/news, April 23, 2001.
6   Mark Katz, *Capturing Sound*, 2010, p3.
7   *Ibid.*, p68.
8   Jane Chapman, *Comparative Media History*, London: Polity Press, 2005, p168.
9   The New King, *Time Magazine*, November 27, 1939.
10 Reuters, January 6, 2008.
11 Goodman, *op. cit.*, p246.
12 Carl Wilson, Kaisers predict riot of interest in bespoke album, *Financial Times*, June 3, 2011, p2.
13 Andrew Edgecliffe-Johnson, *Financial Times*, June 13 2010.
14 Goodman, *op. cit.*, p18.

2.12 Radio
1   David Bodanis, *Electric Universe*, 2005, p89.
2   Gleason Archer, *History of Radio to 1926*, www.davidsarnoff.org.
3   Briggs & Burke, op. cit., p131.
4   Elizabeth McLeod, *From Hawthorne to Hard Sell*, www.midcoast.com, 1998.
5   John Reith, *Broadcast over Britain*, London: Hodder & Stoughton, 1924, p34.

6　Richard J Hand, *Terror on the Air!: Horror Radio in America, 1931–1952*, Jefferson, NC: Macfarland, 2006.

7　Joseph Goebbels, *Der Rundfunk als achte Großmacht: Signale der neuen Zeit*, Munich: Zentralverlag der NSDAP, 1938, pp197–207, cited by calvin.edu/academic.

8　Georg Szalai, Howard Stern, *Hollywood Reporter*, December 9, 2010.

9　www.radiocaroline.co.uk.

2.13 Cinema

1　Hollywood, the Remake, *Wall Street Journal*, December 29, 2005, pA10.

2　Mihir Bose, *Bollywood: A History*, 2006, p38.

3　David Puttnam, *Movies and Money*, 1997, p18.

4　Bose, *op. cit.*, p92.

5　*Ibid.*, p31.

6　Frank Manchel, *Film Study*, Fairleigh Dickinson University Press, 1991, p237.

7　Matthew Sweet, Fancy a quickie, *Guardian*, 2 January 2007.

8　Matthew Garrahan, A pointer to profits, *Financial Times*, August 25, 2010, p7.

2.14 Television

1　*Media Revolution*, BBC2, February 19, 2009.

2　Annan Report, 1977, p26.

3　Brooks Boliek, *Hollywood Reporter*, June 23, 2005.

4　Michele Hilmes, *The Television History Book*, 2003, p33.

5　Richard G. Hubler, Jack Webb: The Man Who Makes Dragnet, *Coronet Magazine*, September 1953.

6　Cable TV companies think outside the box, *Financial Times*, June 21, 2011, p23.

2.15 Video Games

1　Lex Column, *Financial Times*, December 13, 2010.

2　*The Edge*, November 2010, p63.

3　Emma Barnett, The mega-profit game machine, *Sunday Telegraph*, November 28, 2010, pB6.

4　http://gamasutra.com/view/news/30386.

5　McLuhan, *Understanding Media*, p266.

6　www.advent-original.tar.gz.

7　The man who invented Playtime, *Sunday Times Magazine*, November 14, 2010.

8　Tom Chatfield, Tom, *Fun Inc.*, London: Virgin Books, 2010, p118.

9　Tristan Donovan, *Replay: The History of Video Games*, Hove: Yellow Ant, 2010, p7.

10　Steven L. Kent, *The Ultimate History of Video Games*, 2002, p25.

11　Donovan, *op. cit.*, p108.

12　Kent, *op. cit.*, p429.

13　19 years after Columbine, *USA Today*, April 13, 2009.

14　Game addicts starve baby to death, *ABC News*, March 4, 2010.

15　Tom Chatfield, Video games are not just for geeks any more, *Evening Standard*, December 11, 2010, p23.

16　Tom Bissell, *Extra Lives*, New York: Pantheon Books, 2010, p201.

2.16 Web

1   Vannevar Bush, As We May Think, www.theatlantic.com, July 1945.
2   www.plentymag.com.
3   Harkin, *op. cit.*, p45.
4   www.stanford.edu/news/2005.
5   Vint Cerf in personal communication with the author, June 2008.
6   BBC News; dot.life, October 8, 2001.
7   Doran Howitt, *InfoWorld*, November 5, 1984, p59.
8   T Campbell, *The History of Webcomics*, San Antonio, CA: Antarctic Press, 2006, p15.
9   Murad Ahmed, *The Times*, October 14, 2009, p11.
10 James Ashton, Oxford turns digital, Sunday Times, August 29, 2010, p8.
11 Chris Anderson, The web is dead, *Wired*, September 2010, www.wired.com.
12 Justin Smith quoted in *Guardian*, August 19, 2009.

Part Three: Future

1   Innis, *op. cit.*
2   McLuhan, *Understanding Media.*
3   Briggs & Burke, *op. cit.*
4   Tim Wu, *The Master Switch*, New York: Knopf, 2010.
5   Mathias Döpfner, CEO Axel Springer, *Die Welt*, May 8, 2006.
6   Ofcom, Annual Communications Marker Report, August 19, 2010.
7   Joan Bakewell, *The New Priesthood*, 1970, p1.
8   Anthony Davis, *Television: Here Is the News*, London: ITN, 1976, pp137–8.
9   Tom Cheshire, *Wired*, August 2010, p88.
10 *The Economist*, November 28, 2009, p79.
11 Anderson, *The Long Tail*, pp18–40.
12 Aristotle, *Politics.*
13 Bill Gates' home page, www.microsoft.com, January 3, 1996.
14 Andrew Walmsley, *Marketing*, July 7, 2010, p12.
15 Daniel Defoe, *Review*, December 6, 1709. Quoted in Tomorrow's Humanities, speech by James Murdoch at University College London, May 20, 2010.
16 USA Pacific Telegraph Act 1860 stated "messages received from any individual, company, or corporation, or from any telegraph lines connecting with this line at either of its termini, shall be impartially transmitted in the order of their reception, excepting that the dispatches of the government shall have priority. "
17 Giles Hattersley, *Sunday Times*, July 25, 2010, p16.
18 *The Autobiography of Benjamin Franklin*, Dover Publications, 1996, p37.
19 Clay Shirky, *Cognitive Surplus: Creativity and Generosity in a Connected Age*, Allen Lane, 2010.

Index